Reclaiming Participatory Governance

Reclaiming Participatory Governance offers empirical and theoretical perspectives on how the relationship between social movements and state institutions is emerging and developing through new modes of participatory governance.

One of the most interesting political developments of the past decade has been the adoption by social movements of strategies seeking to change political institutions through participatory governance. These strategies have flourished in a variety of contexts, from anti-austerity and pro-social justice protests in Spain, to movements demanding climate transition and race equality in the UK and the USA, to constitutional reforms in Belgium and Iceland. The chief ambition and challenge of these new forms of participatory governance is to institutionalise the prefigurative politics and social justice values that inspired them in the first place, by mobilising the bureaucracy to respond to their claims for reforms and rights. The authors of this volume assess how participatory governance is being transformed and explore the impact of such changes, providing timely critical reflections on: the constraints imposed by cultural, economic and political power relations on these new empowered participatory spaces; the potential of this new "wave" of participatory democracy to reimagine the relationship between citizens and traditional institutions towards more radical democratic renewal; where and how these new democratisation efforts sit within the representative state; and how tensions between the different demands of lay citizens, organised civil society and public officials are being managed.

This book will be an important resource for students and academics in political science, public administration and social policy, as well as activists, practitioners and policymakers interested in supporting innovative engagement for deeper social transformation.

Adrian Bua is Lecturer in Urban Politics in the Department of Politics and International Relations, and a member of the Centre for Urban Research on Austerity, at De Montfort University, UK. His latest work spans democratic theory, urban studies and political economy.

Sonia Bussu is Associate Professor in Public Policy at INLOGOV at the University of Birmingham, UK. Her research and published work focus on participatory governance, coproduction and participatory research.

Routledge Studies in Democratic Innovations

Representative democracy faces several major challenges in contemporary times. Two of the most prominent challenges are the problematic functioning of its institutions and the decreasing popular legitimacy of its decision-making process. The gap between citizens and institutions widens and has major impact on politics and society. This book series aims to bridge the gap between various perspectives on democratic innovations, and examines the determinants, functioning and consequences of democratic innovations from both a theoretical and empirical perspective.

Series editors: *Sergiu Gherghina, University of Glasgow, UK and Camille Bedock, Sciences Po Bordeaux, France.*

The Future of Self-Governing, Thriving Democracies
Democratic Innovations By, With and For the People
Brigitte Geissel

Reclaiming Participatory Governance
Social Movements and the Reinvention of Democratic Innovation
Edited by Adrian Bua and Sonia Bussu

For more information about this series, please visit: https://www.routledge.com/Routledge-Studies-in-Democratic-Innovations/book-series/RSDI

Reclaiming Participatory Governance

Social Movements and the Reinvention of Democratic Innovation

Edited by Adrian Bua and Sonia Bussu

LONDON AND NEW YORK

First published 2023
by Routledge
4 Park Square, Milton Park, Abingdon, Oxon OX14 4RN

and by Routledge
605 Third Avenue, New York, NY 10158

Routledge is an imprint of the Taylor & Francis Group, an informa business

© 2023 selection and editorial matter, Adrian Bua and Sonia Bussu; individual chapters, the contributors

The right of Adrian Bua and Sonia Bussu to be identified as the authors of the editorial material, and of the authors for their individual chapters, has been asserted in accordance with sections 77 and 78 of the Copyright, Designs and Patents Act 1988.

With the exception of Chapter 11, no part of this book may be reprinted or reproduced or utilised in any form or by any electronic, mechanical, or other means, now known or hereafter invented, including photocopying and recording, or in any information storage or retrieval system, without permission in writing from the publishers.

Chapter 11 of this book are available for free in PDF format as Open Access at www.taylorfrancis.com. It has been made available under a Creative Commons Attribution-Non Commercial-No Derivatives 4.0 license.

Trademark notice: Product or corporate names may be trademarks or registered trademarks, and are used only for identification and explanation without intent to infringe.

Every effort has been made to contact copyright-holders. Please advise the publisher of any errors or omissions, and these will be corrected in subsequent editions.

British Library Cataloguing-in-Publication Data
A catalogue record for this book is available from the British Library

Library of Congress Cataloging-in-Publication Data
Names: Bua, Adrian, editor. | Bussu, Sonia, editor.
Title: Reclaiming participatory governance : social movements and the reinvention of democratic innovation / edited by Adrian Bua and Sonia Bussu.
Description: Abingdon, Oxon ; New York, NY : Routledge, 2023. | Series: RSDI | Includes bibliographical references.
Identifiers: LCCN 2022057005 (print) | LCCN 2022057006 (ebook) | ISBN 9781032111216 (hardback) | ISBN 9781032111254 (paperback) | ISBN 9781003218517 (ebook)
Subjects: LCSH: Political participation--Case studies. | Deliberative democracy--Case studies.
Classification: LCC JF799 .R436 2023 (print) | LCC JF799 (ebook) | DDC 323/.0420723--dc23/eng/20230208
LC record available at https://lccn.loc.gov/2022057005
LC ebook record available at https://lccn.loc.gov/2022057006

ISBN: 978-1-032-11121-6 (hbk)
ISBN: 978-1-032-11125-4 (pbk)
ISBN: 978-1-003-21851-7 (ebk)

DOI: 10.4324/9781003218517

Typeset in Times New Roman
by Deanta Global Publishing Services, Chennai, India

The Open Access version of chapter 11 was funded by College of Social Sciences, University of Birmingham.

Contents

List of Figures		viii
List of Tables		ix
Acknowledgements		x
Notes on Contributors		xi
1	**Introduction to the Volume** ADRIAN BUA AND SONIA BUSSU	1

SECTION 1
Conceptualising Democracy-Driven Governance 17

2	**Challenging the "Rules of the Game": The Role of Bottom-Up Participatory Experiments for Deliberative Democracy** DANNICA FLEUß	19
3	**Innovations in Participatory Governance and the (De) commodification of Social Wellbeing** NICK VLAHOS	35
4	**Can Local Participation Disrupt Neoliberalism?: The Politics and Ethics of Caring for Democracy** MARKUS HOLDO	51
5	**The Democratic Multiverse: Governance, Associations and the Prospects for Progressive Democratic Renewal** HENDRIK WAGENAAR	67

SECTION 2
Tracing the Emergence of Democracy-Driven Governance   87

6   Towards Participatory Transition Governance: The Role of Social Movements as "Collaborators" for Democratic Innovation   89
PAOLA PIERRI

7   "Be Like Water": Participatory Arts, Prefigurative Social Movements and Democratic Renewal   104
LUCY CATHCART FRÖDÉN

8   Whose and What Right to the City?: Insights from Lisbon on the interplay of movements and institutions within participatory processes   120
ROBERTO FALANGA

9   De-POLARising Civic Participation?: Lessons from the Incomplete Experience of Greenland   136
GIOVANNI ALLEGRETTI

10   Collective Candidacies and Mandates in Brazil: Challenges and Pitfalls of a *Gambiarra*   154
RICARDO F. MENDONÇA, LUCAS GELAPE AND CARLOS ESTEVÃO C. CRUZ

11   Democracy-Driven Governance and Governance-Driven Democratisation in Barcelona and Nantes   170
ADRIAN BUA, SONIA BUSSU AND JONATHAN DAVIES

SECTION 3
Assessing the Challenges to Projects of Radical Reform   189

12   Expanding Participatory Governance through Digital Platforms?: Drivers and Obstacles in the Implementation of the Decidim Platform   191
JOAN BALCELLS, ROSA BORGE AND ALBERT PADRÓ-SOLANET

13   The Embeddedness of Public-Common Institutions: The Citizen Assets Programme in Barcelona   209
MARINA PERA, IOLANDA BIANCHI AND YUNAILIS SALAZAR

14 How Can Democracy-Driven Governance Turn into
    Technopopulism?: Arguing on the Case of *Ahora Madrid*   225
    FABIOLA MOTA CONSEJERO AND CRISTINA HERRANZ

15 Surfing Disappointment: The Uneasy Inclusion of Social
    Movement Activists in Local Participatory Institutions: A Case
    Study of Madrid (2015–2019)   242
    PATRICIA GARCÍA-ESPÍN

16 Institutionalising Participation from Below: From the Shack to
    Municipal Elections in Commercy, France   259
    SIXTINE VAN OUTRYVE

SECTION 4
Conclusion   275

17 Towards the Messy Middle: The Next Generation of
    Democracy-Driven Governance Research   277
    GIANPAOLO BAIOCCHI

    Index   285

Figures

9.1	Photo of Hans Egede Statue taken by an anonymous activist on 21 June 2020, defaced with red paint, a graffiti reading "decolonize" and the cane in his right hand transformed into a whip	138
10.1	Percentage of city council candidacies per race/ethnicity and age in the Brazilian 2020 elections	158
12.1	Biplot of Indexes	201
12.2	Distribution of Cases in the Biplot	202
14.1	Percentages of participation by year and district, and relative variation by district	235
15.1	The Process of SMAs Disappointment	254

Tables

6.1	Key Elements of Adversarial and Collaborative Forms of Countervailing Power	92
11.1	A Framework to Understand Emergence of DDG	182
12.1	List of Catalan Municipalities That Have Implemented the Decidim Platform (March 2019)	198
12.2	List of Indices and Corresponding Questionnaire Items	200
12.3	Regression Analysis. Dependent Variable: Percentage of Registered Citizens	203
15.1	Interviews and Profile of Informants	247

Acknowledgements

We are profoundly indebted to all the authors for contributing so generously to this volume. The innovative and inspiring cases they shared and the insightful analyses their work provides helped us answer the questions underpinning this book while raising new questions and challenges that will undoubtedly inform future research agendas.

We are grateful to the UK Political Science Association's Participatory and Deliberative specialist group for supporting our work and publishing a series dedicated to the volume on their blog Agora, also syndicated on De Montfort University's Centre for Urban Research on Austerity's blog.

Errors and omissions are our responsibility, as editors, but the quality of the chapters owes much to the internal review process carried out by many of the authors who contributed to the book. Thank you for your punctual comments and constructive suggestions. Some of the most brilliant ideas were developed through the collegiality among the different contributors, who engaged with each other's work so generously.

We thank Koen Bartels, John Boswell and Selen Ercan, who, as convenors of the ECPR's Standing Group on Theoretical Perspectives in Policy Analysis, sponsored panels to support work on the book at the 2021 Interpretive Policy Analysis conference and the 2022 ECPR Joint Sessions of Workshops. Exchanges at these panels were vital to support the development of a coherent volume.

We are profoundly grateful to our partners, friends, mentors and colleagues, for their continuous support, their inspiring work, their generous comments and advice: Sadiya Akram, Hans Asenbaum, Anna Bussu, Nicole Curato, Rikki Dean, Anastasia Deligiaouri, James Duggan, Catherine Durose, Oliver Escobar, Dayo Eseonu, Renata Feijoo, Andrea Felicetti, Maria Tullia Galanti, Jean-Paul Gagnon, Brigitte Geissel, Arianna Giovannini, Steven Griggs, Valeria Guarneros Mesa, Martin Marshall, Jennifer Martinez Lopez, Rodrigo Nuñez Bea, Dominic Richardson, Liz Richardson, Graham Smith and Marta Wojciechowska.

Finally, our deepest gratitude to the Routledge publishing team, Hannah Rich and Emily Ross, for their interest in this work, their patience and their support throughout.

Notes on Contributors

Giovanni Allegretti is Senior Researcher at the Centre for Social Studies at Coimbra University, Portugal. His latest work spans urban studies, participatory planning, environmental policies and platform economy.

Gianpaolo Baiocchi is a scholar and activist. He directs Urban Democracy Lab at NYU, USA, and works closely with organisations such as Right To The City, Housing Justice For All and The Action Lab. A sociologist by training, he has written extensively on participatory democracy.

Joan Balcells is Lecturer in Political Science at the Universitat Oberta de Catalunya (UOC), Spain, and a member of the research group "eGovernance: electronic administration and democracy". His research interests focus on democratic theory, digital democracy, public opinion and deliberation.

Iolanda Bianchi currently holds a Marie Skłodowska-Curie SoE postdoctoral fellowship at the Urban Studies Institute, University of Antwerp. She works in the field of urban governance, urban policy and collective action.

Rosa Borge is the leader of the research group Communication Networks and Social Change (CNSC) at the Internet Interdisciplinary Institute (IN3), and Associate Professor in Political Science in the Law and Political Science Department, both at the Universitat Oberta de Catalunya (UOC), Spain. Her main areas of research are online deliberation and participation, and the use of social media and participatory platforms by public administrations, political parties and social organisations.

Adrian Bua is Lecturer in Urban Politics in the Department of Politics and International Relations, and a member of the Centre for Urban Research on Austerity at De Montfort University, UK. His latest work spans democratic theory, urban studies and political economy.

Sonia Bussu is Associate Professor in Public Policy at INLOGOV at the University of Birmingham, UK. Her research and published works focus on participatory governance, coproduction and participatory research.

Fabiola Mota Consejero is Associate Professor in Political Science in the Department of Political Science and International Relations, and a member of the research group Democracy, Participation and Government at the Universidad Autónoma de Madrid, Spain. Her recent publications explore the impact of social movements on political decision-making.

Carlos Estevão C. Cruz is a PhD candidate in Political Science at the Federal University of Minas Gerais, Brazil. His research interests focus on political theory, democratic theory and social movements.

Jonathan Davies is Director of the Centre for Urban Research on Austerity and Professor of Critical Policy Studies at De Montfort University, UK. His research interests span critical issues in governance, urban studies and public policy.

Patricia García-Espín is Lecturer in Political Sociology in the Department of Sociology at the University of Granada (Spain). Her latest work focuses on social inequalities and access to different forms of political participation.

Roberto Falanga is Assistant Research Professor at the Institute of Social Sciences at the University of Lisbon, Portugal. His research focuses on citizen participation in policymaking, and he is a member of several international projects on related topics.

Dannica Fleuß is Postdoctoral Researcher at the Institute of Future Media, Democracy and Society at Dublin City University, Ireland, and Research Associate at the Centre for Deliberative Democracy and Global Governance at the University of Canberra, Australia. Her research focuses on theories of democratic legitimacy, theoretical and empirical studies of deliberative democracy and approaches aiming at decolonising democratic theory.

Lucy Cathcart Frödén is a Postdoctoral Fellow in the Department of Musicology at the University of Oslo, and an affiliated researcher at Malmö University's School of Arts and Communication. Her research currently focuses on the role of music, sound and voice in social change, particularly in relation to carceral systems.

Lucas de O. Gelape has a PhD in Political Science from the University of São Paulo, Brazil. His research focuses on elections, brokers and local politics.

Cristina Herranz has been Teacher Assistant in the Department of Political Science and International Relations at the Universidad Autónoma de Madrid (UAM), Spain (2017–2022). Her research interests focus on democratic theory and digital democratic innovations.

Markus Holdo works at Lund University, Sweden, where he teaches in the Department of Political Science and leads research projects on activism and democracy. An important question in this work is how to build a shared ethic of solidarity when public discourse is becoming more and more focused on individual success and individual responsibility. He aims to gather insights valuable to people working to make societies more inclusive, equal and caring.

Ricardo F. Mendonça is Associate Professor in the Department of Political Science at the Federal University of Minas Gerais, Brazil, and Fellow at CNPq, Fapemig and INCT.DD, all in Brazil. He is the coordinator of Margem – Research Group on Democracy and Justice. He is interested in democratic theory, contentious politics and political communication.

Sixtine Van Outryve is a PhD Candidate at the Centre for Philosophy of Law at UCLouvain, Belgium. Her PhD focuses on the theory and practice of direct democracy from a communalist perspective, specifically on social movements struggling for local self-government in France and North America.

Albert Padró-Solanet is Lecturer in Political Science at the Universitat Oberta de Catalunya (UOC), Spain, and a member of the research group "eGovernance: electronic administration and democracy". His research is mainly focused on the impact of information and communications technologies (ICTs) on political parties, public opinion and deliberation.

Marina Pera is Postdoctoral Fellow at the IGOP at the Universitat Autónoma de Barcelona, Spain and a visiting scholar at INLOGOV, University of Birmingham. Her main lines of research are urban commons, coproduction policies and community development.

Paola Pierri is Director of Research at Democratic Society, Germany, working in the field of deliberative democracy as well as participatory governance. She specialises in social movements and digital activism, and her current work focuses on open data governance and the impact of digitalisation on our public space and democracy.

Yunailis Salazar is a PhD Student in Politics, Policies and International Relations at the Institute of Government and Public Policies (IGOP) at the Autonomous University of Barcelona, Spain. Her research focuses on the capacity of the new municipalism to implement an agenda of change in the management of public services through socially responsible public procurement in the Barcelona City Council.

Nick Vlahos is Postdoctoral Fellow at the Centre for Deliberative Democracy and Global Governance at the University of Canberra, Australia. His current work focuses on the interconnection between political economy and participatory and deliberative democracy.

Hendrik Wagenaar is Fellow at the Institute for Advanced Studies in Vienna, Austria, and Adjunct Professor at the Centre for Deliberative Democracy and Global Governance at the University of Canberra, Australia. He is also an academic advisor for the International School for Government at King's College London, UK. His research focuses on the relationship between the commons, the political economy and democracy. He also publishes about Deliberative Policy Analysis.

1 Introduction to the Volume

Adrian Bua and Sonia Bussu

Our world is experiencing multiple pressing crises, from the climate crisis to the economic crisis with socio-economic inequalities now reaching unbearable levels within most advanced democracies. Political elites' inability, or unwillingness, to address such crises has contributed to sharply diminishing trust in representative institutions. Democratic innovations (DIs) (Smith 2009; Elstub and Escobar 2019), or processes of participatory and deliberative democracy that engage citizens directly in politics and policymaking, have been increasingly hailed by policymakers, across democracies and authoritarian regimes alike, as an antidote to elected representatives' plummeting legitimacy (Font et al. 2018; Sintomer et al. 2013). However, they have also attracted much criticism. Often discrete, ad hoc and generally top-down, these "invited spaces" (Cornwall 2002) are accused of giving too much power to commissioning organisations, who design the process and choose who to invite. In this way, DIs can limit the scope of the debate (Chambers 2009; Papadopoulos 2012; Lee et al., 2015) and crowd out organic forms of civic life (Hendriks and Lees-Marshment 2019). There is increasing interest in sortition, or using stratified random selection to populate citizen assemblies and citizen juries – so-called mini-publics – that develop policy recommendations for representative bodies at different tiers of government (OECD 2020). There are increasingly loud calls for these spaces to be given decision-making power (Landemore 2020), although some authors warn against important issues of democratic legitimacy that sortition inevitably also raises (Lafont 2020). The self-selection bias of mini-publics is still huge and marginalised groups continue to struggle to be part of the conversation (Bussu et al., 2022a). There is also a risk that these sanitised processes of participation end up depoliticising citizen engagement.

In no small part as a response to these concerns, radical participatory politics has seen a strong resurgence, particularly as a reaction to the 2008 financial crisis and the punishing austerity measures that followed across many advanced economies. "Bottom-linked" forms of collaboration and social innovation (Pares et al. 2017), led by social movements and grassroots politics and often grounded in the everyday democracy of the commons, attempt to institutionalise more prefigurative politics with a renewed emphasis on social justice and bringing issues of political economy centre stage. They aspire to deeper changes to current political,

DOI: 10.4324/9781003218517-1

social and economic structures with a strong focus on strengthening people's (material) capacities to participate, which have been conveniently overlooked by much of the thinking on, and practice of, DIs.

This volume explores what happens when grassroots politics and progressive movements try to reclaim and renew forms of participatory and deliberative democracy, and whether, in so doing, they can open up space for a deeper critique of minimalist liberal democratic institutions and the neoliberal economy that underpins them (Sintomer 2018; Bua and Bussu 2021). In this respect, the cases presented in the book reflect democratic ambitions that often go beyond democratising political institutions, as we see efforts to embed participation within the economy and society at large (Bussu et al. 2022b).

This introduction begins by providing an overview of the relationship between social movements and democratisation, developing an account of the ways in which they have provided inspiration for participatory and deliberative democratic theory and practice and the flourishing of much democratic innovation. We argue that recent developments in the relationship between social movements and forms of participatory governance (Heinelt 2018) can be encapsulated by the concept of "democracy-driven governance" (DDG) (Bua and Bussu 2021). In the following section we define DDG and explain how it acts as a bridge between grassroots politics, the commons and institutions, making visible the everyday democracy that is often invisible to political centres of power (West et al. 2019). The aim is to expand the scope of democratic regulation through institutional reforms inspired by prefigurative politics. The diverse contributions to this volume are more or less loosely vertebrated by this idea and analyse several empirical cases to illuminate these recent developments and help further conceptualisations of DDG. In the last section, we reflect on some of the challenges and opportunities that the various chapters engage with.

Social Movements and Participatory Deliberative Democracy: A Long-Term and Growing Relationship

Social movements and civil society groups have long contributed to democratic life in different ways (Felicetti 2016) advancing demands for democratisation and more substantive citizen engagement through horizontal forms of political and economic organisation and participation (Baiocchi and Ganuza 2016; della Porta and Felicetti 2019). A rich literature has examined their role within conventional political processes (Tarrow 1994; Giugni, McAdam, and Tilly 1999; Goldstone 2003). This scholarship interprets collective action not simply as the formulation of political demands through protests but also as the direct production of collective goods, for instance through forms of mutual help, service delivery and experimentation with communitarian lifestyles (della Porta and Diani 2015) to address current socio-economic and ecological crises (Obeng-Odoom 2021).

Social movements play a pivotal role within democratic theories rooted in the critical tradition – whether participatory (Pateman 1970; Barber 1988), deliberative (Dryzek 2000; Mansbridge 2020), agonistic (Laclau and Mouffe 2001) or

Marxist (Wood 1996) – that promote the expansion of democracy into different spheres of life (Vick 2015). Concessions made by propertied elites to stave off working-class militancy were foundational to the development, expansion and consolidation of representative democracy in the 19th and early 20th centuries (Pilon 2013; Rueschmeyer et al. 1992), and della Porta (2020) has highlighted how social movements, from the labour movement to recent anti-austerity protests, have contributed to a broader conceptualisation of democracy. Their prefigurative politics and their work in facilitating grassroots participation have helped shape more inclusive and transparent forms of internal decision-making, often based on consensus building, which have informed much practice of participatory and deliberative democracy (della Porta 2015). Mansbridge (1996) and Dryzek (2000) had already recognised deliberation within social movements, and their privileged position to build deliberative spaces, as their critical view of institutions can mitigate risks of co-optation.

In recent years, there has been increasing and explicit interest among grassroots groups in adopting deliberative and participatory practices, not just for their own internal decision-making but to engage with institutions (della Porta and Felicetti 2019; Bua and Bussu 2021). In 2011, the Indignados (Indignant) movement in Spain captured the imagination of many progressive observers, as social movements and grassroots groups engaged in experiments in deliberative and direct democracy and crowd-sourced constitutional processes to build movement parties' platforms against austerity measures. The New Municipalism movement that ensued (Bua and Davies, forthcoming; Russell 2019), spreading since across many different countries, attempts to democratise the economy as well as political institutions through mobilising support for practices such as community-wealth building, whereby public institutions can use public procurement to strengthen the local economy, prioritising cooperatives and social enterprises.

The link between environmental protection, socio-economic equality and an inclusive participatory democracy has been at the centre of much global collective action since, particularly during the COVID-19 pandemic, which has laid bare structural injustice along class, gender and racial lines. The pandemic years have been a time of heightened populism, misinformation and scapegoating. A lack of transparency and low accountability, as emergency laws have been used to curb dissent, has highlighted the need for greater citizen participation to strengthen democracy. At the same time, with COVID our societies witnessed an outpouring of bottom-up social action, not least through autonomous mutual support networks, providing a stark contrast with the more visible centralisation of power as governments entered crisis management. Indeed, in the context of continued attacks on public services and growing inequalities, as we emerge into a post-pandemic world shaken by overlapping urgent crises generating spiralling living costs and pushing many into poverty, there is a renewed emphasis on the idea of the commons as public goods that need to be managed through the active participation of citizens, users and the workers.

The volume captures this growing synergy between social movements' mobilisations, the commons and participatory deliberative democracy, and how grassroots democratic action is mobilising to foster alternative forms of participatory politics and economics. The different chapters provide theoretically grounded and empirical analyses of these processes. In this introduction we first develop a conceptual framework through which to analyse these developments and we later articulate the book's overall contribution to both the literature on social movements and the theory and practice of participatory democracy.

Democracy-Driven Governance: Embedding Participation

The concept of *democracy-driven governance* (DDG) (Bua and Bussu 2021) describes the kinds of participatory projects that arise when social movements engage with participatory deliberative institutional design, as part of their strategy to reclaim the state (Wainwright 2003). We use the term as a counterpoint to Warren's (2009) *governance-driven democratisation* (GDD), which refers to democratic innovations mostly initiated by public agencies to respond to specific policy issues and enhance epistemic value. GDD forms of engagement have confronted an important paradox. As new and innovative forms of citizen participation in policymaking and public service delivery are used globally and at different tiers of government, the space for meaningful citizen input is increasingly constrained by technocratic decision-making and global economic pressures (Baiocchi and Ganuza 2016; Streeck 2014). Rather than providing channels to challenge existing socio-economic inequalities, these processes have often been embedded within the neoliberal rhetoric of transparency, good governance and open government (Pateman 2012). Within this context issues of social justice and redistribution of wealth and power, or De Sousa Santos' (1998) "redistributive democracy", let alone the socio-economic and cultural factors that might affect people's capacity to participate meaningfully, have often been side-lined (Fung 2015; Lee et al. 2015; Wampler and Touchton 2019).

Redistributive democracy had been a fundamental feature of early practice of participatory democracy in local politics in the 1960s, with an emphasis on expanding democracy to all spheres of life, starting with the workplace (Pateman 1970). Some radical democrats such as Sheldon Wolin (2008) have pointed out that the 1960s may have been just a moment in which space emerged for meaningful participatory democratic politics, and this space has since closed down or has been fundamentally altered. During the early 1990s, isolated experiences of radical participatory governance emerged in the global South, with initiatives such as Participatory Budgeting (PB) in Porto Alegre (Baiocchi 2001). However, the literature tracing the diffusion and globalisation of PB (Baiocchi and Ganuza 2016) found that, as it travelled the globe, it dropped its critical edge, shifting its focus from social justice to "good governance", as global institutions such as the World Bank started to include it in their open government toolkit. The political has been taken out of politics, in what Wolin (2008) describes as "inverted totalitarianism" or a "managed democracy". We can see these processes of radical change and co-optation throughout the history of participatory governance (Baiocchi 2018). Processes enthusiastically initiated and embraced by radical activists as ways to reclaim the state, were made functional to neoliberalism and its social inequities (Lee et al. 2015). Scholars of a critical political economy tradition warned against the risks of decoupling the practice of democracy and politics from socio-economic constraints, and they developed critiques arguing that, far from deepening participation, these processes might in fact advance neoliberal governmentalities and mystifications (Davies 2011; Swyngedouw 2005). By the same token, the theory and practice of democratic innovation has produced ever-innovative designs, using digital and analogue spaces, pushing the boundaries of what is possible in terms of expanding the reach and scale of direct participation (Elstub and Escobar 2019).

Often reconciling bottom-up practice and top-down designs, there has been a rise in democratic experiments involving activists and practitioners coming together to develop more inclusive approaches to democratic innovations. The grassroots-led deliberative process G1000, for instance, in 2011 brought together Belgian citizens through a series of participatory spaces, including randomly selected citizen assemblies and panels, to discuss a range of policies at a time of political vacuum in the country (Reuchamps et al. 2014). In cases where this grassroots action was successful in building movement parties and winning elections, such as with the New Municipalism movement in Spain (Roth 2019), it produced a social movement-rooted, participatory politics. As social movements learn from theory and recent practice of deliberative democracy, they are developing innovative ways of using and combining these spaces. They are "developing alternative visions of democracy", based on the commons, including the digital commons (Russon-Gilman and Peixoto 2019) prefiguring participatory and deliberative conceptions and engaging in what Wagenaar and Healy (2015) and Wagenaar (2019) call "civic enterprise" referring to the bottom-up production of goods and services.

Democracy-driven governance (DDG) is closely linked to both the traditions of participatory democracy (Pateman 1970; Barber 1984) and radical democratic theory (Wolin 2008), which both provide particularly useful insights to flesh out this concept and its potential as an analytical framework. Albeit sympathetic to the ideals of participatory democracy, radical democrats point to the challenges of its institutionalisation. They argue that the preconditions for the institutionalisation of greater participation that partly characterised the 1960s have given way to a polity dominated by corporations, with unprecedented economic and political inequality, therefore precluding genuine opportunities for inclusive participation and tangible change (Vick 2015). Faced with the doomed stance of radical thought, participatory democracy's lesson lies in the importance of continuing to strive for institutional change and democratisation of diverse spheres of life to empower citizens (Pateman 1970).

DDG builds on these different perspectives. On the one hand, we can understand it as a form of "participation by irruption" (Blas and Ibarra 2006) that establishes the centrality of collectives and groups in an oppositional stance to the state. On the other hand, it seeks to engage with and influence the state, by reclaiming routinised participatory governance. It, therefore, lies somewhere in between the "critical" and "incumbent" forms of democracy as theorised by Blaug (2002), whereby incumbent democracy attempts to preserve and improve existing institutions, whilst critical democracy challenges it through prefigurative politics. DDG is not a top down, or engineered (Blaug 2002), form of participation, but it does seek to gain leverage over the power of the state, within and against it. It acknowledges the critique advanced by radical democratic theory but embraces the challenges of institutionalisation supported by participatory democracy. It incorporates radical democratic calls for diluting the artificial boundaries between economy and politics put in place by liberalism (Wood 1996), with an explicit focus on social justice and structural change, and processes that focus on realising what Smith (2009) referred to as the "democratic good" of "popular control". DDG therefore might provide an analytical frame that helps understand interconnections between forms of citizen participation that have so far been analysed through different theoretical frames and by scholarships that hardly ever speak to one another, e.g., democratic innovations, coproduction, social movements, the commons. DDG places emphasis on the role of grassroots and social movements in generating bottom-up institutional engagement that aims to democratise not just politics, but the economy and wider society. Through DDG we recognise that, if the goal is to widen the scope and reach of democracy, reforms have to be pursued through action that embeds political and institutional, as well as economic and societal changes (Bussu et al. 2022b).

In our article (Bua and Bussu 2021), we emphasise that these different interpretations of participatory governance are neither fixed nor mutually exclusive; they exist in a dynamic relationship. We move beyond a static and dichotomous understanding of top-down and bottom-up participation and instead reflect on this relationship as part of broader processes of contestation and change. Newly claimed spaces can close through assimilation or co-optation (Gaventa 2004), whilst top-down spaces can generate "new fields of power" (Barnes et al. 2007), opening new opportunities for democratisation and space for meaningful change. Therefore, far from being dichotomous or insulated from each other, these understandings interact and overlap through processes of change and co-optation, rooted in "cycles of contention" (Tarrow 1998).

Challenges and Opportunities for Democracy-Driven Governance

The volume examines how this grassroots-led governance works in the real world, accepting that democratisation is always fraught with difficulties within regimes of power in institutions, technology and practice, and there are important challenges "in the fragmentation of the potential social bases, the need to build a new collective identity as well as to establish channels of access to power" (della Porta et al. 2019: 3). Contributions examine how these grassroots movements engage in democratic practice with, within and beyond institutions, promoting alternative modes of governance.

If working with institutions may often be a necessary condition to ensure impact, it is not a sufficient one. It is also difficult to identify clear indicators of impactful participation, and this is still a question under debate. Direct effects on policymaking have long been seen as the benchmark of substantive participation and deliberation (Arnstein 1969), but recent scholarship has pointed out that this should not be interpreted as the only indicator (Goodin and Dryzek 2006; Dryzek 2009; Niemeyer 2014), and other forms of societal and political impact should be considered. In fact, Arnstein's ladder has been criticised for giving quite a simplistic representation of participatory roles and a very linear and hierarchical measure of citizen empowerment. Other scholars have suggested a "star of participation" as an alternative metaphor, with no ideologically validated top (May 2006: 312), whereby citizens can choose to participate in different, more or less intensive, ways without necessarily ending at the bottom of the ladder. Thus, as illuminated by some of the cases presented in this book, DDG might make an equally important contribution in raising public support for deeper public participation and a more radical understanding of democracy, as much as in trying to change structures of governance. It inspires more democratic innovation as it generates global interest in local projects rooted in public demands for democratic engagement to address pressing political problems (della Porta and Felicetti 2019: 13).

Engagement with institutions raises several dilemmas for grassroots groups and social movements. It provides participatory experiments with substantial resources, but it also carries risks of co-optation and absorption into state structures, whereby social movements are required to adapt to state rules and practice, and institutions impose administrative logics and continue to formulate and implement the parameters for citizen participation (Boltanski and Chiapello 2005; Fraser 2015; Lima 2019; Bua and Bussu 2021).

The book provides an analysis of diverse social movement-led processes for democratisation and their potential, limits and opportunities. We initially developed the concept of democracy-driven governance (DDG) in the particular context of the political crisis and wave of contestation witnessed in Spain in the 2010s. Especially important in this context was the "radical municipalist" experience mentioned above (Roth et al. 2019), or new municipalism (Russell 2019), whereby many of Spain's large- and medium-sized cities experimented with, and attempted to radicalise, participatory policies, introducing novel forms of participatory budgeting, sortition chambers, associative democracy, public-commons partnerships and techno-democracy. The contributions reflect on the extent to which the DDG concept travels to other cases, where the material fallout from the Great Recession might not have been a crucial factor and where we might see different political cultures and usages for democracy-driven governance. The book thus explores through different cases and theoretical frames:

- what occurs when social movements are involved in shaping processes of participatory democracy, reflecting on the extent to which such initiatives can sustain the radical potential of citizen participation for social transformation;

- whether we see new forms of participation emerging, or new usages for participatory institutional design;
- the obstacles that DDG ambitions encounter as they try to broaden the scope of democracy;
- the political and institutional impacts on social movements of engaging with participatory governance;
- the tensions between the different demands of lay citizens, organised civil society and public officials.

The book is structured into three main sections. The first section applies different theoretical frameworks to expand conceptualisations and deepen the understanding of democracy-driven governance. In Chapter 2, Fleuß provides a "deliberative account" of institutional/constitutional change emerging through bottom-up political action. She uses exemplary cases in Iceland and Germany to highlight how the theory and practice of deliberative democracy can inform radical reform. As activists reclaim and reinvent these spaces, they have to navigate a fundamental dilemma as they attempt to both counteract and cooperate with political elites. Vlahos (Chapter 3) situates GDD and DDG within a broader conceptual discourse of political economy. He draws on Polanyi's (2001) notion of the "double movement" and Esping-Andersen's (1990) notion of de-commodification to develop nuanced interpretations of how both GDD and DDG can influence processes of (de)commodification and how they work within welfare systems of stratification, providing an innovative reading of how contemporary participatory governance operates in a capitalist democracy. Holdo (Chapter 4) suggests thinking of participation as a form of "democratic care". He draws on works by feminist theorists on the ethics of care to examine participation as both a form of transformative politics and inadvertently complicit in sustaining a neoliberal economy. To participate is to defend solidarity against the neoliberal understanding of people as only caring about their self-interest. However, acts of caring for the community and democracy might also be covering up the consequences of neoliberal policies. Participation in itself is neither disruptive nor supportive of neoliberalism. To be genuinely disruptive and foster DDG regimes, people need to use participatory spaces to renegotiate the terms of their cooperation. Wagenaar (Chapter 5) closes this section with a sober assessment of the steep challenges that both GDD and DDG encounter in advancing their different projects of democratic reform, in the context of the neoliberal political economy. He describes democracy as suspended "within a triangle of distinct operational orders formed by civil society, the state and the corporate-financial sphere". The chapter traces how over the past 50 years the economic sphere has gradually encroached onto the other two to develop into a hegemonic complex that constrains democracy and is immune to its influence. Wagenaar sets out a broader theory of progressive democratic reform that emerges piecemeal through a democratic "multiverse" of commons-based democratic practice.

The second section explores how DDG experiences emerge and develop across different socio-political, economic, cultural and policy contexts. Pierri (Chapter 6) reflects on environmental protection, a policy area which has seen growing state- and social movement-led experimentation with various forms of (more or less radical) participatory governance. The chapter presents empirical findings from an 18-month project to promote climate resilience and reflects specifically on the innovative form of governance for ecological transition in France, which developed as a response to social movement pressure. In Pierri's account social movements act as a "collaborative countervailing power" playing a crucial role in shifting the political discourse and creating space for DDG regimes to emerge. Froden (Chapter 7) presents a very different empirical realisation of DDG, by illuminating interconnections between participatory arts practices and prefigurative social movements. Her short vignettes of political song writing within temporary autonomous zones of resistance within prisons and among immigrants explore the interface between these two realms, demonstrating the benefits of bridging arbitrary disciplinary separations to contribute to radical democratic renewal. Here, democratic reforms emerge from "democratic ecosystems" (Asenbaum 2022) characterised by "complex interactions, porous boundaries, cyclical processes, vitality, mutual dependence and constant change, and as such this notion holds potential for all kinds of participation to be recognised – not just sites that are explicitly political".

The remaining chapters of this section provide very different cases of opposition and resistance to economic, political and colonial oppressions to foster democratic change. Falanga (Chapter 8) uses the conceptual framework of the "right to the city" to analyse the case of Lisbon and explore how social movements' demands emerged and interplayed with the local council's participatory agenda. The "right to the city" frame helps shed light on "emerging socio-political dynamics within and at the border of the participatory setting". Allegretti's (Chapter 9) contribution explores the case of Greenland (Nuuk). Here anticolonial protests in 2020 opened up new space for political participation, where there were traditionally limited opportunities for citizen engagement, within a very closed society. This unorganised community chose to focus on the institution of Nuuk's mayor, forcing it to engage in more structured dialogue and laying the groundwork for more innovative participatory spaces going forward. Mendonça, Gelape and Cruz (Chapter 10) introduce us to collective mandates in contemporary Brazilian politics. Under Brazilian law, a group of individuals can run together for the same seat in Parliament in what is called a *collective candidacy*. If elected, they exert a *collective mandate*. Social movements are making creative use of this institution and the chapter traces their strategies and challenges to, with varying degrees of success, translate multiple voices into one vote in Parliamentary processes. They explore how this innovation is emerging as a creative solution deployed by social movements to strengthen their voice and claims within representative institutions, a pragmatic response that acknowledges the vulnerabilities and limitations of ad hoc participatory processes and tries instead to strengthen the inclusivity of representative politics. The authors examine how these experiments generate ruptures in politics as usual, disrupting the inner workings of the legislative chamber and opening space for DDG-like change. The last chapter of this section by Bua,

Bussu and Davies (Chapter 11) charts the transitions from GDD to DDG reforms through comparative analysis of Nantes and Barcelona, identifying the conditions under which DDG-like forms of participatory governance develop, flourish and are sustained or undermined.

The final section looks at more advanced experiences of DDG to provide a detailed analysis of the challenges they encounter, from bureaucratic resistance to pressure to adapt to the existing policy infrastructure and activist fatigue. Economic and political decisions are hardwired in laws, regulations, fiscal arrangements, customs and practices that inevitably constrain any projects of radical democratic reform. Not only are these processes vulnerable to political cycles and co-optation, as discussed above, but they also have to navigate resistance from bureaucracies, mainstream media and business. This resistance is not always on ideological grounds; often participatory approaches to policymaking and service delivery clash against existing and routed practices of governing and working routines. Understanding how we can engender and embed a participatory culture within policymaking and public service delivery is a crucial challenge (Bussu et al. 2022b). Even sympathetic bureaucrats might resist when participatory policymaking or new public-commons partnership appears to create more work for them, or if they feel new procedures lack clarity and might incur legal restrictions. For this, we need to understand better the interwoven practices of public officials, practitioners and activists that shape and contest processes of embedding participatory institutions in policymaking and the wider society (ibid.).

Many of the cases featured in this section are from Spain. This is because the Spanish experience of DDG is the most advanced, following electoral victories for social movements and grassroots-led coalitions across many major cities in 2015. These chapters reflect on the clash between activist and bureaucratic cultures, or the tensions between different approaches to participatory governance, whether based on organised participation mediated by civil society or individual citizens being invited directly, for instance through online participatory platforms like Decidim, in ways that might bypass civil society organisations. Balcells, Borge and Padró-Solanet (Chapter 12) focus on the use both social movements and local institutions make of participatory digital platforms and how they both contribute to changing the patterns of local governance. The chapter looks at how the participatory platform Decidim has been used by Catalan local governments. This is a platform originally designed by free software movements and 15-M activists protesting against austerity measures post-2008 financial crash. The analysis brings into focus the tensions between the different understanding of participatory governance from both social movements and public administrations, which the authors conceptualise as democracy-driven governance versus governance-driven democratisation. They coexist and interact with each other, though not unproblematically. Through a combination of quantitative and qualitative methods, the analysis traces the obstacles, drivers and trade-offs that condition the development of Decidim as a tool for expanding participatory governance. The study focuses specifically on the perspective of public managers implementing Decidim, whose role often ends up bridging between local administrations and civil society. One of the most interesting findings is that those municipalities with high percentages of citizens registered on the platform are more likely to find resistance from local associations due to "fear of disintermediation" and being bypassed. Pera, Bianchi and Salazar (Chapter 13) examine the case of the Citizen Assets Programme (CAP) in Barcelona, a new policy supporting the urban commons and how this facilitates embeddedness of participation in the local political culture (Bussu et al. 2022b). CAP is understood as a clear example of DDG, as it proposes "an institutional design to recognise and protect urban commons, through the Barcelona en Comú (BeC) government". Under CAP, commons-led management of services and facilities is recognised and promoted by the City Council through so-called public-commons institutions to create new democratic spaces. However, there are several challenges to embedding citizens' led practices into the policy realm. Trust (or lack thereof) plays a crucial role in brokering relationships among the actors participating in DDG policies.

Mota and Guernes (Chapter 14) look at Spain's capital city under the "Ahora Madrid" (Madrid Now) coalition that developed from the 15-M or Indignados movement. The coalition won elections in May 2015 with a manifesto focused on addressing social and territorial inequalities by supporting and expanding a participatory governance infrastructure. This represented a clear attempt at implementing a DDG regime. The authors provide a critique of the approach, which was mainly based on individual – mostly digital – participation, and reflect on whether the new participatory instruments genuinely deepened democracy or rather turned into a management tool. Their findings based on mixed methods covering the length of Ahora Madrid's mandate, between 2015 and 2019, detail how DDG drifted into techno-populism, as the technopolitical or cyberactivist soul of the movement ended up dominating the approach to participatory democracy. The rich analysis identifies three drivers of these dynamics: the plurality of collective action traditions contained within the 15-M movement struggled to coexist within the digital platform; conflicting visions of citizen participation conveyed by the two City Council departments in charge of implementing participatory governance; and the mayor's own technopopulist style of leadership.

The last two chapters of the section take the perspective of activists. The literature highlights both benefits and challenges for activists engaging with participatory mechanisms, particularly when these primarily foster participation on an individual basis, as in the case of Ahora Madrid: on the one hand, there is increased transparency and increased information for non-organised citizens, and on the other hand, activists' aims and ambitions are inevitably contained and moderated. García-Espín (Chapter 15) specifically explores one aspect that has received less attention: the problem of disappointment for activists where ambitions for social justice clash against the limited powers of local participatory institutions, which often do not have the remit and capacity to implement and sustain radical reforms. To examine this puzzle, she explores the case of local forums in Madrid, under the Ahora Madrid government (2015–19). Her analysis also provides ideas to address these issues in practice, from the activists' own unique perspective. Finally, Van Outryve (Chapter 16) moves away from the Spanish experience and presents a case of grassroots-led citizen assembly in the French town of Commercy. The chapter follows this process of radical participatory democracy from its emergence as a result of the 2018 Yellow Vests movement until its demise following the municipal elections of March 2020, detailing this group of activists' determination and creativity in designing inclusive spaces of dialogue and decision-making and the practical challenges they faced in building community support for a very different approach to political engagement.

In the contemporary context of accelerated, deepening, multifaceted and interlinked political, economic, environmental and social crises (Fraser 2022), it is more imperative than ever to ask whether these developments help advance democracy at a time when it is under such severe pressure. The contemporary situation makes the search for transformative projects rooted in, and inseparable from, democratic deepening and expansion (Baiocchi 2018) all the more important. All these cases provide many insights into the contested space to advance democracy. In his concluding remarks, Gianpaolo Baiocchi (Chapter 17) notes that many of the chapters point to the importance of "domain-specific enabling and constraining features". All these cases, however, emphasise how social movements and citizen participation continue to play a crucial role in furthering the cause of critical theory: to challenge incumbency and demonstrate the possibility of other worlds (Horkheimer 1939).

References

Arnstein, S.R. (1969). "A ladder of citizen participation." *Journal of the American Planning Association* 85(1): 24–34.
Asenbaum, H. (2022). Beyond Deliberative Systems Pluralizing the Debate. *Democratic Theory* 9(1): 87–98.
Baiocchi, G. (2001). "Participation, activism, and politics: The Porto Alegre experiment and deliberative democratic theory." *Politics & Society* 29(1): 43–72.
Baiocchi, G. (2018). *We, the Sovereign*. Cambridge: Polity Press.
Baiocchi, G. and Ganuza, E. (2016). *Popular Democracy: The Paradox of Participation*. Stanford: Stanford University Press.
Barber, B.K. (1984). *Strong Democracy: Participatory Politics for a New Age*. Berkeley: University of California Press.
Barnes, M., Newman, J. and Sullivan, H. (2007). *Power, Participation, and Political Renewal*. Bristol: The Policy Press.
Blaug, R. (2002). "Engineering democracy." *Political Studies* 50(1): 102–116.
Boltanski, L., Chiapello, E. and Elliott, G. (2005). *The New Spirit of Capitalism*. London: Verso.
Bua, A. and Bussu, S. (2021). "Between governance-driven democratisation and democracy-driven governance: Explaining changes in participatory governance in the case of Barcelona." *European Journal of Political Research* 60: 716–737. https://doi.org/10.1111/1475-6765.12421
Bua, A. and Davies, J. (forthcoming). "Understanding the crisis of new municipalism in Spain: The struggle for urban regime power in A Coruña and Santiago de Compostela." *Urban Studies*, Online before print, https://doi.org/10.1177/00420980221123939

Bussu, G. et al. (2022a). *Understanding developments in Participatory Governance, MMU.* https://www.mmu.ac.uk/sites/default/files/2022-08/Understanding%20developments%20in%20participatory%20governance_Bussu%20et%20al-06-08-22_final.pdf

Bussu, S., Bua, A. Dean, R. and Smith, G. (2022b). "Introduction: Embedding participatory governance." *Critical Policy Studies* 16(2): 133–145, DOI: 10.1080/19460171.2022.2053179

Chambers, S. (2009). "Rhetoric and the Public Sphere Has Deliberative Democracy Abandoned Mass Democracy?" *Political Theory* 37(3): 323–350.

Cornwall, A. (2002). "Making Spaces, Changing Places: Situating Participation in Development." IDS working papers 170. https://www.ids.ac.uk/publications/making-spaces-changing-places-situating-participation-in-development/

Davies, J. (2011). *Challenging Governance Theory: From Networks to Hegemony.* Bristol University Press.

de Sousa Santos, B. (1998). "Participatory budgeting in Porto Alegre: Toward a redistributive democracy." *Politics & Society* 26(4): 461–510.

Della Porta, D. (2015). *Social Movements in Times of Austerity: Bringing Capitalism Back into Protest Analysis.* Cambridge, Malden: Polity Press.

Della Porta, D. (2020). "Protests as critical junctures: Some reflections towards a momentous approach to social movements." *Social Movement Studies* 19(5–6): 556–575.

Della Porta, D. and Diani, M. (Eds.) (2015). *The Oxford Handbook of Social Movements.* Oxford: Oxford University Press.

Della Porta, D. and Felicetti, A. (2019). "Innovating democracy against democratic stress in Europe: Social movements and democratic experiments." *Representation.* https//doi.org/10.1080/00344893.2019.1624600

Della Porta, D. and Felicetti, A. (2022). "Innovating Democracy Against Democratic Stress in Europe: Social Movements and Democratic Experiments." *Representation* 58(1): 67–84.

Dryzek JS (2000). *Deliberative Democracy and Beyond: Liberals, Critics, Contestations.* Oxford: Oxford University Press.

Dryzek, J.S. (2009). "Democratization as deliberative capacity building." *Comparative Political Studies* 42(11): 1379–1402.

Elstub, S. and Escobar, O. (2019). *Handbook of Democratic Innovation and Governance.* Edward Elgar Publishing.

Esping-Andersen, G. 1990. *The Three Worlds of Welfare Capitalism.* Cambridge: Polity Press.

Font, J., et al. (2018). "Cherry-picking participation: Explaining the fate of proposals from participatory processes." *European Journal of Political Research* 57(3): 615–636.

Fraser, N. (2015). "Legitimation crisis? On the political contradictions of financialized capitalism." *Critical Historical Studies* 2(2): 157–189.

——— (2022). *Cannibal Capitalism.* London: Verso.

Fung, A. (2015). "Putting the public back into governance: The challenges of citizen participation and its future." *Public Administration Review* 75(4): 513–522.

Gaventa, J. (2004). "Strengthening participatory approaches to local governance: Learning the lessons from abroad." *National Civic Review* 93(4): 16–27.

Giugni, M., McAdam, D. and Tilly, C. (Eds.). (1999). *How Social Movements Matter* (NED-New edition, Vol. 10). University of Minnesota Press. http://www.jstor.org/stable/10.5749/j.ctttt706

Goldstone, J. (Ed.). (2003). *States, Parties, and Social Movements (Cambridge Studies in Contentious Politics).* Cambridge: Cambridge University Press. doi:10.1017/CBO9780511625466

Goodin, R.E. and Dryzek, J.S. (2006). "Deliberative impacts: The macro-political uptake of mini-publics." *Politics & Society* 34(2): 219–244.

Heinelt, H. (2018). *Handbook on Participatory Governance*. Edward Elgar.

Hendriks, C.M. and Lees-Marshment, J. (2019). Political leaders and public engagement: The hidden world of informal Elite–citizen interaction. *Political Studies* 67(3): 597–617. https://doi.org/10.1177/0032321718791370

Horkheimer, M. (1939). "*The social function of philosophy*", Critical theory, selected essays. Available at https://www.marxists.org/reference/archive/horkheimer/1939/social-function.htm, accessed 18/10/2022

Laclau, E. and Mouffe, C. (2001). *Hegemony and Socialist Strategy*. London: Verso.

Lafont, C. (2020). *Democracy Without Shortcuts: A Participatory Conception of Deliberative Democracy* (First). Oxford: Oxford University Press.

Landemore Hélène. (2020). *Open Democracy: Reinventing Popular Rule for the Twenty-first Century*. Princeton University Press. Retrieved October 15 2022 from http://search.ebscohost.com/login.aspx?direct=true&scope=site&db=nlebk&db=nlabk&AN=2441142.

Lee, C.W. (2015). "Participatory practices in organizations." *Sociology Compass* 9(4): 272–288.

Lima, V. (2019). "The limits of participatory democracy and the inclusion of social movements in local government." *Social Movement Studies* 18(6): 667–681.

Mansbridge, J. (1996). *In Defense of "Descriptive" Representation (96–18)*. Institute for Policy Research at Northwestern University.

Mansbridge, J., (2020). "A citizen-centered theory." *Journal of Deliberative Democracy* 16(2): 15–24. doi: https://doi.org/10.16997/jdd.411

May, J. (2006). "Ladders, stars and triangles: Old and new theory for the practice of public participation." *International Journal of Market Research* 48(3): 305–319.

Nyemeyer, S. (2014). "Defence of (deliberative) democracy in the Anthropocene." *Ethical perspectives* 21(1): 15–45.

Obeng-Odoom F. (2021). "The commons in an age of uncertainty: Decolonizing nature economy and society." University of Toronto Press. Retrieved October 10 2022 from http://public.eblib.com/choice/PublicFullRecord.aspx?p=6384633

OECD (2020). Innovative Citizen Participation and New Democratic Institutions. https://www.oecd.org/gov/innovative-citizen-participation-and-new-democratic-institutions-339306da-en.htm

Papadopoulos, Y. (2012). "On the embeddedness of deliberative systems: Why elitist innovations matter more. Deliberative systems: Deliberative democracy at the large scale." In *J. Mansbridge and J. Parkinson*. Cambridge, Cambridge University Press: 125–150.

Pares, M. Ospina, S. and Subirats, J. (2017). *Social Innovation and Democratic Leadership: Communities and Social Change from Below*. Northampton, Massachusetts: Edward and Elgar.

Pateman, C. (1970). *Participation and Democratic Theory*. Cambridge: Cambridge University Press.

Pateman, C. (2012). "Participatory democracy revisited." *Perspectives on Politics* 10(1): 7–11.

Pilon, D. (2013). *Wrestling with Democracy: Voting Systems as Politics in the 20th Century*. Toronto: University of Toronto Press.

Polanyi, K. 2001. *The Great Transformation: The Political and Economic Origins of Our Time. Foreword by Joseph E. Stiglitz*. Boston: Beacon Press.

Roth, L. (2019). "Democracy y Municipalismo." In L. Roth, A. Monterde and A. Calleja López, (eds),*CiudadesDemocraticas. La Revuelta Municipalista en el Ciclo post-15M*. Barcelona, Spain: Icaria Publishers.

Rueschemeyer, S. and Stepher. (1992). *Capitalist Development and Democracy*. Chicago: University of Chicago Press.

Russell, B. (2019). "Beyond the local trap: New municipalism and the rise of the fearless cities." *Antipode* 51: 989–1010. https://doi.org/10.1111/anti.12520

Russon-Gilman, H. and Peixoto, T. (2019). "Digital participation." In S. Elstub and O. Escobar (eds), *The Handbook of Democratic Innovation and Governance*, 105–118. Cheltenham, UK; Northampton, MA, USA: Edward Elgar.

Sintomer Y., et al. (2013). *Learning from the South: Participatory Budgeting worldwide: An Invitation to Global Cooperation*. Bonn, Germany, Service Agency for Communities

Sintomer, Y. (2018). "From deliberative to radical democracy? Sortition and politics in the twenty-first century." *Politics & Society* 46(3): 337–357. https://doi.org/10.1177/0032329218789888

Smith, G. (2009). *Democratic Innovations: Designing Institutions for Citizen Participation: Theories of Institutional Design*. Cambridge: Cambridge University Press.

Streeck, W. (2014). *Buying Time: The Delayed Crisis of Democratic Capitalism*. London, UK: Verso Books.

Swyngedouw, E. (2005). "Governance innovation and the citizen: The Janus face of governance-beyond-the-state."*Urban Studies* 42(11): 1991–2006.

Tarrow, S (1994). *Power in Movement. Social Movements, Collective Action and Politics*. Cambridge and New York: Cambridge University Press.

Vick, J. (2015). "Participatory versus radical democracy in the 21st century: Carole Pateman, Jacques Rancière, and Sheldon Wolin." *New Political Science* 37(2): 204–223.

Wagenaar, H. (2019). "Special issue on: Social movements and the third sector." *Partecipazione e Conflitto* 12(2): 298–324.

Wagenaar, H and Healey, P. (2015). "Interface: The transformative potential of civic enterprise." *Planning Theory and Practice* 16(4): 557–561.

Wainwright, H. (2003). *Reclaim the State*. London: Verso.

Wampler, B. and Touchton, M. (2019). "Designing institutions to improve well-being: Participation, deliberation and institutionalisation." *European Journal of Political Research* 58(3): 915–937.

Warren, M.E. (2009). "Governance-driven democratization." *Critical Policy Studies* 3(1): 3–13.

West, S., van Kerkhoff, L. and Wagenaar, H. (2019). "Beyond "linking knowledge and action": Towards a practice-based approach to transdisciplinary sustainability interventions." *Policy Studies* 40(5): 534–555. DOI: 10.1080/01442872.2019.1618810

Wolin, S. (2008). *Democracy Incorporated: Managed Democracy and the Specter of Inverted Totalitarianism*. Princeton: Princeton University Press.

Wood E.M. (1996). *Democracy Against Capitalism: Renewing Historical Materialism*. London: Verso.

——— (2002). *The Origin of Capitalism: A Longer View* ([New ed.]). London: Verso.

Section 1
Conceptualising Democracy-Driven Governance

2 Challenging the "Rules of the Game"
The Role of Bottom-Up Participatory Experiments for Deliberative Democracy

Dannica Fleuß

Introduction

Deliberative democrats put bottom-up legitimacy at the very heart of their normative project. This suggests that all policies and constitutionally fixated "rules of the democratic game" ultimately must be rooted in inclusive procedures and discourses. It also suggests that these inclusive procedures are not exclusively or mainly driven by the state, but by civil society actors such as social movements. I will take this "normative core" of deliberative theory as a point of departure and provide a critical assessment of "classical", Habermasian deliberative democracy, particularly of Habermas' account of institutional and constitutional change. I shall argue that Habermas' proposals for institutional and constitutional reform display a severe *status quo* bias and only allow for incremental reforms that carry on the project of the existing constitution's "founding fathers".

This chapter will explore how deliberative democrats can respond to contemporary democratic crisis phenomena (e.g. increasing levels of citizen dissatisfaction and distrust) – and how concrete reform proposals can be developed on the basis of deliberative theorising. Despite all critiques of Habermas' approach to constitutional reform and institutional renewal, I shall argue that deliberative democratic theory can figure as a normative bedrock for citizen-led initiatives and participatory experiments that aim at constitutional and/or institutional reforms. To this aim, I will proceed in two basic steps. First, I outline an understanding of deliberative democracy that avoids the shortcomings identified in Habermas' approach. I suggest that the core political ideals at play should not be the "closure" of disagreements and "rational consensus", but participants' open-mindedness in communicative exchanges and the open-endedness of political debates and processes. Second, I argue that this "refocused" understanding of deliberative democracy provides a suitable basis for an account of constitutional and institutional reform that is true to deliberative democracy's normative core – i.e. bottom-up legitimacy – and thereby provides a novel perspective on constitutional or institutional reforms.

This approach to institutional reform and constitutional change values citizen-led initiatives and acknowledges the contributions of social movements and civil society actors. Based on two exemplary cases – the Icelandic Initiative for

DOI: 10.4324/9781003218517-3

Constitutional Reform and the recent and ongoing endeavours of the German "Bürgerrat Demokratie" – I will illustrate how bottom-up, citizen-led reform initiatives can instigate *genuinely democratic* institutional or constitutional change. I will emphasise that social movements and civil society actors can play a productive role in challenging the "rules of the democratic game". Citizen-led initiatives for democratic renewal and reform not only align with the core values and ideas of deliberative theory. They also provide a more promising point of departure than "governance-driven democratic innovation" (Warren, 2014) for addressing current democratic crises such as citizen disaffection and distrust in the very tenets of democratic governance (Campus & André, 2014; Dalton, 2004; Ercan & Gagnon, 2014; Foa & Mounk, 2019). These phenomena, as well as the results of recent citizen-led initiatives, indicate that foundational changes to contemporary liberal democracies' institutional and constitutional architecture are required – and that these changes amount to expanding citizens' participatory opportunities. Yet government-led initiatives can rarely be expected to challenge existing constitutional arrangements and institutions at a foundational level. The cases studied will also illustrate a fundamental tension or dilemma that civil society actors must cautiously navigate: to achieve democratic reform, citizen-led, bottom-up initiatives must both uphold their commitment *to counteract* and *to cooperate with* established political elites.

To unfold this deliberative perspective on bottom-up democratic reform, this chapter proceeds as follows. In the section "Refocusing Deliberative Theory: Bottom-Up Legitimacy and Radical Openness", I provide a brief reconstruction of Habermas' "classical" deliberative theory, its shortcomings vis-à-vis deliberative core values and an alternative normative-theoretical account. The section "Constitutional Change and Democratic Institutional Reform Reconsidered" features the implications of this understanding for processes of institutional and constitutional reform and their essential aims, agents and limitations and illustrates how these ideals can be put into practice. I shall refer to two citizen-led processes aiming at democratic renewal and specifically highlight the ways in which they made use of the "toolkit" of democratic innovations and participatory governance approaches. The section "Conclusion and a Look Ahead: Democratic Dilemmas to Live (and Work) With" summarises these considerations and takes them as a basis for a "look ahead", calling for measures that make the "toolkit" of democratic innovations more available to social movements and civil society actors.

Refocusing Deliberative Theory: Bottom-Up Legitimacy and Radical Openness

"Classical" Deliberative Theory – and Its Shortcomings

Jürgen Habermas' approach to democratic norms, processes and institutions in *Between Facts and Norms* (1996) constitutes the "classical" reference point for most contemporary deliberative theorising. In Habermas' work, all collectively binding rules must be justified by inclusive democratic procedures. More specifically, they must be justifiable in "rational discourses" (Habermas, 1996, 107). His understanding of democratic legitimacy is articulated in the "principle of democracy", stating that legal norms must be acceptable to "all citizens in a discursive process of opinion- and will-formation" (Habermas, 1996, 135). Habermas highlights that procedures which bring about legitimate laws must be inclusive and firmly rooted in the broader civil society as well as in informal "lifeworld" contexts. The theory thereby places prime value on bottom-up legitimation: ideally, all legislation that takes place in "formal" democratic institutions emerges from inclusive, society-wide communicative exchanges. Discourses in the public sphere channel, scrutinise and "filter" the arguments and political preferences that are articulated by various civil society agents and groups in the "periphery". Ideally, representatives in empowered institutions then draw from citizens' arguments and preferences when they deliberate about and decide upon collectively binding laws. Consequently, a healthy "flow in communication" within democratic systems and a "deliberative uptake" (Scudder, 2020) in empowered institutions warrant "that the addressees of the law [… can] understand themselves as its authors", thereby guaranteeing the democratic legitimacy of collectively binding regulations (Habermas, 2001, p. 767).

This brief outline already indicates that Habermas' understanding of democracy and self-determination not only recognises the crucial value of bottom-up legitimation and emphasises the importance of an "anarchic" public sphere and a vibrant civil society, but it also strongly emphasises the *legal regulations* and *law-creating procedures* (Habermas, 1996, 6; see Fleuß, 2021, 92; Honig, 2001, 799). Further, Habermas highlights that his account "does not give united citizens of a democratic polity a voluntaristic, carte blanche permission to make whatever decision they like" (Habermas, 2001, p. 767). Rather, democratic decisions' "reasonableness" is warranted due to "rationalizing" deliberations and "filtering" mechanisms that select and organise the claims and arguments put forward by lay citizens. The institutional architecture that realises these requirements in political practice ascribes distinct functional roles to, and formulates different normative standards for, "institutionalized deliberative bodies and the informal communication of the public sphere" (Flynn, 2004, p. 439). As a result, this vision of democratic politics is characterised by a comparatively clear-cut distinction between political or judicial elites and lay citizens (Fleuß, 2021, pp. 81–82; Landemore, 2020, p. 5). In principle, *all citizens'* perceptions, arguments and preferences are supposed to figure as the ultimate source of collectively binding rules. Yet the political institutions envisioned by Habermas are designed to facilitate and promote "*reasonable* will-formation" (Habermas, 2001, p. 767; emphasis in the original) – even when this requires *excluding* particular agents or claims (Fleuß, 2021, p. 98; also see Young, 2002).

Habermas' focus on *reasonable law* and *law-creating procedures* also takes effect in his assessment of constitutional provisions and constitutional change. At least at first sight, the principle of democratic self-legislation seems to be at odds with fixed constitutional provisions. Constitutional provisions define "the scope of action for current democratic citizens" and thereby determine (and, potentially, limit) the *range* of political results that "legitimate" processes can bring about at the end of the day (Fleuß, 2021, p. 91). Yet Habermas famously conceives of constitutionalism and democracy as "co-original". He argues that legal regulations that result from democratic procedures enable citizens to exercise and express their political autonomy and, therefore, do not impose restrictions on peoples' self-determination (Habermas, 1996, pp. 121–122; see Fleuß, 2021, pp. 91–92).

Habermas undoubtedly acknowledges "the tense relationship between constitutionalism and democracy" (also see Honig, 2001, pp. 792–793). He claims that deliberative theorists can, however, resolve this tension by understanding democratic constitutions as "open", "future-oriented" projects of political communities who are engaged in a "self-correcting learning process" (Habermas, 2001, p. 774). Yet this process of ongoing "tradition building", constitutional learning and (re-)interpretation presupposes that "all participants [… are] able to recognize the project as the same throughout history and to judge it from the same perspective" (Habermas, 2001, p. 775). In other words, current and future generations must be "'in the same boat' as their forbearers" and as such, reinterpret and reform their constitution in line with the normative standards and intentions of its founders (Habermas, 2001, p. 775).

In sum, classical deliberative theory paints a positive picture of contemporary Western democracies' basic institutional architecture. Despite warning against "idealizing" constitutional courts and judges (Habermas, 1996, p. 280), this affirmative stance also extends to the idea that constitutional courts are normatively adequate institutions for deliberating about foundational constitutional reforms (Fleuß, 2021, p. 153; also see Lafont, 2019, pp. 220–234).

Against the backdrop of deliberative theory's emphasis on inclusive bottom-up legitimacy, a closer look at Habermas' understanding of institutional and constitutional reform processes enables us to identify three more specific points of concern.

First, Habermas rejects "voluntarism" on behalf of democratic citizens: popular sovereignty does not mean that the people get a "carte blanche permission to make whatever decision they like". Rather, both legislation and the continuation of constitutional projects must result from "*reasonable* will-formation" (Habermas, 2001, p. 767). Young famously argued that the reasonableness requirements spelled out by Habermas essentially represent "the speech culture of white middle class men" and, more specifically, of Western intellectual discourses (Allen, 2016; Young, 1996, p. 124, 2002; also see Fleuß, 2021, p. 98). Consequently, the apparently innocent requirement that legislation as well as constitutional and institutional reform projects shall be based on "*reasonable* will-formation" arguably bears problematic consequences: it allows the exclusion of constitutional projects and reform proposals that do not conform to a particular set of (Western, European Enlightenment) traditions based on being considered "unreasonable".

Second, due to Habermas' focus on legislative procedures in "the center", democratic action in the "periphery" – for example, direct action, legal protest or civil disobedience – tends to play a subordinate role. In consequence, "radical democracy [is displayed as] foreign to the institution it beleaguers" (Gerstenberg, 2019,

p. 1059; also see Fleuß, 2021, p. 81). With this, Habermas' deliberative theory gives us little leverage to conceptualise citizen-led initiatives that challenge the *status quo* of democratic politics and to ascribe them a positive role or function.

Third, Habermas' understanding of "autonomy" and "self-legislation" may support the conclusion that democracy requires the rule of law (and vice versa, as both principles are "co-original") (Habermas, 1996, pp. 121–122). This, however, does not warrant the claim that *any particular constitution* is "legitimate" and/or preferable to alternative constitutional arrangements (Honig, 2001, p. 793). Yet Habermas' theory fails to provide an account, especially for situations where "political contexts, actor' lifeworlds and preferences change such that they feel alienated vis-à-vis the interpretations of basic rights and rules of the game embedded in their country's present democratic constitution" (Fleuß, 2021, p. 118). While he highlights the "future-oriented character, or openness, of the democratic constitution" (Habermas, 2001, p. 774), his vision of concrete democratic institutions and constitutional change nevertheless displays a strong *status quo* bias. The institutions that are considered favourably in *Between Facts and Norms* are precisely those institutional arrangements which characterise contemporary Western democracies. These are, in turn, understood as manifestations of "historical progress" and "modern consciousness" (Allen, 2016, p. 51; Fleuß, 2021, p. 92; Habermas, 1996, p. 6).

Based on this assessment, Habermas argues that the (already) "reasonable" foundation of contemporary (Western) democracies must be respected and protected in future projects aiming at political change. Present generations are thereby asked to acknowledge "their" constitution as an essentially legitimate historical project and are merely ascribed "the task of actualizing the[ir] still-untapped normative substance" (Habermas, 2001, p. 774). Thereby, Habermas "arguably sabotages the very idea of open-endedness" of constitutional projects (Fleuß, 2021, p. 119; also see Honig, 2001, p. 795) – and significantly restricts the range of political practices and agents that are considered justified in pursuing institutional reform and constitutional change (Fleuß, 2021, p. 119; Honig, 2001, p. 799).

Refocusing Deliberative Ideals: Theoretical Restraint and Radical Openness

Classical deliberative theory's understanding of constitutional change imposes rather narrow limitations with regard to (a) the direction of constitutional change, (b) the practices that may be employed to pursue reform and renewal and (c) the agents that are considered relevant and justified in engaging in constitutional reform projects. Habermas may characterise "his hoped-for future in progressive terms" (Honig, 2001, p. 797). Yet a closer look at his account of constitutional change reveals that this approach comes with a severe "paternalistic threat" (Fleuß, 2021, pp. 85, 104–105):

> The present generations may be politically active, but their activism takes the form of agitation for the expansion of rights. They have participation rights,

but they must exercise them in the "right" way. [...] Their medium is law and so they agitate for change by way of constitution-oriented practices.

(Honig, 2001, p. 794)

In consequence, Habermas' deliberative theory appears to leave little room for democratic creativity that transcends the status quo – and it does not provide the normative and conceptual resources for viewing constitutional reform and institutional change as a bottom-up, citizen-led project. Throughout the following paragraphs, I aim at providing an alternative, "refocused" understanding of deliberative democratic ideals that does justice to these requirements and conceives of constitutional or institutional reform processes as a predominantly citizen-led endeavour. At this point, it is crucial to keep in mind that Habermas' account hardly constitutes the only strategy for specifying the core values of deliberative democracy or for putting them into practice: alternative accounts show that deliberative democracy's core values require neither a stark division between "political professionals" and "lay citizens" nor an account of constitutional change that leaves the task of institutional renewal and reform largely in the hands of judicial elites (Dryzek, 1990; Dryzek & Niemeyer, 2010; Fleuß, 2021; Landemore, 2020; Parkinson & Mansbridge, 2012).

In what follows, I shall take Waldron's characterisation of modern, pluralistic societies' "circumstances of politics" as a point of departure: there is no "correct" or "right" answer to questions about "what should be done" – be it with regards to concrete policies or the design of foundational "rules of the democratic game" (Waldron, 1999, pp. 112, 178–179). This point of departure arguably calls for "theoretical restraint": there is *no one right, just or correct way* to organise democratic politics and reform its institutional or constitutional foundations that could be derived from theoretical reasoning (Blaug, 1999). Against this backdrop, I suggest to reconsider some basic notions and ideals of deliberative theorising to develop an understanding of deliberative democracy that takes the requirements of inclusive bottom-up legitimation more seriously: instead of "rational reason-giving", deliberative democrats should focus on the ideals of "communicative action" as the normative foundation of their theorising (Fleuß, 2021, pp. 105–120; also see Dryzek, 1990). In contrast to strategically operating agents, "*communicative action participants* are not primarily oriented towards their own successes" but adopt a *collaborative approach* to coordinating action plans (Habermas, 1984, p. 115; emphasis added). On this account, communicative exchanges about disputed policies and principles do not primarily aim at a "rational consensus" that closes down all disagreement about the right course of action. Rather, communicative exchanges pursue the goal to *understand others'* (potentially) *diverse viewpoints* and perspectives:

One crucial goal of deliberative procedures is to "harmonize" action-plans by establishing a mutual understanding of other participants' perspectives and of the ways different perspectives may (or may not) translate into political action.

(Fleuß, 2021, p. 115; see Dryzek & Niemeyer, 2007, pp. 500–501)

This notion allows us to view "openness" as a *positive political ideal*: "openness" here is a feature of the individual or collective cognitive structures that are open to criticism, correction and learning, to "seeing the other side" (Muradova, 2021). This ideal does not prescribe a particular mode of ("rational" or "reasonable") communication that risks excluding part of a constituency's members. It also does not formulate limitations for what kind of political results can count as "legitimate" results of democratic procedures.

Yet, from normative theorists' perspective this ideal of "radical openness" may also be a double-edged sword: as there is no "right" or "correct" way to determine policies or principles on the basis of theoretical reasoning, the ideal articulated above does not allow for substantive recommendations or action-guiding proposals for institutional and/or constitutional reform. On the positive side, this allows deliberative theorists to avoid overstepping the "limits to theory" and to avoid paternalism. Yet at the same time, this also means that "everything is up for grabs": even fundamental rights and procedural determinations that democratic theorists and citizens usually take for granted must be open for continuous, open-ended reinterpretation and contestation (Fleuß, 2021, p. 120; Waldron, 1999, p. 308).

A deliberative theory that embraces "radical openness" undoubtably bears fairly limited implications for questions regarding the destination of the "constitutional project". I argue that this, however, points towards the need to reconsider the role of political theory in democratic societies. Concrete proposals for democratic renewal and reform should emerge from the perspectives, needs and preferences of affected people. Accordingly, my assessment of deliberative core ideals also requires a methodological turn: theorists cannot offer "blueprint strategies" for reforming institutions but "merely" provide *conversation starters* for the democratic public: they need to "democratize theorizing about democracy" and hand the task of specifying institutions and reform proposals over to affected citizens (Fleuß, 2021, pp. 131–132, 134–137). This, however, only at first glance "simplifies" political theorists' job: theorists still need to provide some idea for how conversations with and among members of a community shall happen and how dialogues about reform perspectives can and should be facilitated. Contestation and debates – particularly those that scrutinise hegemonical discourses and understandings of "good" democratic processes – need facilitating structures which must, in turn, be created and nurtured. In what follows, I will outline strategies for bottom-up, citizen-led constitutional reforms. In doing so, I shall particularly feature the productive role that civil society associations and social movements can play in inclusive, open-minded and open-ended challenges to the very "rules of the democratic game".

Constitutional Change and Democratic Institutional Reform Reconsidered

Radical Openness, Methodological Turns and Bottom-Up Constitutional Reform

In Habermas' theory, constitutional change is conceptualised as an incremental process that carries on our "forebearer's" constitutional project (Habermas,

2001a, p. 775). Consequently, little theoretical efforts go into the question of how *radical* constitutional or institutional change may come about. Habermas' normatively and metaphysically laden understanding of "progress" and "reasonableness" – which allegedly manifest in Western democracies' institutions – has attracted much criticism on behalf of radical democrats, feminist and decolonial scholars (see e.g. Allen, 2016; Mouffe, 2000; Phillips, 1995). This view of political change bears particularly troubling consequences with regard to the concerns and viewpoints of future generations:

> when Habermas characterizes his hoped-for future in progressive terms, he turns that future into a ground. Its character as a future is undone by progress' guarantee. The agency of the present generation, on behalf of which Habermas lays out his argument is now in the service of a set of forces quite beyond itself […]. History moves on and our actions just place us on the right or wrong side of it. Thus, Habermas legitimates constitutional democracy by way of a promised future reconciliation, but what if democratic agency is the price of this particular solution to the problem?
>
> (Honig, 2001, p. 797)

When deliberative theorists avoid these problematic assumptions about progress and reasonableness, they also lose the foundation for supporting a *particular way* of realising deliberative ideals, e.g. with the help of established liberal-democratic political institutions and practices (Allen, 2016, p. 52). In the section "Refocusing Deliberative Ideals: Theoretical Restraint and Radical Openness", I suggested to "refocus" the political ideals of deliberative democracy and see "radical openness" and "open-endedness" as core ideals of deliberative theorising. This enables and requires deliberative democrats to engage in a truly open-ended and inclusive quest for reform proposals that transcend established institutional and constitutional frameworks.

Against the backdrop of the "limits to theory" (Blaug, 1999, p. 75) that I featured in the previous section, I advocate for "Participatory Institutional Design" approaches (also see Dryzek, 1990) that systematically integrate the perspectives of members of a particular constituency or community in developing proposals for democratic renewal and reform. Any concrete reform proposal will be the contingent result of fallible, open-ended processes that take place in particular social, socio-economic, cultural and technological environments. Accordingly, the reform proposals that we may arrive at on the basis of Participatory Institutional Design processes are highly context-dependent and cannot figure as "blueprints" for reforming liberal democracy as such. They can, however, enable theorists to flesh out visions for democratic renewal that have a solid foundation in real-world citizens' perspectives and can thereby figure as "conversation starters" for open-ended debates about alternative ways of "doing democracy" (Fleuß, 2021, pp. 136–144).

Participatory Institutional Design should conform to the following basic rationales: bottom-up design processes should be open to all affected members of a community and promote participants' reflectiveness and open-mindedness. Concrete procedural and decision rules, however, will be both context-dependent and open to participants' contestation and reconsideration. Lay citizens must be the central agents in these open-ended processes, even when they may wish to consult experts and mediators. Generally, Participatory Institutional Design can re-define institutions for routinised law-making as well as constitutional principles and foundational "rules of the democratic game" (Fleuß, 2021, pp. 137–144). While all results of such processes must be considered contingent, reversible and open to further adjustment and contestation, analyses of exemplary processes can nevertheless provide indications or hints, allowing for cautious conclusions about what citizens want and what democratically generated reform proposals may look like. In very brief terms, the Participatory Institutional Design processes that I studied in previous assessments (in Germany and Iceland) indicated that citizens advocate for democratic institutions that allow for more immediate and more meaningful participatory opportunities – with regards to individual policies, but also when it comes to reforming and redesigning the rules of the "democratic game" (see Fleuß, 2021, pp. 148–158).

Constitutional review and the status of constitutional provisions are undoubtably important issues in debates about the "rules of the democratic game". Yet Colon-Rios (2011) rightly remarks that 20th-century democratic and constitutional theory has frequently led these debates at the expense of discussions about an even more fundamental, basic question: *what can a genuinely democratic approach to institutional renewal and constitutional reform look like – i.e. how can "ordinary citizens [be allowed] to propose, deliberate, and decide on important constitutional transformations through the most participatory methods possible"?* (Colon-Rios, 2011, p. 33) Deliberative theorists who wish to do justice to the ideals of democratic inclusion and openness must pay closer attention to processes in the "anarchic public sphere" and provide strategies for linking them with the institutional infrastructure of "empowered" democratic politics. Accordingly, democratic institutions should be "open" or "accessible" for citizen-led initiatives and embrace the – admittedly paradoxical – task to *promote and facilitate counteraction* to existing institutional arrangements (also see Dean, 2018). Civil society agents and social movements here should play a prominent role as they are particularly well-suited for developing practical proposals that creatively go "beyond the critique of hegemonic thinking" (Della Porta, 2020, p. 12; also see Woodly, 2015).

Recent research particularly points towards social movements' "innovative capacity in terms of nurturing and spreading new ideas – about, among other things, democratic institutions" (Della Porta, 2020, p. 3). Yet for a long time, social movement research and democratic innovations scholarship have been fairly disconnected. This may partially result from the fact that many scholarly assessments and practical initiatives in "innovating democracy" have focused on what Warren (2014) termed "governance-driven democratization", i.e. attempts at innovating democracy where "policymaking and administration are [...] moving to the front lines of the project of democratization" (Warren, 2014, p.

38). By now, there is, however, also a broad array of participatory experiments that are "more critically oriented and bottom-up" (Bua & Bussu, 2021, p. 717). Democracy-driven approaches "open […] up opportunities for bottom-up agenda setting", are less prone to follow the rationales of powerful agents or pre-defined "rules of the democratic game" and are more likely to effectively transform traditional institutions "rather than adding to their legitimacy" (Bua & Bussu, 2021, p. 719). Crucially, these approaches to innovating democracy "emerge […] from collective action", e.g. from social movements or civil society associations' initiatives (Bua & Bussu, 2021, p. 718). Following suit, the next section will, based on a brief analysis of two illustrative cases, explore the contributions of social movements and civil society organisations to reforming the "rules of the democratic game".

Putting Ideals into Practice: Citizen-Led Initiatives for Democratic Renewal and Reform

The current democratic malaise is, among other things, a result of a "disconnect" between political-economic elites and the people (e.g. Crouch, 2004, 2016). Against the backdrop of deliberative theory's core values, institutional or constitutional reforms that respond to these crisis phenomena should emerge "bottom-up" and be based on lay citizens' needs, perspectives and preferences. Habermas' theory fails to systematically reflect upon the "anarchic public sphere's" potential to contribute to constitutional reform processes (see the section "'Classical' Deliberative Theory – and Its Shortcomings"). The refocused deliberative account outlined in the section "Refocusing Deliberative Ideals: Theoretical Restraint and Radical Openness" highlights openness and citizens in challenging, contesting and reforming "the rules of the democratic game" (see the section "Radical Openness, Methodological Turns and Bottom-Up Constitutional Reform").

While this understanding of deliberative theory still leaves open the question of how agents in "the anarchic public sphere" may in practice contribute to democratic renewal, recent political developments illustrate how citizen-led initiatives and social movements can instigate changes and challenge "the rules of the democratic game". This potential has manifested itself in substantive proposals for complementing and adapting decision-making procedures in representative democracies or, even more ambitiously, in "redrafting" a comprehensive new constitutional document. In what follows, I shall briefly illustrate the merits – and potential challenges – of two such bottom-up initiatives: the Citizens' Assembly on the Future of Democracy ("Bürgerrat Demokratie") conducted in Germany in 2019 and the Icelandic Initiative for Constitutional Reform which took place between 2010 and 2013 (Della Porta, 2020; Della Porta & Felicetti, 2019; Fleuß, 2021; Geißel et al., 2019; Landemore, 2015, 2017, 2020).

Institutional experimentation and "designing" democratic innovations have received much attention from deliberative and participatory scholars in past decades and often managed to instigate substantive political change (Dryzek et al., 2019). Yet initiatives such as the Citizens Assembly on Electoral Reform in British Columbia (Warren & Pearse, 2008), the Irish Citizen Assemblies that dealt with constitutional reforms concerning gender equality and abortion rights (Farrell et al., 2019; Suiter, 2018; Suiter et al., 2016), or the Belgian G1000 project (Caluwaerts & Reuchamps, 2015) constituted "more piecemeal" efforts targeting individual rights or procedural regulations. The German and the Icelandic initiative, by contrast, take on a more ambitious project, i.e. to "rethink […] democratic principles in a systematic way and, indeed, at the foundational constitutional level of a nation" (Landemore, 2020, pp. 152–153; also see Fleuß, 2021, pp. 147–148).

Despite these similarities, both initiatives differ with regard to (a) the depth of their roots in social movements, (b) their concrete goals and (c) their relationship to established institutions and political elites. The Icelandic initiative emerged in the context of Iceland's political and financial crisis in 2008 and from protests that have later been labelled the "pots and pan revolution". It is deeply rooted in this social movement (see (a)) which called for more, more immediate citizen involvement in political decision-making and thereby opened up a new discursive space (Della Porta, 2020, pp. 36–38). After several referendums on constitutional amendments instigated by government elites had failed, drafting a novel constitutional document with the help of an inclusive crowdsourcing process became the primary goal (see (b)). This process emerged from a combination of "disruptive protests" and interventions of government elites (Della Porta, 2020, pp. 37–38) (see (c)). A National Assembly whose participants were either randomly selected or "chosen as representatives of companies, institutions and other groups" outlined the basic rationales and values of the emerging novel constitution. The Constitutional Assembly then took the results of the crowdsourcing process as well as expert recommendations as points of departure for re-writing the constitutional document.

The reforms and constitutional amendments proposed transcended the frameworks of established representative-democratic institutions and included, for example, a variety of direct democratic instruments (Landemore, 2020, pp. 152–153). At the end of the day, constitutional reform was blocked by conservatives in the Icelandic parliament (Della Porta, 2020, pp. 39–43). Despite this failure in implementing the novel constitution, this case demonstrates that social movements are able to exercise "constituent power" and can utilise the toolkit of democratic innovations in formulating alternative visions for democratic politics (Della Porta, 2020, p. 54). The case also illustrates the tensions that civil society agents must navigate when they cooperate with established political elites: "collaboration with the state is not simply a resource to secure even the highest type of impact (i.e. constitutional change). The state actually exposes democratic experiments to legal, political and administrative dynamics that might halt the process of change" (Della Porta & Felicetti, 2019, p. 12) In the Icelandic case, one particularly graphic example of these dynamics was "the political decision of the ruling party to abandon the constitutional reform process for partisan calculation" (Della Porta & Felicetti, 2019, p. 12).

The German "Bürgerrat Demokratie" (2019) was initiated by *Mehr Demokratie e.V.*, i.e. a charitable civil society organisation that aims at "co-developing"

German democracy with citizens and strengthening lay citizens' impact on collectively binding decision-making. The initiative to gather randomly selected citizens in regional and national assemblies did not evolve out of a particular political protest movement or social movement. Nevertheless, it certainly did not take place in a political vacuum and can at least in part be seen as a response towards German citizens' increasing disinterest, dissatisfaction and distrust vis-à-vis established institutions and elites that surfaced, for example, in electoral gains of far-right populists or young people's disengagement in conventional party politics (see (a)). The process's goal was not a comprehensive novel constitutional document, but a "citizen report" outlining perspectives for institutional reform (see (b)). This report indicates that citizens hold strong preferences for expanding and complementing the participatory toolkit of contemporary German representative democracy: the report proposed to combine citizen participation with referendums at the federal level, advocating for "citizens' councils with randomly selected citizens at the federal level", "nationwide referenda" and "an independent staff unit for citizen participation and direct democracy" (Fleuß, 2021, p. 148; also see Bürgergutachten, 2019). With regard to strategies for putting these proposals into practice, *Mehr Demokratie e.V.* pursued a different route which, very briefly put, combined a public relations campaign, acquiring support in the broader public sphere, with targeted interactions and partnerships with established political elites (see (c)). A core aim here consists in "changing hearts and minds" of citizens and public officials – not so much in *ad hoc* implementations of all citizen recommendations. While the long-term impact on Germany's constitutional and institutional infrastructure is to be seen, the – still ongoing – initiatives managed to raise awareness for alternative ways of doing democracy both among political professionals and among lay citizens. The initiative managed to engage, for example, the then-president of the German parliament as a spokesperson. A representative of *Mehr Demokratie e.V.* specifically highlighted that "it is crucial that well-connected people in positions of power embrace the project and say – *Yes, I go for it!*".

All differences aside, both cases demonstrate that citizens who are involved in the process of agenda setting and are provided with resources and opportunities to "think things through" can come up with constructive reform proposals that significantly transcend the *status quo* of current liberal-democratic practices. What also became visible in both cases is that the citizens involved want *more democracy* and more immediate engagement in determining concrete policies but also cherish the opportunity to have a say in determining and adjusting the foundational "rules of the democratic game" that structure routinised democratic processes (also see Geißel et al. 2019).

These initiatives must frequently face similar obstacles in implementing their proposals such as the opposition of constitutional courts or of (conservative) political party elites who already are in positions of power. These forces may, at least in the first instance, hinder citizen-led initiatives from realising their visions. At the same time, this *opposition* on behalf of established political or judicial elites may also often indicate that citizen-led reform initiatives *did their job well:* they outlined pathways for political change that would, if implemented, fundamentally disrupt established power structures and dynamics. Bottom-up initiatives for institutional or constitutional change here must carefully navigate a fundamental dilemma: citizen-led initiatives should carefully balance the risk of co-optation that may result from close collaborations with (government) elites. Yet they must, at the same time, find *some* strategy to affect the structures of empowered decision-making. However, for citizen-led initiatives, being "successful" must not necessarily mean that they immediately manage to change the constitutional or institutional infrastructure of a polity. Rather, "affecting the public sphere is a very important outcome that citizen-led democratic experiments might be well placed to attain" (Della Porta & Felicetti, 2019, p. 12). Against this backdrop, the Icelandic and the German initiative have been "successful" in the sense that they managed to raise public awareness for political alternatives and reform options by utilising online and offline mass media forums and by forming alliances with prominent party politicians sympathetic to their cause who then figured as "spokespersons" for reform proposals demanding more and more immediate citizen involvement in democratic politics.

Conclusion and a Look Ahead: Democratic Dilemmas to Live (and Work) With

Deliberative theorists put the idea of "bottom-up legitimacy" at the very heart of their project – all legislation, but also the fundamental "rules of the democratic game" must ultimately be rooted in affected citizens' perspectives, needs and preferences. Yet Habermas' "classical" account of deliberative democracy displays a severe *status quo* bias and pays little attention to how precisely the "anarchic public sphere", civil society associations and social movements can actually "feed into" democratic reform processes.

This chapter claims that deliberative theory nonetheless has the potential to provide a crucial normative bedrock for citizen-led, bottom-up reform processes. My reconceptualisation of deliberative democracy's core ideals calls for "radical openness": democratic procedures should not aim at a rational consensus among all participants but at facilitating open-mindedness and mutual understanding. Particularly in pluralistic societies, there may be no such thing as "the right" or "best" solution to a conflict about disputed policies or principles. Accordingly, deliberative theorists should also be committed to "theoretical restraint": political theorists cannot determine concrete action guidelines, "the rules of the democratic game" or the direction of political change. Rather, institutional designs and constitutional provisions must emerge from *actual discourses* among members of a particular community. While the outcomes of such participatory processes may not always please normative theorists, a genuinely democratic approach to constitutional reform will have to bite this bullet. Colon-Rios (2011) argued that the fundamental question of how constitutional change might happen in a genuinely inclusive and democratic manner has been sidelined in much of 20th-century political theorising. This gap may also result from a systematic problem:

as long as theorists presuppose that they *already know* the answer to the question "what are reasonable, good institutions for a democratic polity?", they will not feel inclined to leave this very question to "the people", to the members of political communities and actual political initiatives.

This chapter does not offer a "blueprint-strategy" for democratic reforms. Rather, it provides a sketch of the core rationales that inclusive reform projects should respect against the backdrop of deliberative democratic core values. It then features recent citizen-led initiatives in Germany and Iceland that pursued comprehensive reforms of the "rules of the democratic game" and utilise the toolkit of democratic innovations and participatory governance approaches. Social movements and civil society agents here played a productive role in counteracting the *status quo* of democratic politics and developed creative proposals for alternative ways of "doing democracy". In consequence, one core strategy for promoting democratic legitimacy consists in enabling social movements and civil society-led initiatives to use the tools of democratic innovations and participatory governance (e.g. citizen assemblies, referendums or crowdsourcing tools) (see della Porta & Felicetti, 2019). These bottom-up initiatives can provide deliberative theorists with a more substantive idea of what concrete reform perspectives for contemporary democracies can and should look like. In practical terms, citizen-led initiatives provide a promising perspective for tackling contemporary democratic crisis phenomena – after all, governance-driven democratic innovations (see Warren, 2014) can rarely be expected to provide foundational challenges to existing constitutional arrangements and institutions. These findings also point towards the need for further research investigating how different societal groups can be empowered and enabled to instigate institutional and constitutional change and access the "toolkit" and the resources of democratic innovations and participatory governance.

References

Allen, A. (2016). *The End of Progress: Decolonizing the Normative Foundations of Critical Theory*. Columbia University Press.

Blaug, R. (1999). *Democracy, Real and Ideal: Discourse Ethics and Radical Politics*. Suny Press.

Bua, A., & Bussu, S. (2021). Between governance-driven democratisation and democracy-driven governance: Explaining changes in participatory governance in the case of Barcelona. *European Journal of Political Research*, 60(3), 716–737.

Caluwaerts, D., & Reuchamps, M. (2015). Strengthening democracy through bottom-up deliberation: An assessment of the internal legitimacy of the G1000 project. *Acta Politica*, 50(2), 151–170.

Campus, A.S., & André, J.G. (eds). (2014). *Challenges to Democratic Participation: Antipolitics, Deliberative Democracy, and Pluralism*. Lexington Books.

Colon-Rios, J. (2011). *The Three Waves of the Constitutionalism–Democracy Debate in the United States (and an invitation to Return to the First)*. Victoria University of Wellington Legal Research Papers, 1 VUWLRP 23/2011, 1–34.

Crouch, C. (2004). *Post-democracy*. Polity Press.

Crouch, C. (2016). The March Towards Post-Democracy, Ten Years On. *Political Quarterly*, 87(1), 71–75.

Dalton, R.J. (2004). *Democratic Challenges, Democratic Choices* (Vol. 10). Oxford University Press.

Dean, R.J. (2018). Counter-Governance: Citizen Participation Beyond Collaboration. *Politics and Governance*, 6(1), 180.

Della Porta, D. (2020). *How Social Movements Can Save Democracy*. Polity Press.

Della Porta, D., & Felicetti, A. (2019). Innovating Democracy Against Democratic Stress in Europe: Social Movements and Democratic Experiments. *Representation*, 1–18.

Dryzek, J. (1990). *Discursive Democracy: Politics, Policy, and Political Science*. Cambridge University Press.

Dryzek, J.S., Bächtiger, A., Chambers, S., Cohen, J., Druckman, J.N., Felicetti, A., Fishkin, J.S., Farrell, D.M., Fung, A., Gutmann, A., Landemore, H., Mansbridge, J., Marien, S., Neblo, M.A., Niemeyer, S., Setälä, M., Slothuus, R., Suiter, J., Thompson, D., & Warren, M.E. (2019). The crisis of democracy and the science of deliberation. *Science*, 363(6432), 1144–1146.

Dryzek, J., & Niemeyer, S. (2010). *Foundations and Frontiers of Deliberative Governance*. Oxford University Press.

Ercan, S.A., & Gagnon, J.P. (2014). The crisis of democracy: Which crisis? Which democracy? *Democratic Theory*, 1(2), 1–10.

Farrell, D.M., Suiter, J., & Harris, C. (2019). 'Systematizing' constitutional deliberation: the 2016–18 citizens' assembly in Ireland. *Irish Political Studies*, 34(1), 113–123.

Fleuß, D. (2021). *Radical Proceduralism: Democracy from Philosophical Principles to Political Institutions*. Emerald Publishing.

Flynn, J. (2004). Communicative power in Habermas's theory of democracy. *European Journal of Political Theory*, 3(4), 433–454.

Foa, R.S., & Mounk, Y. (2019). Democratic deconsolidation in developed democracies, 1995–2018, 1995–2018, Working paper, *Harvard Center for European Studies Open Forum*. Online access: https://ces.fas.harvard.edu/uploads/art/Working-Paper-PDF-Democratic-Deconsolidation-in-Developed-Democracies-1995-2018.pdf

Geißel, B., Dean, R., Jung, S., & Wipfle, B. (2019). *Abschlussbericht der wissenschaftlichen Evaluation*. [Scientific report "Bürgerrat Demokratie"].

Gerstenberg, O. (2019). Radical democracy and the rule of law: Reflections on J. Habermas' legal philosophy. *International Journal of Constitutional Law*, 17(4), 1054–1058.

Habermas, J. (1984). *The Theory of Communicative Action: Reason and the Rationalization of Society* (Vol. 1). Beacon Press.

Habermas, J. (1996). *Between Facts and Norms: Contributions to a Discourse Theory of Law and Democracy*. Polity Press.

Habermas, J. (2001). Constitutional democracy: A paradoxical union of contradictory principles? *Political Theory*, 29(6), 766–781.

Honig, B. (2001). Dead rights, live futures: A reply to Habermas's "constitutional democracy". *Political Theory*, 29(6), 792–805.

Lafont, C. (2019). *Democracy Without Shortcuts: A Participatory Conception of Deliberative Democracy*. Oxford University Press.

Landemore, H. (2015). Inclusive constitution-making: The Icelandic experiment. *Journal of Political Philosophy*, 23(2), 166–191.

Landemore, H. (2017). Inclusive constitution making and religious rights: Lessons from the Icelandic experiment. *Journal of Politics*, 79(3), 762–779.

Landemore, H. (2020). *Open Democracy: Reinventing Popular Rule for the Twenty-First Century*. Princeton University Press.

Mansbridge, J., Bohman, J., Chambers, S., Christiano, T., Fung, A., Parkinson, J., ... Warren, M.E. (Eds.). (2012). *Deliberative Systems: Deliberative Democracy at the Large Scale*. Cambridge University Press.

Mouffe, C. (2000). *The Democratic Paradox*. Verso.

Muradova, L. (2021). Seeing the other side? Perspective-taking and reflective political judgements in interpersonal deliberation. *Political Studies*, 69(3), 644–664.

Niemeyer, S., & Dryzek, J.S. (2007). The ends of deliberation: Meta-consensus and inter-subjective rationality as ideal outcomes. *Swiss Political Science Review*, 13(4), 497–526.

Phillips, A. (1995). *The Politics of Presence*. Clarendon Press.

Scudder, M.F. (2020). The ideal of uptake in democratic deliberation. *Political Studies*, 68(2), 504–522.

Suiter, J. (2018). Deliberation in action–Ireland's abortion referendum. *Political Insight*, 9(3), 30–32.

Suiter, J., Farrell, D.M., & O'Malley, E. (2016). When do deliberative citizens change their opinions? Evidence from the Irish Citizens' Assembly. *International Political Science Review*, 37(2), 198–212.

Waldron, J. (1999). *Law and Disagreement*. Oxford University Press.

Warren, M. (2014). Governance-driven democratization. In S. Griggs, A.J. Norval, & H. Wagenaar (Eds.), *Practices of Freedom: Decentered Governance, Conflict and Democratic Participation*. Cambridge University Press, 38–60.

Warren, M.E. and Pearse, H. (2008). *Designing Deliberative Democracy: The British Columbia Citizens' Assembly*. Cambridge University Press.

Woodly, D.R. (2015). *The Politics of Common Sense: How Social Movements Use Public Discourse to Change Politics and Win Acceptance*. Oxford University Press.

Young, I.M. (1996). Communication and the other: Beyond deliberative democracy. In S. Benhabib (Ed.), *Democracy and Difference*. Princeton University Press, 120–135.

Young, I.M. (2002). *Inclusion and Democracy*. Oxford University Press.

3 Innovations in Participatory Governance and the (De)commodification of Social Wellbeing

Nick Vlahos

Introduction

Can innovations in participatory governance lead to the decommodification of social wellbeing? This is an important question, given the fact that socio-economic inequality within capitalist societies is a severe problem. Innovations in participatory governance aim to improve the quality of democracy, deepen citizen participation in the political decision-making process and reimagine the role of citizens in representative democracies (Elstub and Escobar 2019). However, in capitalist democracies, participatory innovations exist in contexts where the pathologies stemming from market-based ideology and strategies of economic adjustment have led to poverty and social exclusion (Levy 2006). Moreover, governments and public administrations support the structural reproduction of gross inequalities because they maintain conditions favourable to capital accumulation (Offe 1984). This ultimately has adverse implications on the potential for democratic innovations to deepen and reimagine the role of citizens in representative democracies. A challenge is that while participatory governance innovations are increasingly being implemented and studied, there are contrasting accounts of why they arise and as a result, what they try to (or can) achieve.

Considering participatory governance is embedded within capitalist economies, we need to be more critical and thorough in how we account for the intersections of capitalism and democracy. This agenda requires an understanding of the preconditions for establishing equal citizen engagement in participatory processes, including how public decision-making can help tame the problems associated with the market economy, elevating the social wellbeing of those being adversely impacted by rising inequality. In addition, there is a necessity to resituate participatory decision-making within welfare state initiatives, as these are programmatically used to alleviate social and material inequity, but they mostly involve elite, rather than public forms of decision-making.

The chapter describes the participatory governance of social wellbeing in the neoliberal era. I examine two urban examples in Toronto, Canada, in terms of how democratic innovations are deployed to tackle structural issues. Both examples seek to improve the social wellbeing of individuals and communities through public participation and deliberation, but they follow different routes, which

DOI: 10.4324/9781003218517-4

respectively align with the characteristics of Warren's (2014) governance-driven democratisation (GDD), and Bua and Bussu's (2021) democracy-driven governance (DDG).

Governance-driven democracy is described as a shift in the mentality of governing, from top-down technocratic decision-making and bureaucratic scepticism of the public's knowledge and problem-solving capabilities, empowering the public to help design policy. GDD entails the recognition by civil servants that, to solve wicked problems in an economic context where staff and resources are limited, affected communities should influence how decisions are made. At the same time, it is recognised that political institutions lack accountability, transparency and inclusivity; public participation and deliberation in policy administration are thus needed to fill in the legitimacy gap of electoral democracy. The concern with this account is that electoral democracy is de-linked from the bureaucracies that implement democratic innovations, and these are quite powerless over the structural influence of capital on the state and have little power in economic regulation (Culpepper 2015).

If a goal is to uncover how participatory governance can help decrease the massive rise of inequality in capitalist societies, scholars and practitioners need to pay attention to the political economy of participation. This is where democracy-driven governance comes in. Bua and Bussu (2020) argue that while commissioning bodies do invite public participation, social movements are simultaneously claiming spaces of participatory governance. DDG is concerned with embedded forms of regulatory democratic decision-making that can lead to social transformation. Politics from the lens of DDG is about power relations and social struggles, and participatory governance comes from tipping points won by social action. Thus, the ontological starting point of what innovations in participatory governance strive to achieve differs between GDD and DDG.

Both GDD and DDG bear the stamp of democratising democracy because they involve the implementation of participatory processes to influence decision-making. However, they differ in their potential to reinforce or alleviate inequality in capitalist societies based on the extent to which they are integrated into or seek to be distanced from the capital-driven logic of capitalist democracy. To appreciate this differentiation, I situate GDD and DDG within a broader conceptual discourse of political economy. In the first section of this chapter, I draw from Karl Polanyi (2001) and Gøsta Esping-Andersen (1990). Both provide nuanced interpretations of (de)commodification in capitalism, and their heuristic devices, namely the double movement (cf. Polanyi), and welfare states as systems of stratification (cf. Esping-Andersen), are relevant for understanding how contemporary participatory governance operates in capitalist democracy.

In what follows, the chapter starts with a discussion of the historical features of capitalist democracy, followed by a section that resituates the main role of democratic innovations within a welfare state paradigm. To demonstrate how innovations in participatory governance are invested in the (de)commodification of social wellbeing, the empirical sections of the chapter describe different applications of GDD and DDG. GDD (government and public sector use of democratic innovation) is examined through the example of neighbourhood planning tables that are part of Toronto Strong Neighbourhood Strategy 2020, implemented by the Social Development Finance and Administration (SDFA) Department at the City of Toronto. By contrast, DDG (locally mobilised democratic innovation) is examined through the example of the Parkdale People's Economy (PPE), a resident-led community governance network.

Both forms of participatory governance are mobilised in response to the severe inequalities observed in capitalist democracy. While they both aim to work around policies within an economy that maintains severe socio-economic inequalities, GDD leverages democratic innovation to make up for other policies that actively commodify the working class and marginalised residents by way of austerity and neoliberal objectives. By contrast, DDG is a countermovement to the political economy of neoliberalism. The PPE aims to be locally rooted, rather than inserted as an arm of government. In this way, DDG in Toronto attempts to elevate social wellbeing by devising alternative governance mechanisms for controlling how markets in land, labour and money, operate and to lessen the reliance on the provision of public goods generally attributed to welfare capitalism, public administration and representative political institutions.

Capitalist Democracy Redux: The Double Movement and Welfare State Decommodification

The beginnings of capitalist democracy are generally to be found in the 19th century, notwithstanding the long history of institutions of representation, when class-divided societies began the process of fitting limited voting franchises onto institutions firmly supporting neoclassical economic ontology (Therborn 1977). This system of political representation, which we now variously term liberal, electoral and representative democracy, allows voters to choose and authorise governments that then nurture a market society (Macpherson 1977). Exact mixtures entail constellations of interventionist policies and regulative institutions, influenced by social and political mobilisation (Huber et al. 1993). Nonetheless, structural contradictions of capitalism, observable in wealth concentration, capital overaccumulation, economic crises and volatility, have little bearing on the power blocs of financial and industrial capital that seek to maintain a separation of political influence on economic production, exchange, circulation and governance (Albo et al. 2010).

There are limits to the manoeuvrability of democratic institutional and governmental apparatuses to pursue socially progressive policies within capitalism, and especially its current neoliberal form. A foundational problem of capitalist democracy is the coexistence of formal political equality with socio-economic inequality (Wood 1995). Economic relations and their connections to political power and socially consequent aspects of life remain a struggle for progressive democrats to overcome. The type of *formal* political equality – suffrage – guaranteed in capitalist democracy coalesces with partisan party politics and is failing to address socio-economic inequality. Capitalist democracy endorses political behaviour appropriate in the marketplace, which is merely the isolated, private expression of prefixed preferences of buying and selling of elites and political parties to govern the market economy (Elster 1997).

As a result, capitalist democracy cannot be comprehensively understood without recognising how structurally unequal agents mobilise power resources to reshape the bases of political and policy decision-making (Korpi 1983). In this perspective, participatory decision-making innovations need to be connected to transformative agendas that seek to reconfigure the operation of politics, administration *and* economics. Here, Polanyi (2001) and Esping-Andersen (1990) can help inform how innovations in participatory governance fit into a critical reading of capitalist democracy.

For Polanyi, while markets are observed throughout human history, capitalist markets are different because they strive to dis-embed the economy from collective control. Moreover, the markets for goods have been extended to include the purchase and sale of labour, land and money in a market economy. The problem with this scenario is that the market economy is claimed to be a naturally occurring phenomenon, whereby the economic system is controlled, regulated and directed solely by market prices. Polanyi takes issue with this on two fronts, the first being that labour and land are not, by nature, commodities. The second is that the notion of a self-regulating market promulgated by economic liberalism is utopian. Indeed, the social history of market economies across industrialised countries indicates that governments consciously intervene in support of capitalism. Polanyi calls this the double movement. It entails the spread of the market economy alongside the implementation of policies and powerful institutions to support private accumulation as well as mitigate the worst impact of the commodification of land, labour and money. The contradictory nature of the double movement means that the state and the market economy influence how social welfare is administered in society.

Polanyi helps us appreciate the need for participatory democratic control – or re-embedding – of commodified goods to ensure that society is not run as an adjunct to the market. However, the slow development of democracy in market societies has meant that there has been initially (or rather only) limited citizen participation in the governance of social wellbeing, which is why public and counter-public struggles have constantly sought to open decision-making to broader portions of the populace. As a result of mass mobilisation, historical variations of civil, political and social citizenship rights have been slowly institutionalised, and the combination of these has come to define the core features of capitalist democracy (Marshall 1950). The nation-state controlled how to address collective needs; as a means for social solidarity, standards of real earnings and living conditions were increased, and social protections like healthcare, pensions, sick leave and employment insurance were provided.

This leads to Gøsta Esping-Andersen's (1990) understanding of decommodification. For Esping-Andersen, while the welfare state involves an ideal picture of state responsibility for securing a basic modicum of welfare for its citizens, it is a system of stratification. Welfare states can be based on targeted or universal programs, as conditions for eligibility. The quality of benefits and services, as well as the extent to which rights are a part of citizenship, also differs across countries. Esping-Andersen's research suggests that nations cluster into regimes, i.e., liberal, corporatist or social democratic, where social assistance or insurance provided to populations depends on public–private mixtures of institutional provisioning. The reason they cluster in the way that they do is that class-coalitional alliances and social struggles inform matrices that differ in the extent to which capitalism is regulated by democratic institutions.

Countries with centralised corporatist arrangements, strong unions and social democratic parties have tended to provide expansive social entitlements to citizens. A key point is that the more "market independence" for an average worker – if the right to an adequate standard of living is guaranteed regardless of previous employment, performance, needs test or financial contribution – the greater their level of decommodification. Yet, in the end, while the politics of commodifying workers has led to collective action to produce a tolerable level of welfare and security, decommodification cannot completely eradicate labour as a commodity so long as capitalism constrains collective social wellbeing (Esping-Anderson 1990).

Resituating the Role of Democratic Innovations

Given the above, how can a participatory consideration of politics, economics and democracy establish new nexuses of decommodification? One way is to expand the realm of double movements of government and welfare systems as systems of stratification, to how democratic innovations operate in capitalist democracy. This relates to who is included and supported by welfare models, how people are involved in decision-making and what decommodification policies encompass.

A prolonged crisis of the welfare state has meant that it struggles to adequately address emerging needs. The problem is that even though welfare state institutions encompass social rights and protections from the throes of the market, it is a limited paradigm for what it means for inclusion and collective participation in politics. Government-directed welfare policies have hinged on racial and gendered privilege, where the parochial universality of social rights was not reflective of the broad diversity of nations (Orloff 1993; Bernhardt 2015).

Furthermore, decommodification indices primarily measure differences across more or less distributive regimes through consumption (of unemployment insurance, sick leave, pensions, health care etc.). Welfare systems are looked at as mechanisms for protecting workers via social benefits. However, expansive notions of decommodification support the pursuit of self-development through diverse social policies (Room 2000). This offers a potential for the public to (re)define relevant social wellbeing activities, supports and protections across multiple indicators, hence not strictly focusing on protecting basic standards of living, but also other social factors.

Welfare states as systems of stratification and double movements can be nuanced in terms of the scale of activities and the public's involvement in the distribution of resources, through innovative participatory and democratic decision-making. For example, localised participatory innovations seek to expand the basis of what welfare or social wellbeing consists of. At the current juncture, this is needed because democratic innovation research suffers from a lack of theoretical, analytical and empirical engagement with critical research on capitalism (with the exception of scholarship concerning participatory budgeting). Concomitantly, literature attending to capitalist democracy is heavily weighted towards democratic mobilisation, participation and decision-making as it relates to voting, cabinets, parties and legislatures.

If we are to learn from both Polanyi and Esping-Andersen to appreciate if participatory governance innovations are to contribute to social wellbeing, we need to consider the multiple ways that stratification and decommodification operate across participants, spaces and systems. Recall that if social policies insulate people from market imperfections, their decommodification can be potentially empowering. Similarly, different forms of civic decision-making should be viewed in terms of the simultaneous production and/or mitigation of stratification. This will invariably be connected to the approaches of participatory governance aligned with GDD and DDG, which entails differences in institutionalised and/or embedded community approaches to participatory governance. This is based on whether institutionalisation connects to or bypasses, community/grassroots participation and whether participatory spaces are merely ancillary/consultative spaces versus given some degree of decision-making power (Bussu et al. 2022). Scholars of democratic innovations have focused on the decommodification of political participation in terms of setting the normative and empirical foundations for a participatory, not simply elective democracy. We must go further and establish the mechanisms of how to collectively govern social wellbeing. The political and the economic cannot remain disparate sources for scholars of democratic innovations.

Even if structured public forums can empower the public, most, if not all, participatory acts will still consist of combinations of inclusion and exclusion or overlapping forms of stratification. Who convenes, creates agendas, determines the control over outcomes, gets to participate (be it a few randomly selected/elected people or the public at large); where and when decisions take place; if accessibility and equity measures are encompassing; how decisions are made (majoritarian, consensus or modified consensus); and the extent of accountability, transparency and evaluative processes involved, all contribute to stratification in participation. Qualifying forms of participation are a facet of justifying who the people are, and how they are allowed to participate, which will reflect upon equity and equality.

Governance-Driven Democratisation in Toronto: The Example of Neighbourhood Planning Tables

The politics of redistribution is multidimensional in Canada, and a complex mix of forces has reshaped the social policy landscape.[1] Keith Banting and John

Myles (2014) note that global economic pressures, ideological change, shifts in the influence of business and labour, the decline of equality-seeking civil society organisations, realignment in the party system, shifting bureaucratic politics and decentralisation in the federation, all these have impacted inequality in Canada. The social system of redistribution coincides with the spatial architecture of (urban) democracy, which involves deployments of governing authority, and we can observe policies of interventionist but substantively anti-statist neoliberal government actions in Ontario since the late 1990s (Horak 2013).

New social risks have involved income and service gaps generated by the transition of labour markets from well-paid jobs to increasingly precarious service jobs (Jenson and Saint-Martin 2006); in the Greater Toronto Area (GTA), the number of people who describe their job as temporary increased by 40% between 1997 and 2013 (Lewchuk et al. 2013). Simultaneously, reductions in personal income taxes, tax exemptions for savings and cuts to consumption taxes have served affluent Canadians the most. The top 1% of income shares have reversed postwar trends, disproportionately concentrating wealth in fewer hands (Yalnizyan 2010). In the GTA, income inequality has outpaced provincial and national trends, growing at double the national rate, prompting a claim that the link between growing income inequality and access to opportunity is the defining challenge of our time (Dinca-Panaitescu 2017). Those living in Toronto face particular challenges, including an affordable housing crisis that is a struggle for hundreds of thousands of renters, a homelessness crisis and childcare that is the most expensive in the country (Wilson 2020). Social assistance in Ontario is focused on supporting individuals and families with very low incomes. The politics of this system is framed around how so-called lower rates incentivise employment and decrease dependence on the system, but the last decade saw caseloads increase by nearly 30% (Kapoor 2020).

The nature of capitalist development in Toronto is heavily connected to tertiary, knowledge services clustering in the inner core of the city. The effect of the way urban capitalism is spatially designed in Toronto is that a strong financial, health and tech sector has cemented its place downtown while pushing outward the more precarious forms of labour, and along with this has been disinvestment in the social geography of certain areas (Cowen and Parlette 2011). As a result, there is mounting evidence about just how divided Toronto is regarding social polarisation and spatial segregation (Hulchanski 2007). There is an intersectional component to this geographic orientation. Toronto is very diverse, with over 200 languages spoken across the city, and close to half of the population are immigrants, but the city is racially segregated. The inner core is particularly expensive to rent, let alone its own residential dwellings. Over the past several decades, the inner suburbs of Toronto have become what some call "ethno burbs"; the further you leave the core, the more racialised and poverty-stricken certain neighbourhoods become. These areas struggle with transportation, social services and local employment accessibility issues.

To address residential sorting and the disparity between neighbourhoods, the City of Toronto collaborated with local service providers and anchor institutions to develop the Toronto Strong Neighbourhoods Strategy (TSNS 2020). To initially determine the wellbeing of each of the 140 neighbourhoods across the city at the time (currently there are 158), the World Health Organization's Urban Heart Index was used to measure key indicators of community health. It was found that 31 neighbourhoods were deemed to be under-developed, and these communities were allocated the status of neighbourhood improvement area (NIA). A new community development approach would be implemented to elevate five themes of neighbourhood social wellbeing: economic opportunities, social development, participation in civic decision-making, physical surroundings and healthy lives (SDFA 2014). The TSNS 2020 is a neighbourhood equity strategy, where a small team of community development officers support residents by connecting them to vital services. In this context, community development operates in terms of managing relationships and building trust.

An interesting facet of the TSNS 2020 is its participatory governance framework that facilitates, connects and enables local activities at 15 neighbourhood planning tables (NPTs) covering the 31 NIAs. NPTs consist of residents, city councillors, community agencies and city staff who work to identify local priorities, plan solutions and create partnerships (SDFA 2017a). NPTs convene monthly to work on their Action Plans to address aspects of the five themes (SDFA 2017b). In addition to working on community action plans, short-term grants for community initiatives are administered through local neighbourhood planning tables (SDFA 2019). The grants support local social networking events and community-led capacity-building activities concerning financial literacy, civic education, digital proficiency, hospitality-related certifications and soft skills related to employment preparedness.

SDFA's work with local communities and residents is very important and respectable; the community development unit (CDU) represents a vast diversity of lived experiences and practitioners seeking practical and systemic solutions to social and racial inequity. But given the socio-economic problems outlined above, the CDU is faced with a difficult, if not impossible task. The work of elevating social wellbeing on the ground, within communities, comes up against a broader economic context whereby the local council (and provincial government) has governed with a neoliberal agenda for well over a decade, and this contributes to the reproduction of the inequality and inequity that the CDU strives to reduce.

There are also a few challenges that the NPTs have experienced. One is that their composition varies in terms of who gets a seat at the table. In principle, these tables are open to NIA residents. However, because they are convened by a community development officer with significant responsibilities that go beyond managing a planning table, the participants tend to be at (least initially) already actively involved community leaders. In addition, demographic representation, and the ratio of residents to organisational representatives, differs depending on where you are in the city. NPTs are therefore used to engage with already-existing partners, and then to use the tables as a vehicle to bring in new allies and residents into the fold and gain connection to other residents, service providers and city staff. To complicate this, some NPTs are almost entirely local service providers.

In one instance, an NPT split into a resident-only and an agency-only table within the same community. This means that voices at the tables can diverge, having both constructive and tenuous effects on collaboration depending on the visions stakeholders have for their communities, and who they want to be the primary decision-makers.

Another challenge revolves around the $5000 community grant that each NPT is given to allocating for social purposes. Every year, the city does an open call where community members go and pitch creative ideas to their improvement area planning table. The table determines who to supply with a limited portion of the pool of funds. Some of the most fascinating and inspiring community projects arise from this community funding program, and they are strictly resident designed and implemented. However, because there are only 15 tables covering 31 NIAs, $5000 must be spread thinly across several NIAs, which amounts to only a few resident projects receiving limited funds.

The nascent goal of neighbourhood planning tables is to decommodify social wellbeing, and they achieve certain milestones in this direction. Still, they struggle with overcoming structural inequalities. The funding available for community grants sponsored by NPTs is unstable, and much of the work was halted during the pandemic. Nonetheless, NPTs are a source of democratic innovation, as there are nascent conversations within the CDU about enhancing the tables, with ambitions either to provide them with an operating budget or to implement participatory budgeting through the tables. Ultimately, NPTs do leverage resources through key anchor institution partnerships. The challenge is that under-development in the periphery requires more than working around the problems of capitalism. The government does have policies in place to tackle issues related to poverty, but as outlined above, there are countervailing economic strategies such as those related to land planning and development, which augment a spatially unbalanced local economy. The spillover effects of the local housing market, the geographical placement of jobs and the lack of diversification make any governance-driven strategy for elevating social wellbeing a difficult one without the requisite integrative macroeconomic agenda that seeks to confront the spatial division of labour in downtown and peripheral Toronto.

Democracy-Driven Governance in Toronto: The Parkdale People's Economy

The challenges facing neighbourhoods undergoing gentrification are significant because "revitalization" generally happens at the expense of low-income populations. In South Parkdale, social tensions surround the displacement of vulnerable tenants (Slater 2005). For several decades, Parkdale has had an influx of higher-income homeowners, and as residents have moved into the community, property values have risen while concentrations of affordable housing have diminished. Since the 2000s, rapid condominium development and new businesses that cater to more high-end clientele have accelerated residential and commercial changes. Parkdale residents have witnessed an increasing wealth gap between the North and South of the neighbourhood, with 90% of residents located in the South being renters, and close to 35% of the population living in poverty (Kamizaki 2016).

This scenario prompted community organisers to develop the Parkdale People's Economy, which consists of a community land trust, a local currency program called the Co-op Cred Program, a movement for Community Benefits and a community-based food distribution and procurement initiative through the Community Flow project. The PPE has built upon community action research. The first of these studies was commissioned in 2010 by the Parkdale-Activity Recreation Centre (PARC). *Beyond Bread and Butter* identified community responses to food insecurity in Parkdale. Interestingly, this report argued for a need to develop a community land trust (CLT) that would provide affordable housing to residents as well as preside over a food coalition and a local food hub (Richer et al. 2010).

The suggestion for a CLT propelled subsequent research: *A Place for Everyone* (2011) and *Cultivating a Governance Model for a Community Land Trust in Parkdale* (2012) established that the rate of value change in Parkdale was higher on average than the rest of the city in terms of commercial property, rent and dwelling value, and as a result of the alarming values of property increases, significant losses to community assets and affordability were something that required systemic and structural change. A community land trust is a non-profit organisation that obtains land, holds it in perpetuity for the community and has the goal of decommodifying land by taking it out of the real estate market. The benefit of a CLT is that it involves the democratic control of land, which is important not only because the private ownership of land is primarily focused on profit, but also because the politics of housing has resulted in no new developments of affordable units in decades, whereas public stocks of Toronto Community Housing have simultaneously been sold off (Goodmurphy and Kamizaki 2011).

The proposed governance of the CLT would be community-based in that people who use the lands or reside in the surrounding areas control its operations. The board of governors would be composed of one-third of leaseholders, one-third of community members at large and one-third of public organisations/officials. Governance would have to foster the inclusion and participation of Parkdale's diverse residents, and the principles for decision-making would have to weigh the pros and cons of majority rule, consensus and modified consensus (Bath et al. 2012). In 2014, the Parkdale Neighbourhood Land Trust (PNLT) was incorporated as a non-profit organisation, and is run by a board of directors, consisting of local organisations and members that represent the diversity of Parkdale. A core value of the PNLT is that the local community is best served by effectively engaging residents and key stakeholders in the decisions affecting them. As of 2023, the PNLT provides 81 single-family homes and small buildings with a total of 153, mostly family-size units of affordable housing for adults with low income and/or who experience mental health and addictions challenges.

In 2015, the neighbourhood-wide Parkdale Community Economic Development (PCED) Planning project was undertaken in collaboration with over 25 organisations, as well as a series of participatory planning workshops with hundreds of residents. The guiding philosophy of the PCED is a systems-based approach that builds community-based initiatives with broad-based economic reforms and ultimately aims to establish alternative institutions that promote collective ownership and democratic control of land, money and labour. For example, the Co-op Cred Program offers work-learn placements, whereby participants earn credit for work activity and exchange credit for healthy food. The PCED aims to shift attention from the centrality of employment to systems and conditions in which the creation and redistribution of wealth are organised. Three series of public forums were held between May 2015 and November 2015. The first involved eight workshops to develop neighbourhood wellbeing indicators as a starting point for community visioning. This set of indicators was used as a guiding framework for a second series of workshops on community needs and assets mapping, identifying trends in Parkdale and key issues that require attention and action. These workshops helped identify key visions, needs and aspirations for Parkdale, and, building on these, a third round of participatory workshops identified community actions that could be worked on collaboratively. The participatory planning workshops established that the local economy should serve seven indicators of social wellbeing: social infrastructure, affordable housing and land use, decent work and economic opportunities, health and food security, community financing, participatory local democracy and cultural development and learning (Kamizaki 2016).

Some of the core action items going forward include: developing a community service hub for co-location and service integration; preserving and strengthening affordable housing through succession planning, initiating community-driven vision and revitalisation of public assets, retaining affordable commercial spaces, linking redevelopment with decent work generation and exploring partnerships with local anchor institutions; starting a community-based food processing social enterprise, as well as developing a food hub for food security in conjunction with an expanded urban agriculture site; creating a community planning board for local decision-making concerning infrastructure development; and promoting narrative-based communication through art to convey community visions and to promote cultural activities in public space.

There is a cross-over between these objectives and the TSNS 2020. The city utilises a mixture of a centralised base of indicators to measure urban health in NIAs, along with a decentralised approach to how local neighbourhoods define their priorities within that scheme. Parkdale was recognised in 2014 as one of the NIAs, and the PPE acts as the local planning table. It is important to note that the PPE does draw support from external funders, local businesses, third sector staff, city community developers and planners, as well as the local city Councillor. That said, the objectives of the PPE are not strictly limited to the interests of cross-organisational interlocutors. The PPE is a community rather than city developed framework. The PPE approach is a long-term, strategic vision that positions itself to be less reliant on the vagaries of state and market ideology. Providing alternative methods to structural issues beyond the scope of the city's TSNS 2020 is the path to addressing inequity and inequality in Parkdale. What makes this agenda interesting from the lens of participatory governance and decommodification is that community members do not separate an equitable local economy from the redistribution of decision-making power away from the local government to the community. It established a neighbourhood land trust to control and preserve affordable single-family homes and small buildings in perpetuity.

Discussion and Conclusion

While scholars of participatory governance do theoretically prioritise their relative effectiveness against normative values, assessments are often abstracted from the broader political-*economic* dynamic that surrounds them (Pateman and Smith 2019). Given the extent of inequality in capitalist democracy, there is a strong need for attending to participatory decommodification of social needs. If we are to comprehensively understand innovations in participatory governance, we need to reflect on the coexistence of discursive arenas and pervasive inequality. Democratic innovations exist within highly stratified societies, so the dialogical health of overlapping participatory processes should not be divested from the stratifications produced by capitalist economies.

If we consider participatory processes as (de)commodifiers, then we are left with how inequality is or is not being addressed to the extent that it could, or in comparison to other spaces, and regimes. Both Polanyi and Esping-Andersen provided the conceptual springboard for a consideration of how, in capitalist democracy, innovations in participatory governance can contribute to collectively defining and pursuing social wellbeing. Based on the case studies outlined above, this depends on capacities, resources, mandates, mobilisation and integration in overlapping political and economic processes. These contextual experiences provide nuanced implications for the literature on governance-driven democratisation and democracy-driven governance.

The way GDD and DDG arise and utilise democratic innovations is differentially linked to a double movement and involves forms of stratification and (de)commodification. In terms of the former, at a political and bureaucratic level, policy objectives and implementation are contradictory; the dis-embedding of market imperatives leads to strategies to offset severe inequalities by controlled forms of resident involvement. Governance-driven democracy in Toronto involves a double movement of the deployment and then mitigation of government policies that have contributed to the perpetuation of inequality. In terms of the latter, spatial forms of resident mobilisation and engagement coevolve to counteract problematic social, economic and political phenomena and are differentiated in how they approach and (can) devise strategies to address systemic problems. Thus, participatory decommodification is not a complete emancipation from capitalism, but the elevation of social wellbeing vis-à-vis empowered public decision-making.

The chapter focused on local innovations in participatory governance, in a liberal welfare state that struggles to structurally address the issues of a stratified society. Mobilising for social wellbeing within communities, therefore, raises questions about the liminal spaces and opportunities of resident involvement and how they both differ from and overlap with formal political and administrative processes. The chapter highlights the importance of discerning between forms of stratification in participation and how this impacts the (de)commodification of social wellbeing. As a form of GDD and DDG, both NPTs and the PPE, respectively, entail stratified participation based on who ends up prioritising local actions, partially because there are divides between wealthier white homeowners and renters (especially racialised social housing tenants), but also considering challenges from limited resources, disconnection between community groups and organisations, as well as the tough task of outreach and drawing in both members and volunteers. The core difference between NPTs and the PPE, despite both being focused on elevating social wellbeing, is that the latter is more poised to meet the challenges of mobilising to address inequality in the context of capitalist democracy.

The case of PPE is unlike other public engagement processes in Toronto because it devised community governance mechanisms to address structural problems. We can begin to appreciate decommodification in terms of the public's involvement in the distribution of resources that fulfil collectively determined social wellbeing indicators. Parkdale's approach is a co-determined path for market independence, seeking to control and own rental buildings, secure affordable and healthy food as well as aid struggling residents with opportunities to participate in a local currency program.

If the goal of the PPE is to detach social life from market dependence and to democratically regulate the economy, one enduring tension involves the form that institutionalisation takes when it comes to the participatory governance of social wellbeing. The two cases presented in the chapter align with Bussu et al. (2022), in that there appears to be a differentiation between the extent of decommodification that can be achieved depending on either the governance-driven or democracy-driven participatory governance processes for elevating social wellbeing. The former is located as an arm of the local government as seen in the TSNS 2020, rather than an organic, community-driven program vis-à-vis the PPE.

While a community-led approach is not the only way to anchor and embed DDG, the latter overlaps with partisan commitments and regime characteristics. By contrast, in Toronto, where municipal political parties are non-existent, there have been difficulties in establishing a transformative left-leaning council agenda that might also institutionalise DDG, which is why the struggle to embed participatory governance continues to rest with residents in their own neighbourhoods. The PPE does overlap with the neighbourhood improvement area and planning table schema, but it is neither dependent, nor its main platform to achieve its goals. This subtle nuance means that DDG in liberal contexts with limited social movement integration within party politics might mean that participatory governance of social wellbeing is better situated in communities rather than integrated into municipal governance. At the same time, the scale of activities that are required for larger levels of decommodification cannot solely rely on the neighbourhood level and requires policy interventions that support actors in collectively devising and securing social wellbeing.

Note

1 This section draws from a portion of the research presented in Vlahos, N. 2022. "Democratic Restructuring and the Triaging Functions of an Urban Deliberative System." Centre for Deliberative Democracy and Global Governance, University of Canberra, Working Paper Series 1: 1–26.

References

Albo, G., Gindin, S., and Panich, L. 2010. *In and Out of Crisis: The Global Financial Meltdown and Left Alternatives.* PM Press.

Banting, K., and Myles, J. 2014 "Introduction: Inequality and the Fading of Redistributive Politics." In *Inequality and the Fading of Redistributive Politics.* Edited by Keith Banting and John Myles. University of British Columbia Press.

Bath, A., Girard, D., Ireland, S., Khan, S., and Major, S. 2012. Cultivating a Governance Model for a Community Land Trust in Parkdale. *Parkdale Activity-Recreation Centre (PARC) and the University of Toronto.*

Bernhardt, N. 2015. "Racialized Precarious Employment and the Inadequacies of the Canadian Welfare State." *Journal of Workplace Rights* 5(2): 1-15.

Bua, A., and Bussu, S. 2021. "Between Governance-driven Democratisation and Democracy-driven Governance: Explaining Changes in Participatory Governance in the Case of Barcelona." *European Journal of Political Research* 60(3): 716-737.

Bussu, S., Bua, A., Dean, R., and Smith, G. 2022. "Embedding Participatory Governance." *Critical Policy Studies* 16(2): 1-13.

Cowen, D., and Parlette, V. 2011. "Inner Suburbs at Stake: Investing in Social Infrastructure in Scarborough." In *Research Paper 220.* Cities Centre, University of Toronto.

Culpepper, P. D. 2015. "Structural Power and Political Science in the Post-crisis Era." *Business and Politics* 17(3): 391–409.

Dinca-Panaitescu, M., Hulchanski, D., Laflèche, M., McDonough, L., Maaranen, R., and Procyk, S. 2017. *The Opportunity Equation in the Greater Toronto Area: An Update on Neighbourhood Income Inequality and Polarization.* United Way Toronto and York Region and Neighbourhood Change Research Partnership.

Elster, J. 1997. "The Market and the Forum: Three Varieties of Political Theory." In *Deliberative Democracy: Essays on Reason and Politics*, edited by James Bohman and William Rehg. The MIT Press.

Elstub, S., and Escobar, O., eds. 2019. *Handbook of Democratic Innovation and Governance.* Edward Elgar Publishing Ltd.

Esping-Andersen, G. 1990. *The Three Worlds of Welfare Capitalism.* Polity Press.

Goodmurphy, B., and Kamizaki, K. 2011. *A Place for Everyone: How a Community Land Trust Could Protect Affordability and Community Assets in Parkdale.* Parkdale Activity-Recreation Centre.

Horak, M. 2013. "State Rescaling in Practice: Urban governance Reform in Toronto." *Urban Research & Practice* 6(3): 311-328.

Huber, E., Ragin, C, and Stephens, J. D. 1993. "Christian Democracy, Constitutional Structure, and the Welfare State." *American Journal of Sociology* 99(3): 711–749.

Hulchanski, J. D. 2007. *Three Cities Within Toronto: Income Polarization Among Toronto's Neighbourhoods, 1970–2005.* Cities Centre, University of Toronto.

Jenson, J., and Saint-Martin, D. 2006 "Building Blocks for a New Social Architecture: The LEGO™ Paradigm of an Active Society." *Policy and Politics* 34(3): 429-451.

Kamizaki, K. 2016. *Parkdale Community Planning Study: Building a Foundation for Decent Work, Shared Wealth, an Equitable Development*. Parkdale Community Economic Development (PCED) Planning Project.

Kapoor, G. T. 2020. *System Transformation in Ontario Works: Considerations for Ontario*. Maytree Foundation.

Korpi, W. 1983. *The Democratic Class Struggle*. Routledge & Kegan Paul.

Levy, J. 2006. "The State after Statism: From Market Direction to Market Support." In The State After Statism: New State Activities in the Age of Liberalization. Edited by Jonah D. Levy. Harvard University Press.

Lewchuk, W., Lafleche, M., Dyson, D., Goldring, L., Mesiner, A., Procyk, S., Rosen, D., Shields, J., Viducis, P., and Vrankulj, S. 2013. *It's More than Poverty: Employment Precarity and Household Well-Being*. Poverty and Employment Precarity in Southern Ontario (PEPSO).

Macpherson, C. B. 1977. *The Life and Times of Liberal Democracy*. Oxford University Press, 1977.

Marshall, T. H. 1950. *Citizenship and Social Class*. Cambridge University Press, 1950.

Offe, C. 1984. *Contradictions of the Welfare State*. Edited by John Keane. The MIT Press.

Orloff, A. S. 1993. "Gender and the Social Rights of Citizenship: The Comparative Analysis of Gender Relations and the Welfare State." *American Sociological Review* 58(3): 303-328.

Pateman, C., and Smith, G. 2019. "Reflecting on Fifty Years of Democratic Theory." *Democratic Theory* 6(2): 1-10.

Polanyi, K. 2001. *The Great Transformation: The Political and Economic Origins of Our Time*. Foreword by Joseph E. Stiglitz. Beacon Press.

Richer, C., Htoo, S., Kamizaki, K., Mallin, M., Goodmurphy, B., Akande, A., and Molale, A. 2010. *Beyond Bread and Butter: Toward Food Security in a Changing Parkdale*. Parkdale-Activity Recreation Centre.

Room, G. 2000. "Commodification and Decommodification: A Developmental Critique." *Policy & Politics* 28(3): 331-351.

Slater, T. 2005. "Toronto's South Parkdale Neighbourhood: A Brief History of Development, Disinvestment, and Gentrification." Centre for Urban and Community Studies, University of Toronto. *Research Bulletin* 28: 1-8.

Social Development Finance and Administration, Social Policy Analysis and Research Division. 2014. *TSNS 2020 Neighbourhood Equity Index: Methodological Documentation*. City of Toronto.

Social Development, Finance and Administration. 2017a. *Toronto Strong Neighbourhood Strategy 2020*. City of Toronto, CD18.4 Appendix 2.

Social Development, Finance and Administration. 2017b. *Toronto Strong Neighbourhoods Strategy 2020 Neighbourhood Action Plans*. 2017. City of Toronto, CD23.10, Revised Appendix 1.

Social Development, Finance and Administration. 2019. *Supporting Toronto's Communities*. City of Toronto, Special Committee on Governance, GV3.2.

Therborn, G. 1977. "The Rule of Capital and the Rise of Democracy." *New Left Review* 103: 3–41.

Vlahos, N. 2022. "Democratic Restructuring and the Triaging Functions of an Urban Deliberative System." Centre for Deliberative Democracy and Global Governance, University of Canberra, Working Paper Series 1: 1–26.

Warren, M. E. 2014. "*Governance*-Driven Democratization." In *Practices of Freedom: Decentered Governance, Conflict and Democratic Participation*. Edited by Steven Griggs, Aletta J. Norval, and Hendrik Wagenaar. Cambridge University Press.

Wilson, B. 2020. *Toronto After a Decade of Austerity: The Good, the Bad, and the Ugly*. Social Planning Toronto.

Wood, E.M. 1995. *Democracy Against Capitalism: Renewing Historical Materialism*. Cambridge University Press.

Yalnizyan, A. 2010. *The Rise of Canada's Richest 1%*. Canadian Centre for Policy Alternatives.

4 Can Local Participation Disrupt Neoliberalism?

The Politics and Ethics of Caring for Democracy

Markus Holdo[1]

What difference can local participation make in a world where inequality increases everywhere, where segregation pulls communities apart and where policymakers marginalise the needs and interests of the people whose lives their decisions affect the most? This question was central two decades ago when research on participatory institutions took off. Leftist scholars described participatory budgeting, in particular, as a rebellion against neoliberal capitalism, and liberal democracy scholars proclaimed enthusiastically that this new invention would refuel citizens' energies and solve democracy's crisis (e.g., Harvey 2012; Fung 2004). Not all these proclamations were grounded in careful analysis of the constraints and obstacles of local politics. But while some scholars were idealistic about what small spaces democratic activism could achieve, critics seemed to dismiss it all too easily. They claimed that participatory practices were too soft, too small and too submissive to make any real difference. Few of them seemed to consider that these spaces might offer something distinct from protests or party politics, something valuable, even disruptive, in its own right.

Two decades later, we have an enormous literature on participatory institutions that offers valuable lessons on what conditions are required for participation to have an impact on people's well-being, as well as on political inclusion and redistribution (see, e.g., Bherer et al. 2016; García-Espín and Sánchez 2017; Touchton and Wampler 2014; Bua and Bussu 2021; Wampler and Goldfrank 2022). New studies have generated various ideas about what kind of design features may positively affect outcomes (e.g., Gilman and Wampler 2020). The debates, nowadays, are less about hyperbolic declarations and more about carefully examining specific conditions and outcomes. But while the research field now appears more sober and mature, it also seems to be losing the spirit that once so deeply animated work on participatory democracy. Have we lost sight of the political questions that once embodied practices of participation in places like Porto Alegre, Brazil, and that awakened the democratic imagination of researchers and policymakers in many parts of the world? Has the field's development come to mirror what some see as a general depoliticisation of participatory practices? Participation has become a "fast policy", easily adopted by governments of different political orientations (Peck and Theodore 2015). The popularity of participation, suggest

DOI: 10.4324/9781003218517-5

Gianpaolo Baiocchi and Ernesto Ganuza, is "paradoxical": participation is a grassroots response to democracy's crisis, yet its meaning has proved so ambiguous that it can be incorporated into any political project, including neoliberal and conservative ones (Baiocchi and Ganuza 2014; 2016). These analyses echo the warning of Carole Pateman (2012), who helped found the field half a century ago, that the meaning of participatory democracy today appears so vague that it risks becoming little more than a functional part of governance practices that are deeply at odds with the project of building a more inclusive, egalitarian society.

Building upon these critical reflections, I want to return to the question of what difference participation can make in a world that, after two decades of experimentation with participatory policies, seems even less democratic than before. Critics, on the one hand, warn that participation is prone to manipulation and undermines the kind of contentious political action needed to achieve change (Cohen and Rogers 2003; Rodgers 2012). Some advocates, on the other hand, have suggested that the skills of cooperation and collaboration fostered through participation may be just as important as the capacity to engage in contestation (Fung and Wright 2003). Neither side appears fully convincing. If total rejection of participation seems careless, the celebration of cooperative practices as such appears incomplete at best and naïve at worst. The point of participation cannot be to accomplish immediate, dramatic change, but in societies characterised by inequality, exclusion and segregation, it also cannot be simply to make citizens more cooperative.

I want to offer an alternative to both of these views. In my own research on participation in Rosario, Argentina, I have been struck by how citizens and public administrators talk about their activism and work as *caring* – caring about one's community, caring about the neighbours and the city and caring about democracy. To participate is similar to how we take responsibility in a family, at a workplace or in friendship. A woman I interviewed in Rosario said, "I take care of the house, I take care of my work, I take care of the church, I take care of participatory budgeting". This notion of caring may seem trivial at first. Isn't it just a form of chest beating or patting one another on the back for all the good work? But what if this notion of caring is more significant than it appears? To be part of something that embodies shared beliefs in solidarity, equality and interdependence may feel as important as defending one's interests in open political contestation. Participation may feel meaningful because the values it embodies are missing in society at large. To be part of a space where they are put to practice may give hope for change. And perhaps something has already changed when people get together and form bonds of mutual trust and solidarity and experience the power of collective action. Where would significant social change begin if not in spaces that make such hope, such bonds and such action possible?

To explore this further, I will draw on works by feminist theorists on the ethics of care (Tronto 1993; Casalini 2019). Seeing participation as a form of *democratic care* can, I feel, deepen our understanding of what is special about participation as a form of politics, its transformative potential as well as its limits. I begin in the next section by discussing in more detail a pair of paradoxes concerning participation. These raise questions that I suggest we can address through the concept of democratic care. In the third section, I draw on interviews and observations from my fieldwork on participatory budgeting in Rosario, Argentina (see Holdo 2014, 2016a, for methodological details). I highlight aspects of democratic care that I think are widely relevant to cases of participation and social cooperation in unequal, segregated societies. In the fourth section, I address the limits of practices of democratic care. Care, I suggest, would play a central part in a radically different society. But it also plays a part today in maintaining and patching together relationships of trust and legitimacy, without which neoliberalism might crumble under its own weight. To make spaces of democratic care transformative and not merely reproductive, participants need to use them to renegotiate the terms of their cooperation. I end by offering reflections on what a society may look like that made more room for democratic care. That radically different – nonviolent, egalitarian and inclusive – society, I argue, could probably not be achieved in any other way.

The Paradoxes of Participation

New participatory institutions have had very different consequences around the world (see Wampler and Hartz-Karp 2012; Baiocchi and Ganuza 2016; Fernández-Martínez et al. 2020). How "participation" is understood and implemented in different local settings depends, in part, on local leaders' authority to take decisions on redistribution, decentralisation and delegation of decision-making to ordinary citizens (Wampler 2010; McNulty 2020). But it also depends on what commitments and ideas they have in the first place. What Gianpaolo Baiocchi and Ernesto Ganuza (2016) have called "the paradox of participation" is that participation is, at the same time, a radical project of grassroots democracy *and* an ambiguous policy tool that can mean almost anything and can be made to fit in almost anywhere, and with almost any kind of politics. This ambiguity is also reflected in the research literature. Some see, in particular in the early practices of participatory budgeting, a radical, insurgent politics of tearing down power structures and building a more egalitarian, inclusive form of government from below. Other scholars have instead conceptualised participation in terms of "innovation", "collaboration" and "design" – a language that has more affinities with an entrepreneurial spirit than radical politics (e.g., Geissel 2012).

Local governments in different parts of the world began inventing and adopting new ways to involve citizens in local decision-making in a period marked not by democratic renewal but by intensified competition, welfare retrenchment, administrative reforms and demobilisation. At the same time as Porto Alegre gained the mythical status of "capital of the global justice movement", it caught the attention of "international audiences of a quite different kind", write Peck and Theodore (2015, p. 147). These included consultants on urban policy, public sector accountants and the so-called Washington consensus organisations, such as the World Bank and the Inter-American Development Bank. The latter organisations, along with UN-Habitat and the European Union, praised participatory budgeting and offered loans to Porto Alegre and virtually every other municipality that wished to try participatory budgeting. Their support was, of course, less due to its consequences for political inclusion than to how it appeared to facilitate efficiency and transparency in financial management (Peck and Theodore 2015, pp. 149–150). Participatory budgeting's "bipartisan credibility", write Peck and Theodore, contributed to its appeal as a "policy brand" for local governments in many parts of the world (2015, p. 227).

This is disturbing for those who see participation as a way to defend the values of equality and inclusion. Participation seems instead often to be used merely as an instrument to patch up the widening social cracks produced by decades of neoliberal policies. This tendency would be no surprise to critical urban scholars and political theorists such as Wendy Brown (2015) and Margaret Kohn (2016), who have pointed out numerous ways that democracy is being undermined through policies that pull citizens apart, break down the possibilities for solidarity and create increasing distrust among people, and between people and political institutions. In the same city, people live increasingly different lives. Their housing situations, access to public infrastructure and public spaces and their chances of making themselves heard are becoming increasingly unequal – not the least in places that have adopted policies of participation. The early literature on participation appeared almost immune to these developments. It treated, as Zander Navarro (2004) has commented, Porto Alegre, in particular, as an "inexpugnable fortress amidst the neoliberal sea". By exaggerating the role of local leaders' revolutionary imagination and ignoring much of the economic and political conditions they had to adapt to, many scholars actually made it hard to learn much about how participation could accomplish something significant under conditions characteristic of local government today (for a critique, see Baiocchi 2003b, p. 208). When case studies elsewhere showed less exciting results, researchers often claimed a lack of radical imagination, which only further segmented the myth of Porto Alegre (see, e.g., Cabannes 2004; Wampler 2010).

It is, of course, not up to local leaders to decide whether to be affected by global capitalism or not, even if they have some freedom to choose how far they want to adjust to it. The paradox that Baiocchi and Ganuza point to seems less puzzling once we realise that the myth of Porto Alegre is just that. Careful empirical analyses tell a more sober story of politically skilful but also realistic local leaders who created alliances not just with civil society leaders but also with the private sector and delivered on promises to fight corruption and increase transparency, much in line with demands from Washington consensus organisations (see Abers 2000, 2003; Baiocchi 2005; Goldfrank and Schneider 2006; DeNardis 2011). Participatory budgeting was instrumental in the Workers' Party's attempt to build deep and broad political coalitions. In other places, local leaders have been able to use more watered-down versions of participation to gain the democratic legitimacy they need as their actual policies prioritise the interests of resourceful investors. Participation is constrained at the outset because it can never accomplish the kind of radical change that local decision-makers pretend it aims for.

This leads us to a second puzzle, or a second paradox, if you will. While the first paradox concerns the spread of participatory institutions – which has not made local governments any more democratic overall – the second paradox concerns citizens' choices to participate despite the absence of democratic deepening. For many citizens, participation is an act of solidarity, defending democratic values of inclusion and equality, and promoting the interests of otherwise marginalised groups. Moreover, studies have shown that participants do not simply accept what they are offered but claim their independence, mobilise collective action to further shared interests and at times take over meetings (Baiocchi 2003a, 2005; Wampler 2010). Yet, at the same time, participation gives the sense that our societies are fine and that the governments that provide spaces for participation are legitimate. Participation, thereby, helps reproduce political structures and policy orientations that generate precisely those social injustices that participants wish to oppose.

The second paradox thus follows from the first. By participating, people at the same time refuse to accept neoliberal values *and* help bring legitimacy to neoliberal policies. They resist yet simultaneously support neoliberalism because they produce precisely what neoliberalism needs to sustain itself but systematically destroys: legitimacy, social trust and capacity for collective action. My experience of interviewing participants in Rosario, Argentina, is that many of them reflect carefully both on the values they associate with participation and on the ways that the interests of the local government may differ from theirs (Holdo 2016a). The paradoxes of participation are not lost on them. But to act ethically in an unjust society may sometimes be to care for the community, the city and the democracy we share even when the consequences are uncertain.

Democratic Care

Joan Tronto writes that care is

> everything we do to maintain, continue and repair our 'world' so that we can live in it as well as possible. That world includes our bodies, our selves and our environment, all of which we seek to interweave in a complex, life-sustaining web.
>
> (Tronto 1993, p. 103)

The ethics of care brings our attention to how societies rely on but often refuse to recognise care as labour. Care has been closely associated with nurturing in a literal sense, and much empirical work on care has focused on the actions of healthcare workers and domestic workers (Pols 2015). When critical scholars speak of a crisis of care, they refer to how austerity policies have devalued and undermined practices and institutions that were instrumental in the development of advanced welfare states (see Casalini 2019; Arruzza 2016; 2020). But the concept of care has also been employed to examine the roles that bonds of trust and mutual support play in other contexts (e.g., Bartos 2021; Nicholson and Kurucz 2019). To frame participation as care is to extend the empirical scope of the concept further and suggest that declines in social and political trust and democratic legitimacy, too, can be seen as part of a general care crisis.

Jane Mansbridge (1991) connected the idea of care and nurturing with democratic theory three decades ago, as she pointed out that the ancient Greek understanding of democracy had much in common with modern feminist thinking – from the suffragists' emphasis on "social motherhood" to a later feminist critique of neoliberal ideology. Several feminist democratic theorists have suggested thinking of democracy as everyday practices of inclusion, egalitarian decision-making, compromise, negotiation and deliberation (see Mansbridge 1983; Pateman 1970; see also Phillips 1998). Recently, Tronto (2013) has used the term "caring democracy" to make the argument that we need to shift the political discourse from narrow economic growth issues to address the distribution of caregiving and care-receiving in society (see also Urban & Ward 2020).

I want to move further in this direction. What I call practising democratic care is to care for democratic ideals of inclusion, empathetic listening, equality and mutual understanding. It is to insist on these ideals, act on them, transmit them, critically reflect on them and resuscitate them. This idea of democratic care, I believe, helps make two simultaneous shifts in the analysis of participation. The first shift is from thinking of cooperation strategically to seeing cooperation in terms of solidarity. Advocates of participation have been hard-pressed to respond to critics, often from rational choice or agonistic perspectives, who attack the softer parts of participatory and deliberative ideas – empathy, trust, mutual understanding, consensus and so on (e.g., Przeworski 1998; Mouffe 2000; for discussion, see Holdo 2019; 2020b). Is cooperation really possible without some form of coercion or domination? At least where participants have different resources and interests or where facilitators seem more powerful than participants, it may be wise to be cautious and carefully protect one's own interests in interaction with those whose interests differ from one's own (see e.g., Cohen and Rogers 2003). This kind of reasoning is why people approach cooperation strategically and feel uneasy about embracing deliberation as a mode of interaction.

Advocates for participation have responded by imagining forms of balancing power or using protests as a "reserve threat" in case participatory spaces come to reproduce patterns of domination (Wampler 2010; see Holdo 2016b). In a similar vein, I have previously sought to make a "realistic" argument for why participation may often not end in co-optation by showing that participants may be so useful to local governments in need of legitimacy that they come to possess substantial power (Holdo 2016b; 2019). These arguments, however, assume that people only cooperate if this serves their own interests, which would make it hard to rid participatory processes of instrumental and manipulative behaviour. Consequently, much work has focused on the question of how to make space for genuine cooperation while at the same time holding people accountable to democratic norms (e.g., Fung 2004). But what if, instead, this contradiction is just an unhelpful way to think about participation? What if what we need is a shift toward a different ethos, a different sensitivity or a different mode of interacting?

Thinking of participation as democratic care shifts the perspective toward solidarity. Accountability gives the idea of objective rules, structural incentives and an impartial facilitator of deliberation to enforce them. By contrast, the democratic care perspective suggests that people can listen empathetically to each other based on a willingness to find out in what ways we need each other and what we want to accomplish together. We cannot achieve a just society without everyone's cooperation. Empathetic listening involves, not the least, creating an environment together where we recognise differences in status and power. Each person needs to consider, through empathetic listening, the needs of all others (Puāwai Collective 2019; see also Bourgault & Robinson 2020). Caring requires us to become sensitive to differences in power, interests and experiences and to learn about one another's perspectives and from each other's experiences through sharing and listening. While accountability is in tension with spontaneity, solidarity suggests becoming more aware, more considerate, more responsive to our differences and thereby more authentic toward each other.

The second shift is from viewing participation as a civic virtue to seeing it as a form of labour that is distributed in society, and whose terms need to be renegotiated. The literature on participation, and public discourse more generally, tends to assume that participation is something praiseworthy, and something to be encouraged. In particular, neo-Tocquevillian ideas of civic commitment and social capital have often been promoted with a sense of reviving a gone-by sense of civic community (e.g., Putnam 2016). While democracy is arguably unsustainable without participation, we also need to ask what kind of democracy, what kind of participation, are people asked to perform and in whose interest? This means to politicise acts of participation and contest ideas of civic virtue that are easily incorporated into and used to support existing policy orientations. The second shift is thus toward a more critical focus on people's possibilities to contest ideas about what participation should mean and be about, to challenge boundaries and reshape participatory spaces so that they reflect their needs, views and interests (see also Holdo 2020b).

The idea of democratic care helps us make this move by rendering the political potentials of democratic care, as well as its political limits, visible. The critical question of whether the terms of cooperation can be renegotiated applies generally to forms of care. Feminist works on care have sought not only to challenge the tendency to devalue the role that care practices play in society but also the tendency to associate caring with sentimental and romantic ideas. Similarly, the idea of caring for democracy may evoke sentimental and romantic ideas of community and solidarity. Theorists of care aim, by contrast, to construct a theory of the social and political roles that care performs (e.g., Tronto 1993; Held 2006). As Tronto (2013) has argued, care needs to be recognised as labour. Then we can politicise it and redistribute it.

The second shift thereby raises critical questions about the politics of democratic care. In a different world, democratic care might have been a cornerstone of a collective project of building a just society based on the recognition of interdependence, but what does it do in *this* world? Is it a form of resistance? Or does care actually help sustain neoliberalism by covering up its social and political consequences?

We are back to the paradoxes of participation. To care for democracy is to resist the neoliberal credo of selfishness and help make space for solidarity and collective mobilisation. But on the other hand, it provides neoliberal societies with the bonds of trust and legitimacy needed to sustain them. The concept of care allows us to situate participation in a more general political context of policies of austerity, welfare retrenchment and public–private partnerships. Even if participation is not neoliberal *per se* – in fact, I argue that it is antithetical to neoliberalism – it still plays a function for neoliberalism by maintaining, continuing and repairing the common world that any political order needs to maintain itself over time. At the same time, care practices embody the ideals of a radically different society. As I will discuss further at the end of the chapter, we cannot know how that society would be structured, only that it would have more space for empathy and collective ethical reflection.

Democratic Care in Rosario, Argentina

Every year in April, the municipality of Rosario invites its residents to come and discuss the problems and needs of their neighbourhoods. This marks the beginning of the participatory budget process, which will continue until December. Thousands of people attend the first meetings, while a few hundred sign up to represent their districts and their neighbourhoods as *councillors* in the assemblies that will convene weekly throughout the year. The councillors' task is to develop a list of projects that will be subject to a public referendum. It involves attending meetings, discussing with neighbours and preparing for debates with the municipality. They devote considerable time and energy to this engagement while often being involved in many other forms of activism too. "You learn to run", as one councillor put it.

Rosario adopted this model of participatory budgeting known from Porto Alegre in the spring of 2002, the year after Argentina's economy collapsed. A few months earlier, at the end of December, the protests had grown so intense that they had made it impossible for the government to function. In Buenos Aires, people defied curfews. Large assemblies gathered outside La Casa Rosada, the presidential palace, night after night, until one evening, the president finally got in a helicopter and left, accompanied only by the cheers of protestors celebrating his resignation as a people's victory. In Rosario, the mayor and his closest associates understood that this was a point of no return. How could things ever be normal again when people's trust in political institutions and representatives had been so badly abused?

But they also saw the crisis as an opportunity to try something new. "It was the worst possible moment. But we went out to the people with the little money that was left. And we said: let us decide together what we can do with it. That is how it started", said one representative of the local government.

In this analysis of participation in Rosario, I want to highlight how the care perspective helps focus, on the one hand, on practices of solidarity, as an ethic of participation, and on the other hand, on how participants can renegotiate the terms of their cooperation. These two parts of the analysis thus reflect the two shifts I have suggested that are entailed in using the concept of democratic care.

Solidarity: The Ethics of Participation

I began interviewing councillors and municipal employees and sitting in on meetings, in 2011. For many of the councillors I interviewed, the answer to the question of why they participate appears self-evident, even provocative. "It is a citizen's responsibility. It is a duty", said Nora. "Many people do not come because they are too comfortable. They stay in their houses and don't do anything. They will not change anything like that". Pablo called it "a vocation". "I think", he said, "that most of us come for the same reason, to help the neighborhood. There are some who might have other interests, but for the majority of us, that is what it is – the solidarity with the neighbor".

To participate is to take a stand for solidarity and reject the apathy, selfishness and dishonesty that the councillors see dominating elsewhere in society. It is also, as theorists of care would emphasise (e.g., Urban & Ward 2020), to make invisible labour visible and create a sense of collective identity around the values attached to it. It means supporting each other in an effort to care for one's community. It also involves recognising differences in social backgrounds, identities and challenges and exploring on what basis they can work together for a shared purpose. A woman from the indigenous Qom community shared with me her experience of overcoming obstacles imposed on her in relation to gender and ethnicity. To speak at meetings required her to process deep feelings of shame. Indigenous people do not usually speak in front of non-indigenous, she said, and women do not usually take on the role of representing their community. With participatory budgeting, this changed. Rosario is, of course, still a segregated city where indigenous people experience discrimination daily. But the councillors have learned to be sensitive, she said, about what it means for her to participate as a Qom woman.

While the councillors insist that participatory budgeting is for anyone who wants to get involved, they also reflect on common practices of exclusion that they need to watch out for. The municipality sets the rules, according to which participatory budgeting is open to all who want to participate. Women and men need to be equally represented. All neighbourhoods should have their own councillors. And if childcare becomes an obstacle to participating, the municipality is obliged to offer assistance. But there are still many potential ways that people could be excluded or silenced at meetings. Councillors I interviewed mentioned several factors that can affect people's possibilities to participate on equal terms, including status differences (for example, based on previous experiences of community organising), unequal resources (including time and knowledge), specific terms used in discussions (concerning, for example, budget matters and the language of evaluating proposals' "feasibility"), political differences, fluency in Spanish and disrespect and unequal treatment based on gender, ethnicity, class or age. These things should not be allowed to affect people's opportunities to be part of the participatory budget, they suggested. "There are codes of respect", said Lydia, a councillor in the Western district, and added that she expects male councillors to be more respectful than men usually are elsewhere. But in practice, the councillors need continuously to call attention to when and how the "codes of respect" are violated.

These testimonies do not prove that participatory budgeting successfully includes all participants on equal terms. Rather, what they suggest is that a sense of reciprocal trust, solidarity and understanding is an important part of what makes participation meaningful. It is what makes it special, what makes it different from other spheres of society. A few councillors suggested that they need to be careful to make everyone feel included because the participatory budget might otherwise lose its credibility as a democratic space. Thus, while some councillors mentioned that previous experiences of participation and activism help to make others listen, often they would stress that it is their shared responsibility to make equal space for everyone. At meetings, councillors are expected to show awareness and sensitivity to the specific issues and interests that need to be represented in participatory budgeting, including issues of deprivation and structural racism. When they fail to show such sensitivity, other councillors make them aware of it. During one meeting, for example, when a councillor suggested a campaign against wasting water, another councillor responded by calling attention to the fact that in this particular district, many residents hardly had access to running water in the first place.

Renegotiating the Terms: The Politics of Participation

Participatory budgeting offers councillors a space in which they can build community with others. They develop a shared sense of purpose by exchanging experiences and views about the needs of their neighbourhoods. To participate is to work toward a healthier, more equal, more inclusive and less violent society. It is to "maintain, continue, and repair our 'world'," as Tronto puts it. But what is the political function of participation in Rosario? The municipality uses it to gain democratic legitimacy. Even before the crisis in 2001, Rosario was developing strategic plans collaboratively with actors in the private sector and civil society to gain a sense of broad-based legitimacy (Holdo 2016b). Like other local governments, Rosario has faced challenges of adjusting to a more vulnerable economic situation due to national and transnational free-market policies. Participation plays an important role for the municipality by giving the sense that despite the economic vulnerability and need to attract investors, Rosario is led by an administration that has the needs of the residents as its highest priority. For all the talk of solidarity, participation might simply give the local government what it needs, in terms of legitimacy, to continue on the path of neoliberalism. Or does participation in any way challenge that path? Can Rosario's residents use participation to pursue goals beyond the municipality's intentions?

One councillor told me that leaders of the Socialist Party, which has now governed Rosario for four decades, sometimes treated her as a party activist. "For how long have you been a *militante*?" one of the party's leaders once asked her. She felt outraged even thinking about this, especially since she was critical of how the participatory budget had worked. Like many other councillors, she pointed out that her task was to represent her neighbours, not to work for the government. In a segregated city, where large parts of the population experience social, economic and political marginalisation, the distinction between the government and the neighbours is crucial. If the councillors are seen as cooperating too closely with the government, their neighbours will not trust that they are working for change and are not part of a scam. "People see what is missing", said Griselda, a councillor in Rosario's most marginalised district. "People no longer believe in politics", says Daniel. "Politics has involved too much dishonesty".

Although many councillors can talk at length about the value of participation and the specific advantages that participatory budgeting, in particular, has brought with it, they also frequently complain. In particular, they complain about projects that were not implemented on time and about the lack of explanations. If the projects are delayed or not even carried out, people may think that participatory budgeting is just another of the government's lies. At one meeting, a councillor says that they should have big parties whenever something is actually done so that people see that it's not just a sham. Compared to other participatory budgets, Rosario's is a case of a well-working process, where people initiate projects that the municipality implements most of the time (Holdo 2016b). But the complaints are crucial for making the municipality see that the councillors' cooperation is not unconditional (see Holdo 2019). Councillors need both to defend participation as something ethical and valuable *and* distance themselves from the government that facilitates participation. The risk, if they fail to do this, is that they will not gain the respect and recognition they need to get from their neighbours, and if they do not get that, then the possibility of using participatory budgeting to accomplish change will be small. An important condition for participatory processes to be transformative is that they are different, and *perceived* as different, from other political projects that may also aim at generating support for the government by co-opting or corrupting civil society leaders.

Several councillors bring up the risk of co-optation. As Jorge from the Western district puts it, "the people in the Socialist Party are not fools. They try to bring you into this machine. They handle participatory budgeting as machinists". In order to make them listen seriously, the councillors need to show that they are not fools either, that they condition their participation and that whatever the intentions of the government to use participatory budgeting for its own purpose, the councillors refuse to play along. Instead, they seek to use the leverage they gain from participating to renegotiate the terms of cooperation. The councillors in the Western district exemplified this at one meeting as they passed around and signed a letter to the mayor. The letter contained a list of demands for changes in participatory budgeting's way of functioning. The mayor was also asked, among other things, to explain why many projects had been waiting for implementation for several years. "I ask you all to sign it", said the author of the letter, "so that the mayor can see that it represents the views of the councilors".

One could, perhaps, think that the government could simply ignore the councillors' complaints. But in Rosario, the municipality appears quite aware that it needs the councillors' cooperation to be able to gain the political benefits of participatory budgeting. Several of the municipal staff who organise the meetings told me that participatory budgeting only works if there is a sense of working together, among the councillors but also among the city's residents more generally. Therefore, they have reasons to listen to the councillors and concede to their views when this is needed to maintain their faith in the process.

The participatory budget works very differently from ideas about contentious politics because the municipality needs people in the city to take the councillors seriously. It needs the councillors to be recognised even if this makes them powerful also in relation to the municipality. The municipality does various things for people to acknowledge and appreciate the work that the councillors do: for example, it distributes maps to the residents that show the implemented projects for each part of the city, and when bigger projects are finalised, it organises public events to celebrate their inauguration and thereby generate positive publicity for the councillors and the participatory budget. The more recognition they get, the more they can generate legitimacy for the government. But they can also use that recognition to push for changes in how the participatory budget works and redefine its boundaries (see also Holdo 2021). By demanding and receiving recognition, the councillors are able to politicise their participation, and, if not redistribute it, at least expand its significance beyond the government's intentions.

Conclusion: The Limits of Democratic Care Work

The question of what difference local participation can make is crucial for citizens in general and movement activists in particular. Today, disruptive protests, from the Indignados and Occupy movements to recent environmental activism, often lead to the participation of some kind. Especially in local politics, new forms of participatory decision-making are becoming more and more common as a way to handle citizens' dissatisfaction with austerity policies, economic inequality and the domination of financial interests in politics. But under what conditions can they become spaces for meaningful political change?

To address this question, I have applied a care perspective that offers a way to move beyond previous debates about whether or not participation can disrupt neoliberal politics. Participation by its nature is not disruptive in the sense that protests can sometimes be. But seen as a form of democratic care, acts of participation question what we think we know about how we can accomplish change. To care for democracy is to defend democratic ideals by giving them space, practising them, reflecting on them and resuscitating them. In a sense, the path is also the goal. But what exactly is the goal? And how does participation take us there? I conclude by addressing these questions.

Joan Tronto (2013) has described a "caring democracy" as one in which the priorities of public discourse would be radically different. Acts of caring would no longer be taken for granted but politicised. The distribution of both provision and reception of care would be much higher up on the political agenda. Extending the idea of care to caring for democracy brings into central focus the politics of participation. A caring democracy would also be one where we give more room for solidarity as opposed to the selfishness dictated by neoliberalism. A caring democracy could be a society where we come together continuously to reflect on what kind of society would correspond to our shared values and what responsibility we as individual members have to achieve its realisation. Care disrupts the neoliberal thought that the best society is produced through everyone's uncoordinated consumer and investment choices. We cannot draw out in detail how our political institutions would look like in a more caring society. But we would listen more empathetically, connect, recognise our different needs, embrace ambiguities and reflect together on difficult ethical problems. It would be a radically nonviolent, inclusive and egalitarian society.

It seems unlikely that we could realise such as society merely through strategies of open contestation or electoral competition – we also need to practise the democratic ideals we preach. But it is also not enough, I have suggested, to recognise the many ways people care for democracy, and how they act to repair our shared world. These acts, too, need to be examined critically. In the worst case, they help reproduce the structures needed for unjust policymaking to continue. It is, I have argued, by politicising participation, that is, by bringing attention to the often-unacknowledged ways that people (civil society and community leaders as well as many municipal employees) help sustain democracy despite the neoliberal policies that undermine it. For participation to be disruptive, people need to use it to renegotiate the terms of their cooperation. In Rosario, participants have done this by reminding the municipality that their cooperation is conditional. They demand recognition in return for participation, and with that recognition, they can challenge patterns of exclusion. This case offers lessons for practices of care in general: let us care for each other and for democracy, but let us also acknowledge that as we do this we are also compensating for a deficit in an uncaring system: in return, we must demand that our actions be recognised, that we can contest political boundaries and extend spaces of caring.

Note

1 Acknowledgements: many people helped and inspired me in working on this chapter. I especially want to thank Priscyll Anctil Avoine, Sonia Bussu, Zohreh Khoban, Johanna Söderström and Ekatherina Zhukova. A sincere thank you to the editors, Adrian Bua and Sonia Bussu, for caring about everything that makes this collective project possible. My work on this chapter was financed by Forte (grant no. 2018-00550).

References

Arruzza, C. (2016). Functionalist, determinist, reductionist: Social reproduction feminism and its critics. *Science & Society*, 80(1), 9–30.
Arruzza, C. (2020). Non vogliamo tornare alla normalità: Il Coronavirus e le lotte delle donne. In Carlotta Benvegnù, Niccolò Cuppini, Mattia Frapporti, Floriano Milesi, Maurilio Pirone (ed.) *La Pandemia*. Bologna: Dipartimento delle Arti Università di Bologna. 81–87.

Baiocchi, G. (2003a). Emergent public spheres: Talking politics in participatory governance. *American Sociological Review*, *68*(1), 52–74.
Baiocchi, G. (2003b). The long march through institutions: Lessons from the PT in power. In GloBal MoVEMENTS, NaTioNal GRiEVaNCES Mobilizing for "Real Democracy" and Social Justice in Baiocchi (ed.), *Radicals in Power: The Workers' Party and Experiments in Urban Democracy in Brazil*. London: Zed Books. 207–226.
Baiocchi, G. (2005). *Militants and Citizens: The Politics of Participatory Democracy in Porto Alegre*. Stanford University Press.
Baiocchi, G., & Ganuza, E. (2014). Participatory budgeting as if emancipation mattered. *Politics & Society*, *42*(1), 29–50.
Baiocchi, G., & Ganuza, E. (2016). *Popular Democracy: The Paradox of Participation*. Stanford University Press.
Bartos, A.E. (2021). Troubling false care. *ACME: An International Journal for Critical Geographies*, *20*(3), 312–321.
Bherer, L., Fernández-Martínez, J.L., García Espín, P., & Jiménez Sánchez, M. (2016). The promise for democratic deepening: The effects of participatory processes in the interaction between civil society and local governments. *Journal of Civil Society*, *12*(3), 344–363.
Bourgault, S., & Robinson, F. (2020). Care ethics thinks the political. *International Journal of Care and Caring*, *4*(1), 3–9.
Brown, W. (2015). *Undoing the Demos: Neoliberalism's Stealth Revolution*. MIT Press.
Bua, A., & Bussu, S. (2021). Between governance-driven democratisation and democracy-driven governance: Explaining changes in participatory governance in the case of Barcelona. *European Journal of Political Research*, *60*(3), 716–737.
Casalini, B. (2019). Care of the self and subjectivity in precarious neoliberal societies. *Insights Anthropol*, *3*(1), 134–139.
Cohen, J., & Rogers, J. (2003). Power and reason. In Archon Fung and Erik Olin Wright (eds.) *Deepening Democracy: Institutional Innovations in Empowered Participatory Governance*, 237–255. London/New York: Verso Books.
DeNardis, L. (2011). Democratizing the municipal budget in Latin America: Citizen participation in Brazil and Mexico. *International Review of Social Sciences and Humanities*, *2*(1), 91–102.
Fernández-Martínez, J.L., García-Espín, P., & Jiménez-Sánchez, M. (2020). Participatory frustration: The unintended cultural effect of local democratic innovations. *Administration & Society*, *52*(5), 718–748.
Fung, A. (2004). Empowered participation. In *Empowered Participation*. Princeton University Press.
Fung, A., & Wright, E.O. (2003). Countervailing power in empowered participatory governance. In Archon Fung and Erik Olin Wright (Eds.) *Deepening Democracy: Institutional Innovations in Empowered Participatory Governance*, 259–289. Verso Books: London/New York.
García-Espín, P., & Sánchez, M.J. (2017). Participatory processes as democracy makers. Exploring effects, mechanisms and evidences in civil society. *Revista de Estudios Politicos*, 177, 113–146.
Geissel, B. (2012). Impacts of democratic innovations in Europe. In Brigitte Geissel and Kenneth Newton (eds.), *Evaluating democratic Innovations: Curing the Democratic Malaise*, 209–214. Abingdon, UK: Routledge.
Gilman, H., & Wampler, B. (2020). The difference in design: Participatory budgeting in Brazil and the United States. *Journal of Deliberative Democracy*, *15*(1).

Harvey, D. (2012). *Rebel Cities: From the Right to the City to the Urban Revolution.* Verso Books.
Held, V. (2006). *The Ethics of Care: Personal, Political, and Global.* Oxford University Press on Demand.
Holdo, M. (2014). *Field Notes on Deliberative Democracy: Power and Recognition in Participatory Budgeting* (Doctoral dissertation, Statsvetenskapliga institutionen).
Holdo, M. (2016a). Deliberative capital: Recognition in participatory budgeting. *Critical Policy Studies, 10*(4), 391–409.
Holdo, M. (2016b). Reasons of power: Explaining non-cooptation in participatory budgeting. *International Journal of Urban and Regional Research, 40*(2), 378–394.
Holdo, M. (2019). Cooptation and non-cooptation: Elite strategies in response to social protest. *Social Movement Studies, 18*(4), 444–462.
Holdo, M. (2020a). Power games: Elites, movements, and strategic cooperation. *Political Studies Review, 18*(2), 189–203.
Holdo, M. (2020b). Contestation in participatory budgeting: Spaces, boundaries, and agency. *American Behavioral Scientist, 64*(9), 1348–1365.
Holdo, M. (2021). An inclusive and participatory approach to counter-radicalization? Examining the role of Muslim associations in the Swedish policy process. *Ethnicities, 21*(3), 477–497.
Kohn, M. (2016). *The Death and Life of the Urban Commonwealth.* Oxford University Press.
Mansbridge, J.J. (1983). *Beyond Adversary Democracy.* University of Chicago Press.
Mansbridge, J.J. (1991). Feminism and democracy. *The American Prospect,* 1/1(Spring), 126–39.
McNulty, S. (2020). An unlikely success: Peru's top-down participatory budgeting experience. *Journal of Deliberative Democracy,* 8(2).
Mouffe, C. (1999). Deliberative democracy or agonistic pluralism. *Social Research, 66,* 745–758.
Navarro, 2004, p. 252. Navarro, Z. (2004). Participatory budgeting in Porto Alegre, Brazil, in Licha, I. (Ed.). (2004). *Citizens in Charge: Managing Local Budgets in East Asia and Latin America.* Washington, DC: Inter-American Development Bank.
Nicholson, J., & Kurucz, E. (2019). Relational leadership for sustainability: Building an ethical framework from the moral theory of 'ethics of care'. *Journal of Business Ethics, 156*(1), 25–43
Pateman, C. (1970). *Participation and Democratic Theory.* Cambridge University Press.
Pateman, C. (2012). Participatory democracy revisited. *Perspectives on Politics, 10*(1), 7–19.
Peck, J., & Theodore, N. (2015). *Fast policy: Experimental statecraft at the thresholds of neoliberalism.* Minneapolis, MN: University of Minnesota Press.
Phillips, A. (Ed.). (1998). *Feminism and Politics.* OUP Oxford.
Pols, J. (2015). Towards an empirical ethics in care: Relations with technologies in health care. *Medicine, Health Care and Philosophy, 18*(1), 81–90.
Puāwai Collective (2019). Assembling disruptive practice in the neoliberal university: An ethics of care. *Geografiska Annaler: Series B, Human Geography, 101*(1), 33–43.
Putnam, R.D. (2016). *Our Kids: The American Dream in Crisis.* Simon and Schuster.
Przeworski, A. (1998) Deliberation and Ideological Domination. In Elster, J. (ed.) *Deliberative Democracy.* Cambridge: Cambridge University Press.
Rodgers, D. (2012). Separate but equal democratization? Participation, politics, and urban segregation in Latin America. In *Latin American Urban Development into the 21st Century* (pp. 123–142). Palgrave Macmillan, London.

Touchton, M., & Wampler, B. (2014). Improving social well-being through new democratic institutions. *Comparative Political Studies*, *47*(10), 1442–1469.
Tronto J.C. (1993). *Moral Boundaries, a Political Argument for an Ethic of Care*. Routledge.
Tronto, J.C. (2013). *Caring Democracy*. New York University Press.
Urban, P., & Ward, L. (Eds.). (2020). *Care Ethics, Democratic Citizenship and the State*. Springer International Publishing.
Wampler, B. (2010). *Participatory Budgeting in Brazil: Contestation, Cooperation, and Accountability*. Penn State Press.
Wampler, B., & Hartz-Karp, J. (2012). Participatory budgeting: Diffusion and outcomes across the world. *Journal of Public Deliberation*, *8*(2).
Wampler, B., & Goldfrank, B. (2022). *The Rise, Spread, and Decline of Brazil's Participatory Budgeting: The Arc of a Democratic Innovation*. Springer Nature.

5 The Democratic Multiverse

Governance, Associations and the Prospects for Progressive Democratic Renewal

Hendrik Wagenaar

Introduction

In the last decade, our understanding of the relationship between democracy and associations has received a new impetus. Two concepts, Governance-Driven Democratisation (GDD) (Warren 2014) and Democracy-Driven Governance (DDG) (Bua and Bussu 2021; this volume; Bua, Bussu and Davies this volume), have been put forward to describe and explain ostensible new developments in the relationship between the political-administrative system and civil society groups. At the root of this renewed interest in the normative and functionalist heart of democratic theory is a growing sense that the capacity of the political-administrative system for managing societal sectors and solving public problems has reached unsurpassable limits. These are limits of diagnosis, design and delivery that impede the effectiveness of government and compromise its legitimacy in the eyes of citizens. Governments cope with a cascade of interlocking crises, such as unaffordable housing, unconscionable income inequality, eroding labour rights, climate breakdown, migration, the COVID-19 pandemic and, since the recent onset of inflation, a cost-of-living crisis for an increasing number of families. There is a growing sense that not only do governments have few effective solutions to these problems, but in many cases they ignore their existence, pursue solutions that violate social justice or attempt to deflect their seriousness by focusing on ideological rectitude in public finance and cultural expression.

GDD and DDG are important and intriguing attempts to address this generalised breakdown of governance capacity by reviving the intricate relationship between government, democracy and association. Both of these developments in democratic theory make important empirical and normative claims, suggesting that we might enter a new phase in the entanglement of civil society with the political-administrative system, and, by implication, the functioning of democracy. These democratic innovations proceed via an intensified involvement of citizen groups in the formulation and implementation of policy-making. In both instances the stated purposes are both functional and normative. By opening up processes of agenda setting, policy formulation and policy delivery to input from citizen groups, administrations seek to expand their knowledge base and operational capacity and adopt new, more inclusive, forms of collective problem-solving,

DOI: 10.4324/9781003218517-6

thereby broadening and deepening the democratic process (Bua and Bussu, Introduction). Governance-Driven Democratisation (GDD) sees the impetus for this development as originating with administrators, while Democracy-Driven Governance (DDG) suggests the pressure from, and creativity of, social movements as the driver of these institutional changes. Both of these innovations in democratic theory boast empirical support. GDD can be seen as the theoretical conceptualisation of four decades of experiments in advanced democracies with interactive, polycentric or network government (Briggs 2008; Ostrom 2010; Agger et al. 2015; Edelenbos and Van Meerkerk 2016). DDG points to detailed case descriptions (Porto Alegre, Barcelona) in which citizen groups have organised themselves on specific issues and managed to gain the support of sympathetic politicians and administrators to design participatory administrative arrangements that reflect the collective needs, experiential knowledge, communicative skills and civic virtues of ordinary citizens (Avritzer 2002; Baiocchi 2017; Bua and Bussu 2021; Zechner 2021).

Reforming political-administrative institutions through civil society initiatives is an ambitious goal where we may expect to encounter many practical, normative and discursive obstacles. At stake is not only the effectiveness and legitimacy of the political-administrative system but also a deepening of our democracy along the well-known dimensions of franchise, scope and authenticity (Dryzek 1996). To fully appreciate the size and nature of these challenges of democratic innovation, we need to put them in a larger perspective.

This chapter lays the groundwork for a theory of democratic institutional reform. I will approach this task by broadening the focus of my analysis in two ways. I will first expand the state-centred approach of these new modes of citizen participation by providing a more encompassing view of the relationship between democracy, government and association (see: "Association and Democracy"). The conclusion will be that although progressive democratic reform should involve the budgetary, legal and organisational power of the state, it can, and should, also occur outside the boundaries of the state. Normatively this means that governance should not be the exclusive domain of the state (Hirst 1994).[1] I will then expand upon this conclusion by moving my analytical gaze to the undertheorised, economic dimension of democracy. I will argue that in almost every instance of collective decision-making, the wider political economy needs to be taken into account to understand the constraints that bear upon particular policy areas (see: "The Mirage of Economic Democracy"). I will show that this widening of perspective reveals serious limitations of the possibilities for successful statist participatory governance, through either GDD or DDG. In the final section I argue for a participatory ecology, a system of associations, both parallel to and in collaboration with the state. I will also revive a tradition of progressive public administration which has been lost in the contemporary quest for a small state ("Conclusion: The Democratic Multiverse"). Taken together these alternatives form a repertoire of progressive reform in the democratic multiverse.

Associations and Democracy

Despite its references to civil society and social mobilisation, the GDD–DDG debate is state-centred. It expects progressive democratic innovation to be anchored in state institutions. However, if we take democracy as our window upon this expansive conceptual field, then in the most general terms, in modern societies democracy is suspended between three poles: the political-administrative system, the financial-economic sector and civil society. Differently put, democracy as a system of collective self-rule has to contend with the effects of, as Mark Warren puts it, three distinct operational orders, three functional domains of social activity. These are the coordination of economic activity through the mechanisms of prices and competition (markets), the hierarchical, legalised and formal procedures of public agencies (bureaucracy) and the voluntary, cooperative interactions of civil society (association) (Warren 2001, 49–50). Each of these three spheres operates according to a distinct functional logic that is constitutive of its nature, output and moral justification, and that is orthogonal to the other two modes. For example, it would be antithetical to the intimate, emotional relationships within the family to subject it to the utility-maximising analysis that characterises the business sphere. Inevitably, the three spheres are in continuous interaction with each other, dominating, exploiting, avoiding, transgressing, influencing or cooperating. The effects of these complex interactions have consequences for the form and depth of democracy, supporting, subverting, emasculating, enriching or, in extreme cases, abolishing democracy altogether.

Among the three spheres, civic associations occupy an ambiguous position. Without the formal powers and financial might of the other two, they are the weakest, yet, they are the source, even in authoritarian regimes, of progressive transformation (Evans and Boyte 1986; Goldfarb 2006). In democracies, associations are not only a major source of regime legitimacy but, at the risk of overgeneralisation, at a more fundamental level a condition of possibility for functioning democratic arrangements. This is evidenced by the frequent entanglements of associations with markets and hierarchies in the course of history. Worker movements at the turn of the 20th century inaugurated social security and anti-monopoly laws. Half a century later corporatism became a form of regulated capitalism in which organised interests negotiated wages and labour rights. Similarly, squatter movements of precarious workers in Brazil developed into constitutionally anchored democratic institutions (Holston 2008). In other words, social struggle has been a central mechanism of progressive reform. This puts the burden on the analyst to explain on what new terrains and by what new means the latest incarnations of the incursion of associations into government bureaucracies transpire.

I will argue that GDD and DDG are the results of the negative consequences, the externalities if one prefers, of the increasing dominance of the corporate sector over the other two (a theme that I will expand on in the next section). The impact of corporate dominance on society and democracy remains somewhat implicit in the literature of GDD and DDG – more so in GDD than in DDG, which acknowledges economic hardship as the impetus and focus of social movements. This is important in so far as it also has left undiscussed two important elements of the current resurgence of associations. The first is the relative absence of the importance of economic democracy in the new forms of public participation. Economic dispossession and its effects on people's life chances, collective identity and, in the case of climate change, their very survival are at the heart of their motivation to organise themselves. Closely related to economic democracy is the risk to the democratic effects of associations that result from hegemony, the cognitive captivity of a population by a powerful neoliberal ideology that has suffused every aspect of life (Mirowski 2014; Brown 2015; Wagenaar and Prainsack 2021). The second is the re-emergence of another type of association, the commons, partly in response to the hegemonic effects of neoliberalism. Commons are interesting because they do not necessarily seek to influence governance, although that doesn't mean that they don't become entangled with the bureaucratic and economic spheres (Zechner 2020). Taken together I think that this will result in a more complete account of the normative and functional contribution of associations to economic activity and democratic governance, an account I call the *democratic multiverse*.

In bare-bone form, democracy is a system of collective self-rule that is informed by the twin ideals of the equal distribution of the possibility to influence collective decisions that affect one's life situation and equal participation in collective judgment (Warren 2001, 60). Both of these ideals are the necessary conditions of a functioning democracy. When one of these ideals is compromised, democracy itself is in jeopardy. For example, when citizens have the possibility to vote but the reigning regime has effectively shut down the media, safe for a few official, regime-friendly outlets, the vote has become more or less meaningless, and democracy has become illiberal democracy. Or, reversely, when a country allows vigorous debate in the public sphere but effectively restricts citizens' right to vote (through first past the post systems, gerrymandering, spurious voter identification and so on), citizens' possibilities to influence collective decision-making are severely compromised. To quote Warren: "Democracy thus involves institutionalized procedures and protections that enable the expression, demonstration, argumentation, and justification through which individuals decide what they want or think is right both as individuals and as members of collectivities" (2001, 60).

For a proper assessment of the reach and possibilities of democracy, it is important to be reminded that in terms of the tripartite distinction of social orders, institutionalised democracy is essentially dissociated from the state, economy and civil society. Even though most advanced economies have constitutions that prescribe in elaborate detail the procedures for periodic elections, the separation of powers, the rule of law and so on, at heart democracy is more an invitation than an obligation. For them to be effective, the ideals that guide institutionalised democracy must be accepted by citizens, officials and businesses alike. Voting, for example, is a right, but in almost all countries citizens have a choice to enact that right or not. Similarly, elected officials who have been defeated in an election step down from office, but in practice this is as much a habit as an obligation and can be subverted, as we have recently seen. Thus, the challenge of institutionalised democracy is to find ways to persuade the three operational spheres to open up their inner workings to democratic procedure. In that sense democracy is dispositional as well as procedural. It is in accomplishing this task that associations play a central role as a subsidiary to state-organised, institutionalised democracy.

The mechanism by which the influence of democracy upon the three social domains proceeds is associational relations. Associational relations are relations based on the norms of voluntariness, trust, mutual respect, consensual agreement and the possibility of exit (Hirst 1994, 50; Warren 2001, 54). In this they differ from the instrumental, utilitarian exchanges that govern markets and the hierarchical, command exchanges of bureaucracies. The distinction between associations, as organisations based on associational relations, and associational relations is important because it explains how democracy can come to invade the three social domains. Although a certain distinct type of relations defines each domain, they also require elements of the other two for their proper functioning. Businesses are organised in hierarchical ways, for example, simply because it expands their capacity for control and coordination (Warren 2001, 50). More important for our argument is that each domain relies to a greater or lesser extent on the normative work of trust, voluntariness and consensual agreement as a condition for its proper functioning and its continuity.

This short digression on democratic theory leads to two conclusions. First, modern administrative bureaucracies are permeated with associational relations. Although nominally organised according to legal rule, formal procedure and merit-based appointments, in their day-to-day functioning there is much emphasis on deliberation, and consensual collective judgment and decision-making (Freeman 2021).[2] From here, it is only a short step to extend this mode of working to citizens and associations outside the bureaucracy. Second, the permeation of associational relations in non-associational spheres, such as a state bureaucracy, is in itself not indicative of a progressive turn of the organisation. At most, it signifies a more mature approach to human resource management, a willingness to introduce a measure of self-governance in the day-to-day management of the organisation that has little bearing on the organisation's actual policies. A state bureaucracy that operates according to associational principles could, for example, very well pursue ideologically informed, hard-bitten austerity policies that hurt most of the population. As we will see in the next section, for the possibility of the progressive reform of administrative bureaucracies, it is more important to pay attention to the *content* of the needs and interests for which civil associations seek to get the ear of administrative bureaucracies and businesses. The more these are at odds with each other, the more difficult it will be to convince the latter to collaborate with civil associations.

Ever since Weber's classic sociological analysis, we are aware of the functional advantages of bureaucracy. Formal written rules create a predictable environment for both employees and the public. Knowledge is secured through appointments based on educational credentials and merit. A hierarchy of authority and constitutionally defined relationships with elected officials guarantee organisational and political accountability. Combined with the power of the state and the rule of law, this produces an operational mode that has the capacity to initiate collective problem-solving and see it through to the delivery stage (du Gay 2000; Warren 2001, 49–50; Meier and O'Toole 2006). The circumstance, that in post-modern societies whole classes of problems (wicked problems) are becoming more and more resistant to bureaucratic management, doesn't detract from the fact that it is still the dominant mode of governance in most public areas. Associations, on the other hand, such as social movements or commons, are almost purely based on informal relationships, governed by peer governance, trust, mutual respect and community values. To open up a state bureaucracy to associations will thus inevitably lead to friction with the bureaucratic mode of governance. Even in the best of circumstances, administrative bureaucracies will find it difficult to expose financial and political decision-making to the normative thrust of citizen participation. The challenge for bureaucrats is not so much to be convinced of the advantages of inclusiveness or widening the epistemic base of collective judgement and decision-making, but to weld together, in practice, two distinct operational modes. For example, what is the role of the citizen or association in the accountability structure of a government bureaucracy? How does the formally described functional role of the bureaucrat combine with the informal role of the citizen? The result is likely to be a governance arrangement that, from a purely operational perspective, will be unstable and/or of limited effectiveness.

Unfortunately there is ample evidence for this. Successful innovatory arrangements such as GDD, empowered participation (Fung 2004), civic capacity (Briggs 2008) or adaptive capacity (Bourgon 2011) are attempts to overcome the operational divide between government bureaucracy and civic association and to maintain the latter's capacity for delivery. This usually means that the latter operates within the agenda of the former, at arm's length, and that the collaboration is usually limited in time so that all participants are aware that it represents an experimental space, a temporary departure from business as usual. In many instances participatory governance is an add-on, though not necessarily an unimportant one, to the administrative bureaucracy (Meier and O'Toole 2006). It also means that in almost all these instances economic policy is off-limits. Participatory experiments in public administration concern topics of a social nature such as prisons, crime, youth services, homelessness and bushfires, but rarely issues that involve the interests of the business sector such as energy, housing or city planning (Bourgon 2011). In cases where social movements have taken over urban administrations, we regularly see that the incoming administration encounters legal jurisdictions as well as active obstruction and hostility of an alliance of sitting administrators and, tellingly, business interests (Bua and Davies 2022).

From the perspective of the progressive transformation of government, this might sound discouraging and rather inconsequential. However, in my own experience of doing action research on GDD initiated by different municipal agencies in the city of The Hague, it has a range of, sometimes unexpected, individual and institutional effects (Wagenaar et al. 2010; Wagenaar and Duiveman 2012). From up close we registered the development among residents and administrators of individual efficacy, critical skills and civic virtues such as attentiveness to the common good, conflict resolution and cooperation across ethnic divides. Institutionally we observed the opening of information channels as well as the development of co-government. For example, a participatory initiative by the Agency for Public Infrastructure to involve citizen groups in neighbourhood management quickly revealed to the officials involved that, through a decade of outsourcing, the organisation had lost considerable delivery power, prompting the reintroduction of shorter lines of command. Another project that sought to steer social services on the basis of need revealed that professional organisations routinely ignored those needs to supplant them with whatever routine services they were organised to supply. Participation offered a counterweight to the dominance of professional organisations in the delivery of social services (Wagenaar et al. 2010; for Amsterdam, see *Samen Wonen Samen Leven* 2019). A third, more bottom-up challenge by residents who were dissatisfied with the police's lack of effort to confront the growing drug trade in their neighbourhood led to enduring collaboration and the creation of a number of successful citizen-led public safety programs along the lines of empowered participation (Wagenaar 2007). Arguably the most important results of GDD were the parallel development of critical political skills and civic virtues among the citizens who were active in the participatory efforts and the change of attitude among agency officials from an internally oriented mode of working to the routine involvement of citizen associations in policy formulation and implementation – however, always within the confines of municipal policy-making as established in the coalition agreement between political partners.

Perhaps these are relatively small achievements, far removed from the redress of deep social inequality or the progressive transformation of municipal government sought by DDG. Yet an event looking back at 10 years of citizen participation in The Hague revealed a general mood of critical satisfaction among citizens and officials, as well as the consolidation of participation as a generalised mode of municipal governance. Yet, GDD has some well-known limitations. When powerful actors are involved, these often resort to forum hopping, obtaining the desired results through backroom deals with government officials. In addition, government and corporate actors do not feel obliged to accept the deliberative outcomes of GDD arrangements (Wagenaar 2022). GDD operates within the agenda of the commissioning agency and may stifle bottom-up citizen initiatives (Bua and Bussu, Introduction, this volume). Finally, GDD participation hardly touches upon the pressing problems affecting large cities in the Netherlands and elsewhere, problems such as unaffordable housing, growing income inequality, the commodification of urban development, the continuing precarisation of work, climate change, excessive tourism and recently handling the COVID-19 pandemic. It is to these that we turn now.

The Mirage of Economic Democracy

There is a third pole in the democratic triangle: the economic sector. The argument I make is threefold: (1) our understanding of democratisation in local, and for that matter national, governance cannot be seen apart from the wider political economy, (2) developments in the political economy since the late 1960s have created a sea change in the structure and functioning of the political economy and state–society relations and (3) these changes have severely impoverished the functioning of local and national democracy by effectively restricting its scope and authenticity. In this section I will discuss these changes and their effects on democratic functioning. In the next section I will discuss the commons, as an associational countermovement that feeds and inspires DDG.

Much democratic theorising focuses on the relation between citizens and the state. Yet, as we have seen in the preceding section, the life of citizens is not only influenced by the activities of governments but also by those of businesses, banks and other economic actors. For example, when a central bank raises the interest rate, a decision taken by a small committee without any democratic debate, this affects millions of mortgage holders by adding to their monthly outlays.[3] Economic democracy, let alone democratic participation in economic activities, is an underdeveloped area (Thorpe and Gaventa 2020, 8; Vlahos 2023). Going beyond the unhelpful and effectively misleading moniker "market", Thorpe and Gaventa helpfully define the economy as

> the production of goods and services, the processes through which they are transferred and exchanged, and the distribution of profits, welfare or other benefits accruing from these activities … as well as the governance of these economic processes at different (macro, meso and micro) levels.
>
> (2020, 8)

They then frame the issue of economic democracy by asking two questions: what is meaningful participation in economic governance? And: "How might participation enable increased social control over the economy, in ways that transform economic relations and meet the needs of all?" The objective of economic democracy is the attainment of a people-centred economy. A people-centred economy "supports community regeneration and wealth circulation, is rooted in democratised ownership, values local assets and supports local agencies …. It often involves citizen self-organising and innovation … and has important 'social and solidarity' aspects" (Thorpe and Gaventa 2020, 8). Its aim is for ordinary people to regain meaningful control over economic governance and "transform economic relations and meet the needs of all" (ibid.). The authors envision three arenas for economic democracy: participation in the management and investment decisions of firms, participation in government economic policy-making, and alternative community or cooperative structures. Instead of expanding on these modes of economic democracy as the road to a people-centred economy, I want to follow a different strategy and argue that we are probably as far removed from any meaningful economic democracy as during the days of Manchester capitalism or the Gilded Age.

My starting point is that the very distinction between "society", as the realm of social values and personal relations, and the "economy" as a realm governed by its own laws and managed by a technocracy of economists, financiers and business experts who possess privileged, objective knowledge that is inaccessible to the layperson, is itself the historical outcome of the very processes that we seek to bring under democratic control.[4] I will argue that a series of deep transformations in business and finance in the last half-century has further cemented the idea of the economy as a separate realm to the point that it has become a taken-for-granted reality. That is, even people who are critical of the negative effects of markets on society still do not question the "Economy" as a separate domain with special status within the public sphere and its associated experts inside and outside of government. This in turn has created serious impediments to a meaningful form of democracy along franchise, scope and authenticity (Dryzek 1996; Kioupkiolis 2020, 15), where scope extends to collective judgements and decisions regarding economic and financial issues. To adequately appreciate the weight of this claim, and the roadblocks it creates for meaningful democratic participation, I need to list these disparate changes to give the reader an idea of the extent to which they have come to cohere into a Gramscian hegemonic block (Hall 2017). In a brief outline, I discern the following major changes.

First, the economic order has become more international, interconnected and multipolar. International regulation, promoted by large corporations and financial institutions, and given intellectual authority by economists, successfully weakened national control over markets and businesses (Glyn 2006; Rodrik 2012; Kuttner 2018). Second, and related, the last 50 years have also seen the rise of the "giant transnational firm" (Crouch 2011, 49). Entry barriers and network externalities have made massive concentrations of corporate power possible (ibid.), which resulted in a "corporate takeover of the market" *and* of national governments (Sanchez Bajo & Roelants 2013; Gamble 2014). Whatever name we prefer to give it, in many policy domains local, national and transnational governments de facto capitulated to corporate and financial interests – or, perhaps more precisely, have chosen to ideologically embrace those interests.

Third, under the influence of economic doctrine, anti-trust legislation was seriously weakened in the 1980s and replaced by shareholder value as a measure of corporate health (Crouch 2011; Stout 2012). The effect of the shareholder value doctrine has been a stagnation in wages as labour costs have been relentlessly driven down, the outsourcing of labour with its concomitant precaritisation, the move of industries to low-wage countries, financial engineering as a corporate strategy and the abandonment of corporate social responsibility (Wagenaar and Prainsack 2021, ch. 7). For ordinary people, this meant that substandard service, financial and other exploitation and indignity at the hands of large corporations with hardly a possibility of redress has become an everyday phenomenon.

Fourth is the rise of a deliberately opaque, speculative financial industry that contributes little to the wellbeing of individuals and the efficiency of businesses (Kay 2015; Vogl 2017). One effect of the dominance of finance in the neoliberal economy is the prominence of debt, both as an idea and a practice, in public and private life. In the barest of outlines, debt has come to occupy a central role in the economy to the point that it is now an "endogenous feature" of the global economic system as well as the political imaginary (Streeck 2013; 2017; Kelton

2020). Governments felt they had to borrow to finance public infrastructure and social assistance programs, through the issuance of sovereign bonds, to make up for the declining share of corporate taxes. In the rhetoric of government officials and professional economists public debt was regarded in the same terms as private debt, a thoroughly misleading ideology that Mary Mellor calls the "handbag economy" (Mellor 2016). This moralisation of public debt ushered in so-called austerity programs allegedly aimed at containing the growth of public debt (Blyth 2015) but that in effect acted as a disciplinary tool for the working population by creating considerable social hardship among low earners and the unemployed. For the state of democracy, the fetishisation of public debt has been ruinous. It has resulted in a limitation by international capital and central banks – through the depoliticisation of socio-economic decisions and adherence to discursive economic orthodoxy – of both the sovereignty of the nation state and the democratic freedom of its citizens to decide over its interests and circumstances (Flinders and Wood 2014).

Finally, the above developments are as much ideational as legal-organisational. These discursive changes took two forms. On the one hand, a powerful neoliberal narrative that depicts the state as oversized, overbearing, inefficient and obstructing "natural" market efficiency has supported the move towards a minimal state (for the origins of this doctrine, see Maclean 2017; Wagenaar and Prainsack 2021, ch. 7). This led to the marketisation of ever more state services and the introduction of corporate management techniques into public sector agencies. At the same time, neoliberalism has also resulted in a strong state that is willing to exert its monopoly on organised coercion (Jessop 2015, 28), and its capacity for electronic surveillance (Zuboff 2019) to safeguard corporate interests and defend itself against alleged external and internal threats (Gamble 1994). On the other hand, we witnessed what historian Philip Mirowski dubbed 'everyday neoliberalism', the expansion of market principles, such as competition, the commodification of individuals and the conflation of individualised notions of property and freedom, into every sphere of social life and personal identity (Brown 2006; Mirowksi 2014).

Wagenaar and Prainsack have argued that these ideational developments have resulted in a situation of hegemony. They define hegemony not as durable political domination, but as a form of cognitive captivity, a horizon of intellectual and practical possibility, moral authority, and collective and individual imagination that includes both political and civil society (2021). These "intersubjective forms of consciousness" are embedded in and sustained by the institutional, practical and linguistic organisation of society. These shared beliefs and practices do not emerge *sui generis* but are imposed and sustained through law, regulation, institutions, professional conduct, surveillance and government technology.

What do these developments mean for the prospects of a functioning democracy or the meaningful participation of citizens in democratic governance? Some observations:

1. The interpenetration of the global corporate-financial order with the state has created a new Leviathan that dominates civil society. Its negative effects,

such as depressed wages, precarious work, unaffordable housing, erosion of basic public services such as health services, social care and education, data exploitation, loss of rights, everyday humiliation and the destruction of the natural environment, are experienced by citizens worldwide. In addition, the discursive hegemony of a neoliberal market ideology has pervaded almost every sphere of public life. Where social-democratic governments in the 1980s were sometimes rudely reminded by international money markets of the limited space for democratic innovation (Kuttner 2018, 77), today most governments don't need to be reminded and tolerate, or even abet, corporate tax avoidance, data exploitation, rising income inequality, the attenuation of the public sector and catastrophic climate change in the name of "balancing the budget" and "bringing down the debt".[5]

The immediate effects on democracy are twofold. The involvement of the state in the global corporate-financial Hegemon has impaired electoral, parliamentary democracy from the inside out. In many countries elections have descended into beauty contests between candidates who more or less occupy the same political platform. Ongoing processes of depoliticisation have removed ever more areas of collective interest, such as the distribution of wealth and income, the imposition of taxes and subsidies or the fight against climate change, from collective decision-making by transferring them to the dictate of transnational agreements, the discipline of credit rating agencies or the "technical" decisions of central banks (Streeck 2013, 113). More pernicious is the hollowing out of the capacity for collective judgment through the effects of hegemony. The neoliberal market ideology that has pervaded collective and private life has severely reduced the options for individual and political autonomy as a condition of democratic collective judgment.[6]

2. The prospects for meaningful participation in democratic governance are mixed. We saw the relative success of GDD. Within a narrow agenda set by local government, citizens were able to exert influence over issues in their immediate environment that affected them. In the process we observed positive individual and institutional democratic effects. But it was also clear that almost all the large political-economic issues that are the result of the transitions in the political economy fell outside of the purview of these GDD experiments. This is no wonder. If we take the affordability crisis in housing as an example – but the argument applies to most other current crises – the state has relatively little influence over what is called the housing "market". The availability and price of housing are determined by a dispersed conglomerate of banks, building societies, construction companies, privatised housing associations, real estate agents, investment banks and offshore equity firms, advertisement agencies and nowadays tourist accommodation platforms, all operating under the dictate of financialisation (Cole 2015). Laws, fiscal arrangements and financial regulation favour homeownership over renting. The whole is supported by a conservative ideology of a property-owning democracy and a hegemonic narrative that links individualised property to freedom (Wagenaar and Prainsack 2021, ch. 4; Jackson n.d.). Municipal

housing departments are an integral part of this sprawling conglomerate and are in no position to take a critical stance towards it. Moreover, as we have seen, the "industry" doesn't hesitate to flex its muscles when it sees its interests threatened and obstruct progressive reform (Bua and Davies 2022).

3. DDG is a more promising alternative to resist the neoliberal Hegemon. DDG has its origins in social movements that resist the reigning cognitive order, formulate alternatives to it, understand its underlying power dimension and are willing to disrupt state and economic institutions to draw attention to its injustices. Bua and Bussu show, for example, how Spanish citizens who, in the wake of the financial crisis of 2008, struggled with unaffordable mortgages organised themselves and reframed their problem from one of individual debt to housing as a collective issue (Bua and Bussu 2021, 724). Similarly, Zechner reports how women in Barcelona, experiencing first-hand the effects of harsh austerity measures, organised themselves in childcare commons (Zechner 2021).

It is important at this point to emphasise a key distinction between GDD and DDG. GDD originates in constraints on administrative decision-making. These constraints, as we have seen, have to do with a lack of legitimacy and the erosion of governing capacity. DDG, on the other hand, originates in the lived experiences of people. Describing the emergence of childcare commons in Barcelona Zechner writes, for example:

> Multiple jobs, temporary and underpaid contracts, informal work arrangements, lack of labour and social rights, rising rents and instable (sic) housing arrangements, all played their part in a crisis of social reproduction that was affecting people's lives ... How to even imagine building a family?
> (2021, 61)

By drawing upon their own everyday, and in the case of social reproduction, literally embodied, experiences and testing them in interaction with others in similar circumstances, these residents escaped the neoliberal narrative about housing and child care and replaced it with a social rights narrative. They not only resisted the neoliberal hegemony by reframing the problem away from its well-known phraseology[7] but also forged new practices and relations governed by community values such as solidarity, inclusiveness and sustainability (Zechner 2021, 39). In short, they created commons. Under certain favourable conditions regarding political leadership, vigorous associational activity, the autonomy of local governments and poor socio-economic performance (Bua et al. this volume), such social movements may be successful in influencing the agenda of the local administration and occupying administrative process.

The problem is in the subsequent administrative consolidation. DDG faces two risks. I will illustrate these with the earlier housing example, but they apply to all areas of administrative delivery. First, to design and implement progressive, just housing programs requires an inevitable shift from associational to bureaucratic organisation. Funds need to be allocated, land purchased, planning permission obtained, construction companies mobilised, contracts drawn up and so on. This requires a high level of bureaucratic organisation and technical expertise. Many activists have little experience with, or taste for, effective bureaucratic delivery, or even its monitoring (Bua and Davies 2022).[8] Second, the progressive transformation of the local administration will inevitably generate resistance from the other actors in the corporate and financial sectors. With easy access to elected officials and higher civil servants, and in the possession of large amounts of money and the promise of well-remunerated jobs in the private sector to sway or bribe government officials (the infamous revolving door), businesses are in an excellent position to organise a counter-offense and activate the levers of hierarchical administration to destabilise or undo the progressive DDG initiative. The upshot is that in the current political economy, DDG is inherently unstable (Bua and Davies 2022).

Conclusion: The Democratic Multiverse

The allure of democracy is its normative promise. That is also its liability. However, the presence of a promise doesn't necessarily imply that it will be realised. For that to happen, many conditions must be met. The purpose of the preceding section is to provide a realistic picture of the political-economic obstacles to the realisation of the democratic promise of the mobilisation of citizen associations. The occupation of the state by an increasingly assertive, detached, exploitative and rapacious globalised corporate-financial sector, and the ideological surrender of the state to this situation, has imperilled democratic governance worldwide. While the obvious failures of the governing and corporate elites in areas such as climate change, pandemic management, income inequality, the suppression of labour rights, affordable housing, health care and education have resulted in public unease, it has not led to a serious attempt to reform our destructive political economy. In fact, the neoliberal capture of the state has seriously undermined administrative capacity and created space for important but in the end limited innovations such as GDD. I will close by briefly arguing that there are two more options for progressive democratic governance in the face of neoliberal hegemony.

The first are commons. Commons are defined by a "triad" of features. They are rooted in the values of community, governed through dialogue, coordination and self-organisation and aimed at meeting needs by producing things or services together. Commons are a different way of relating with each other, a form of everyday politics that is affective, caring and playful (Zechner 2020, 15).[9] They form a needs-based, people-centred economy (Bollier and Helfrich 2019; Thorpe and Gaventa 2020). In their structure, functioning and values they are the antithesis of the profit-driven, exploitative market economy. Their organisation and operating principles escape the neoliberal hegemony in our society. In that sense they are a subversive commentary on the neoliberal order. Commons can be found in areas such as renewable energy, social and childcare, housing, city planning, banking and the internet (Wagenaar and Healey 2015; Bollier and Helfrich 2015; Zechner 2021). Many commons don't aspire to collaborate with the state or the corporate sector, but they don't eschew it either when it doesn't violate the spirit of the commons. Under certain conditions, commons can be one of the roots of DDG and open up a perspective on an alternative, more emancipatory, democratic politics (Kioupkiolis 2020, 4). Zechner describes a reciprocal relationship between commons and progressive municipal politics in Barcelona. Bruised by harsh austerity politics, women forged new relations and new narratives about vulnerability, shared needs and reproductive rights. In this they were actively supported by Ada Colau, the then future mayor of Barcelona, and a "range of radical women councillors" (2020, 7; 2021, 34). Through "incessant educational and consciousness-raising work amongst their male colleagues as well as the general population", a "feminist groundwork" was laid for a progressive takeover of Barcelona's government apparatus and a redefinition of municipal politics. As Zechner concludes: the concomitant changes in relationality and subjectivity formed the basis for "lasting and sustainable social and systemic change" (Zechner 2020, 8).

The second is a progressive public administration. This may come as a surprise given my critique of the capture of the political-administrative system by powerful economic interests, but in the early part of the 20th century in cities such as Vienna and Amsterdam, administrations emerged that designed and delivered comprehensive programs that successfully implemented integrated housing, public health, education and culture policies for the working class. In an article on "Red Vienna" the historian Florian Wenninger and I analysed the elements of the remarkable success of the relatively short-lived city administration, whose legacy endures until today (Wagenaar and Wenninger 2020).[10] We describe the training of a knowledgeable cadre of civil servants imbued with strong administrative ethos (a masterstroke of the young administration to countervail the corrupt and conservative imperial civil servants), progressive taxation (including various creative wealth taxes), state construction of housing, hospitals, public schools, parks and swimming pools, affordable public transport and cultural institutions. We also noted that these activities were comprehensive and informed by a grasp of the fundamental interrelatedness of urban problems and the needs of working men and women. But, above all, they were guided by a compelling vision, both ethical and practical, of emancipating the working class, a vision that was sufficiently attractive to appeal to non-socialist sympathisers. The enabling conditions for Red Vienna were a solid majority for the socialist party in the city council and financial autonomy from the federal state.[11] One of the purposes of our article was to present, in an age of ideological distrust of government and the deprecation of civil servants, a real-world example of a highly effective progressive city administration.

Progressive public administration differs from GDD in that the existing institutions, laws, procedures, fiscal powers, networks and experience of a municipal administration are put in the service of fair, inclusive and sustainable democratic governance. Councillors and administrators do not have to learn to manage and govern on the job or measure the inevitable work of negotiation and compromise against the camaraderie and enthusiasm of street protest. When the socialist party took over Vienna's government after WWI, it inherited a discredited and defeated but intact city administration. In contrast to the alliance of modern government with corporate interests, the young government of Red Vienna developed a highly effective, comprehensive suite of policy tools, while it articulated a coherent vision of the physical, social and cultural emancipation of the working class. It did this because it chose to do so. Nothing but ideological capture prevents current urban administrations from similarly putting their administrative institutions, experience and powers in the service of a progressive, and nowadays, sustainable vision.

To sum up, I described how democracy is suspended within a triangle formed by civil society, the state and the corporate-financial sphere. Within this triangle, democracy needs to persuade the three spheres to accept it practices, rules and values. We saw that in the last half-century the economic sphere has gradually insinuated itself into the other two spheres to the point that the whole triangle forms a dense hegemonic complex of self-referential practices, insulating itself against democracy. But we also saw that democratic innovation occurs within a wider participatory ecology that encompasses both associations and hierarchical public administration.

For democracy, this larger picture of democracy in its wider political-economic environment is good news and bad news. Barring a cataclysmic global disaster, there is no realistic prospect that liberal electoral democracy will suddenly change course, constrain the global corporate-financial complex and reverse the neoliberal hegemony. However, the wider perspective on democracy that I sketched in this chapter offers a number of leverage points that taken together might make inroads into the neoliberal Hegemon. GDD, DDG, the commons and progressive public administration, each by itself and in combination with each other, are able to offer a viable alternative to the negative social and climatological effects of neoliberalism. There is obviously no blueprint for and guarantee of success.[12] These are dispersed, chaotic, scattered processes that, one hopes, inspire and encourage. There is only the promise of just and fair governance that is constitutive of the democratic multiverse.

Notes

1 Although the state should use its regulatory and budgetary powers to protect and facilitate this kind of associational democracy (Hirst 1994, 56).
2 I am aware that there are considerable cultural differences at work here. My description is particularly apposite to administrations in Western Europe and the Scandinavian countries. My experiences in the UK administration showed a much more hierarchical way of working. From scattered observations, I assume that Southern Europe has yet another kind of prevailing work mode.
3 See https://twitter.com/richardjmurphy/status/1570663396957384704?s=11&t=yYJ tyskrwMNC6wMtXNnCjA for a critique of this taken-for-granted state of affairs.
4 Polanyi famously described the genealogy of this split and how it was engineered through the commodification of work (one of the three famous "fictitious commodities", land, work and money) so that it could be brought under a market regime. He also

describes pre-capitalist societies where economic activity was governed by community values (Polanyi 2001 [1944]; Rogan, 2017).
5 The inexplicable and disastrous abandonment by social democratic parties of their core principles since the 1980s is of course another instance of the hegemony of market capitalism (Hall 2017; Kuttner 2018, ch. 7).
6 Individual autonomy "has to do with individuals' capacities to take part in critical examination of self and others, to participate in reasoning processes, and to arrive at judgments they can defend in public argument". These are ever so many "political achievements" (Warren 2001, 63). Political autonomy is the extension of individual autonomy, a process of "collective judgement" that is the result of "public reasoning and justification … among individuals who recognize the validity of a claim and thus its authority" (op. cit. 65). When many insights and claims are decreed to be out of bounds, declared to be subversive or unacceptable, or unavailable to the collective imagination, individual and political autonomy, and thus democratic collective judgement is impaired.
7 In housing: "Increase the supply of affordable housing". "Give young families the opportunity to get on the housing ladder". "I buy a house to start building equity". In childcare: "The government should provide affordable childcare". "Grandparents should look after their grandchildren".
8 To illustrate this point, Gerbaudo describes how within the disappointing tenure of Podemas as junior coalition partner of the socialist party (PSOE), Podemos' labour minister Yolande Diaz stood out, and achieved general popularity, for her effective delivery of a series of labour laws and income support programs (Gerbaudo 2022).
9 As Zechner puts it: "[C]ommons are about 'putting life at the center' of our activities (a key phrase of the Spanish-speaking feminist movements), which hinges on radical collective care and the capacity for doing situated politics" (2020, 15).
10 It came to power in 1919 and was unseated in 1933 in a fascist coup. On the 5th of March that year the Austrofascist chancellor Dolfuss suspended parliament. A short but violent civil war ensued that centred on the council housing estates, the proud symbols of Red Vienna.
11 With regard to fiscal powers, it is important to note that Vienna is both a city and a federal state ("*Land*"). The latter status gives it access to federal funds.
12 Kioupkiolos, in his excellent overview of the political dimension of progressive politics takes a similar position when he says: "A synthetic approach is the most apt for our times, composing (a) opposition, insurrection and rupture with (b) congenial state reforms and (c) the formation of new social relations and practices here and now, which lay the groundwork for a different future" (2020, 7). However, if synthetic means an amalgamation or coordination of these three progressive approaches, I am sceptical. The best we can expect is a series of scattered, discordant but important and inspiring initiatives that might at some point reach critical mass. That, in itself, is a reason to be hopeful.

References

Agger, A., Damgaard, B., Krogh, A. and Sørensen, E. (eds.) (2015) *Collaborative Governance and Public Innovation in Northern Europe*, Sharjah, U.A.E: Bentham Books

Avritzer, L. (2002) *Democracy and the Public Space in Latin America*, Princeton, NJ: Princeton University Press

Baiocchi, G. and Genuza, E. (2017) *Popular Democracy: The Paradox of Participation*, Redwood City, CA: Stanford University Press

Blyth, M. (2015) *Austerity: The History of a Dangerous Idea*. Oxford: Oxford University Press

Bollier, D. and Helfrich, S. (eds.) (2015) *Patterns of Commoning*. Amherst, MA: Levellers Press

Bollier, D. and Helfrich, S. (2019) *Free, Fair and Alive. The Insurgent Power of the Commons*. Gabriola Island, BC: New Society Publishers

Bourgon, J. (2011) *A New Synthesis of Public Administration. Serving in the 21st Century*, Montreal: McGill-Queens' University Press

Brown, W. (2015) *Undoing the Demos. Neoliberalism's Stealth Revolution*, New York: Zone Books.

Briggs, X. (2008) *Democracy as Problem Solving. Civic capacities in Communities Across the Globe*, Cambridge, MA: MIT Press

Bua, A. and Bussu, S. (2023) "Introduction to the Volume", in A. Bua and S. Bussu (eds), *Reclaiming participatory Governance. Social Movements and the Reinvention of Democratic Innovation*, Milton Park, Abingdon: Routledge.

Bua, A. and Bussu, S. (2021) "Between governance-driven democratisation and democracy-driven governance: Explaining changes in participatory governance in the case of Barcelona", *European Journal of Political Research 60*: 716–737

Bua, A. and Davies, J. (2022) "Understanding the crisis of new municipalism in Spain: The struggle for urban regime power in A Coruña and Santiago de Compostela", *Urban Studies*, Online before print, https://doi.org/10.1177/00420980221123939

Bua, A., Bussu, S. and Davies, J. (2023) "Democracy-driven governance and governance-driven democratization in Barcelona and Nantes", in A. Bua and S. Bussu (eds), *Reclaiming participatory Governance. Social Movements and the Reinvention of Democratic Innovation*, Milton Park, Abingdon: Routledge.

Cole, I.C. (2015) "Whatever happened to housing policy?", *Public Lecture to Celebrate the 50th Anniversary of the Department of Urban Studies and Planning/Town and Regional Planning 21 October 2015, unpublished*

Crouch, C. (2011) *The Strange Non-Death of Neoliberalism*, Cambridge: Polity Press

Dryzek, J.S. (1996) *Democracy in Capitalist Times: Ideals, Limits, and Struggles*, Oxford: Oxford University Press.

Du Gay, P. (2000) *In Praise of Bureaucracy: Weber – Organization – Ethics*. Thousand Oaks, CA: Sage

Edelenbos, J. and van Meerkerk, I., (eds.) (2016) *Critical Reflections on Interactive Governance. Self-Organization and Participation in Public Governance*. Cheltenham: Edward Elgar.

Evans, S.M and Boyte, H.C., (1986) *Free Spaces. The Sources of Democratic Change in America*. New York: Harpers & Row

Flinders, M. and Wood, M. (2014) "Depoliticisation, governance and the state", *Policy & Politics*, 42(2): 135–149

Freeman, R. (2021) *Doing Politics*. https://doingpolitics.space

Fung, A. (2004) Empowered Participation: Reinventing Urban Democracy. Princeton, NJ: Princeton University Press

Gamble, A. (1994) *The Free Economy and the Strong State. The Politics of Thatcherism*, London: Macmillan

Gamble, A. (2014) *Crisis Without End? The Unravelling of Western Prosperity*, London: Palgrave MacMillan

Gerbaudo, P. (July 28, 2022) "A new Sorpasso?", New Left Review. https://newleftreview.org/sidecar/posts/a-new-sorpasso

Glyn, A. (2006) *Capitalism Unleashed: Finance, Globalization, and Welfare*, Oxford: Oxford University Press.

Goldfarb, J.C. (2006) *The Politics of Small Things. The Power of the Powerless in Dark Times*, Chicago, IL: The University of Chicago Press.

Hall, S. (2017) "Gramsci and Us, https://www.versobooks.com/blogs/2448-stuart-hall-gramsci-and-us

Hirst, P. (1994) *Associative Democracy. New Forms of Economic and Social Governance*, Cambridge: Polity

Holston, J. (2008) *Insurgent Citizenship. Disjunctions of Democracy and Modernity in Brazil*, Princeton, NJ: Princeton University Press.

Jackson, B. (n.d.) "*Property-Owning Democracy: A Short History*, Oxford: University College, (unpublished manuscript): https://www-users.york.ac.uk/~mpon500/pod/Jackson.pdf

Jessop, B. (2015) *The State: Past, Present, Future*, Cambridge: Polity

Kay, J. (2015) *Other People's Money. Masters of the Universe or Servants of the People?* London: Profile Books

Kelton, S. (2020) *The Deficit Myth. Modern Monetary Theory and How to Build a Better Economy*, London: John Murray

Kioupkiolis, A. (2020) "Heteropolitics", *Refiguring the Common and the Political*, European Research Council, ERC-COG-2016-724692. Report

Kuttner, R. (2018) *Can Democracy Survive Global Capitalism?* New York: W.W. Norton & Company.

Maclean, N. (2017) *Democracy in Chains. The Deep History of the Radical Right's Stealth Plan for America*, Melbourne: Scribe.

Meier, K.J. and O'Toole, L.J. (2006) *Bureaucracy in a Democratic State: A Governance Perspective*, Baltimore, MD: Johns Hopkins University Press

Mellor, M. (2016) *Debt or Democracy. Public Money for Sustainability and Social Justice*, London: Pluto Press.

Mirowski, P. (2014) *Never Let a Serious Crisis Go to Waste*, London: Verso.

Ostrom, E. (2010) "A Long Polycentric Journey", *Annual Review of Political Science* 13, 1–23

Polanyi, K. (2002 [1944]) *The Great Transformation: The Political and Economic Origins of Our Time*, Boston, MA: Beacon Press

Rodrik, D. (2012) *The Globalization Paradox: Why Global Markets, States, and Democracy Can't Coexist*, Oxford: Oxford University Press.

Rogan, T. (2017) *The Moral Economists. R.H. Tawney, Karl Polanyi, E.P. Thompson and the Critique of Capitalism*, Princeton, N.J.: Princeton University Press.

Samen Wonen, Samen Leven (2019) *Inclusie en democratie in de wijk. Samen werken aan een inclusieve solidaire samenleving. Stimuleren van lokale democratie en een inclusieve wijkeconomie*, Amsterdam: Stichting Samen Wonen, Samen Leven

Sanchez Bajo, C. and Roelants, B. (2013) *Capital and the Debt Trap. Learning from Cooperatives in the Global Crisis*, Palgrave Macmillan

Stout, L. (2012) *The Shareholder Value Myth. How Putting the Shareholders First Harms Investors, Corporations and the Public*, San Francisco, CA: Berrett-Koehler Publishers.

Streeck, W. (2013) *Gekaufte Zeit: Die Vertagte Krise des Demokratischen Kapitalismus*, Berlin: Suhrkamp Verlag.

Thorpe, J, and Gaventa, J. (2020) "*Democratising Economic Power: The Potential for Meaningful Participation in Economic Governance and Decision-Making*, IDS Working Paper 535, Brighton: Institute of Development Studies.

Vlahos, N. (2022) "*Innovations in Participatory Governance and the (De)commodification of Social Wellbeing*", in A. Bua and S. Bussu (eds), Reclaiming participatory

Governance. Social Movements and the Reinvention of Democratic Innovation, Milton Park, Abingdon: Routledge.

Vogel, J. (2017) *The Ascendency of Finance*, Cambridge: Polity

Wagenaar, H. (2022) "Deliberative policy analysis", in: S. A. Ercan, H. Asenbaum, N. Curato, and R. F. Mendonça (eds.) *Research Methods in Deliberative Democracy*, Oxford: Oxford University Press: 423–437

Wagenaar, H., (2007) "Governance, complexity and democratic participation: How citizens and public officials harness the complexities of neighbourhood decline", *American Review of Public Administration*, 37(1): 17–50.

Wagenaar, H. and Duiveman, R. (2012) "De Kwaliteit van een Stadswijk: Good governance door stedelijke daadkracht in Den Haag", (The Quality of a Neighbourhood: good governance through developing civic capacity"), in F. Hendriks, and G. Drosterij (eds.), *De Zucht naar Goed Bestuur in de Stad*, Den Haag: Boom Lemma

Wagenaar, H and Healey, P. (2015) "Interface: the transformative potential of civic enterprise", *Planning Theory and Practice*, 16(4): 557–561

Wagenaar, H. and Prainsack, B. (2021) *The Pandemic Within. Policy Making for a Better World*, Bristol: Policy Press.

Wagenaar, H. and Wenninger, F. 2020. "Deliberative policy analysis, interconnectedness and institutional design: Lessons from 'Red Vienna'", *Policy Studies*, 41(4): 411–437

Wagenaar, H., van Schijndel M., Kruiter, H. (2010) *Bewonersparticipatie en Veiligheid. Tussen Droom en Daad in een Complexe Bestuurlijke Context (Citizen Participation and Safety. Policy Challenges in a Complex Urban Environment.)*, Campus The Hague: University of Leiden. (52 pages. In Dutch)

Warren, M.E., (2001) *Democracy and Association*, Princeton: Princeton University Press

Warren, M.E., (2014) "Governance-driven democratization", in S. Griggs, A. Norval, and H. Wagenaar (eds.) *Practices of Freedom: Democracy, Conflict and Participation in Decentred Governance*, Cambridge: Cambridge University Press, 38–60.

Zechner, M. (2020) "Heteropolitics", *Refiguring the Common and the Political*, European Research Council, ERC-COG-2016-724692. Report

Zechner, M. (2021) *Commoning Care & Collective Power*, Vienna: Transversal Texts

Zuboff, S. (2019) *The Age of Surveillance Capitalism. The Fight for a Human Future at the New Frontier of Power*, New York, NY: Basic Books.

Section 2
Tracing the Emergence of Democracy-Driven Governance

6 Towards Participatory Transition Governance

The Role of Social Movements as "Collaborators" for Democratic Innovation

Paola Pierri

Introduction: Climate Crisis or Democracy Crisis?

The mass public mobilisations for climate action observed since 2018 have highlighted the inextricable link between climate change, democracy and social justice. Despite renewed attention in more recent years, the call for public participation in climate action is not entirely new (from the 1992 Rio Declaration, to the 2015 Paris Agreement through to the 2020 European Climate Pact). What is new is that after many years of social movements, inter-governmental agencies and NGOs struggling to make environmental issues a global priority for political debates and governments' actions, climate change has recently risen to the top of the political agenda and public debate.

Part of this success is also due to a new way of framing the environmental issue as a question of climate "emergency" (Doherty, De Moor and Hayes, 2018). The use of this particular framing has resonated with many people and has been very effective in capturing the attention of a wider public and motivating people to act or to demand action from governments. Alignment, as we know from social movement theory (Snow et al., 1986), is the complex process through which political actors find the right narratives and the right tones that resonate with people and motivate them to mobilise. This framing of "emergency" has also raised interesting debates in the democratic field. The narrative based on the idea of "climate crisis/emergency" has raised support for immediate, coordinated and strong action, which, some would argue (Fiorino, 2019), might be more effectively led by experts and implemented through authoritarian forms of government. Some scholars are now questioning whether democracy is actually "fit for purpose" to address climate change and the ecological breakdown (Malm, 2021); others have built an argument for a new *social contract* between governments and their citizens on climate action (Willis, 2020); and others still have been asking whether climate movements might contribute to the emergence of the post-political and post-democratic scenarios supported by the framing on emergency (Swyngedouw, 2010, 2009; Schlembach, Lear and Bowman, 2012).

The relationship between the climate and democracy has been the object of scholarly debate for a long time (Iwińska et al., 2019). Traditionally these debates have been growing in the field of studies that look at environmental struggles

DOI: 10.4324/9781003218517-8

and processes of democratisation and regimes transition, and scholars in this field have already highlighted how "Several arguments suggest that climate change can be troubling for democracy and democratization, directly and indirectly through adverse impact on for instance livelihoods, human development and, ultimately, social harmony" (Burnell, 2012: 818).

Without the pretence of addressing the question of *whether* democracy is good for the environment, this chapter aims at contributing to the debates in this field by exploring the role of social movements and grassroots politics in mobilising support for and informing climate action. After introducing theories on modes of governance, the chapter looks specifically at the role of social movements in politicising the debates around climate. In the second part of the chapter, I will introduce the case study from the metropolitan area of Orléans and their model of the *Assises pour la transition écologique*, which is a democratic design for governance that has taken momentum in France across different metropolitan areas. This case study is particularly interesting as it presents an unusual example of democratic innovation emerging from an unexpected place: a local metropolitan area in France that has a long tradition of conservative governments, low-level citizen engagement and previously modest records of climate initiatives. The chapter theorises a role for social movements and civil society in influencing conservative governments to act against climate change. This is particularly important, as support for environmental policies is traditionally less strong among conservative administrations compared with left-wing and progressive governments (Talpin, 2015), whilst these conservative governments are still crucial actors holding power to intervene at the local or system level. If not activated to act against climate change, they either will stay inactive – as by-standers – or might even block significant climate change action to happen.

This chapter, therefore, aims to put forward a case study of innovative and participatory transition governance from a local area that draws on Empowered Participatory Governance (Fung and Wright, 2003) to define the importance of "*collaborative countervailing power*" (2003: 282).

Questions of Governance

Innovation in participatory governance can be considered one of the most important developments in public policy and administration of the past decades. Participatory governance has been defined as "participatory forms of political decision making, involving organised and non-organised citizens, to improve the quality of democracy" (Geissel, 2009: 403).

This section aims to briefly introduce two modes of participatory governance that will be used to assess the case study of the Orléans Metropole Assises for the Ecological Transition: empowered participatory governance (EPG) and democracy-driven governance (DDG).

The work of Archon Fung and Erik Olin Wright (2003) is particularly useful to assess modes of innovative and democratic governance. Through the analysis of several experiments with governance from across different countries, the authors advance a proposal for an innovative re-design of our governance institutions that they label as "Empowered Participatory Governance" (EPG). These forms of governance, which aim to be at once more participatory and more empowering in motivating action, are based on three key principles: (1) the focus on specific problems, (2) the involvement of ordinary people who are affected by the problems and (3) the use of deliberative tools to advance possible solutions.

Many recent developments in participatory governance initiated by public agencies have been characterised by a functionalistic approach, as citizens are invited to strengthen the democratic legitimacy and problem-solving capacity of the commissioning body, in what Warren (2014) describes as "governance driven democratisation". Bua and Bussu (2021) develop the concept of democracy-driven governance (DDG) to capture what happens when social movements reclaim these spaces of participatory governance to respond to bottom-up claims.

Bringing EPG and DDG (and also Governance Driven Democratisation (GDD) to a certain extent) in comparison with each other might raise interesting possibilities to advance theorisation and practice of governance for transformation. EPG and DDG, for instance, both present interesting characteristics and design principles that have been used to analyse the case study presented in this chapter, namely:

- they problematise the question of *power*, challenging common objections from the literature (Cohen and Rogers, 2003) about the power-neutralising claim against deliberative and more collaborative modes of governance.
- they do not aim to advance *universal solutions* to all issues of governance, as they recognise that institutional arrangements are a shifting terrain, where different needs, constellations of actors and power dynamics can change that will require accordingly changes in the institutional design.
- they are equally interested in the question of *processes* as well as the question of *outcomes*, as the two should not be assumed to be directly dependent variables.
- finally, they both recover – although in different ways – a role for more critical voices (and specifically *social movement* approaches) in the space of collaborative governance.

This last point is the main one that this chapter is exploring, as the theorisation of the role of social movements in EPG might in fact enrich and contribute to advancing a role for DDG governance models, in less conducive political contexts and even in conservative ones, as the case study illustrated in this chapter aims to exemplify.

The role of social movements in advancing democracy-driven governance is framed to be instrumental in providing channels to formal governance for non-state and non-private actors to define priorities and advocate for more democratic control. Interestingly, in the EPG model of Fung and Wright, on the other hand, movements have a role only as long as they accept to dismiss their adversarial tones and tactics and become what the authors define as "*collaborative countervailing power*" (2003, p. 282). Countervailing power in Fung and Wright's definition refers to "*a variety of mechanisms that reduce, and perhaps even neutralize, the power-advantages of ordinarily powerful actors*" (idem:p. 260).

Key in the case study presented in this chapter is the role of what Fung and Wright (2003) call collaborative forms of countervailing power (p. 280). Differently from *adversarial* forms of countervailing power that develop through rigid and maximalist frames that are oppositional towards institutional actors and elites, collaborative forms, although still countervailing, develop ways to build collaborations with institutional actors and towards meaningful forms of Empowered Participatory Governance (EPG).

"*Collaborative countervailing power*" might seem – as the authors themselves say– "*a bit of an oxymoron*" (2003: 263) as the concept incorporates two elements seemingly in opposition. Collaborative and adversarial forms of countervailing power require different skills set and political attitudes that have attracted less research (Fung and Wright, 2003).

Table 6.1 illustrates the main difference between the two forms of countervailing power.

The EPG model, this chapter will argue, can provide a useful bridge to the gap between the DDG and GDD models that are needed to better understand the role (and the skills) that social movements can play as "agenda setters" also within more conservative governance regimes. In these contexts, forms of collaborative countervailing power can create a political space that is conducive to introducing transformative interventions that might otherwise not happen.

The Role of Movements as Actors of Governance

Democratic innovation and the field of collective action have been depicted to be on opposing sides (Mouffe, 1999), as their logics have been long considered to be

Table 6.1 Key Elements of Adversarial and Collaborative Forms of Countervailing Power

Forms of Countervailing Power	Political Scale	Organisational Competencies	Political Meaning
Adversarial	Engaging central points of decision-making (less focus on the administrative level)	Influencing high-level policy and legislative decisions	Injustice frames (rigid diagnostic, prognostic and motivational frames)
Collaborative	Operating at local *and* at larger scales	Problem-solving competencies and implementation (which also requires deep local knowledge)	Less rigid frames (testing hypothesis, creating locally tailored solutions)

Source: Fung and Wright, 2003.

in conflict and almost undermining each other's approach. But this relationship has more recently been reconsidered in all its complexity and as one that presents many nuances (Corry and Reiner, 2021; della Porta and Felicetti, 2019; Talpin, 2015; della Porta, 2013; Talpin, 2015). Questions of power and political opportunity structure are central to more collaborative approaches to participatory and deliberative democracy (Polletta, 2016; Fung and Wright; 2003), as the latter also needs to consider the asymmetries of power and the role of forces of *countervailing power*.

Despite the potential connections between the two fields, practical examples of social movements' participation in democratic innovation experiments are still the exception and not the rule (Talpin, 2015). Social movements and institutional democratic innovations in fact have rarely occurred together or have been interpreted as being linked to each other (della Porta and Felicetti, 2019). Interesting cases in this direction have recently emerged – e.g., the engagement of a group from Extinction Rebellion (also XR) in the Scottish Climate Citizens Assembly process, or the Gilets Jaunes' mobilisation in France (della Porta and Felicetti, 2019). In both cases movements advocated the use of citizens' assemblies with binding decision-making power (Extinction Rebellion, 2019). But the XR experiment did not advance further since XR withdrew from the assembly processes before this started.[1]

Modes of *institutionalisation* of social movements have often been highlighted as critical in ensuring the emergence, sustenance and long-term impact of collective action. When it comes to assessing the role and tactics of environmental movements, one should first acknowledge their problematic identity as they cover a diverse range of movements (e.g. "green" and more recently "climate" movements) that have specific forms of organisation, strategies and ambition (Rootes and Nulman, 2015). The climate movements that have recently become more prominent in the Global North present some interesting characteristics compared to more global environmental movements from the 1970s and after. First, they seem to have a strong local focus, predominantly directing their actions to cities (Tokar, 2015; Agyeman and Angus, 2003). This is part of a wider trend towards *decentralising* climate action (Martin et al., 2018) that emerged as a result of the struggle to achieve impact at the global level and the need to diversify the movement logics and tactics, to ensure immediate harm reduction as well as maintaining the focus on achieving more radical goals in the long-term. This is in fact a key characteristic of recent climate movements, as research shows that even more radical groups seem to display an appetite for piecemeal policy measures within the policy systems in which they operate (Corry and Reiner, 2021).

These movements in the climate field are increasingly recognising the need to develop new modes and processes that help strengthen opportunities for the institutionalisation of their requests, which intersect in complex ways with policy processes, knowledge production and the promotion of innovative democratic design. Drawing on the wider literature on collective action four roles might emerge for groups and movements in climate-related governance processes, namely:

- *guardians of inclusivity*, because movements traditionally aim to highlight questions of social justice and equality, avoiding interventions that can

deepen inequalities and social exclusion. When it comes to climate movements, a justice-centred perspective ensures that the demands and the rights of those around the world who suffer the most severe consequences of climate change are included (Parks, 2020; Tokar, 2015; Schlosberg and Collins, 2014; Agyeman and Angus, 2003).
- *providers of alternative spaces* for political debates, which for climate movement and action means to ensure that also adaptation and mitigation are framed as political and not merely as technical questions (Corry and Reiner, 2021 Biesbroek, Peters, and Tosun, 2018; Smith, 2015).
- *providers of alternative knowledge* (Corry and Reiner, 2021; della Porta & Pavan, 2017) since – despite the increased scientific evidence – climate change can still be considered a highly contested and polarised knowledge domain, where different systems of knowledge are still developing in conflict (Parks, 2020; Jamison, 2010).
- *agenda setters* (Walgrave and Vliegenthart, 2019), which is one of the roles that social movements aim to play and that has usually been linked to the size, media coverage and the actions that protests instantiate and the extent to which these can capture the public and therefore the political interest to the point of affecting the agenda-setting process.

In the next pages I will be drawing on a case study of innovation in governance for climate action based in France, which could be considered a case of innovation in *reaction* to social movement pressure, and which presents interesting points of reflection to learn more about the link between movements and democracy-driven governance models.

Towards Participatory Transition Governance

The case study presented in this chapter draws on the work of the "*Healthy, Clean Cities Deep Demonstrations*" programme, supported by the European Institute of Innovation and Technology (EIT) and delivered through the Climate-Knowledge and Innovation Community (Climate-CKIC). The programme aimed at identifying and advancing innovation that helps society mitigate and adapt to climate change. It is based on an ambitious plan to work with mayors and municipalities to support cities across Europe which face the challenge of becoming healthy places to live whilst reaching net-zero emissions by 2030. Initially developed together with 10 cities, the plan of the multiannual programme is to engage 100 cities in 10 years.[2]

The programme brought together expertise in financing, technical innovation, architecture, carbon accounting and citizen participation to design and conduct strategic experiments with cities.[3] These portfolios of experiments were designed to work together and achieve systemic change in areas as diverse as mobility and logistics, housing and the built environment, waste and the circular economy, energy and urban greening. The programme – initially 18 months long – was based on the overarching premise that questions of climate change and climate adaptations, although global by their own nature, materialise and take shape at the local scale, where key policies and decisions are implemented and sometimes contested.

Drawing on different democratic designs that were developed by the cities during the project (from Citizens Lab to Participatory Hubs or Participatory Budgets, and others), the programme has been delivering interesting innovation in transition governance across Europe.

In the next section I present some reflections on the key elements of democratic design for transition, based on the case of the Orléans metropolitan area, and their work on Transition Governance.[4] Although these reflections do not aim to advance universal solutions to all issues of governance, as they recognise that institutional arrangements are a shifting terrain, what was common across the different cities is that action was built on the back of strong national and local grassroots climate movements.

The case study from the Orléans metropolitan area can be considered an example of democratic innovation driven by social mobilisation and protests, as the shift in the political will to initiate a participatory governance process to foster climate action was a direct response to the escalation of climate protests. Over the years, a growing number of activists had been taking to the streets through a mix of international groups (e.g. linked to Extinction Rebellion) and local collectives and initiatives – like "*Il est encore Temps Orléans*"[5] or "*Les mouvement zéro*"[6] – which advocated the urgency of bold local climate actions.

The case study from Orléans should be framed within a wider context in France that can be traced at the national and local level, made of increased grassroots climate action, on the one hand, and a *new wave* (OECD, 2020) of deliberative and participatory climate interventions are sweeping the country, on the other. These requests were in fact in line with recent waves of consultations around Sustainable Energy, Climate and Air Plans (SECAP) and the growth in deliberative and participatory democracy across France (Décider Ensemble, 2020). These initiatives all underlined the need for transition governance to be empowered by a diversity of grassroots climate actions underpinned by greater citizen participation.

Transition Governance "à l'orléanaise"

Orléans Métropole (from now on also OMET) consists of 22 local councils/municipalities. OMET adopted a Sustainable Energy and Climate Action Plan (SECAP) in 2018 to become an energy-positive territory with a 100% renewable energy supply by 2050. To reach this goal, and to ensure a bold yet resilient climate transition, OMET has been developing a new approach to governance that supports the long-term mobilisation of Orléans citizens, with participation and systemic innovation at its core.

There is no "one-fits-all" approach to designing a more participatory governance model for ecological transition. Changes in political opportunities and shifts in political alignments can present unique "*tipping points*" (Bua and Bussu, 2021: 2), which are moments of the *shift* of a political process from stability and slow, incremental change, to speeding up to more dramatic cascading effects. In the case study from OMET a window of opportunity materialised with the results of local elections in the summer of 2020, which saw the green and left coalitions gain momentum and an increased vote share, despite a right-wing coalition still securing the majority. These unprecedented results – especially for the green party – changed the political conditions and pushed towards a shared ambition to open up a participatory process towards green transition governance. This crystallised in the foundational steps and iterative design of an "*Assises de la transition écologique*",[7] a participatory process *à l'orléanaise* that was driven by a politically diverse Steering Group and designed to shape the priorities of the metropolitan government for the next 5 years around climate action.[8]

The main ambition of the Assises was to accelerate the ecological transition for a durable, dynamic and resilient metropolitan area. The method of the Assises revolved around creating the opportunity for diverse actors to mobilise around the topics of nine different thematic *ateliers*. Alongside these official ateliers, which were led by Orléans Métropole and advertised as the *Assises "ON"* (since part of the official programme from the start), civil society actors were also invited to organise various forms of interactive and deliberative events to mobilise local residents around climate-related issues (termed the *Assises "OFF"*). The Assise OFF were bottom-up initiatives that were introduced in the official agenda and used as space to generate learning and inspiration and allow for practical solutions.

However, this model of territorial governance for climate transition also raised challenges, as metropolitan areas are one step removed from citizens' engagement, and most of the OMET processes have been in fact so far driven by political élites and civil servants at the metropolitan level. The French "Institut de la concertation et de la participation citoyenne" also noted the creation of a gap at the local democracy level between spaces for debate (i.e. the local councils) and spaces for decision (i.e. the metropolitan areas).[9] These metropolitan areas have been defined as "*a laboratory of post-democracy*" (Desage, 2017), and this is especially true when it comes to addressing climate change, since responsibility over climate action rests with the *Métropole* level, whilst citizen participation initiatives are organised at the municipality level. Running an Assises process at the metropolitan level is therefore not without its challenges, but it presents a promising approach to improve public ownership over decision-making and policymaking on climate action at the inter-municipal level. Moreover, when a local or regional administration engages with more participatory governance processes for the first time – like in the OMET case – specific skills and thematic knowledge (both on citizens engagement and climate action) should not be assumed as being already there and building capacity is a necessary step for policymakers and elected officials to address confidently the challenges ahead.

The Role of Collaborative Countervailing Power in Governance

OMET is an example of democratic innovation for climate governance "*in reaction to popular mobilisation*" (della Porta and Felicetti, 2019: 14), which had in turn impact on the political election and landscape. On 20 September 2019, as part of the global mobilisation, the NGOs "*Il est encore temps Orléans*" and "*Youth for climate Orléans*" organised a March for Climate. In late 2019 and early 2020, Democracy innovator Philippe Rabier, the founder of the local NGO *CiTLab*, attempted to set up a full citizen candidate list. With this group called "*Orléans Ensemble*", he and his list's candidates eventually merged with the lead Green Party (EELV) list ahead of the March 2020 municipal elections. In addition to that, NGO Alternatiba Orléans published a visual explainer assessing each candidate's climate-related pledge and "grading" each programme accordingly.

These modes of collaborative countervailing power seem to fit very well with the role of local associations, groups and movements in Orléans, which in fact were strongly rooted in local-level policy and action, as well as being connected with international movements and ideas. Through the Assise process, local movements and actors also demonstrated high skills in problem-solving, as they took part in the co-design and co-creation of practical solutions. Finally, they brought to the Assise a specific framing of the issues at stake but did not shy away from engaging in multi-stakeholder groups to test those ideas, compromise on some of them and co-create locally tailored solutions.

The adoption of more collaborative forms of countervailing power by local groups and movements in Orléans was also in line with recent studies, which reveal how "When it comes to climate action, radicalism (belief in the necessity of system- change and use of extra-institutional methods) and science-led policy are increasingly seen as not contradictory" (Corry and Reiner, 2021: 211).[10] The relationship between more radical forms of engagement, such as protests, and more collaborative forms of participation in institutional politics that took shape through OMET could be understood as "*mutually co-constitutive*" (Roth and Saunders, 2019: 527). Local actions and protests generated the right pressure points that led to the organising of the Assise, whilst the design of the process set the tone for the ways in which more radical groups could take part.

Whilst the literature covers several examples of democratic innovation developed through direct cooperation with left-leaning governments (Talpin, 2015), instances of social movements developing a dialogue with conservative administrations are sporadic. This is potentially a limitation when it comes to swinging the balance towards an ecological transition as support is needed from across the political spectrum. Climate denial and inaction are usually associated with governments that are closer to more conservative and liberal ideologies (Carrus, Panno and Leone, 2018).

Design Principles for *Participatory* Transition Governance

Democratic innovation stemming from protests, as illustrated in Talpin's (2015) work, risks producing little more than procedural concession from above, which do not translate into the broader democratisation of the political process. What Orléans case illustrates is that whilst collaboration among institutional actors, associations and social movements might be a necessary condition for democratic innovations to directly affect policymaking, this is by no means a sufficient one (della Porta and Felicetti, 2019). In the next and concluding section, I turn to discuss some lessons that can be drawn regarding the challenges and opportunities of institutionalising forms of participatory governance, reflecting on the tensions between the different demands of lay citizens, organised civil society and public officials.

Firstly, the increased local mobilisation and protests were a key factor in shifting the political will and attitude within the metropolitan area. Since 2019, civil society had become more active in Orléans and the other local municipalities. These initiatives demonstrated a clear intention of the local climate movements to establish direct connections with political parties and influence the upcoming elections, since movements can play a key role as a catalyst of political crises and realignment of political forces (Kriesi, 2015).

The most interesting findings from the OMET case study arguably emerged from some notable process design choices and principles that were introduced in the Assise, like the "Assise OFF". These formats provided an open space for groups to self-organise and propose a topic or run an event, and they represented possibly the most interesting feature of the design of the Assises in OMET as an alternative space created *by design*. Similarly to the *vrai débat*[11] organised by social movements in France on the occasion of the Grand Débat, the "Assises OFF" could be seen as an opportunity to provide an alternative forum that is still designed *within* the original model of the Assises. The "Assises OFF" also aimed at engaging a wider and diverse public that was possibly out of reach and felt excluded from the more institutionally led events and arguably played a part in counterbalancing the presence of more powerful business and industry interest groups. This could be equally seen as a sign of the difficulty to engage more radical positions and movements within more institutional spaces and top-down processes, and perhaps a tactic to pre-empt those alternative initiatives organised by movements outside of the invited space of the Assise.

Finally, when it comes to assessing impact, the Assise model might look more like a "*messy political compromise*" (Karkainnen, 2003). Civil society and groups did arguably find their space through the "Assise OFF", but the risk of being dominated by political and administrative logics frustrating the original spirit of the interventions – as warned by della Porta and Felicetti (2019) – is very real. At the time of writing, it is too early to assess the impact of the Assise for the Transition on actual policies. A workshop to share the political responses to the many inputs and ideas that the Assise generated was held in June 2021, but no clear commitment can be yet identified. As della Porta and Felicetti remind us (2019), "a very important outcome of these experiments concerns their ability to inspire further democratic innovations elsewhere and to generate interest in these projects".

As the Assise model keeps growing in France, these design features might be embedded and become key elements of other participatory governance approaches. Future research might expand on the trigger, the dynamics and the impact of so-called "*protester policy engagement*" (Corry and Reiner, 2021: 199) in the climate space and what forms of participation are most conducive to climate governance.

Towards Governance Strategies for Engaging Conservative Elites

This chapter presented a practical example of how more critical stances (and social movement approaches) could find a space to be heard and to be acted upon in less receptive and conducive local contexts, through certain modes of collaborative governance. Movements in the Orléans context demonstrated useful skills for collaborative countervailing power. They managed to put pressure on the local conservative government by translating the global demands of climate movements to the local political context, through the climate pledge for political candidates and other local campaigns (as illustrated above). Compared to other international examples the climate movements did adopt in Orléans a less rigid and less ideological framing, offering possibilities to collaborate with the existing government (for instance by promoting and making use of the Assise OFF spaces), in order to address the local problems with local knowledge and ad-hoc solutions. Their actions also managed to galvanise support among the local population for the left and green parties, which played a stronger role in the last election.

This case study has illustrated three important implications. Firstly, it shows the journey and the "tipping points" that allowed a shift to happen; what could have previously been considered an "unexpected place" for bold climate action became an interesting place "to watch" in order to learn more about transition governance. Secondly, Orléans Métropole with its conservative/left-wing ruling coalition paints an interesting picture, in a context where several large French cities are currently led by green mayors, and it demonstrates that climate action can gather sufficient consensus and transcend partisan differences. The emergence of innovative and bold action on climate from outside what might be considered the "usual suspects" should in fact be welcomed, since the action that focuses only on traditionally progressive cities and regions with long-standing tradition and competence both on participatory governance practice and climate action will not be sufficient to achieve the ecological transition that is needed. Finally, the experience of OMET also raises interesting reflections on the role of movements when they become "*collaborative countervailing power*" (Fung and Wright, 2003).

Social movements play a key role in advancing democracy-driven governance (Bua and Bussu, 2021), but how this relationship pans out in political contexts dominated by more conservative governments is not clear. To answer this question, this chapter has argued that we need to draw on the EPG model as a useful bridge between the DDG and GDD models to accomplish that *dynamic relationship* between the two models, which Bua and Bussu also talk about (2021, p. 10). The EPG model of governance highlights one crucial point that arguably remains partially unclear in the conceptualisation of DDG, that is the role and the skills needed for social movements to advance their agenda within top-down and more conservative governance structures, whereby collaborative countervailing

100 *Paola Pierri*

power can help them move beyond more adversarial modes of relationship and towards engagement with state institutions. Through the notion of "*collaborative*" countervailing power, EPG provides improved sensitivity to the political context and increased flexibility to adapt to the movements' demands in a complex and shifting political landscape. These are key elements that would benefit a future fine-tuning of the DDG model, beyond only adversarial approaches and for less conducive political settings.

Organising and sustaining support for climate action in more conservative administrations requires finding allies and coordinating action across party lines and among residents who hold different and even conflicting views. In these contexts, the minimising conflict has proved already successful (Koslov, 2019), and the prospect of debates turning too agonistic could risk blocking any future actions. In these *conflict-averse* conditions, the solution-oriented approach of the Assise could be understood as another tactic to address a polarising topic, such as climate change, in a less ideological manner and with more collaborative approaches.

Since climate policy has become a central issue in the political and public agenda, studying how strategies for mobilising more conservative elites will evolve together with movement strategies and roles in governance will be crucial. The case of OMET is a case in point since the political tradition and context of the Orléans metropolitan area were possibly less conducive to more adversarial movements' tactics and had a tradition of low-level citizens' engagement and modest records of climate initiatives. Given the context, more adversarial tactics would have arguably had less space to develop and considerably less potential to achieve impact within a short time.

Notes

1 Extinction Rebellion decided to leave the Stewarding Group of Scotland's Climate Citizens Assembly as the group considered the Assembly process to be *'not good enough'*. According to the XR group the Assembly Secretariat was not setting an ambitious target for the discussion and certain key experts suggested by XR were not included. A good summary of the debate can be found here: https://www.bbc.com/news/uk-scotland-54830823.
2 The first cohort of city partners includes Amsterdam, Edinburgh, Kraków, Leuven, Madrid, Malmö, Milano, Orléans and Vienna, as well as Future Cities South-East Europe city partners, Križevci, Maribor, Niš, Sarajevo and Skopje.
3 The *Healthy, Clean Cities Deep Demonstration* programme was delivered by a consortium of design partners with different expertise, which included Democratic Society, Bankers Without Boundaries, Dark Matter Labs and Material Economics.
4 Transition governance refers to a governance approach that aims to facilitate and accelerate sustainable large scale and long-term societal change (transitions) towards more ecologically socio-technical systems.
5 This is a citizens' collective bringing together several movements and associations in Orléans working on different themes of the climate emergency (e.g. preservation of biodiversity and the environment, social and fiscal justice, training and citizen participation, mobility, agriculture and food). The aim of the collective is to represent a citi-

zens' lobby on the Orléans territory and the local elected representatives to take actions on these topics. More information on their website: https://ilestencoretempsorleans.weebly.com/.
6 'Les Mouvements Zéro' was founded in July 2015 by Justine Davasse in Orléans (France). Initially a radio show, Les Mouvements Zéro kept growing to become a blog, a series of sustainable events and workshops to learn about zero waste lifestyle. The goal of the movement is to bring knowledge to the people and to highlight that change is possible (and required) in business, in politics and within consumption. More information on the movement can be found here: https://lesmouvementszero.com/english/.
7 See more information here: https://transition.orleans-metropole.fr/),
8 More detail about the design and the process of the Assise have been already published here: https://carnegieeurope.eu/2021/04/22/novel-approach-to-local-climate-action-in-france-pub-84363.
9 See n. 6: https://i-cpc.org/wp-content/uploads/2020/10/Manifeste-des-m%C3%A9tropoles-participatives-ICPC-1.pdf.
10 Citing a viewpoint from Deepa Shah accessible here: https://europepmc.org/article/med/31249083.
11 See more information here: https://www.le-vrai-debat.fr/.

References

Agyeman, J. and Angus, B. (2003) The role of civic environmentalism in the pursuit of sustainable communities, in *Journal of Environmental Planning and Management*, 46:3, 345–363, https://doi.org/10.1080/0964056032000096901
Biesbroek, R.; Peters, B.G. and Tosun, J. (2018) Public bureaucracy and climate change adaptation, in *Review of Policy Research*, 35:6, 776–791 https://doi.org/10.1111/ropr.12316
Bua, A. and Bussu, S. (2021). Between governance-driven democratisation and democracy-driven governance: Explaining changes in participatory governance in the case of Barcelona, in *European Journal of Political Research*, https://doi.org/10.1111/1475-6765.12421
Burnell, P. (2012) Democracy, democratization and climate change: Complex relationships, in *Democratization*, 19:5, 813–842, https://doi.org/10.1080/13510347.2012.709684
Carrus, G., Panno A. and Leone, L. (2018) The moderating role of interest in politics on the relations between conservative political orientation and denial of climate change, in *Society & Natural Resources*, 31:10, 1103–1117, https://doi.org/10.1080/08941920.2018.1463422
Cohen, J., and Rogers, J. (2003) Power and reason, in *Deepening democracy: Institutional innovations in empowered participatory governance*, Fung, A. and Wright, E.O. (Eds), London Verso, 237–255.
Corry, O. and Reiner, D. (2021) Protests and policies: How radical social movement activists engage with climate policy dilemmas, in *Sociology*, 55:1, 197–217
Décider Ensemble (2020). La démocratie bousculée: Quel renouvellement pour notre démocratie et nos systèmes de décisions? Ouvrage coordonné par Décider Ensemble. Retrieved from: https://www.decider ensemble.com/page/996272-notre-ouvrage
della Porta, D. (2013). *Can Democracy be Saved*? Cambridge: Polity
della Porta, D. and Felicetti, A. (2019) Innovating democracy against democratic stress in Europe: Social movements and democratic experiments, in *Representation*. https://doi.org/10.1080/00344893.2019.1624600

della Porta, D. and Pavan, E. (2017). Repertoires of knowledge practices: Social movements in times of crisis, in *Qualitative Research in Organizations and Management: An International Journal* 12:4, 297–314, https://doi.org/10.1108/QROM-01-2017-1483

Desage, F. (2017) Le gouvernement des métropoles, laboratoire de la postdémocratie, *CERAPS-Université Lille*. Retrieved online at https://lilloa.univ-lille.fr/handle/20.500.12210/14873 (accessed on 11th December 2020)

Doherty, B., De Moor, J. and Hayes, G. (2018) The 'new' climate politics of extinction rebellion? In *Open Democracy*, retrieved from the internet https://www.opendemocracy.net/en/new-climate- politics-of-extinction-rebellion/ (accessed 14th November 2020)

Extinction Rebellion (2019) *The Extinction Rebellion Guide to Citizens' Assemblies*. Extinction Rebellion. Retrieved from https://extinctionrebellion.uk/wpcontent/uploads/2019/06/The-Extinction-Rebellion-Guide-to-Citizens-Assemblies-Version-1.1-25-June2019.pdf

Fiorino, D.J. (2019)Improving Democracy for the Future: Why Democracy Can Handle Climate Change, in *International Relations*, June, 4.

Fung, A. and Wright, E.O. (2003) *Deepening Democracy: Institutional Innovations in Empowered Participatory Governance*. London: Verso

Geissel, B. (2009). Participatory governance: Hope or danger for democracy? A case study of local agenda 21, in *Local Government Studies* 35:4, 401–414.

Iwińska, K.; Kampas, A. and Longhurst, K. (2019). Interactions between democracy and environmental quality: Toward a more nuanced understanding, in *Sustainability*, 11:1728, https://doi.org/10.3390/su11061728

Jamison, A. (2010). Climate change knowledge and social movement theory, in *Wires Climate Change*, 1:6, 811–823, https://doi.org/10.1002/wcc.88

Karkainnen, B.C. (2003). Toward ecological sustainable democracy? in Fung, A. and Wright, E.O. (eds.) *Deepening Democracy: Institutional Innovations in Empowered Participatory Governance*, pp. 208–224. London: Verso

Koslov, L. (2019): Avoiding climate change: "Agnostic adaptation" and the politics of public silence, in *Annals of the American Association of Geographers*, https://doi.org/10.1080/24694452.2018.1549472

Kriesi, H. (2015) Party systems, electoral systems and social movements, in della Porta, D. and Diani, M. (ed.) *The Oxford Handbook of Social Movements*, pp. 667–680. Oxford: Oxford Handbooks.

Malm, A. (2021) *How to Blow Up a Pipeline. Learning to Fight in a World on Fire*. London: Verso Book

Martin, E., Perine, C., Lee, V. and Ratcliffe, J. (2018) Decentralized governance and climate change adaptation: Working locally to address community resilience priorities. In Alves, F., Leal Filho, W., and Azeiteiro U. (eds.) *Theory and Practice of Climate Adaptation. Climate Change Management*, pp. 3–22. Springer, https://doi.org/10.1007/978-3-319-72874-2_1

McAdam, D. (2017) The politicization of climate change: Problem or solution?, In *The Annual Review of Political Science*, 20, 189–208, https://doi.org/10.1146/annurev-polisci-052615-025801

Mouffe, C. (1999). Deliberative democracy or agonistic pluralism, in *Social Research*, 66:3, 745–758

OECD (2020). *Innovative Citizen Participation and New Democratic Institutions: Catching the Deliberative Wave*. Retrieved from: https://www.oecd.org/gov/open-government/

innovative-citizen-participation-new-democratic-institutions-catching-the-deliberative-wave-highlights.pdf

Parks, L. *Benefit-sharing in Environmental Governance Local Experiences of a Global Concept*. London – New York: Routledge

Polletta, F. (2016). Social movements in an age of participation, in *Mobilization: An International Quarterly*, 21, 485–497

Rootes, C. and Nulman, E. (2015). The impacts of environmental movements, in della Porta, D. and Diani M. (eds.) *The Oxford Handbook of Social Movements*, pp. 729–742. Oxford: Oxford Handbooks.

Roth, S. and Saunders, C. (2019). Gender differences in political participation: Comparing street demonstrators in Sweden and the United Kingdom, in *Sociology*, 53:3, 571–589

Schlembach, R., Lear, B. and Bowman, A. (2012) Science and ethics in the post-political era: Strategies within the camp for climate action, in *Environmental Politics*, 21:5, 811–828, https://doi.org/10.1080/09644016.2012.692938

Schlosberg, D. and Collins L.B. (2014). From environmental to climate justice: Climate change and the discourse of environmental justice, in *Wires Climate Change*, 5:3, https://doi.org/10.1002/wcc.275

Smith, J. (2015). *Social Movements and the Multilateral Arena*, in della Porta, D. and Diani M. (eds.) *The Oxford Handbook of Social Movements*, pp. 605–618. Oxford: Oxford Handbooks

Snow, D.A., Burche, Rochford, E., Worden, S.K. and Benford, R.D. (1986) Frame alignment processes, micromobilization, and movement participation, in *American Sociological Review*, 51:4, 464–481

Swyngedouw, E. (2010) Apocalypse forever? Post-political populism and the spectre of climate change, in *Theory Culture & Society*, 27, 2–3.

Swyngedouw, E. (2005) Governance innovation and the citizen: The Janus face of governance-beyond-the-State, in *Urban Studies*, 42:11, 1991–2006

Talpin, J. (2015) *Democratic Innovations*. In della Porta, D. and Diani M. (eds.) *The Oxford Handbook of Social Movements*, pp.781–792. Oxford: Oxford Handbooks.

Tokar, B. (2015) Democracy, localism, and the future of the climate movement, in *World Futures*, 71:3–4, 65–75, https://doi.org/10.1080/02604027.2015.1092785

Walgrave, S. and Vliegenthart, R. (2019) Protest and agenda-setting. In Baumgartner, F.R., Breunig C. and Grossman E. (eds.) *Comparative Policy Agendas: Theory, Tools, Data*. Oxford: Oxford University Press.

Warren, M. (2014). Governance-driven democratization, in S. Griggs, A.J. Norval & H. Wagenaar (Eds), *Practices of freedom: Decentered governance, conflict and democratic participation*. Cambridge, UK: Cambridge University Press, 38–6i.

Willis, R. (2020). *Too Hot to Handle? The Democratic Challenge of Climate Change*. Bristol: Bristol University Press

7 "Be Like Water"
Participatory Arts, Prefigurative Social Movements and Democratic Renewal

Lucy Cathcart Frödén

Introduction

The practices and values of prefigurative social movements and participatory arts projects share similar features. Both are loosely bordered contexts made up of shifting communities and networks that broadly pursue goals of social transformation in diverse and localised ways. Both aspire to create countercultural spaces where the collective imagination can be nurtured, where relationships and mutual care can be prioritised, where voices from the margins can become more audible and where inequalities can be addressed. Both share a language of process, improvisation, inclusion, open-endedness and performance. Both can also be considered contested spaces, where utopian aspirations can prove difficult to achieve. Despite this common ground, these realms are discussed and theorised in largely separate spaces. The aim of this chapter is to map out some of this common ground, to question boundaries created when certain practices are constructed as "political" or "apolitical", and to consider how thinking together might support democratic renewal more broadly.

The chapter will begin by identifying in broad brush strokes how these contexts conceptualise the interplay between the creative and the political in different ways and will go on to lay out some of the critiques of participatory practices. It will then sketch three areas in which dialogue between participatory arts and prefigurative social movements might prove productive – each one accompanied by a short vignette from participatory arts practice. This account makes no apology for being partial, subjective and situated; my own expertise is not in political science or democratic innovation, but in the theory and practice of participatory arts.

The reflections here complement the discussions in the wider volume regarding the shift from *governance-driven democratisation*, or GDD (Warren, 2014), to *democracy-driven governance*, or DDG (Bua and Bussu, 2021). Some of the key critiques of participatory approaches in the arts find resonance in Bua and Bussu's discussion of GDD – for example, that such approaches are elite-led, entrench unequal power dynamics, serve to increase the legitimacy of existing institutions and structures, close down spaces for transformative social change and may also contribute to a de-politicisation of collective action. By contrast, democracy-driven governance is a way of conceptualising participatory governance that is

DOI: 10.4324/9781003218517-9

bottom-up, critically oriented and social justice-focused (Bua and Bussu, 2021). Similar shifts in values, direction and power dynamics can be observed in participatory arts contexts, and this chapter will explore some of these similarities.

Locating the Politics in Shared Creative Practice

Carl Boggs defined prefiguration as "the embodiment, within the ongoing political practice of a movement, of those forms of social relations, decision-making, culture and human experience that are the ultimate goal" (1977, p. 2). In other words, in prefigurative social movements, how movement actors relate to one another *in the moment* – how power and resources are shared, how decisions are made, how voices are heard – is understood to be a way to enact in the present the future society the movement strives towards. In the decades since, prefiguration has been practised and defined in diverse ways, within a network of interconnected social movements. Since the Seattle WTO protests in 1999 and the Alterglobalisation and Occupy movements, awareness of prefigurative practices has become more widespread (Graeber, 2004). Although there are common themes such as opposition to neoliberal capitalism and contempt for mainstream representative democracy, it is generally agreed that there is no "singular goal, adversary or identity that is shared by all movement actors except at the most abstract level of desiring '(an)other world(s)'" (Maeckelbergh, 2011, p. 2).

Arts-based interventions have played a key role in enriching and mobilising prefigurative movements all over the world. Creative practice has been used in a myriad of subversive and thought-provoking ways to galvanise social movements, strengthen group identities and communicate with a wider audience. Examples range from the many forms of culture jamming (see Delaure and Fink, 2017); to graffiti and other visual interventions in public space (Gordon, 2018; Petropoulou, 2018; Cory, 2020); and to musical expressions of solidarity across the globe that help to claim public space (Green, 2016), to enrich prefigurative communities (Yates, 2015) and to encourage participation (Turino, 2008). Crucially though, discourses on the role and value of art in prefigurative social movements tend to focus on outcomes that contribute directly to the goals of the movement in question, such as engagement, education, outreach, awareness raising and inclusion; thus, creative practice and artistic expression are commonly conceptualised as part of the "strategic toolkit" (Sanz and Rodriguez-Labajos, 2021) of a movement.

The term *participatory arts* covers a broad set of practices that have emerged across the globe since the early 1990s under many names, including "socially engaged art, community-based art, experimental communities, dialogic art, littoral art, interventionist art, participatory art, collaborative art, contextual art and (most recently) social practice" (Bishop, 2012, p. 1). Despite the proliferation of names and approaches, these practices share a common focus on inclusive and collaborative modes of art production, often with transformative or emancipatory aims. Some of these collaborations connect established artists in new constellations, but this chapter is primarily concerned with "the specific and historically-recent practice that connects professional and non-professional artists in an act of co-creation" (Matarasso, 2019), in particular working with groups that have experience of marginalisation and social exclusion.

The contribution of participatory arts to political goals may be less easily identified, not least because the form and content of what is created in such contexts may not be explicitly political. Far from being "apolitical", however, participatory arts praxis is better conceptualised as having a different locus of politics, where art is not a "toolkit" but a way to include and amplify voices, perspectives and narratives that are frequently excluded from formal political participation. Here, inclusion in the *making* of the work is as crucial as, or indeed more crucial than, the artefact itself (Cohen-Cruz, 2002).

Tyrannies and Entanglements

Participatory approaches have become widespread in recent decades, in the arts, in politics and in local and international development, and their frequently idealistic rhetoric makes them vulnerable to critique. Cooke and Kothari (2001) described participation as "the new tyranny", drawing attention to unequal power dynamics, tokenism and approaches that may be formulaic, manipulative or harmful. Participatory processes, they contend, "can both conceal and reinforce oppressions and injustices in their various manifestations" (p. 13). This forms part of a longstanding discourse critiquing participatory development as an "anti-politics machine" (Ferguson, 1994), where participatory practices are seen as offering a veneer of equality that masks or even entrenches structural injustices by emphasising the personal over the political, concealing power differences, and claiming emancipatory outcomes without critical analysis of the wider neoliberal context (Williams, 2004).

The growth in the commissioning of participatory art under New Labour could be seen as a form of "democratisation of culture based on predefined economic, aesthetic and social values" (Hope, 2011, p. 3) – in other words, a top-down approach that did not allow participants to set the agenda. Such projects often assumed uncritically that positive outcomes of improved individual wellbeing and broader social change were a given. Collaboratively crafted art, however, is far from a universally ameliorative force. Rather, it should be considered "a power, not a good" (Matarasso, 2019) and should be subject to ongoing critical examination.

The discourse on participation in the arts suggests that an uncritical approach to participation is likely to support the status quo and unlikely to stimulate social transformation (see Bishop, 2010, 2012 and Kester 2011, 2013). There is no question that participatory arts methods can be made to serve the interests of financial donors or those in political power, through "co-option, compromise or complicity" (Kester, 2011, p. 2). At its most insidious, participatory art can achieve the opposite of what it sets out to do, becoming complicit in the shift in responsibility for social welfare onto individuals and local-level projects. Indeed, art historian Claire Bishop expresses a "profound ambivalence about the instrumentalisation of participatory art as it has developed in European cultural policy in tandem with the dismantling of the welfare state" (2012, p. 5).

In the context of late capitalism, then, socially engaged arts work is often inescapably "grafted onto the market" (Cultural Policy Collective, 2004, p. 11), either through the ways in which it is funded and thus entangled with corporate, state or third sector bodies, or through the channels by which the work created is expected to reach an audience. This can involve uncomfortable compromises, including requirements to produce work that is "apolitical". These entanglements merit further exploration, as they represent a complex interface where power and influence are enacted. Prefigurative social movements, by contrast, often operate by withdrawing altogether from engagement with capitalist mechanisms (Soborski, 2019).

An emergent understanding of participatory arts as a social practice of commoning highlights a critical engagement with the wider political context in participatory arts contexts. "Commoning art" not only represents a community but strengthens and mobilises it at the same time, through acts that "(re)produce a community while performing them" (Eynaud et al., 2018). This understanding distances participatory arts from complicity with capital, partly by conceptualising commoning as the accumulation of "dialogical practices, rather than [...] resources" (Carras, 2020, p. 3). Whereas community art before 2008 was often co-opted to mask or compensate for the depletion of the welfare state and promote social cohesion, "commoning art" has emerged in the age of austerity and demonstrates more activist and radical political tendencies (Otte and Gielen, 2018).

Prefigurative social movements have also been critiqued with regard to uncomfortable entanglements with power, paradoxically, for being either too closed or too open to the wider context. Some sites and practices of prefiguration, such as the creation of small-scale sustainable communities, have been critiqued as too inward-looking and tending "towards a type of social closure" (Jeffrey and Dyson, 2021). This sense of closure is deemed to be problematic both because it prioritises a small, closely connected few and excludes broader alliances, and because community economies may end up "(re)producing neoliberal conditions" (Argüelles et al., 2017, p. 30). Certain kinds of media refusal (such as quitting social media) can represent another kind of social closure, critiqued as a tactic of resistance that is more available to some than others, and as such can be read as "an expression of elitism" (Portwood-Stacer, 2013, p. 1054).

A different set of critiques could be summed up in terms of the risks of openness. Jeffrey and Dyson (2021) draw on various studies (Kulick, 2014; Van de Sande, 2015; De Wilde and Duyvendak, 2016; Vasudevan, 2015) to point out instances where prefigurative movements have been open to dilution – for example, through scaling up to become more institutionalised versions of themselves, or through funding that aligns them with dominant forces of state and capital. Similarly, Naegler (2018) discusses critiques of prefigurative practices as ineffective when "opening the way for co-optation and incorporation into the very consumer paradigms they mean to oppose" (p. 508). Both the "too closed" and "too open" forms of critique point to broader concerns of power imbalances and structural inequality, and how to manage interfaces between prefigurative communities and their wider contexts in ways that allow the communities at stake to retain their integrity while also exercising their desire to catalyse social change. Such tensions constitute another site where participatory arts and prefigurative communities could productively think together.

Such a process of thinking together, with a view towards transformative social change and democratic renewal, could engage with the contrasting notions of governance-driven democratisation (GDD) and democracy-driven governance (DDG) as discussed elsewhere in this volume. It is easy to see parallels between GDD and uncritical, co-opted participatory projects, as top-down, bureaucratic approaches that generally serve to preserve the status quo and entrench existing power differentials and social structures. DDG, on the other hand, is described as "efforts by social movements to invent new, and reclaim and transform existing, spaces of participatory governance" (Bua and Bussu, 2021, p. 716). Interestingly, these two contrasting approaches do not constitute a simple binary opposition. DDG does take a bottom-up approach, but it does not retreat altogether from existing power structures. Rather, it "opens up opportunities for bottom-up agenda setting, by ways of hybrid processes where invented spaces of citizenship interact with traditional institutions to transform them rather than adding to their legitimacy" (Bua and Bussu, 2021, p. 719).

This hybridity and refusal of boundaries is of particular interest here in considering parallels with participatory arts and prefigurative social movements. The question of how to engage with existing power structures is often framed as a binary one: between complicity or total retreat, engagement or dismissal, co-optation or separation. However, DDG presents a model that seeks to transgress, disrupt and transform these structures of governance from inside and outside simultaneously, working within the pragmatic assumption that engagement with them is and will continue to be necessary. This more porous conceptualisation of political action moves the discourse away from questions of inclusion or exclusion, towards more capacious understandings of what might constitute political action.

Beyond Binaries: Towards Connected Creative Communities

Having established common ground in critiques of participatory arts and prefigurative social movements, the remainder of this chapter constitutes a kind of interdisciplinary thought experiment, exploring how bringing these realms together might help to trouble some of the binary oppositions that frequently emerge in both discourses, such as political/apolitical, rehearsal/performance, public/private, present/future, process/product.

Political and Apolitical

Both prefigurative social movements and participatory arts can be said to engage in "the struggle for social change" (Trott, 2016), but as discussed previously, the nature and focus of their political intentionality differ. Participatory arts projects have been recognised to engage and overlap with informal, grassroots politics (Rimmer, 2012) and have been said to constitute a mechanism for "cultivating political literacy and nurturing engaged citizenship" (Flinders and Cunningham, 2014, p. 5). However, the problematic subtext of this point of view is that participants – primarily from marginalised communities – are assumed to be a monolithic and homogenous group who are by nature uninformed and disengaged until "activated" by some external force:

> To argue, in the manner of funding bodies and the advocates of collaborative art alike, that social participation is particularly suited to the task of social inclusion risks not only assuming that participants are already in a position of impotence, it even reinforces this arrangement.
> (Bishop, 2012, p. 38)

The reduction of participatory arts to a kind of conveyor belt that transports people over an imagined boundary from "passive" to "active" or "apolitical" to "political" is to overlook the inherently political nature of including and amplifying the perspectives and imaginations of under-represented communities. This includes those who are subject to hostile systems of state control and are thus excluded from formal political participation, such as people in the criminal justice system or the asylum system, as well as communities that face other forms of marginalisation.

It is generally agreed that prefigurative social movements are concerned with "the imagining, production and circulation of political meanings" (Yates, 2015, p. 1). Holloway (2010) too suggests that political intentionality is what sets prefigurative politics apart from "other doings" (p. 17). However, some scholars argue that prefigurative principles "can be applied to a variety of activities, beyond those explicitly deemed 'political' or 'activist'" (Green and Street, 2018). It is in this grey area of how "political" is defined that prefigurative politics and participatory arts intersect, where "the political aspirations of community art-making are rooted foremost in a view of cultural democracy as comprised of, and reflecting, people's dreams and desires" (Kirakosyan and Stephenson, 2019, p. 377) and where art holds potential to "rehumanise a society rendered numb and fragmented by the repressive instrumentality of capitalist production" (Bishop, 2012, p. 11).

A broader understanding of the political to include types of collective action that are not formally organised can be found in theories on "practice movements" (Eckert, 2015). Such movements focus on "some improvement of everyday possibilities of living" and seek to expand "the space of action of those who pursue them" (p. 568). This more capacious understanding of political action goes beyond resisting or transgressing the status quo, towards "potentially polyvalent normative and projective dimensions" that hold transformative potential (p. 573). This more expansive understanding of political action opens up interfaces with participatory arts.

A further way to trouble the political/apolitical binary is to see participatory arts and prefigurative social movements as adjacent and intersecting "epistemic communities", spaces in which individuals of different backgrounds and forms of expertise can "make sense of the world, and contribute to collective (interactive) efforts to deal with shared problems" (Haas, 2016). This resonates with accounts of free and democratic social structures as spaces where people can experience enjoyment and empowerment, leading to "a radical new need for the freedom, equality, community, and democracy that they embody" (Raekstad, 2018, p. 366). Participatory arts lend themselves here as sites of experimentation, ideas and memorable experiences.

"We Don't Want to Write a Political Song"

Protest songs from Bella Ciao to Shosholoza swell through the Wednesday morning quiet in Glasgow's spectacular Riverside Museum. I am spending the day with the Joyous Choir, a group of women with roots all over the world, many with experience of the brutality of the UK asylum system. We start the day by wandering the collections and in doing so we come across a number of historical artefacts relating to transportation during the Atlantic slave trade. Facing these displays – the horrors of the diagrams of bodies shackled and packed tight in the ship's hold – that's when the choir members begin, quietly at first, to sing.

Later, we move into the museum's collaborative space to begin writing our own song together. I assume that there will be an element of protest to our song, but Mina assures me – "We don't want to write a political song". There are about ten of us gathered to write a song together, as one part of a larger collaboration between Glasgow Sculpture Studios, artist Alberta Whittle[1] and Maryhill Integration Network[2]'s Joyous Choir. Our only starting point is the theme of "water". We share our experiences, from the insistent tapping of the Glaswegian rain, to memories of journeys on waterways, to wider concerns about climate change or migration, and to feminist metaphors illustrating the power of connectedness and care. Slowly we weave these threads together into a shared reflection on care, movement, connection, rest and hope. We begin to understand water as a force of both connection and separation, nurture and danger. At the same time, water holds a wealth of metaphors for our own agency and capacity to flow, to nourish, to move and to disrupt.

At some point, we start to think more about the sound of water, and the sonic qualities of the words that describe it. Suddenly there is a sense of the room opening up, recalibrating, as people start to share and play with words and phrases from other languages. We begin teaching each other our words for water – pani *in Gujarati,* nsuo *in Twi,* vatten *in Swedish. As the creative process opens up to multilingual input, some of the more reserved participants become more animated and the sonic environment of our shared space gains layered, multidirectional, multivocal textures, as participants with overlapping linguistic repertoires interpret unfamiliar words for the group. This shift towards multilingual lyrical content allows group members who had previously been watching from the margins to participate more fully in our collective decision-making. Gradually, our song takes shape, ending on the recurring refrain of "udha vade ska", a line in*

Albanian that means "wherever the road may lead". At the end of the songwriting process, Boatemaa, a co-writer who speaks English and Twi (a Ghanaian language), reflected, "I will value my language now".

So, did we write a political song? We did not write a protest song, but there are aspects of our song that are political. The way the lyrics express feminist ethics of care and solidarity, for example, or the enthusiasm for finding new words from outside the dominant colonial language. Opening up to words and sounds other than English can also be seen as a political act, in a wider context where a deficit-based approach to language learning remains widespread (Scanlan, 2007) and multilingualism is viewed with suspicion (Said, 2018) and multilingual people are "under siege in a worrisome world where threats to human difference have risen to the mainstream" (Ortega, 2019). When the choir went on to perform the song at cultural events around Scotland, they contributed to normalising multilingualism in our public life and urban soundscapes.

Rehearsal and Performance

There is a shared performance-related dimension between participatory arts and prefigurative social movements. Varying modes of performance are central to most participatory arts projects, and prefigurative practices too have been described as performative (Jeffrey and Dyson, 2021), involving open-ended processes of improvisation (Maeckelbergh, 2011; Silver, 2014; Vasudevan, 2015). Traditionally in the performing arts there is a separation between rehearsal (private) and performance (public). However, both prefigurative and participatory contexts blur this boundary, in creating non-linear and iterative processes where often the rehearsal and the performance are one and the same.

In new social movement theory, the fluidity and contingency of the boundary between public and private have long been recognised, particularly in relation to the expansion of the role of the state and its increasing interventions and intrusions into private life (Della Porta and Diani, 2006). As early as 1980, Melucci theorised an end to the separation of the public and the private, recognising this as a site of mobilisation and political action:

> Sexuality and the body, leisure, consumer goods, one's relationship to nature – these are no longer loci of private rewards but areas of collective resistance, of demands for expression and pleasure which are raised in opposition to the instrumental rationality of the apparatuses of order.
> (Melucci, 1980, p. 219)

This goes against assertions that when collective action is removed from public space, it can be "perceived as losing its political animus" (Trott, 2016), instead recognising the personal as political. This elision of the public/private divide is recognised as a site of creative and political potential in participatory arts. The invitation to participate unsettles the separation between performer/audience, rehearsal/performance and, by extension, public/private. Augusto Boal's vision of turning spectators into "spect-actors", and theatre into "rehearsal of revolution" is a case in point (Boal, 1974/2019).

Temporary Autonomous Zones

It doesn't take long to realise that the prison environment is marked by hierarchies. Power differentials are expressed in myriad ways – in the carefully calibrated nicknames that demonstrate familiarity or contempt; in the folded arms and defiant postures of prison officers watching a distressed prisoner who has dropped a pile of important papers in a corridor; in the caricatures pinned to the staffroom noticeboard; in who has keys, who has access and who is allowed to raise their voice.

Over the years of being involved in regular Vox Sessions[3] – 3-day intensive songwriting workshops in criminal justice settings – we have deliberately cultivated practices of care and mutual recognition that allow the space we occupy within the prison to become associated, albeit temporarily, with experiences of greater equality and humanity. We recognise this as sharing some features with the anarchist concept of the Temporary Autonomous Zone: an ephemeral space that eludes formal structures of control, where interpersonal and structural hierarchies are minimised, and the focus is on the present moment. The refusal of power differentials in this context is thought to lead to a more creative environment (Bey, 1985).

In this context, we are both rehearsing and performing an alternative set of social relations. Whoever enters the workshop space is required to participate on the same terms as everyone else, regardless of their status in the labyrinthine prison hierarchy. We are all songwriters here. Other labels are left at the door – at least to the extent that this is possible in an institution where even clothing colours are used as a tool of categorisation and control. We undertake a kind of place-making through simple rituals of collective creativity, conviviality and hospitality, which, although only momentary, offer a glimpse of an altered set of social relations. There is value in such moments because they "materialize just long enough to open up new relationalities" (Brown, 2019, p. 81), aligning in this sense with transformative justice movements.

In this particular participatory arts project, there is minimal separation between rehearsal and performance – partly because circumstances prevent us from inviting an audience to the final sharing of our new songs but also because of an informal social contract whereby everyone in the space is expected to take an active role. Here, participatory arts intersect with prefigurative practices, not only as a "rehearsal for revolution" or for a future "other world" but also as a performance of that other world in the now, that allows a temporary community to recognise itself as different, against the backdrop of prison hierarchies. Here, "the role of artworks is no longer to form imaginary or utopian realities but to actually be ways of living and models of action within the existing real" (Bourriaud, 2009, p. 56).

Present and Future

The convergence of rehearsal and performance leads to another significant point of synergy. Attention to ethical, inclusive relations and micropolitics based on equality is a central feature that participatory arts share with prefiguration. In prefiguration, this is described as means-ends equivalence or "being the change that you wish to see in the world". This can be understood as a kind of temporal collapse, where the present and the future become overlaid, and has been theorised as "present tense politics" (Trott, 2016) or "collapsing the future into the present" (Swain, 2019, p. 55). Springer poetically describes this as "fold[ing] protest and process together in an integral embrace" (2014, p. 3).

In this emphasis on the present moment, the daily interactions between community members become a site in which to enact the fairer society desired by the movement, summed up in ongoing critical reflections on the importance of *process*, a term which "becomes coupled with passion, anger, hope, and power, so much so that the term becomes impossible to ignore" (Maeckelbergh, 2011, p. 2).

There is a parallel conversation in participatory arts with regard to the relationship between *process* and *product*, long characterised as a tension in community music in particular (see for example Schippers and Bartleet, 2013; or Rimmer et al., 2014). In this context, the process can be understood as prioritising the present, in the form of interpersonal relationships and participant wellbeing, and product as prioritising the future results, in the form of performance or artefact. The separation of product and process into two parts in direct opposition to one another rests on all sorts of flawed assumptions – not least that the "professional" artist or musician will naturally create a more "attractive" artefact or performance or that a decision to prioritise one necessarily requires some degree of neglect of the other.

There is no question that both process (how we make) and product (what we make) are important to consider, but the construction of a binary opposition between "good art" and "good participation" is unhelpful. Kester's (2013) proposition of a *dialogical aesthetic* opens up a new way of conceptualising creative collaboration, shifting focus from the virtuosity of the individual artist or the attractiveness of the artefact towards the exchange of shared creativity:

> We typically view the artist as a kind of exemplary bourgeois subject, actualizing his or her will through the heroic transformation of nature or the assimilation of cultural difference—alchemically elevating the primitive, the degraded, and the vernacular into great art. Throughout, the locus of expressive meaning remains the radically autonomous figure of the individual artist. A dialogical aesthetic suggests a very different image of the artist; one defined in terms of open-ness, of listening and a willingness to accept dependence and intersubjective vulnerability. The semantic productivity of these works occurs in the interstices between the artist and the collaborator.
> (Kester, 2013)

This conceptualisation broadens the site of "the artwork" to include process, including all the interactions that take place in the liminal spaces between collaborators. Such a shift takes participatory arts closer to prefigurative practices in two ways. Firstly, by dismantling the hierarchy between, for example, the "lead artist" and the participants, space is created for a more horizontal and representative set of relations to emerge, thus democratising the creative process. Secondly, by framing the journey as part of the destination – or the process as part of the artwork – the linearity of the creative process is helpfully disrupted, through the same kind of temporal collapse that we see at work in means-ends equivalence.

Some scholars have perceived tensions between means and ends in prefigurative politics – for example, in movements where goals and outcomes tend to be prioritised over interpersonal relationships and process-oriented perspectives (Power, 2016), or where focus on the means and the present moment is considered to be in opposition to the strategic (e.g. Breines, 1989; Polletta, 2002). This supposed tension between the prefigurative and the strategic has been critiqued by scholar-activists including Maeckelbergh (2011), who have shown that the prefigurative can by its very nature be strategic, not in the sense of linear progress towards singular, pre-determined goals, but rather as flexible, interconnected networks engaged in "practices of social change that bring new political structures into existence bit by bit, improving those structures as they go along" (2011, p. 16).

In the same way that a dialogical aesthetic can help defuse the supposed tension between product and process in participatory arts, perhaps it also offers a way to conceptualise the prefigurative as strategic. The dialogical aesthetic suggests that the richer and more inclusive the process, the better the resultant product. In other words, these supposed binary dichotomies between present relational goals and future political or aesthetic goals can be collapsed when we consider the relational foundations of either project as vital to its success.

Sounds of Solidarity

There are six of us engaged in a remote songwriting experiment as part of the Vox Unbound[4] community. We are all in lockdown, and one of us is also in prison, one recently released and one in a different country. Some of us know each other, and some of us don't. Our task is to write a song together on the theme of "solidarity" – and one of many interesting things about this challenge is the invitation to recognise and discuss the power dynamics as the creative process progresses.

Under the "email a prisoner" scheme, people in prison are only allowed one sheet of paper to reply to a message, but our prison-based co-writer squeezes a wealth of lyrical ideas into the small space available to him, in response to some creative prompts. Our writing snowballs from here, pinging across group messaging and video calls, and even over a garden fence when the technology fails. It is easy to fall into a focus on the product – the what *we will make together rather than the* how *of it – but the more we slow down and focus on the process, the more experimental space this creates in the present moment.*

There is a lot of waiting in this process, a lot of liminal, in-between space. Time stretches and contracts as we wait for replies, wonder if messages have arrived, play with chord progressions in the meantime. Cyclical time makes more sense than linear time here – not only because there is a sense that process and product, present and future, are being folded into one. But also because of the unstable and unspoken backdrop to our collaboration: the brutally cyclical nature of short-term sentences on repeat, which some of our group have experienced. Our process is not perfect: when we examine the power dynamics, we see they are not equal; those of us with more resources or time or freedom or energy or data are able to participate more fully. We keep shifting, keep trying to open up the process and find ways towards equality where we can. Along the way, we reflect on how everyone can be represented sonically: through lyrical contributions, guitar riffs, vocals spoken or sung and found sounds of footsteps and birdsong. Slowly, the process becomes audible in the product.

Conclusion

Participatory arts practices and prefigurative social movements clearly share common ground, and both can be considered vital sources of renewal in our collective democratic life. This chapter has sought to map out commonalities and differences between these realms and to demonstrate some ways in which they might benefit from thinking together, not least in response to critiques of the "participatory turn". Participation is of course always "tied up with power" (Jenkins and Carpentier, 2013, p. 265). Critiques of participatory practices, in the arts and the political sphere alike, coalesce around questions of power, voice and representation. These discourses frequently feature binary oppositions – top-down vs bottom-up, or political vs apolitical, or open vs closed, or active vs passive – when the reality is more complex and multifaceted than these categories suggest. Greater porosity is required not only in theory but also in relation to the boundaries that divide people into participants vs non-participants or citizens vs non-citizens. Here, the radical inclusivity to which participatory arts aspire, combined with the rich collective imaginaries they express, can play a vital role in addressing questions of inequality and exclusion in the context of democratic renewal.

The emerging notion of "democratic ecosystems" (Asenbaum, 2022) offers a lively and dynamic way of understanding democratic renewal. Ecosystems are characterised by complex interactions, porous boundaries, cyclical processes, vitality, mutual dependence and constant change, and as such, this notion holds potential for all kinds of participation to be recognised – not just sites that are explicitly political. All ecosystems need water, and so perhaps participation can be imagined as the water needed to sustain democratic ecosystems. In writing *Udha Vade Ska*, one of the co-writers, Anastasia, referenced Bruce Lee's well-known exhortation to "be like water", and we enjoyed a moment of collectively imagining ourselves and our voices as water: combining, flowing, swelling and subsiding. Water nurtures and sustains life, it transgresses boundaries and it also slowly erodes structures that seem impenetrable. Perhaps this is exactly what our democracies need.

Acknowledgements

Profound thanks to all the individuals and communities with whom I have had the pleasure of working in creative collaboration, through Maryhill Integration

Network, the Joyous Choir, Vox Liminis, Vox Unbound, and Distant Voices. I have learned so much from your insight, openness and imagination. Thanks also to Alison Urie, Fergus McNeill, and the editors and other authors of this volume for valuable feedback on earlier drafts of this chapter.

Notes

1 See https://www.albertawhittle.com/.
2 Maryhill Integration Network (MIN) is a community development organisation in North Glasgow. It aims to nurture connections between people from different backgrounds in the local community, through participatory arts projects, activities focused on wellbeing and connection, and advocacy and campaigning. MIN was at the forefront of the successful campaign for people with refugee status to be allowed to vote in Scotland. Encompassing the cultural and the political, MIN's work has been described by DeBono and Mainwaring (2020) as part of a broader network of 'transgressive solidarity work that challenges EU border practices and concomitant categories to reimagine a more welcoming Europe' (p. 90). Find out more at www.maryhillintegration.org.uk.
3 Vox Sessions are a model of collaborative songwriting developed by arts organisation Vox Liminis. Working primarily in criminal justice-related settings, their work explores the role that the arts can play in shaping a more just society. From 2017-2021, Vox Liminis was involved in the Distant Voices project, a collaborative action research project undertaking songwriting-as-research in Scottish prisons, in partnership with the Universities of Glasgow, Edinburgh and the West of Scotland. Find out more at www.voxliminis.co.uk and www.distantvoices.org.uk.
4 Unbound is the ongoing creative community of Vox Liminis. It is a diverse group that meets weekly to eat and be creative together. Unbound began as a response to people who had been involved in Vox Liminis projects while in prison getting in touch after release. It provides a place to make positive connections, to build community, to make and learn together. During the COVID-19 lockdowns, Unbound had to figure out new ways of working, and the 'Sounds of Solidarity' project is one of the things that emerged from this period. Find out more at www.voxliminis.co.uk/projects/unbound.

References

Argüelles, L., Anguelovski, I., Dinnie, E., 2017. Power and Privilege in Alternative Civic Practices: Examining Imaginaries of Change and Embedded Rationalities in Community Economies. *Geoforum* 86, 30–41. https://doi.org/10.1016/j.geoforum.2017.08.013

Asenbaum, H., 2022. Beyond Deliberative Systems: Pluralizing the Debate. *Democratic Theory* 9, 87–98. https://doi.org/10.3167/dt.2022.090106

Bey, H., 1985. T.A.Z.: The Temporary Autonomous Zone, Ontological Anarchy, Poetic Terrorism. *The Anarchist Library*. https://theanarchistlibrary.org/library/hakim-bey-t-a-z-the-temporary-autonomous-zone-ontological-anarchy-poetic-terrorism.

Bishop, C., 2012. *Artificial Hells: Participatory Art and the Politics of Spectatorship*. Verso Books, London; New York.

Bishop, C. (Ed.), 2010. Participation, in: 3. pr. ed, *Documents of Contemporary Art*. Whitechapel, London.

Boal, A., 2019. *Theatre of the Oppressed*. Pluto Press, London.

Boggs, C., 1977. Marxism, Prefigurative Communism and the Problem of WORKERS' Control. *Radical America* 6 (Winter), 99–122.

Bourriaud, N., 2009. Relational aesthetics, in: Nachdr. ed, *Collection Documents sur l'art*. Les Presses du Réel, Dijon.
Breines, W., 1989. *Community and Organization in the New Left, 1962-1968*. Rutgers University Press.
Brown, M., 2020. Transformative justice and new abolition in the United States. In *Justice Alternatives*, Carlen, P., and Ayres França, L., 2020. . Abingdon, Oxon; New York, Ny: Routledge.
Bua, A., Bussu, S., 2021. Between Governance-driven Democratisation and Democracy-driven Governance: Explaining Changes in Participatory Governance in the Case of Barcelona. *European Journal of Political Research* 60, 716–737. https://doi.org/10.1111/1475-6765.12421
Carras, C., 2020. Sonic Counterpublics and Commoning Practices. *International Review of the Aesthetics and Sociology of Music* 51, 3–18.
Cohen-Cruz, J., 2002. An Introduction to Community Art and Activism. Community Arts Network / Art in the Public Interest, North Carolina.
Cooke, B., Kothari, U. (Eds.), 2001. *Participation: The New Tyranny?* Zed Books, London; New York.
Cory, Erin, 2020. Street Solidarity: A Report on Lebanon's 'October Revolution' | FIELD. *FIELD Journal*.
Cultural Policy Collective, 2004. *Beyond Social Inclusion: Towards Cultural Democracy*. Cultural Policy Collective.
DeBono, D. and Mainwaring, Ċ., 2020. Transgressive Solidarity: From Europe's Cities to the Mediterranean Sea. *Nordic Journal of Migration Research*, 10(4), pp.90–106. DOI: http://doi.org/10.33134/njmr.360
de Wilde, M., Duyvendak, J.W., 2016. Engineering Community Spirit: The Pre-figurative Politics of Affective Citizenship in Dutch Local Governance. *Citizenship Studies* 20, 973–993. https://doi.org/10.1080/13621025.2016.1229194
DeLaure, M., Fink, M., Dery, M., 2017. *Culture Jamming: Activism and the Art of Cultural Resistance*. New York University Press, New York.
Della Porta, D., Diani, M., 2006. *Social Movements: An Introduction*, 2nd ed. Blackwell Publishing, Malden, MA.
Eckert, J., 2015. Practice Movements, in: Della Porta, D., Diani, M. (Eds.), *The Oxford Handbook of Social Movements*. Oxford University Press, Oxford. https://doi.org/10.1093/oxfordhb/9780199678402.013.46
Eynaud, P., Juan, M., Mourey, D., 2018. Participatory Art as a Social Practice of Commoning to Reinvent the Right to the City. *Voluntas* 29, 621–636. https://doi.org/10.1007/s11266-018-0006-y
Ferguson, J., 1994. *The Anti-politics Machine: "Development," Depoliticization, and Bureaucratic Power in Lesotho*. University of Minnesota Press, Minneapolis.
Flinders, M., Cunningham, M., 2014. *Participatory Arts and Political Engagement*. Arts and Humanities Research Council.
Gordon, U., 2018. Prefigurative Politics between Ethical Practice and Absent Promise. *Political Studies* 66, 521–537. https://doi.org/10.1177/0032321717722363
Graeber, D., 2004. *Fragments of an Anarchist Anthropology, Paradigm*. Prickly Paradigm Press: Distributed by University of Chicago Press, Chicago.
Green, A., Street, J., 2018. Music and Activism: from Prefigurative to Pragmatic Politics, in: *The Routledge Companion to Media and Activism*. Routledge, London, pp. 171–178.

Green, A.J., 2016. Activist Musicianship, Sound, the 'Other Campaign' and the Limits of Public Space in Mexico City. *Ethnomusicology Forum* 25, 345–366. https://doi.org/10.1080/17411912.2016.1236350

Haas, P.M., 2016. *Epistemic Communities, Constructivism, and International Environmental Politics*. Routledge, London: New York.

Holloway, J., 2010. *Crack Capitalism*. London: Pluto Press.

Hope, C.S., 2011. Participating in the 'Wrong' Way? *Practice Based Research into Cultural Democracy and the Commissioning of Art to Effect Social Change*. Birkbeck: University of London.

Jeffrey, C., Dyson, J., 2021. Geographies of the Future: Prefigurative Politics. *Progress in Human Geography* 45, 641–658. https://doi.org/10.1177/0309132520926569

Jenkins, H., and Carpentier, N., 2013. Theorizing Participatory Intensities. *Convergence: The International Journal of Research into New Media Technologies* 19 (3): 265–86. https://doi.org/10.1177/1354856513482090.

Kester, G.H., 2013. *Conversation Pieces: Community and Communication in Modern Art, With a New Preface*. ed. University of California Press, Berkeley Los Angeles London.

Kester, G.H., 2011. *The One and the Many: Contemporary Collaborative Art in a Global Context*. Duke University Press, Durham.

Kirakosyan L., Stephenson M. Jr., 2019. Arts as Dialogic Practice: Deriving Lessons for Change from Community-based Art-making for International Development. *Psych*. 2019; 1(1): 375–390. https://doi.org/10.3390/psych1010027

Kulick, R., 2014. Making Media for Themselves: Strategic Dilemmas of Prefigurative Work in Independent Media Outlets. *Social Movement Studies* 13, 365–380. https://doi.org/10.1080/14742837.2013.831754

Maeckelbergh, M., 2011. Doing is Believing: Prefiguration as Strategic Practice in the Alterglobalization Movement. *Social Movement Studies* 10, 1–20. https://doi.org/10.1080/14742837.2011.545223

Matarasso, F., 2019. *A Restless Art: How Participation Won, and Why it Matters*. Calouste Gulbenkian Foundation, UK Branch, London.

Melucci, A. 1980. The New Social Movements: A Theoretical Approach. *Social Science Information* 19 (2): 199–226. https://doi.org/10.1177/053901848001900201.

Naegler, L., 2018. 'Goldman-Sachs Doesn't Care if You Raise Chicken': The Challenges of Resistant Prefiguration. *Social Movement Studies* 17, 507–523. https://doi.org/10.1080/14742837.2018.1495074

Ortega, L., 2019. SLA and the Study of Equitable Multilingualism. *The Modern Language Journal 103 (January)*: 23–38. https://doi.org/10.1111/modl.12525.

Otte, H., Gielen, P., 2018. *When Politics Becomes Unavoidable: from Community Art to Commoning Art*. pp. 269–280. In Dockx, N. and Gielen, P. (eds), *Commonism, a New Aesthetics of the Real*. Amsterdam: Idea Books.

Petropoulou, C., 2018. Social Resistances and the Creation of Another Way of Thinking in the Peripheral "Self-Constructed Popular Neighborhoods": Examples from Mexico, Argentina, and Bolivia. *Urban Science* 2, 27. https://doi.org/10.3390/urbansci2010027

Polletta, F., 2002. *Freedom Is an Endless Meeting: Democracy in American Social Movements*. University Of Chicago Press.

Portwood-Stacer, L., 2013. Media Refusal and Conspicuous Non-consumption: The Performative and Political Dimensions of Facebook Abstention. *New Media & Society* 15, 1041–1057. https://doi.org/10.1177/1461444812465139

Power, C., 2016. The Integrity of Process: Is Inner Transition Sufficient? *Journal of Social and Political Psychology* 4 (1): 347–63. https://doi.org/10.5964/jspp.v4i1.538.

Raekstad, P., 2017. Revolutionary Practice and Prefigurative Politics: A Clarification and Defense. *Constellations* 25 (3): 359–72. https://doi.org/10.1111/1467-8675.12319.

Rimmer, M., 2012. The Participation and Decision Making of 'at risk' Youth in community Music Projects: An Exploration of Three Case Studies. *Journal of Youth Studies* 15, 329–350. https://doi.org/10.1080/13676261.2011.643232

Rimmer et al., 2014. Whatever Happened to Community Music. *AHRC Research Network Report*. 10.13140/RG.2.2.13999.94886.

Sanz, T., Rodriguez-Labajos, B., 2021. Does Artistic Activism Change Anything? Strategic and Transformative Effects of Arts in Anti-coal Struggles in Oakland, CA. *Geoforum* 122, 41–54. https://doi.org/10.1016/j.geoforum.2021.03.010

Schippers, H. and Bartleet, B.L., 2013. The nine domains of community music: Exploring the crossroads of formal and informal music education. *International Journal of Music Education*, 31(4), pp.454–471.

Silver, J., 2014. Incremental Infrastructures: Material Improvisation and Social Collaboration Across Post-colonial Accra. *Urban Geography* 35, 788–804. https://doi.org/10.1080/02723638.2014.933605

Soborski, R., 2019. Prefigurative Politics in Anti-Neoliberal Activism: A Critique. *Perspectives on Global Development and Technology* 18, 79–92. https://doi.org/10.1163/15691497-12341506

Trott, C.D., 2016. Constructing Alternatives: Envisioning a Critical Psychology of Prefigurative Politics. *Journal of Social and Political Psychology* 4, 266–285. https://doi.org/10.5964/jspp.v4i1.520

Turino, T., 2008. *Music as Social Life: The Politics of Participation, Chicago Studies in Ethnomusicology*. University of Chicago Press, Chicago.

van de Sande, M., 2015. Fighting with Tools: Prefiguration and Radical Politics in the Twenty-First Century. *Rethinking Marxism* 27, 177–194. https://doi.org/10.1080/08935696.2015.1007791

Vasudevan, A., 2015. The Autonomous City: Towards a Critical Geography of Occupation. *Progress in Human Geography* 39, 316–337. https://doi.org/10.1177/0309132514531470

Warren, M.E., 2014. Governance-Driven Democratization, in: Griggs, S., Norval, A.J., Wagenaar, H. (Eds.), *Practices of Freedom*. Cambridge University Press, Cambridge, pp. 38–59. https://doi.org/10.1017/CBO9781107296954.002

Williams, G., 2004. Evaluating Participatory Development: Tyranny, Power and (Re)Politicisation. *Third World Quarterly* 25, 557–578.

Yates, L., 2015. Rethinking Prefiguration: Alternatives, Micropolitics and Goals in Social Movements. *Social Movement Studies* 14, 1–21. https://doi.org/10.1080/14742837.2013.870883

8 Whose and What Right to the City?

Insights from Lisbon on the interplay of movements and institutions within participatory processes

Roberto Falanga

Introduction

The "right to the city" is one of the most well-known and debated concepts in social and urban studies. As Henri Lefebvre (1968; 1973) put it, the *œuvre* is the call for citizen participation against the reduction of urban life to capitalist transactions and market-led strategies. In the last few decades, many scholars have discussed the role of urban movements in reclaiming the city. In parallel, the diffusion of government-led processes of participation has inspired a wider debate on new forms of bringing together multiple actors to deliberate on urban changes. Despite the mushrooming of urban movements and participatory processes, little is known about whether and how movements have played a role within participatory settings in pushing forward the right to the city. In fact, the interplay of movements and institutions within invited spaces of participation can unlock a new understanding of the transformation of urban claims. To fill this gap, the chapter discusses a recent participatory process promoted by the Lisbon city council for the regeneration of the Martim Moniz Square, an iconic space in the city. This was one of the few participatory processes addressing urban transformations implemented during the first wave of the COVID-19 pandemic in Europe. In addition, this was the only participatory process implemented at the city scale and the first to be implemented almost entirely online in Lisbon in 2020.

The chapter is structured into three main sections. The first presents the conceptual framework, which builds upon the theory of the right to the city from its original formulation proposed by Lefebvre at the end of the 1960s to the following scholarly debate interrogating the role of urban movements and participatory processes. The second section zooms in on the main urban transformations in Lisbon, the capital city of Portugal, by shedding light on the trajectory of movements and participatory processes in the city. The regeneration of the Martim Moniz Square is introduced by highlighting the main terms of contention between the "Garden Martim Moniz Movement" – a movement raised by activists, experts, local NGOs – and the Lisbon city council. Focus on the participatory process initiated at the end of 2020 illuminates whose and what right to the city was claimed within this specific participatory setting. In the third and last section, I argue that while the movement advanced a new debate on environmental justice through the

DOI: 10.4324/9781003218517-10

creation of a new garden in the square, some issues were left outside the scope of action. The inclusion of the most marginalised groups of the society who are living and working in that area was not a primary goal of the movement, which raises concerns about the social impacts of a new garden. While the city council countered, to a certain degree, risks of social exclusion from the participatory process, the potential aggravation of structural inequalities in that area was not placed at the centre of the official discourse.

This case study shows that the right to the city claimed by some members of the movement and political parties in Lisbon paid little attention to the multiple effects of capitalism in the city. However interconnected, some effects build on a long track of segregation and the exclusion of some groups of migrants, aggravated by the recent boom of tourism and housing speculation in the city; some others are directly connected to the results of this participatory process, as the request for a green space may overlook social exclusion in that area. Despite the centrality of capitalism in the right to the city, neither the movement nor the city council set out the conditions to scale the debate on the potential consequences of the regeneration of the square. Their interplay was rather based on the pursuit of conciliatory solutions supported by a large consensus about the new garden.

The Right to the City: Setting Out the Conceptual Frame

When in the late 1960s Henri Lefebvre (1968; 1973) introduced the concept of the "right to the city", students' mobilisations and workers' protests fuelled the first big crisis of western democracies after the Second World War. Younger generations, low-skilled workers and groups at the margins of society claimed a new political turn and a radical change in society. In fact, the claim for the right to the city arose amid the growing influence of big financial institutions over politics (Harvey, 2008). Despite the crash of the global property market between the end of the 1960s and the beginning of the 1970s, the primacy of capitalism confirmed a huge power at the hands of some economic agents. Against this backdrop, protests drew inspiration from Marxist theory and contended the replacement of "exchange value" with "use value" (Purcell, 2003; Krieger et al., 2021). Accordingly, the city was to be valued not as a market product, but rather as a space to be lived, perceived and conceived by its inhabitants (Lefebvre, 1974). The right to the city aimed at aggregating the "cry and demand" of inhabitants against urban injustices and contradictions. In so doing, the postulation of the right to the city sought to stimulate the action of urban social movements towards the radical restructuring of social, political and economic relations in the city.

Lefebvre's original formulation of the right to the city was explicit about the need to change the status quo. The revolutionary ethos of this concept, however, was subdued in the years that followed, by academic and political actors (Belda-Miquel et al., 2016). In parallel, movements increasingly sought more conciliatory rather than disruptive solutions with political institutions. While during the 1970s movements were clear about the need to combat capitalist forces and looked for strong alliances with labour unions and political parties, the 1980s marked a shift in their repertoires of social action. Many movements preferred programme strategies instead of protests (Mayer, 2009), in compliance with competitive ideals of urban development (Uitermark, 2004). Nonetheless, in those years movements often understood that by adopting more conventional strategies, they could capitalise on opportunities opened by political institutions, including participatory processes (Polletta, 2007). In the 1990s, as the market discipline became imperative and global, movements tended to reframe their scope in cities that became key targets for new financial assets.

Despite some economic stagnation, global capitalist trends crystallised in the 2000s, and activism intercepted changes coming from new international networks that eventually reignited the debate on the right to the city in a globalised world (Della Porta and Felicetti, 2022). Throughout the financial crisis, square occupations have represented an important opportunity to experiment with new interactions between movements and participatory processes, as well as with the political system more broadly (Della Porta, 2019). As shown by the Spanish case, movements have increasingly interacted with political institutions and created additional opportunities for participation for all citizens. In fact, some movements joined under the umbrella of "new municipalism" with the aim of reconfiguring urban governance with the heavy support of digital technologies, which stimulated a new culture of cyberactivism within public institutions (Mota Consejero and Janoschka, 2022). In the last two decades, global struggles have increasingly relied on the development of new technologies and have often built up new interconnections. As a result, movements are interrogating the role of the digital sphere for urban communities and activists, fostering a new debate on the role of "netizens" and the pursuit of the "right to the digital city" (Foth et al., 2015).

Whose and What Right to the City?

The right to the city proposed by Lefebvre opposed the accumulation of capital in the city. According to the author, citizens should be in a position to produce and use the urban space against rising oligarchies (Purcell, 2013). The depoliticisation of the public debate on the right to the city, however, was often paralleled by tame movements co-opted in urban development projects (Mayer, 2009). One of the principal strategies put in place to decrease the revolutionary ethos of the right to the city was the extension of its meaning. Against those arguing that the right to the city was for everything and everyone, Marcuse (2009) defends that the many should defy the few capital owners. In particular, the author contends the specificity of who the main actors should be: the deprived (immediately exploited, unemployed, impoverished) and discontented (disrespected and treated unequally) people. Once it has been established who should be at the forefront of collective struggles, some scholars clarify what rights should be reclaimed. According to Lefebvre, this is not an ascribed legal right, but rather an outcome of political struggle. Likewise, Mayer (2009) says that this right should not be held as a juridical right, but rather as an oppositional one. In addition, the author acknowledges potential traps in the proliferation of advocacy groups that frame their struggles in the exclusive terms of rights, often backed by mainstream discourses of international organisations. This point is echoed by Belda-Miguel and colleagues (2016), who contend that the incorporation of the right to the city in a growing number of political claims leads to its depoliticisation and deradicalisation.

The Marxist roots of this right disclose another important aspect of whose and what right to the city is claimed. According to Attoh (2011), the right to the city embodies the potential breakdown of state law. Purcell (2005) adds that beyond challenging state injustices on a local scale, movements should set out cross-sectional actions against capitalism and foster a multi-scale strategy. As the privatisation and reduction of the welfare state against which movements raise their voice is not a prerogative of the local scale, the author reminds us that the city is today the most important political and economic battleground where urbanisation processes are taking place. As a result, the right to the city should not fall into the "local trap" and, as argued by Harvey (2008), rather acknowledge the absorption of capital surpluses and the dispossession of the urban masses as a multi-scale phenomenon activated by a wide range of actors. The right to the city, as the author stresses, cannot help but be a collective right in opposition to trends of neoliberalism-driven disinvestment in the public realm and in favour of public–private partnerships.

Citizen Participation for the Right to the City

The collective nature of the right to the city is nurtured by the opposition to the inequalities produced by multi-level capitalist forces within the city. Scholars stress how the many deprived and discontented inhabitants should raise their voice against the dispossession of the city in the hands of a few private investors. According to Lefebvre, the only manner in which this can be achieved is by changing power relations. Purcell (2005) elaborates on this point and argues that power relations change when people appropriate and occupy spaces by improving their physical access and use. Such goals can be achieved by strengthening social connections, mobilising inhabitants and promoting active participation in decision-making. According to Lefebvre (1968), citizenship is the act of inhabiting the city rather than a "membership" to a nation-state. Likewise, Subirats (2011) adds that citizenship is politically co-produced by forging links with others and experiencing mutual responsibility and solidarity. The civic awakening of citizenship can enhance collective consciousness in contrast to the common ideology and practice of citizen acquiescence (Purcell, 2014). As a consequence, citizen participation holds the potential to expand the limits of politics and increase chances of citizen control over the city for a full urban experience (Purcell, 2003).

The scientific debate on citizen participation in the right to the city has specifically focussed on grassroots movements. Nevertheless, the rise of a variety of participatory settings in the last few decades has advanced new questions and opportunities to expand the debate. As Cornwall (2002) put it, to "popular" spaces of participation reclaimed by civic groups, political institutions have increasingly counterposed "invited" spaces. The flourishing of participatory processes organised by public authorities with invited citizens and stakeholders has attracted an increasing number of scholars, practitioners, policymakers and international organisations. According to Smith (2009), a wave of democratic innovations in the last few decades has had the merit to shift from state-led government to society-led governance with ordinary citizens through official frameworks. Spaces of participation do not only hold a political aspect, as they often address spatial issues, as in the case of participatory planning initiatives and community engagement in urban regeneration. The coming together of multiple interests and goals in such processes shows the potential overlapping of multiple "spaces of participation" within and/or for the same physical place, as well as the rise of new mobilisations on contested urban issues (Miraftab, 2020). At the edge of the multiple spaces of participation, citizens often mix official and alternative settings, as counter-publics constitute new identities and generate new claims (Fraser, 1997). In fact, as highlighted by Bua and Bussu (2020), while participatory processes can trigger both democracy and governance-driven goals, today citizen participation more clearly stands at the intersection of multiple spaces that give the stage to multiple actors holding different degrees of power.

Urban Movements and Participatory Processes

According to Polletta (2007), social movements in western democracies shifted from a revolutionary ethos in the 1960s to a search for transforming what counts as politics since the 1990s. Such a shift required new repertoires of social action and scholars have long debated about whether and how movements can transform social structures at the local level. Castells (1983) early stressed the benefits of scaling local struggles through international connectivity (Castells, 1983). Nonetheless, other scholars contend that movements should be consistent with the specific problems raised in their locale rather than embracing universal struggles. According to Pruijt (2007), in pursuing the "use value" of the city, urban movements should be oriented by instrumental goals and try to be effective on a local scale. Different understandings about the scopes of action of movements are conditioned by their goals, whether they are openly oppositional to the state or not. In both cases, movements share the common challenge to find adequate strategies so as not to miss the opportunity to influence public authorities without either sacrificing or compromising their struggles (Polletta, 2016). Some movements have a repertoire based on squatting and occupying spaces, while others prefer to negotiate conciliatory solutions with public authorities. The latter advocate for living improvements in the city and are more likely to find decision-makers inclined to integrate their requests into the public agenda (Andretta et al., 2015).

Despite the transformations of activism and the growth of government-led participatory processes, little is known about whether and how urban movements play a role in such formal settings. More precisely, the debate on the interplay between urban movements and political institutions in participatory processes has been surprisingly limited hitherto (Talpin, 2015). Nevertheless, evidence shows multiple ways through which these players can come to an agreement. In some cases, spontaneous forms of civic action are not prone to conciliatory solutions and keep a distance from the state. Miraftab (2020) points to the spread of insurgent practices of citizenship that struggle to create a common ground of understanding with the most marginalised groups. As she argues, "[w]hen the formal citizenship rights supposedly granted by the state are irrelevant to realities of poor communities, people use interstitial spaces of power not to merely ask for but to practice their rights to dignified life from below" (ibidem, 436). In other cases, public authorities intercept grassroots instances in search of a compromise between radical changes and functionalist goals. Movements may find a way in which their struggles can gain visibility and put pressure on governments by transforming democratic innovations (Smith, 2009) into "citizen-led innovations", as Della Porta and Felicetti (2022) put it. Such innovations hold the potential to transform participatory processes by introducing potentially disruptive claims through legitimate state mechanisms.

Unpacking Citizen Participation for the Right to the City in Lisbon

In this chapter, I focus on the participatory process enacted by the Lisbon city council for the regeneration of an iconic space in the city centre: the Martim Moniz Square (MMS hereafter). In the last decade, the city of Lisbon has become a highly contested space at the centre of tremendous socio-political transformations. The local economy was preserved, in the aftermath of the 2008 financial crisis, through the action of public and private agents mainly in the real estate and tourism sectors. Since the mid-2010s, Lisbon has experienced a significant economic recovery and today the city is acknowledged as one of the most attractive and competitive destinations in Europe. Real estate and tourism sectors continue to play a major role, and this rapid transformation has brought significant improvements in the living quality of citizens. Nevertheless, the rise in living costs has raised growing concerns mostly due to the housing inflation cycle, which has forced many residents to leave their homes (Falanga and Tulumello, 2017). Growing discontent among lower and middle classes has fuelled new mobilisations against pro-developers and pro-tourism measures, which have echoed international struggles in big cities (Falanga et al., 2019).

The recent rise in housing movements in Lisbon has built on diffuse poverty and cases of segregation of some migrant communities mainly at the borders of the city. Data from the 2021 Census shows that foreigners in the metropolitan area represent around 45% of the foreign population in Portugal. However, despite general concerns about participation in tailored initiatives or activities, there is a lack of integrated strategies to engage migrants in public life.[1] As regards political life, the European Social Surveys show low rates of citizenry trust in democratic institutions and participation in political elections at the national level. The outlook was particularly negative during the financial crisis (2011–14), while the strength of social mobilisations was not comparable to neighbouring countries (Baumgarten, 2013). According to Moury and Standring (2017), the alienation of grassroots groups grew as austerity was presented as a *fait accompli* by the central government. The convergence of some key actors, including labour unions, political parties at the opposition, business sectors and the Constitutional Court, eventually encouraged the Socialist Party to stop supporting austerity, contributing to their victory at the following national elections in 2015 (De Giorgi et al., 2015). The attraction of private investment in the tourism and real estate sectors had some setbacks. Mobilisations spread in Lisbon and Porto in opposition to the "touristification" of the urban environments and spreading evictions. In parallel, the Lisbon city council triggered new forms of dialogue with citizens through participatory processes.

The growth of participatory processes pushed forward by a new generation of local Mayors aimed to compensate for the strong centralisation of the central state (Allegretti, 2021). In Lisbon, citizen participation has been a key pillar of urban governance in the last 15 years. The main reason behind the implementation of the first-ever participatory budget at the city level in a European capital was related to the decrease in citizen trust towards political institutions (Falanga and Lüchmann, 2020). Negative outlooks of political participation in national elections were aggravated by the austerity measures imposed under the readjustment programme agreed upon by major parties and the so-called Troika.[2] While this outlook was essentially true at the national level, local authorities used participatory processes to strengthen the relationship between decision-makers and citizens at a time when austerity cut local budgets and personnel (Falanga, 2018). Against this backdrop, the participatory agenda of Lisbon was internationally acknowledged for advancing democratic innovations that became flagships, such as the participatory budget and the BipZip programme. The latter is based on annual calls for local NGOs and local partners to join together and propose area-based initiatives in deprived areas of the city. Local partnerships are funded and required to implement the initiatives by ensuring community engagement (Falanga, 2020).

Despite the success of both participatory budget and BipZip, social movements have limited involvement. Generally, the gap between movements and participatory processes is often a result of perceptions of white and middle-class stakeholders dominating formal settings (Polletta, 2007). In Lisbon, the reasons behind this distance can be traced back to the level of institutional designs. Empirical analysis of both participatory processes illuminates some aspects worth understanding. Regarding the participatory budget, Lisbon does not provide any formal mechanisms to engage associated citizens, and participation is promoted on a one-to-one basis. The sought-after interaction between each citizen and public authorities may have discouraged movements from taking a stage in this participatory process. Regarding the BipZip programme, while the poor conditions of neighbourhoods where local partnerships are invited to implement community projects may encourage the presence of grassroots groups to reclaim better living standards, the emphasis on the implementation of an already agreed project may have equally discouraged the participation of movements. A pragmatic orientation may reduce the space of debate on structural inequalities and discourage the mobilisation of alternative groups.

As Valesca (2019) put it, the quantity and quality of information shared with grassroots groups may further hinder full participation in participatory processes. However, the lack of grassroots support undermines sound and credible outcomes, as elites continue to control decision-making. In Lisbon, some community groups composed of householders and local stakeholders used participatory processes to get some funding in deprived areas and made the best out of "interstitial spaces" around participatory processes to put additional pressure on decision-makers. For example, on the eastern side of the city, community groups have used the participatory budget to reclaim quality public spaces and, in parallel, have raised public awareness about the impact of the undeveloped supply of public services through alternative channels (Falanga, 2022).

The Martim Moniz Square

The Martim Moniz Square (MMS) is an iconic space of the city. It connects the city centre to one of the most regenerated and cool urban areas of Lisbon, as echoed by the "*Time Out*" magazine in 2019. This area, however, holds a relatively low number of inhabitants, confirming trends of depopulation in the historic centre as pointed out by the Social Atlas of Lisbon. Moreover, an ageing local population in the area is a considerable issue, contrasted with growing settlements of migrants, who represent around 25% of the local community. Social diversity characterises daily life on this site, as shown by the many cultural initiatives organised by migrant communities. Nonetheless, the MMS is also a hotspot of poverty in the city. In an initial attempt to regenerate the square, the Lisbon city council gave a concession to use the square to the NCS ("Número de Ciclos por Segundo") enterprise in 2012. The NCS inaugurated the "Fusion Market" composed of ten stands selling food from all over the world, which attracted new public. Sound and soil pollution, however, motivated neighbours and the district government to publicly complain about the use of the square. The slow decay of the market eventually convinced the city council to welcome a new project for the square by the joint venture Moonbrigade – which included NCS. The new project was called "Martim Moniz Market" and was based on the increase in the number of stands, with a new modern appearance, covering more than 50% of the square.

As soon as the project was made public in 2018, some activists, local NGOs and political parties on the left of the political spectrum raised their concerns. Both social and political actors – especially the communist party – referred to the "right to the city" in opposition to the perceived democratic deficit in the decision taken by the city council.[3] Between 2018 and 2019, formal and informal meetings were organised to discuss the risks of privatisation of the public space, which fuelled a larger debate on the desired uses of the square. Social groups and experts were encouraged to take an active part in this debate by publishing their testimonies online and in public debates. At the beginning of 2019, the idea of a green public space gained public support against the "Martim Moniz Market" project, as corroborated by around 1600 signatures on a public petition launched by the new "Garden Martim Moniz Movement" (GMMM hereafter). The GMMM gathered activists, local NGOs, experts and citizens advocating for a new political turn in that area. To this end, the GMMM publicly requested the city council to promote a participatory process on the future of the MMS.

The Participatory Process for the Regeneration of the Martim Moniz Square

As soon as the city council acknowledged the growing social pressure and credibility of the GMMM in the eyes of citizens and media, it announced the end of the "Martim Moniz Market" project in July 2019. The newly appointed deputy mayor for urban planning declared the intention to implement a participatory process for the regeneration of the MMS shortly afterwards. This process would take place on-site through a mix of consultative and deliberative settings. The outbreak of the COVID-19 pandemic at the beginning of 2020 convinced the organising committee to seriously consider more adequate and safe measures.[4] The shift from in-presence to online modes of interaction required careful consideration of the positives and negatives of e-participatory tools. An ex-ante appraisal of the inclusiveness of the process was made in light of the sociodemographic data of the area. The committee was especially keen to find an effective way to reach out to and engage migrant communities and marginalised people while ensuring wider participation at the city level. To this end, some members of the committee ensured their presence on-site at the first stage of the process and made sure the district government helped in having local organisations on board to facilitate contacts with locals whenever needed.

The participatory process was structured into three main stages backed by a public exhibition of key historical and present facts regarding the MMS.[5] At the outset, some members of the organising committee were physically present in the square to provide information and help to those who wanted to take part in the online participatory process. Face-to-face contact opportunities were created to reach people living and working in the square, as well as local organisations involved in social work with the most vulnerable groups. The first stage of the participatory process attracted a wide diversity of participants, 29% belonged to migrant communities. Data collected allowed for a better understanding of key social and spatial issues regarding the square.[6] In particular, the participatory process made clear that the MMS was mainly perceived as an uninviting "crossroad" within the city, as few people chose to spend time there. Nevertheless, some aspects were positively rated by participants, such as shopping and eating out around the square. More green space, cleanliness and better air quality were pointed out as primary needs. The multicultural environment was equally identified as a very positive feature of this space, along with more technical issues, such as the good opportunity to keep the underground car park. Citizen proposals for the regeneration of the MMS resulted in a large consensus around the creation of a garden, followed by requests for more public facilities, cultural and multicultural activities, mobility solutions, and cleanliness and safety.

Inclusiveness was a priority of the city council which tried to reach the local community and ensure a balanced representation of citizens' voices. To this end, some choices were made that were reflected in the constitution of public (Barnes et al., 2003). All Lisbon residents were invited to participate, including those working, studying or just visiting the city; at the neighbourhood level, a strong emphasis was placed on involving migrant communities and marginalised groups. At both levels, the city council looked for one-to-one interaction without the intermediation of groups and movements. As a result, the GMMM was taken as a player in the public contention, but it was not given any formal role in the design and implementation of the participatory process. Nevertheless, the city council acknowledged the opportunity to organise two internal workshops with a few representatives of the GMMM and city council departments in order to share knowledge on some of the most contentious technical issues related to the regeneration of the square. Workshops did not have any direct implication on the final results and rather served as a way to build a common understanding of some key issues emerging from the participatory process. Out of the participatory process, the GMMM did not organise any specific events, such as protests and demonstrations against the city council and/or the participatory process. In contrast, the GMMM supported the process by sharing news with activists and followers on its social networks, which confirmed interest in the initiative.

In this endeavour, the city council took advantage of the accumulated knowledge and know-how on the design and implementation of participatory processes. The new initiative built on these legacies and innovated, at least, three interrelated domains. First, this was one of the few participatory processes in Europe implemented during the first wave of the COVID-19 pandemic which focussed on urban transformations, contrasting with the massive interruption of local processes of citizen participation as well as with the many informal local initiatives focussing on goods and service delivery at the neighbourhood level (cf. Falanga, 2020). Second, this was the only participatory process implemented on a city-wide scale in Lisbon during the first wave of the pandemic, which complemented community initiatives at the neighbourhood level promoted through the BipZip programme. Third, this was the first participatory process in Lisbon developed almost exclusively online, thus marking a significant step forward for online modes of interaction in citizen participation.

Discussion: Whose and What Right to the City of Lisbon?

The GMMM and the Lisbon city council have been key players in creating the conditions for a new participatory process in Lisbon about the regeneration of the MMS. Public contention cast light on different, opposite on occasion, ideas for the production and use of the MMS. On the one hand, the city council legitimately conceded the square to a private actor in 2012 and aimed at renovating the deal years later. On the other hand, however, civil society legitimately stopped the initial private sector-led project and claimed a new political turn to regenerate an iconic space of the city. Such a claim was underpinned by concerns for environmental justice and translated into proposals for a new green space in a central area of the city that hosts many different migrant communities and marginalised groups. The support gained by the GMMM's petition in the city was backed by the endorsement of experts and practitioners, which eventually convinced the city council to cease the project for the new Martim Moniz Market. In this succession of events, both social and political actors recalled the right to the city as the "northern star" to qualify decision-making in Lisbon. The interplay of the GMMM and the city council within this process, in fact, raises questions as to whose rights were claimed and what right they have to the city.

The GMMM advocated the right to make citizens reappropriate the square by underlining the need to get back its "use value". This right intercepted different, however, interconnected, issues, such as the lack of public green spaces in that urban area. By invoking principles of environmental justice, the GMMM moved towards conciliatory goals with the city council and openly requested a participatory process. As soon as the city council acknowledged the opportunity to give citizens a voice, the GMMM immediately persuaded public opinion on the potential benefits of a garden in that place. Conciliatory goals, therefore, are built on the persuasion of society and the "endorsement" given by experts, political parties and the district government to the GMMM (see Polletta, 2016). In addition, these factors explain the success that the creation of green space had in the participatory process, because the GMMM succeeded in constructing a collective claim by becoming a credible player in the eyes of both citizens and the city council. Public legitimacy and social acceptance of the GMMM led to the incorporation of social instances in the public debate and the local agenda, thus determining the decision to open a "citizen-led innovation" (Della Porta, 2019).

The other legitimate player was the city council, which harvested the opportunity to open a public discussion with citizens, without losing its credibility. Such an endeavour was shaped by concerns about inclusiveness (see Valesca, 2019). The socio-spatial characteristics of the MMS were acknowledged by the city council and efforts were made to involve both individuals and organisations representing migrant communities and marginalised groups living and working in the area. Despite the heavy constraints due to the COVID-19 pandemic, physical presence in the square was secured at a first stage to disseminate and invite people and local NGOs in the neighbourhood to take an active part. Such an inclusive ethos, however, also meant recalibrating the role of the GMMM in the participatory process as no formal role was given to the movement in the design and implementation of the participatory process. This decision was taken by the city council in order to ensure a balanced and equitable process for all participants. While the GMMM raised some initial concerns about this decision, it essentially agreed on stepping back and giving support to the dissemination of the participatory process, which paved the way towards a conciliatory result.

The main result of the participatory process was to confirm citizens' aspirations to see a new green public space in the square. This process also epitomises a specific interplay between movements and political institutions in Lisbon. On the one hand, there was a claim for the public reappropriation of the square as a public space against the perceived privatisation of city space. Activists and local NGOs first and the GMMM later aligned on concrete urban problems, showing little interest in either scaling the claim up or connecting with international partners (Castells, 1983). The GMMM advanced its claim by opposing the Martim Moniz Market project based on international standards for environmental justice in urban settings. Despite being opposed to the new market project, the movement's strategy moved along non-conflictual lines. There was no intention to break the "state law", but rather to influence public opinion, and public authorities (Andretta et al., 2015). In fact, this strategy sought wide support from citizens and conciliatory goals with the city council (Pruijt, 2007). The organisation of public debates, the launch of the GMMM's website and the involvement of experts to give their testimony to the cause helped make the claim a collective one.

Concluding Remarks

The case of Lisbon discussed in this chapter sheds light on whether and how social movements can play a role in state-led participatory processes and specifically what type of interplay can take place with political institutions. By pushing forward a legitimate protest, the GMMM constructed a collective claim for (more) public spaces in the city centre. While advancing a conciliatory strategy with the city council, the movement was determined to stop the project of a new market. Its discourse developed around the lack of green areas, which found a large consensus among citizens. Such a result informed the participatory process opened by the city council in 2020, which echoed citizens' aspirations for a new public green space in the square. Despite the decision taken by the city council to give neither a formal role nor a privileged stage to the movement in the design and implementation of the participatory process, the formal exclusion did not affect the outcome of the participatory process. In fact, the conciliatory strategy pursued by the GMMM not only succeeded in convincing the city council to open a participatory process, but it also succeeded in persuading public opinion on the legitimacy of its claim. These two factors suggest that the GMMM adopted what Della Porta (2019) calls "participatory skills" developed by social movements that aim to co-produce citizen-led innovations with political institutions (Della Porta and Felicetti, 2022).

Is the public green space the most fitting solution to the right to the city claimed by social and political actors? To answer this question, we should ask to what extent the impact of capitalism on the (re)production of structural inequalities was addressed by the key players. According to Lefebvre (1968; 1973), the cry and demand of the inhabitants should be oriented towards the (radical) change of social structures. Marcuse (2009) added that the right to the city should lead to the reappropriation of the urban space by the most deprived and discontented. Accordingly, while a considerable effort has been made by both GMMM and the city council to engage with migrant communities and marginalised groups, their relative weight in the final result is unclear. Likewise, whether the green space represents a radical change in power relations is a question worth answering by considering both positives and negatives. Along with benefits, green areas can however further new processes of gentrification connected to urban development processes, which were barely addressed in the public debate. Such risks speak of potentially negative impacts on the inhabitants and may boost new investments in the real estate and tourism sectors in the surroundings (García-Lamarca et al., 2022).

This chapter is based on a single case study through the angle of the right to the city. As such, it is difficult to generalise findings. However, future research on the interplay of movements and political institutions within participatory processes can unlock aspects that were not entirely developed here. Is the lens of the right to the city useful in the analysis of participatory processes developed around contentious urban issues? How do movements build their legitimacy and choose the repertoire of social action within and at the borders of participatory processes? How do political institutions behave with movements advancing more radical changes rather than conciliatory goals?

Notes

1 More information is available from the Observatory of Migration: https://www.om.acm.gov.pt/documents/58428/177157/Estudo+OM+70.pdf/f7d3dad1-248e-4c97-a30a-565e0653a478.
2 The adjustment programme was agreed between the government and the Troika in 2011. Troika was the name given to the supervision of the International Monetary Fund, European Commission and European Central Bank over the 3-year economic adjustment programme signed in May 2011 for a bailout package of 78€ million. The programme aimed to consolidate domestic finances and improve international competitiveness.
3 Link to the debate launched by the communist party on the right to the city in the MMS: https://www.am-lisboa.pt/302000/1/011386,000419/index.htm.
4 The organising committee was composed of public officials from the citizen participation, urban planning, public space, environment, cultural heritage and communication departments.
5 The first stage aimed to collect qualitative and quantitative data on the perceived negative and positive aspects of the square, along with proposals for its future regeneration (December 2020–February 2021). This goal was operationalised through an online survey questionnaire and 11 online focus groups. In addition, two workshops were organised between the organising team and the GMMM to discuss further the main issues of the square. The second stage concerned an open call for drawings submitted by citizens on the basis of the outputs retrieved from the previous stage (March–June 2021). As the local elections held in September 2021 formalised a new political majority, the Lisbon city council is expected to steer the regeneration of the MMS, the third and last stage of the process.
6 The survey questionnaire collected 1009 responses. Most respondents were 18–50 years old holding higher degrees (Bachelor and/or Master), while less than 1% of participants were under 18 years old and around 11% were less educated people. Eighty-nine percent of respondents were Portuguese, as 11% were from 21 different countries. Focus groups gathered 147 participants and were either scheduled by citizens via the official website or organised by the coordinating team with public and private organisations. One focus group was held with 73 pupils of a primary school close to the MMS.

References

Allegretti, Giovanni (2021) "Common Patterns in Coping with Under-Representation in Participatory Processes: Evidence from a Mutual Learning Space for Portuguese Local Authorities (LAs)" *Innovation: The European Journal of Social Science Research*, 34(5), 729–765

Andretta, Massimiliano; Piazza, Gianni; Subirats, Anna (2015) "Urban dynamics and social movements" *The Handbook of Social Movements*, ed. Donatella della Porta and Mario Diani. New York: Oxford University Press, 201–216

Attoh, Kafui A. (2011) "What kind of right is the right to the city?" *Progress in Human Geography*, 35(5), 669–685

Barnes, Marian, Newman, Janet; Knops, Andrew; Sullivan, Helen (2003) "Constituting 'the public' in public participation" *Public Administration Review*, 81(2), 379–399

Baumgarten, Britta (2013) "Geração à Rasca and beyond: Mobilizations in Portugal after 12 March 2011" *Current Sociology* 61(4), 457–473.

Belda-Miquel, Sergio; Peris Blanes, Jordi; Frediani, Alexandre (2016) "Institutionalization and Depoliticization of the Right to the City: Changing Scenarios for Radical Social Movements"*International Journal of Urban and Regional Research*, 40(2), 321–339

Bua, Adrian; Bussu, Sonia (2020) "Between governance-driven democratisation and democracy-driven governance: Explaining changes in participatory governance in the case of Barcelona" *European Journal of Political Research*, 60(3), 716–737

Castells, Manuel (1983) *The City and the Grassroots: A Cross-cultural Theory of Urban Social Movements*. Berkley: University of California Press

Cornwall, Andrea (2002) "Locating citizen participation" *IDS Bulletin*, 33(2), i–x

De Giorgi, Elisabetta; Moury, Catherine; Ruivo João Pedro (2015) "Incumbents, opposition and international lenders: governing Portugal in times of crisis" *The Journal of Legislative Studies*, 21 (1), 54–74

Della Porta, Donatella (2019) "For participatory democracy: some notes" *European Political Sciences*, 18, 603–616

Della Porta, Donatella; Felicetti (2022) "Innovating democracy against democratic stress in Europe: Social movements and democratic experiments" *Representation Journal of Representative Democracy*, 58(1), 67–84

Falanga, Roberto (2018) "Critical trends of citizen participation in policymaking: Insights from Portugal", *Changing Societies: Legacies and Challenges. Citizenship in Crisis*, ed. Lobo, Marina Costa, Silva, F. C. da, Zúquete, J. P. Lisbon: Imprensa de Ciências Sociais, 295–318

Falanga, Roberto (2020) "Formulating the success of participation in urban regeneration: Insights from Lisbon" *Urban Research and Practice*, 13(5), 477–499

Falanga, Roberto (2022) "Understanding place attachment through the lens of urban regeneration. Insights from Lisbon" *Cities*, 122, 103590

Falanga, Roberto; Ligia H. Lüchmann (2020) "Participatory Budgets in Brazil and Portugal: Comparing Patterns of Dissemination", *Policy Studies*, 41(6), 603–622

Falanga, Roberto; Tulumello Simone (2017) "Portugal and austerity: What European model?" *Centre for Urban Research on Austerity Blog*, available at: https://cura.our.dmu.ac.uk/2017/11/20/portugal-and-austerity-what-european-model/

Falanga, Roberto; Tulumello Simone; Inch, Andy; Alves, Rita; Jorge, Silvia; Kühne, Jannis; Silva, Rita (2019) "The "Caravana pelo Direito à Habitação": Towards a new movement for housing in Portugal?" *Radical Housing Journal*, 1(1), 171–187

Foth, Markus; Brynskov, Martin; Ojala, Timo (eds.) (2015) *Citizen's Right to the Digital City: Urban Interfaces, Activism, and Placemaking*, Singapore: Springer

Fraser, Nancy (1997) *Justice Interruptus: Critical Reflections on the "Postsocialist" Condition*. New York: Routledge

García-Lamarca, Melissa; Anguelovski, Isabelle; Cole, Helen V.S.; Connolly, James J.T.; Pérez-del-Pulgar, Carmen; Shokry, Galia; Triguero-Mas, Margarita (2022) "Urban green grabbing: Residential real estate developers discourse and practice in gentrifying Global North neighborhoods" *GeoForum* 128, 1–10

Harvey, David (2008) "The right to the city", *New Left Review*, 53, 23–40.

Krieger, Morgana G. Martins; Pozzebon, Marlei; Gonzalez, Lauro (2021) "When social movements collaborate with the state towards the right to the city: Unveiling compromises and conflicts" *EPA Economy and Space*, 53(5), 1115–1139

Lefebvre, Henri (1968) *Le droit à la ville*. Paris: Anthropos.

Lefebvre, Henri (1973) *Espace et politique*. Paris: Anthropos.

Lefebvre, Henri (1974) "La production de l'espace", *L'Homme et la société*, 31–32, 15–32

Marcuse, Peter (2009) "From critical urban theory to the right to the city", *City*, 13(2–3), 185–197

Mayer, Margit (2009) "The "Right to the City" in the context of shifting mottos of urban social movements", *City*, 13(2–3), 362–374

Miraftab, Faranak (2020) "Insurgency and Juxtacity in the Age of Urban Divides" *Urban Forum*, 31, 433–441

Mota Consejero, Fabiola and Janoschka, Michael (2022) "Transforming urban democracy through social movements: The experience of Ahora Madrid", *Social Movement Studies*, ahead of print

Moury, Catherine; Standring, Adam (2017) "'Going beyond the Troika': Power and discourse in Portuguese austerity politics" *European Journal of Political Research*, 56(3), 660–679

Polletta, Francesca (2007) "Participatory democracy in social movements" In *Encyclopedia of Sociology*. Hoboken (New Jersey): Wiley-Blackwell.

Polletta, Francesca (2016) "Social movements in an age of participation" *Mobilization: An International Quarterly*, 21, 485–497

Pruijt, Hans (2007) "Urban movements" In *Blackwell Encyclopaedia of Sociology*, ed. George Ritzer. Malden: Blackwell, 5115–5119

Purcell, Mark (2003) "Citizenship and the right to the global city: Reimagining the capitalist world order" *International Journal of Urban Regional Research*, 27, 564–590

Purcell, Mark (2005) "Urban Democracy and the Local Trap" *Urban Studies*, 43(11), 1921–1941

Purcell Mark (2013) "The right to the city: The struggle for democracy in the urban public realm" *Policy & Politics*, 41(3), 311–327

Purcell, Mark (2014) "Possible Worlds: Henri Lefebvre and the Right to the City" *Journal of Urban Affairs*, 36(1), 141–154

Smith, Graham (2009) *Democratic Innovations: Designing Institutions for Citizen Participation*. Cambridge: Cambridge University Press

Subirats, Joan (2011) *Otra sociedad ¿otra política?: De "no nos representan" a la democracia de lo común*. Barcelona: Icaria Asaco

Talpin, Julien (2015) "Democratic innovations" In *The Oxford Handbook of Social Movements*, ed. Donatella della Porta and Mauro Diani. New York: Oxford University Press, 781–792

Uitermark, Justus (2004) "The co-optation of squatters in Amsterdam and the emergence of a movement meritocracy: A critical reply to Pruijt" *International Journal of Urban and Regional Research*, 28(3), 687–698

Valesca, Lima (2019) "The limits of participatory democracy and the inclusion of social movements in local government" *Social Movement Studies*, 18(6), 667–681

9 De-POLARising Civic Participation?
Lessons from the Incomplete Experience of Greenland

Giovanni Allegretti

Introduction

Building on decades of variegated participatory and deliberative practices at different latitudes, in the last decade there has been a broadening in the way democratic innovations (DIs) are defined. Originally viewed as "routinised participation" (Blaug 2002), a growing literature recognised that DIs (1) can originate in different fields and moments of the institutional transformation, which can even imagine some state bodies as a "brand new social movement" (Santos, 2006), but (2) can also take shape as a result of forms of critical democracy (Blaug 2002), through which social movements and local civil society enter local state institutions and try to reshape them, to better respond to bottom-up demands for reforms and rights (Bua & Bussu, 2021).

Hence, as proved by empirical examples in this book, DIs are today imagined as referring both to self-organised and "invented" forms of citizens engagement "by irruption" (Blas & Ibarra, 2006) and to "invited spaces" opened by institutions (Gaventa, 2005). Often, they also emerge as intermedium meeting points between these two generative processes, and as arenas where different tools and governance modes interact (Bouwma et al. 2015; Lascoumes et al., 2011; Lascoumes & Le Gales, 2007), generating larger strategies to produce innovative changes in polities. In fact, the agency which concretely shapes the two main families of participatory arenas that one could gather under the label of "governance-driven democratization" (GDD) or "democracy-driven governance" (DDG) does not necessarily respond to a single logic, often encompassing hybrid dynamics of interaction and mutual learning (Sorice, 2019). Possibly, during the COVID pandemic, the capacity of these two main generative paths to interact grew (Falanga & Allegretti, 2021).

Although the normative orientation of the two main generative paths of participatory and deliberative practices remains different (Bua, 2019; Bussu, 2019), the devices through which GDD and DDG play out are often similar and mutually borrowed (Nez, 2015). An important interpretative support to read their use comes from tracing back which "tipping points" or "inflection points" mark the transition from different modes of introducing meaningful and incisive spaces of social dialogue into the polity domain: in fact, this can help to better examine the dynamic relationship between GDD and DDG and their significative overlapping and mutual transformations (Bua & Bussu, 2021).

This chapter narrates a story which is paradigmatic of how different forms of agency can interact, opening new spaces to gradually shape and enroot democratic innovations in a specific context, where a willing institution accepts to start confronting itself with more radical logics. The peculiar context is Greenland (Kalaallit Nunaat or KN, from now on), a nation and a "constituent country" of the Kingdom of Denmark, which – despite growing self-government capacity (through various reforms between 1979 and 2009) – is still confronted with Danish supremacy in many nonlinear forms and through "distinct contact zones that have emerged through the many encounters between locals and newcomers" (Hastrup, 2019: 243). The case helps to trace how critical democracy (in this case, anticolonial sentiments) can push for a rethinking of top-down DIs and move towards more DDG-like regimes. It also captures how the concept of DDG can be relevant to social movement-led participatory governance beyond material concerns (Della Porta & Felicetti 2019): but it does it in a peculiar context, marked by a scattered panorama of organised social movements and critical voices against the mainstream representative politics.

Departing from an episode that inspired headlines in newspapers worldwide –the unprecedented anticolonial protest against the statue of the missionary Hans Egede, in the summer of 2020 – through an *inductive* approach, the chapter will discuss some of its consequences in reimagining and reshaping the stagnant panorama of democratic innovations in KN.

This chapter will present findings from 37 interviews and focus groups conducted by the author in 2020, as part of a Short-Term Scientific Mission of a COST Action.[1] The views of over 50 protagonists of the local scene of Nuuk – politicians, administrative personnel, religious leaders as well as artists and other activists – help to substantiate a discussion on the limits and challenges of the attempts to institutionalise new forms of social dialogue.[2]

The section "An Anticolonial Protest and Its Follow-Ups" describes the episode of the anticolonial protest and its immediate follow-ups; the section "A 'Turning Point'? Legacies of the Poll on Hans Egede's Statue" addresses the debate in the local community about the directions that these follow-ups could have taken and on what strategies could help respond to diffuse concerns about democracy in KN. The concluding remarks summarise some meaningful dimensions emerging from local voices and a reflection on the contributions that Greenland can offer to the consolidation of the DDG concept.

An Anticolonial Protest and Its Follow-Ups

On June 21st, Kalaallit Nunaat celebrates the day in which (in 2009) the official language changed from Danish to Greenlandic and the KL autonomous government took a new series of responsibilities. On the eve of 21 June 2020, during the wave of protests promoted by the Black Lives Matter movement (Gronholt-Pedersen,

2020: 1), a statue of the missionary Hans Egede in Nuuk was marked with blood-like red paint and the word "decolonize", while the cane carried in the figure's right hand was turned into a whip (Enge, 2020). The episode – a reminder of the remaining tensions between Greenland's mostly indigenous Inuit residents and the former colonisers – happened in a central area of the capital sadly known as "the Colonial Harbour" (Kolonihavnen), which locals prefer to call "Old Nuuk".

The pictures of the landmark statue posted on social media (much used in KN) drew hundreds of mostly approving comments, despite the episode being labelled by mainstream media as an anonymous (hence cowardly) vandalism act.[3] At the time, few public voices (the majority female) spoke out to comment on the episode. Among the most radical, the young member of the Danish Parliament, Aki-Matilda Høegh-Dam (Hills, 2021: 4) described the prominent position of the statue as a provocative "symbol of colonial power", while the tattoo artist Paninnguaq Lind Jensen linked the outcry with the recognition that "Inuit are constantly silenced and never given the opportunity to process the traumas that have been passed down for generations".[4]

Unexpectedly, one of the public figures who took the outcry seriously was the mayor of the Sermersooq municipality (which includes the capital), Charlotte Ludvigsen. Recently entered into office, she organised a referendum-like poll about the destiny of that statue built in 1922 to commemorate the founding of

Figure 9.1 Photo of Hans Egede Statue taken by an anonymous activist on 21 June 2020, defaced with red paint, a graffiti reading "decolonize" and the cane in his right hand transformed into a whip. *Source:* https://kunstkritikk.com/no-coloniser-deserves-to-be-on-top-of-a-mountain

Nuuk. Driven by the "curiosity" to understand why the painting had been carried out, she took advantage of the episode to inaugurate a Service Area and a municipal portal[5] that were almost ready at the time, "where people could express their opinions with words and arguments" (Ludvigsen, 2023). The anticolonial protest appeared as an opportunity to enrich the original scope of the pro-participative platform, initially shaped around the public hearing model used for several years, due to the requirements of planning legislation (ACA4, 2020).

Indeed, the local poll – like many referendum-like processes in KN – was not binding and had a binary formulation, as voters could choose between the removal of the statue or its maintenance. Voting happened mainly online; postal bulletins were also distributed, especially to older residents in hospices. The "instant poll" collected votes between 3 July and 21 July 2020 and was criticised by the local opposition political party, Siumut, for being rushed. It had a relatively low turnout (1,649 votes out of a municipal population of 23,123).[6] Of those who voted, 62% opted to keep the statue and 38% suggested to remove it. Registration on the platform aimed to avoid the phenomena of double voting, which could reduce the credibility of the process, and a clear timeline and a process diagram were published to explain the voting procedure and next steps,[7] if the vote were to be pro-removal (Hills, 2021: 2). Only on the eve of the last voting day was a public event held in the Katuaq Cultural Center, to raise awareness. The workshop's methodology was simple, with small tables to allow participants to feel at ease in discussing the central topic of the poll with other fellow citizens. Several artists took part (including famous singers like the Moroccan/Greenlandic rapper Josef Tarrak-Petrussen), but no provision was taken for enriching the deliberative quality, for example through the interaction of experts with different positions.

The Council committed to ratifying whatever decision would be indicated by voters, no matter the quorum reached. The ratification occurred in early September 2020 in an "undramatic Municipal Council vote" (Hyldal, 2020) without any debate. The online discussion pages and the town hall meeting created to facilitate the community discussion were lively and well used, although an even more lively confrontation occurred on social networks and in spaces that were possibly considered by citizens as more neutral and reliable than those offered by political/administrative bodies. The mayor herself – noticing the younger generation was generally leaning towards removal – suggested that such a debate should be continued beyond the end of the poll (Hills, 2021: 7). Despite the formal decision to maintain the statue where it still stands, the referendum increased the debate on Hans Egede's legacy, and Greenlandic authorities later decided not to celebrate the 300-year anniversary of his arrival to Greenland on 3 July 1721.[8]

The consolidation of the Municipal Platform for Civic Dialogue "Kommuneqarfiga" (whose motto is "The Municipality of Sermersooq is listening to you. Now it's your turn to be heard!") advanced at a fast pace, reaching more than 5,000 registered users in 1 year (almost 1/3 of Nuuk population) and improving its privacy policies and users' rights. An official presentation of the restructuring at the end of August 2020 unveiled a new important section, allowing citizens to make proposals in any area of municipal competence and committing the City Council to discuss officially any idea which reaches 250 signatures of support within 90 days. Proposals of debates on city transformations are filed and displayed on the platform both by the city administration (there were 15 debates between July 2020 and August 2022, of which 4 were still open at the time this chapter was closed) and by individual citizens and groups (6 proposals were presented in the same time-frame[9]). Each proposal has a clear space for fostering debate and receives official feedback and justifications at any stage of formal decisions made by the elected representatives.

Until now, the majority of dialogues are related to town planning transformations. So, they look at an extension of the "public hearings" required by legislation as a formal step for every decision in planning policies. As for now, the memory of the referendum on Hans Egede's statue is the only process with broader implications related to cultural issues, and it still appears to be the "hottest topic", as it collected a number of comments higher than the sum of all those received on other debates.[10]

In March 2021, on the eve of local and national elections, the city administration approved the "Strategy for Citizens Involvement"[11], which includes the platform, and will be gradually implemented over the new political mandate. Other public services linked to the municipal government contributed to extending the scope of pre-existing forms of social dialogue to more complex and contentious topics, such as those related to coloniality, memory, reconciliation and social asymmetries. For example, following the anticolonial protest, the Katersugaasivik Nuutoqaq (Nuuk Lokalmuseum) hosted important exhibitions on "hot topics", accompanied by public debates[12], which demonstrated how hard it was to speak out in public on conflictual issues, especially for the youngest. Activists convinced the museum administration to organise some workshops about "the difficulties of being an activist in the specific environment of Nuuk and Greenland in general" (ADM4, 2020). The Nuuk Art Museum displayed a collection on "Art of Nordic Colonialism" in collaboration with Danish-Caribbean artists, giving continuity to previous events co-organised with the "Nuuk Nordic Culture Festival" and the Ilisimatusarfik (University of Greenland) as part of a research project intended to counterbalance "the pervasive lack of awareness of colonial history typical of the Nordic self-image" (Enge, 2019).

Although establishing a clear cause–effect relation between the multiplication of institutionally led events and similar bottom-up initiatives is difficult, a visible acceleration took place on both sides. The opening of new institutional spaces of debate became a pivotal reference point for informal groups that took shape as a response to the protest around the statue. Among them, one can quote the association "Nalik Kalaallit Nunaat" (Haahr Pedersen, 2021a) founded in the wake of the debate on Hans Egede's statue to put decolonisation on the agenda to work "towards an independent future", moving from debates with a practical orientation – as the abandonment of food traditions and against the import of products produced in KN. To "connect the dots" with the revolutionary work of the music group Sume – which, in the 1970s, had put art at the forefront of education to freedom and awareness of coloniality (Silis Hoegh, 2014) – the new group focuses on the belief that in the decolonisation process "no one else speaks on one's behalf", emphasising direct citizens' participation. A second example regards the "Inuit Nutaat" collective, a recent-born group of activists who describe themselves as non-partisan ordinary citizens. Stating that "many of the challenges we face in our society are rooted in the fact that we are not treated as equals", they try to imagine a "new normal" centred on talking "constructively and respectfully and future-oriented about the next steps for Kalaallit Nunaat".[13] Among the goals of such organisations, there is that of becoming "ambassadors for decolonizing the environmental movement" (MOV4, 2020), also through discussing how much added dependence was brought to KN by international mainstream environmentalist campaigns (such as those against whale and seal hunting). Different types of collectives are also gaining visibility and protagonism through youth-led action. This is the case of "Greenland4Nature"[14], created by four young women who – in September 2020 – organised public workshops on "What is the youth's stand on biodiversity in KN", involving in the dialogue the KN national government (Nukappiaaluk, 2020). In domains valuing art for social change, a youth Group Theatre was created in Tasiilaq (situated in the far-eastern part of Semersooq municipality) by a young intersexual director, to face with young peers the taboo topics of family violence and youth suicide, imagining forms of community participation led by artistic performances.

A "Turning Point"? Legacies of the Poll on Hans Egede's Statue

KN is a large nation with low-density urbanisation, whose 57,000 inhabitants concentrate in small settlements along the coastal line and fjords. Geographical constraints and sociocultural traditions require us to take into adequate account peculiar ways to structure the concept of "leadership", the challenges posed by the dynamics of social self-control that characterise small settlements, and other factors like the importance of oral culture in the transmission of values and traditions. Therefore, struggle repertoires of civil society differ from those usually existing in denser countries and in large urban/metropolitan milieus. The harsh climate makes inter-settlement connections difficult, which in turn increases the isolation of micro-societies. In this perspective, some problems linked to the management of everyday life (such as the scarcity of spare parts for production machinery, the slowness and high costs of ordinary maintenance) acquire a more important dimension than in other contexts and can become a "strategic" focus of citizens attention in participatory settings, as they are central for the quality of their daily lives. Political-administrative relations with the Danish Kingdom, and their economic interdependence, add complexity to this panorama.

These intertwined aspects configure the risk that KN could be seen by inhabitants as "the Land of Retaliation and potential blackmailing by part of a small group of powerful agents" (MOV5, 2020), which suggests that the majority of citizens keep a low profile in public debates. Such aspects also explain why – traditionally – the people who dared to speak out in public spaces, were mainly belonging to aged social groups, and "the majority of activists are elderly persons, often retired: people who have nothing to lose and may express themselves with more freedom" (MOV5, 2020). However, things are gradually changing and the youth, whose recruitment opportunities often depend on mainland Denmark and foreign enterprises, are starting to become more visible in the public sphere. Partially, an anchor for such transformation is provided by those social networks which seem to partially provide a "safe forum" for active and collaborative engagement (Skjervedal, 2018).

Indeed, in the decade following the conquest of further degrees of political-administrative autonomy and decentralisation (2009), Kalaallit Nunaat "saw a gradual growth in the centrality of citizens involvement in public policies", although it is not yet "a pivot around which governance frameworks are being reshaped" (ADM2, 2020). As several authors stressed, in a nation highly pressured by international political and economic interests in its natural resources (Breum, 2021a, 2018, 2015), the direct involvement of citizens in policy-making is somehow kept at the margins, almost becoming one of the cross-cutting "sacrifice zones" (Rasmussen & Gjertsen, 2018) of national democracy. This is true for a different range of issues, which includes environmental-sensitive territorial transformations and decisions on mining exploitation[15] (Pelaudeix et al., 2017; Hansen et al., 2016), such as the work of the Constitutional Committee[16] (McGwin, 2020). The joint report "To the Benefit of Greenland", produced in 2014 by the Universities of Greenland and of Copenhagen, pointed to a massive lack of transparency in decision-making processes, especially when it comes to natural resource management, and it advocated for more comprehensive and earlier citizen involvement in decision-making. Calls for greater public participation have grown along with Greenland's increased political autonomy from Denmark, remarking that the joint interests of the two political apparatus on delicate sectors have certain "conservative elements" (Rasmussen & Gjertsen, 2018: 201), which contribute to their maintenance and continuity, but also prevent innovation towards a more open social management of resources and economic development at the national and local level.

Some traditional characteristics of the participatory approaches in KN have remained unchallenged also after the change of majority in 2021, when KN moved to the left, and the experience accumulated at local level by similar coalitions (as is the case of Nuuk) could have become a significant starting point for a gradual restructuring of citizens participation. One can say that path dependence remains significant (Hansen, 2016), and few creative forms of structured social dialogue potentially involving individual citizens have been experimented in the last two years. This immovability is not symmetrical in all sectors. For example, in a country where almost 50,000 out of 57,000 inhabitants maintain close ties with their Inuit origin (IWGIA, 2022; IWGIA/IIPFWH/IPACC, 2022), participation in the protection of material and immaterial heritage has shifted, in line with international practice, to better involve indigenous population. This is proved by the ongoing process for structuring a new UNESCO heritage area linked to hunting traditions in Tasiilaq (a settlement of Semmersoq distant from Nuuk).

What are the main unchallenged characteristics of the prevalent participatory formats adopted in KN? The interviews conducted among civic organisations and political-administrative actors converge on this: (1) all experienced processes are consultative, and people's inputs – requested as a pre-requirement by governmental planning procedures – are usually collected in advanced phases of the decisional procedures, when the option of abandoning the project or the policy is hardly a real option. (2) The contributions from stakeholders are collected prevalently through written statements, expected to express well-justified and expert-grounded points of view. Such "cold spaces" of consultation can barely be viewed as interactions and hardly offer open and collective spaces for confrontation. This reveals the prevalence of GDD forms of participation, whose conception and coordination remain in the hand of institutional actors. In rare cases, a more output-oriented approach matches the rhetoric related to the creation of participatory spaces with formal tools of direct democracy, which have been rarely (although successfully) used to support important decisions on the future of the country – as in the case of the referenda for leaving the European Community (1985) and for the confirmation of the Self-Ruling Agreement (November 2008). In such occasions, the rhetoric centred on civic participation clashed with the tools used, presenting mere Yes/No options.

Given such a stagnant/inertial panorama, what are the potential contributions that the anticolonial protest could have suggested to ignite and consolidate a meaningful switch? Players located in civil society, the artistic milieu and the mass media in Nuuk concentrate attention on three key dimensions of the episode and its legacies:

1) the protest can be observed as a "vandalic act", or through the lens of an act of "irruption" or "disruption", a bottom-up and unexpected form to conquer visibility (Blas & Ibarra, 2006) which uses artistic repertoires for catching larger attention, without generating permanent and irreversible damages to the material artefacts involved. The latter vision was chosen by the mayor and other supporters of the following debate; but, there was not enough reflection on the repertoires of the "irruption act", which could have helped to shape the poll as a variable geometry of differentiated actions to optimise its provocative capacity of fostering a larger engagement of the local community.

2) the episode showed the possibility to trigger new procedures of participation, anchored to a DDG perspective, and based on the will of an institutional actor to build on the anxieties and priorities expressed by traditionally under-represented voices, in order to open a "virtuous circle" of multiple interactions with society. Nevertheless, the courage of mayor Ludvigsen in responding quickly to the anticolonial protest, so to leverage a public debate on the symbolic destiny of the statue, only partially revealed the capacity of a public administration to abandon its comfort zones (composed of stiff and codified tools of public consultation) and expand the possibility of meaningful and sustainable dialogue with citizens.

3) the "tipping point" that triggered a change of perspective in the political agency anchored to the KN isolation deepened by the pandemic emergency, which catalysed the attention of many citizens on the cultural values and opportunities of

a nation that often underestimates its potential. Many convergent debates in KN, during 2020, brought to the surface cultural and post-colonial topics, which are reflected also in the anticolonial protest referred to here. The latter was capable to provoke a reflection which – simultaneously – goes beyond material concerns (Della Porta & Felicetti, 2019) but also embeds strong concrete issues related to power distribution, Eurocentric supremacy, employment and epistemicides (Santos, 2014).

Indeed, the respectful approach that the Semmersoq Mayor adopted in commenting on (and building on) the anticolonial protest had broader potential than the consequences that followed. For example, an imprudent public statement from Mrs. Ludvigsen changed some rules of the poll during the course of the voting procedures, lowering the credibility of the process and the trust of some potential participants. Possibly, the critics of such a mistake benefited the configuration of future rules for the Kommuneqarfiga portal, which today appears "more rigorous, clear and reliable for users" (ACA3, 2020). Indeed, the municipality capitalised on some critics. For example, several councillors and civic groups requested that the poll should end with a face-to-face event and a drawing competition on "how the mountain top of the future should look like?".[17] Both suggestions were accomplished, even if in a rush. Instead, a still unchallenged limitation refers to the centrality of the platform, a contested dimension of the new offer of participatory arenas in Sermersooq, despite the efforts made in 2021 to improve security protocols and clarify data storage and privacy policies. Possibly, the reasons why limiting the offer of participation to online tools is criticised rely on two factors. The first refers to the prevalence of the written dimensions on the oral and visual ones, which would better match the Inuit culture. The second is the consequence of a slow-evolving and complex panorama of tense relations between Greenlanders and the use of technology as a form of domination. As shown by recent literature (Møller Jørgensen, 2017; Doel et al., 2016; Hansen, 2003), in KN the process to shape a national platform service that supports political institutions and administrative services has been slow and incomplete, mostly relying on Danish-based operators. Hence, a "visible mistrust surrounds the black-boxes of ICTs in the country, as if they could favour control and blackmailing by part of powerful gatekeepers" (ACA7, 2020). In the case of the poll on Egede's statue – as remarked by the rapper Tarrak-Petrussen (in Allegretti, 2022) – the lack of accuracy in shaping online devices could have generated a spreading fear "of being controlled", preventing the new website to create "spaces where people feel safe in expressing their opinions": that is why, the debates on private social networks appeared freer and more intense than the process promoted by the mayor.

Establishing cause–effect relations between the local poll on Egede's statue and the following transformations of the new Kommuneqarfiga portal is not easy. The polling process was formally built as a consultative arena, but – from a substantive point of view – was shaped as an almost-codecisional space, as far as the municipal administration committed to ratifying whatever decision was going to emerge from the vote. In light of the critics that the polling process received, it proved to be an important learning opportunity for institutional and civic appraisal. As such, DDG characteristics become evident, and the contribution that the anticolonial protest offered to increasing the quality of the participatory platform that was already under construction was a joint effort of civil society and local institutions which cooperated in making the effects of this short episode of irruption more "permanent".

The absence of *forms of co-design with future users* has been considered a missing element in the poll on Egede's statue and – until now – has not been overcome by the conception of the participatory tools provided by the "Kommuneqarfiga" portal. The majority of participatory instruments used in Nuuk still look organiser driven rather than citizens oriented. To address the risk that such an approach could reduce the attractivity, legitimacy and potential impact of participatory processes, co-designing tools and methods with active citizens could play a positive role and reinforce DDG-like ambitions. Eventually, it could lead to a major politicisation of the discourse on the platform itself, putting under discussion its ethical protocols and procedures, the sovereignty of data, as well as the construction of a community of developers around the platform, who could increase its liveability, resilience and adaptivity to citizens' needs (Bussu et al., 2022a). At the moment, the new municipal "Strategy for Citizen Involvement", approved on March 2021[18], does not propose formal steps to go in this direction, and it does not give attention to monitoring and evaluation as a key step for improving the panoply of devices envisaged and their coordination.

Given this incomplete capitalisation of previous experiences by the Semmersoq municipality, the question of how the present transformations can be scaled at higher levels of the KN Self-ruling Government (Naalakkersuisut) remains an exercise in rhetoric. As for now, we do not know yet if the new left-wing government elected in April 2021, which is led by Inuit Ataqatigiit (AI), the party of the Nuuk's mayor (Breum, 2021b) will show greater commitment to promoting and championing participatory and deliberative democracy processes.

An Open Conclusion

Successful participatory initiatives rarely grow in a vacuum (Smith & Martin, 2021) but germinate over a long period of grassroots and institutional activity and as a result of an organic culture of democratic exchange and experimentation among different actors, which often include tensions and mechanisms of action–reaction–counteraction. Contexts and conjunctures can provide differentiated support to the incremental evolution of such dynamics and favour (or not) transitions between modes of citizen engagement that respond more to GDD- or DDG-like logics.

This chapter focussed on a context which is rather unusual to encounter in the literature on citizen engagement and DIs. In fact, Kalaallit Nunaat is often ignored as a self-ruling constituent nation and a political-institutional significant environment by many international indexes and mapping exercises.[19] Yet, the complicated situation of its recent "colonial moment" (Hastrup, 2019) is widely recognised as a paradigmatic example, especially for the ambiguities concerning the rights, autonomy and sociocultural imbalances that refers to its large indigenous population (IWGIA, 2020, 2021).

Looking to KN as a "South-of-the-North" nation and a semi-peripheral democracy marked by the presence of deep "abyssal lines" (Santos, 2014) that unbalance the capabilities of, and the power relation among different ethnic, age and gender groups which constitutes its population, one must recognise that there is a long way to go, in order to increase the quality of the ecosystem of participatory and deliberative tools (Boni et al., 2019), through an interaction between invited and invented spaces (Bussu, 2019). Indeed, literature about governance and participation in KN highlights the inadequate nature of the participatory spaces opened until now, in terms of quality of deliberation and capacity of attracting the majority of the indigenous population – especially the youth – and valuing their knowledge (Dahl & Hansen, 2019). Yet, a consistent network of civic actors is also lacking, who could impact polity by presenting skilled and organically developed proposals for reimagining goals and reshaping methods for fostering major civic engagement in public decision-making. Thus, talking about the existence of a consistent DDG-like approach able to impact institutional behaviour, would sound disproportionate. This is true even if its capital Nuuk shows higher levels of experimentation in the field of citizen participation. Indeed, KN remains hovering between the presence of a growing number of institutionalised tools for guaranteeing citizens the right of having their voice heard by institutions and a visible incapacity of granting effectiveness – and therefore attractiveness, credibility and authoritativeness – to such arenas.

The anticolonial protest against Hans Egede's statue in June 2020 was a spark, an outcry from the margins and a way through which some actors (traditionally absent from the polity scene) claimed the need to switch public debate to re-embed topics often neglected in the invited spaces of participation existing in KN. Such form of "irruption" – read from a multiculturalist perspective – qualified demands for autonomy from indigenous communities (Martí & Sanahuja, 2005; Sieder, 2002), and a quest for new methodological endeavours that allow them to participate, in a different way and with a newly recognised protagonism, in the elaboration of strategic policies (Blas & Ibarra, 2006: 16). Although the authors of the statue's painting remained anonymous, their action brought together a community of different actors (activists, artists, some national and local politicians and bureaucrats) who wished to contribute to imagining proactive "consequences" for the sake of Nuuk governance system and its future developments.

Two key factors guaranteed positive impacts:

1) this unorganised community chose to interact with a specific institution (the Nuuk's mayor) using the irruption episode to question some limits of existing participatory procedures, exactly when the Sermersooq municipality was building its new participatory strategy.

2) those who more actively participated in the debate on the statue also exposed their critical views on the limits of the referendum-like poll and its reduced capacity to challenge and overcome the poor deliberation quality of other traditional channels. Thus, they acted as independent watchdogs for the

process, providing monitoring and evaluation procedures which had not been established by the municipality. In this perspective, the main critics were that a traditional referendum-like approach polarised positions and lowered the deliberative quality of the process and its potential to trigger a deeper analysis of the underlying conflict. Some activists wondered whether it could have been possible to leave space for third ways: for example, imagining art inventions that could provoke a more permanent debate (using the statue's basement for locating explanatory plates with different visions on the figure of Egede, or the counter-presence of art-works that could reinforce the visibility of Inuit culture vis-à-vis the colonisers' supremacy) instead of reducing the process to a stay-or-go dilemma. Such modalities would have better reflected the cultural peculiarities of the Greenlandic milieu, which privileges orality, humour, art and body language (Tarrak-Petrussen in Allegretti, 2022).

If politics is an "above all relationship" (Blas & Ibarra, 2006: 23), the collective action that maintained alive the flame lit by the anticolonial protest demonstrated that Nuuk's social fabric had developed. Building on Subirats (2005), one could say that the fact of "not simply challenging conventional politics", but also "working within the limits of what is conventional" paved a path to reinforce the "spaces of autonomy" of social actors, pointing out which participatory methods could be strengthened in the future, as useful to grant "more power to them" and not "(just) to further legitimize institutions" (id, p. 8). Therefore, the episode described in this chapter had a maieutic dimension, acting as a catalyst/accelerator to influence the growth of a mutual dialogue between a scattered and semi-unorganised group of stakeholders and the local institutions, influencing the degree of awareness (and mobilisation) of both about the need of rethinking the range of participatory practices in a more DDG-like perspective. It shows that irruptions can be one pathway towards DDG.

Two years later, results still show ambiguities, but the system of participatory spaces consolidated in the Sermersooq municipality (those formally enrooted, and the more fluid spaces designed by other actors, such as the local museums) demonstrates acknowledgement of the anticolonial protest and its follow-ups. The Kommuneqarfiga portal is still a stiff space, designed by commercial intermediaries, but it is gradually incorporating some requests that emerged from the debate on the statue. In this perspective, the anticolonial spark was not a change of paradigm, but it represented a step towards sustainable changes. This is not meaningless, for a context where – until a few years ago – an approach to "ocular democracy" (Green, 2010), and a long tradition of passivity and disenchantment (Hansen, 2016) prevailed.

If we wonder which is the direction pointed out by local actors to give continuity to what happened in 2020, the answer points to what Asenbaum and Hanusch (2021: 1) defined as "democratic playgrounds and democratic ateliers", i.e. participatory spaces that value "playfulness and creativity as two aspects that established democratic innovations rarely incorporate". Rather than focussing on output-oriented DIs for expected change, these spaces prefer "a logic of democratic serendipity, an exploratory, open-ended mode of participatory engagement, which promises to open democracy for unexpected change" (ibid.). In such approaches, oriented towards building a throughput legitimacy (Iusmen & Boswell, 2016), serious gaming and critical artistic practices can generate "prefigurative" settings (Lerner, 2014, p. 42) that go beyond discursive expression, where immersive and embodied performances engage sensations, emotions and actions in novel formations (Lester, 2013: 28). This can help explore "a crucial dimension of the radical democratic project" (Mouffe, 2007: 6).

In a tense post-colonial conjuncture where it is important to not replicate the power dynamics of the larger societal context they are situated in (Hastrup, 2019), such approaches could better unfold the agentic potential of participants, and its interconnections with new forms of inclusion and transparency (a traditionally missing link in KN).

New formats of participation need to incorporate non-Western forms of play and arts (Asenbaum & Hanusch, 2021: 9), to tackle and overcome profound structural inequalities and epistemic injustice, and to rescue different structural meanings of participation as a "way of everyday living", and not only as a dimension of political confrontation (Allegretti et al., 2022: 66). Thus, future participatory arenas in KN need to be more sensitive to cultural diversity and learn from experiences around the world (Gaskins, Haight, & Lancy, 2007). The critics that followed the poll on Egede's statue implicitly stressed the need for joint planning of participatory formats and their monitoring and assessment. In fact, co-design and a gradual and permanent replanning of participatory spaces with targeted participants appear as a precondition for better responding to their needs, guaranteeing the creation of new comfort zones that make them feel at ease in the process and stimulate their gradually growing involvement (Saward, 2021). This seems particularly necessary for the technological dimension, provided the centrality given to the Kommuneqarfiga portal: components of further anonymisation (Asembaum, 2018; Ruesch & Märker, 2012) could play as a means to favour the attractiveness, credibility and authoritativeness of a device that – conversely – can appear as a dangerous "black box" which clip out the public commitment of the most fragile societal groups.

Explicit efforts for co-designing future spaces of participation could be seen also as a leverage that contributes to reconfiguring current societal and political organisations to produce alternative futures (Bussu et al., 2022a). This is, somehow, the main disruptive contribution provided by the irruptive action of June 2020 – and its DDG-oriented follow-ups.

This case constitutes a *largely incomplete experiment*. In fact, the institutional methodological proposal to manage an orderly public debate on the anticolonial protest lacked creativity, being not oriented towards epistemic goals, and substantially aligned with a referendum that "polarized" opinions around binary choices, giving to "voting" excessive weight compared to the value and the space recognised to deliberation. Additionally, it did not commit to conducting any assessment or evaluation, which could help to build new developments out of the lessons learned. A recent dialogue between some European universities and local organisations (addressed to organise seminars to improve KN local knowledge about participatory and deliberative methodologies and tools)[20] might constitute a promising space to co-design future practices marked by higher levels of embeddedness (Bussu et al., 2022b). These could help engage with the expectations of different actors, preventing elite manipulation of participatory energy.

Summarising, social movement-led participatory governance in Kalaallit Nunaat is still a "mirage", but the interventions of social groups giving an opinion on the quality and the challenges of the invited processes of social dialogue are growing in intensity and frequency (as exemplified by radical informal groups such as "Angisunnguaq Qujanaq" or "Inuit Nutaat"). They claim a switch from an organisers-driven range of institutionalised tools for civic engagement to more participant-oriented ones.

The word pun in the title of this chapter ("dePOLARizing participation") has a precise meaning. It recalls the need to reduce the polarisation which today characterises the panorama of practices of social dialogue in KN, with a neat prevalence of top-down processes "by invitation" and of binary referendum-like procedures which do not forge proper spaces for the emergence of "third-way" solutions to deal with conflicts. At the same time, to reach these goals, a "re-polarization" of participatory/deliberative processes is required. This means reembedding the DIs both in the specificities of a "polar environment" (i.e., the constraints of low-density places) and the peculiarities of the sociocultural milieu of Kalaallit Nunaat, marked by high inequalities and power imbalances, epistemic injustice and contentious legacies of the colonial construction of the national identity (Gad, 2009).

Acknowledgements

This article was made possible by the Short-Term Scientific Mission (STSM) "Arctic perspectives on citizens engagement: the incomplete experience of Greenland", funded by COST ACTION "Constitution-making and deliberative democracy" (CA17135). PHOENIX project, funded by the Horizon 2020 programme (grant agreement N. 101037328), also contributed. Gratitude goes to all interviewees, to Javier Arnaut (University of Iceland) and Runa Svaert (Sermersooq Municipality), but also to Ruth Ann Montgomery-Andersen and Priscila Delgado Carvalho (who helped to review and shorten the article). I thank the editors of this book, Adrian Bua and Sonia Bussu, whose patience proved a real interest in this contribution. Draft versions benefited from the comments made by participants of events organized by the International Political Science Association, the Interpretive Policy Analysis network, the International Arctic Social Sciences Association and the European Consortium of Political Research.

Notes

1 The Short Term Scientific Mission dedicated to analyse the case here described was part of a COST Action entitled, "Constitution-making and deliberative democracy" (CA17135), an interdisciplinary research network that brings researchers and innovators together to investigate experiences related to the construction of democratic inno-

150 Giovanni Allegretti

vations in different countries, with particular attention to those involving citizens on topics related to central constitutional values.
2. The quotes report statements of 51 interviewed persons, safeguarding anonymity. ACA identifies members of the KN academic community; ART a variegated group of artists; POL local/national politicians; MED local and Greenlandic media system; and MOV activists.
3. The Greenlandic artist Aqqalu Berthelsen (Uyarakq) was chosen to pass on an anonymous statement from the group responsible: "It is about time that we stop celebrating colonisers and that we start taking back what is rightfully ours. It's time to decolonise our minds and our country. No coloniser deserves to be on top of a mountain like that. We need to learn the truth of our history" (Enge, 2020). Berthelsen – who lives in Inari, Finland, argued for years that all statues of Egede ought to be removed.
4. https://www.facebook.com/paninnguaq.jensen (Gronholt-Pedersen, 2020: 1).
5. https://kommuneqarfiga.sermersooq.gl/da-DK/.
6. This number includes also the inhabitants of the farer parts of the municipal territory (as Tasiilaq) and the persons without voting age. In Nuuk, in 2020, inhabitants were 18,000.
7. https://kommuneqarfiga.sermersooq.gl/da-DK/projects/hans-egede-statuen-1/5.
8. The municipality had taken in 2019 the decision to divert elsewhere the 2.7 million kr. for celebrations. But the emphasis used by the mayor to confirm the measure in the 2021 Budget Plan was stronger than before the protest (Haahr Pedersen, 2021b).
9. https://kommuneqarfiga.sermersooq.gl/da-DK/initiatives.
10. They were 160 in September 2022. See https://kommuneqarfiga.sermersooq.gl/da-DK/projects/hans-egede-statuen-1/5.
11. Strategi for Borgerinddragelse: https://sermersooq.fra1.digitaloceanspaces.com/wp-content/uploads/2021/03/03132459/Borger-dk.pdf.
12. The project "Qimmeq" related to the historical importance and disappearance of sled dogs (Meldgaard, 2020); another described the demolition of "Blok P" social housing (Doel et al., 2016; Jensen & Diemer, 2014); the exhibition of the architect/photographer Peter Barfoed targeted abandoned villages of Grønnedal and Ivittuut (Brogaard Buhl, 2018).
13. http://inuitnutaat.org.
14. https://www.facebook.com/Greenland4Nature-105966731275165/.
15. From 2013 to early 2022, only 15 public hearings occurred at national level – usually on mining projects and environmental plans; two happened in 2021, during and immediately after the election of April 2021 (Consultation Archive of the Greenlandic Self-Government).
16. https://ina.gl/udvalg/lovpligtige-og-staaende-udvalg/forfatningskommissionen/?lang=en.
17. Opened until 10 August 2020, its results (never exposed in public) were sent to council members before their final decision.
18. https://sermersooq.fra1.digitaloceanspaces.com/wp-content/uploads/2021/03/03132459/Borger-dk.pdf.
19. The Freedom House reports include Greenland in Full Democracies as part of Denmark (https://freedomhouse.org); the Democracy Index by the Economist Intelligence Unit (EIU – https://www.eiu.com) shows NO DATA; the International IDEA only shows few data about Legal provisions for mandatory and optional referenda at national level (https://www.idea.int/data-tools/country-view/113/45).
20. Within the "PHOENIX" EU-funded project (www.phoenix-horizon.eu), the Centre for Social Studies of Coimbra University – in May 2022 – started to plan a series of event, together with some representative of the University of Greenland, the Bahá'í community of Nuuk and some other social collectives.

References

Allegretti, G. (2022). "Viaggio in Groenlandia". *Urbanistica Informazioni*, 305 (forthcoming)

Allegretti, G.; Meloni, M.; Dorronsoro, B. (2022). "Civic participation as a travelling ideoscape. Which direction?". In Mkoni, S.; Kaiper-Marquez, A.; Mokwena, L. (eds., 2022), *The Routledge Handbook of Language and the Global South/s*. Routledge, 57–71

Asenbaum, H. (2018). "Anonymity and Democracy: Absence as Presence in the Public Sphere". *The American Political Science Review*, 112(3), 459–472

Asenbaum, H.; Hanusch, F. (2021). "(De)futuring democracy: Labs, playgrounds, and ateliers as democratic innovations". *Futures*, 134. https://doi.org/10.1016/j.futures.2021.102836

Blas, A.; Ibarra, P. (2006)."La participación: Estado de la cuestión". *Cuadernos Hegoa*, 39, 5–35

Blaug, R. (2002). "Engineering democracy". *Political Studies*, 50(1), 102–116

Boni, A.; López-Fogués, A.; Fernández-Baldor, A.; Millan, G.; & Belda-Miquel, S.; (2019). "Initiatives towards a participatory smart city. The role of digital grassroots innovations." *Journal of global ethics*. 15:2, 168–182.

Bouwma, I.M.; Gerritsen, A.L.; Kamphorst, D.; Kistenkas, F. (2015). *Policy Instruments and Modes of Governance in Environmental Policies of the European Union*. Statutory Research Tasks Unit for Nature & the Environment

Breum, M. (2015). *The Greenland Dilemma*. Royal Danish Defence College

Breum, M. (2018). *Cold Rush. The Astonishing True Story of the New Quest for the Polar North*. McGill-Queen's University Press

Breum, M. (2021a). *Grønland og den amerikanske forbindelse*. Gyldendal

Breum, M. (2021b)."Greenland's new leadership will be challenged by a push for faster Independence". *Arctic Today*, 9/4/2021

Brogaard Buhl, A. (2018). *Grønnedal Arctic Resort Feasibility Study*. Arsuk Fjord Real Estate IVS

Bua, A. (2019). "Democratic innovations and the policy process". In Elstub, S.; Escobar, O. (eds), *Handbook of Democratic Innovation and Governance*. Edward Elgar, 282–296

Bua, A.; Bussu, S. (2021). "Between governance-driven democratisation and democracy-driven governance: Explaining changes in participatory governance in the case of Barcelona". *EJPR*, 60, 716–737

Bussu, S. (2019). "Collaborative governance: Between invited and invented spaces". In Elstub, S.; Escobar, O. (eds), *Handbook of Democratic Innovation and Governance*. Edward Elgar, 60–76

Bussu, S.; Bua, A.R.; Dean, R.; Smith, G. (2022a). "Introduction: Embedding participatory governance". *Critical Policy Studies* 16(2), 133–145

Bussu, S.; Golan, Y.; Hargreaves, A. (2022b). *Understanding Developments in Participatory Governance*. Report of Manchester Metropolitan University

Dahl, P.; Hansen, A. (2019). "Does indigenous knowledge occur in and influence impact assessment reports? Exploring consultation remarks in three cases of mining projects in Greenland". *Arctic Review on Law and Politics*, 10, 165–189

Della Porta, D.; Felicetti, A. (2019). "Innovating democracy against democratic stress in Europe: Social movements and democratic experiments". *Representation*, 58(1), 67–84

Doel, R.; Harper; K.; Heymann, M. (2016, eds.). *Exploring Greenland: Cold War Science and Technology on Ice*. Palgrave Macmillan

Enge, M. (2019). "Lions in the Arctic". *Kunstkritikk/Nordic Art Review*, 11/11/2019, https://kunstkritikk.com/lions-in-the-arctic/

Enge, M. (2020). 'No coloniser deserves to be on top of a mountain'. *Kunstkritikk/Nordic Art Review*, 22/06/2020, https://kunstkritikk.com/no-coloniser-deserves-to-be-on-top-of-a-mountain/

Falanga, R.; Allegretti, G. (2021). "Democracia participativa em tempos de covid-19: A procura de uma nova ritualização". In Mota Almeida, L.F.; Ferreira Ramos, M.; de Sousa, L. (eds), *Poder local em tempos de Covid-19- Vol.1*. Almedina, 63–95.

Gad, U. (2009). "Post-colonial identity in Greenland?: When the empire dichotomizes back — Bring politics back in". *Journal of Language and Politics*, 8, 136–158

Gaskins, S.; Haight, W.; Lancy, D.F. (2007). "The cultural construction of play". In Göncü, A; Gaskins, S. (Eds.) *Play and Development: Evolutionary, Sociocultural, and Functional Perspectives*. Erlbaum, 179–202.

Gaventa, J. (2005). "Reflections of the uses of the 'power cube'". *CFP Evaluation Series*, 4, pp.1–46

Green, J. (2010). *The Eyes of the People: Democracy in an Age of Spectatorship*. New York: Oxford University Press

Gronholt-Pedersen, J. (2020). "A statue in Greenland is marked with anti-colonial statements". *Arctic Today*, 22/06/2020

Haahr Pedersen, S. (2021a). "Ny forening: Vi skal reflektere over 300-års kolonihistorie". *KNR*, 06/01/2021

Haahr Pedersen, S. (2021b). "Nuuk dropper al markering af 300-året for Hans Egedes ankomst". *KNR*, 26/01/2021

Hansen, A.; Vanclay, F.; Croal, P.; Skjervedal, A.-S. (2016). "Managing the social impacts of the rapidly-expanding extractive industries in Greenland". *The Extractive Industries and Society*, 3(1), 25–33

Hansen, K.G. (2003). "ICT, citizenship and democracy in Greenland". In L. Pekkala, L. Kullerud, & O. Snellman (Eds.), *Bridging the digital divide: sharing best practices for developing ICT in the rural areas of the north and south: Proceedings of the SCOPE-UARCTIC workshop 09-12 may, Mpumalanga, South Africa*, (ppNIHE, . 60–66).

Hansen, K.G. (2016). *Fra passiv iagttager til aktiv deltager*. PhD Thesis, Aalborg University

Hastrup, K. (2019). "Colonial moments in Greenland: Mutable tensions in the contact zone". *Itinerario*, 43(2), 243–261

Hills, T. (2021). "Hans Egede statue. Nuuk, Kalaallit Nunaat, Greenland". *Contested Histories. EUROCLIO Case Study n. 27*, 1–11, https://contestedhistories.org/wp-content/uploads/Greenland_-Hans-Egede-Statue-in-Nuuk.pdf

Hyldal, C. (2020). "Lokalpolitikere nikkede ja: Hans Egede-statuen rokker sig ikke en centimetre". *KNR*, 1/09/2020, https://knr.gl/da/nyheder/lokalpolitikere-nikkede-ja-hans-egede-statuen-rokker-sig-ikke-en-centimeter

Iusmen, I.; Boswell, J. (2016). "The dilemmas of pursuing "throughput legitimacy" through participatory mechanisms". *West European Politics*, 40, 1–20

IWGIA (2020). *IWGIA Annual Report 2020*. IWGIA

IWGIA (2021). *The Indigenous World 2021*. IWGIA

IWGIA (2022). *Recognising the contributions of Indigenous Peoples in global climate action? An analysis of the IPCC report on Impacts, Adaptation and Vulnerability*. IWGIA

IWGIA/IIPFWH/IPACC (2022). *Indigenous Peoples' Rights and UNESCO World Heritage Sites*. IWGIA/IIPFWH/IPACC

Jensen, P.; Diemer R. (2014). *Blok P Erindringer*. Documentary. Nordatlantens Brygge

Lascoumes, P.; Le Gales, P. (2007), "Introduction: Understanding Public Policy through Its Instruments—From the Nature of Instruments to the Sociology of Public Policy Instrumentation". In *Governance: An International Journal of Policy, Administration, and Institutions*, Vol. 20 (1), pp. 1–21.

Lascoumes, P.; Simard, L.; McCoy, J. (2011). "Public policy seen through the prism of its instruments: Introduction". *Revue française de science politique*, 61, 5–22

Lerner, J. (2014). *Making Democracy Fun*. MIT Press

Lester, S. (2013). *Rethinking children's participation in democratic processes: A right to play, sociological studies of children and youth*. Emerald Group Publishing Limited. https://doi.org/10.1108/S1537-4661(2013)0000016006.

Ludvigsen, C. (2023). "Intervista alla Sindaca della capitale groenlandese". *Urbanistica Informazioni*, 306 (forthcoming)

Martí S.; Sanahuja J.M. (eds) (2005). *Etnicidad, autonomia y gobernabilidad en América Latina*. Ediciones Universidad de Salamanca

McGwin, K. (2020). "Work resumes on a constitution for Greenland, with a request for a new deadline". *The Arctic Journal*, 19/05/2020

Meldgaard, M. (2020). "Stories of life and death in the Arctic". In Krupnik, I.; Crowell, A. (eds). *Arctic Crashes: People and Animals in the changing North*. Smithsonian Inst. Press, 25–42

Møller Jørgensen, A. (2017). "Competing Visions of eDemocracy in Greenland: Negotiations of Power in Online Political Participation". *Policy & Internet. V.*, 9(2), 210–231

Mouffe, C. (2007). "Art and democracy: Art as an agnostic intervention in public space". *Open*, 14, 1–7

Nez, H. (2015). *Podemos, de l'indignation aux élections*. Les Petits Matins

Nukappiaaluk, N. (2020). "Unge vil have større fokus på biodiversitet". *Sermitsiaq AG*, 23/09/2022

Pelaudeix, C.; Basse, E.; Loukacheva, N. (2017). "Openness, transparency and public participation in the governance of uranium mining in Greenland: A legal and political track record". *Polar Record*, 53, 1–14

Rasmussen, R.O.; Gjertsen, A. (2018). "Sacrifice Zones for a Sustainable State? Greenlandic Mining Politics in an Era of Transition". In: Dale, B., Bay-Larsen, I., Skorstad, B. (eds) *The Will to Drill - Mining in Arctic Communities*. Springer

Ruesch, M.A.; Märker, O. (2012). "Making the Case for Anonymity in E-Participation". *EJournal of EDemocracy and Open Government*, 4(2), 301–317

Santos, B. (2006). *A Gramatica do Tempo - Para Uma Nova Cultura Politica*. Cortez

Santos, B. (2014). *Epistemologies of the South. Justice Against Epistemicide*. Routledge

Saward, M. (2021). *Democratic Design*. Oxford University Press

Sieder, R. (ed., 2002). *Multiculturalism in Latin America*. Palgrave

Silis Hoegh, I. (2014). *Sumé: The Sound of a Revolution*. Anorak Film/Bullitt Film/Jabfilm

Skjervedal, A.-S. (2018). *Towards Meaningful Youth Engagement: Breaking the Frame of the Current Public Participation Practice in Greenland*. Master Thesis. University of Greenland

Skjervedal, A.-S; Hansen, A. (2014). "Perceptions of public participation in impact assessment: A study of offshore oil exploration in Greenland". *Impact Assessment and Project Appraisal*, 32(1), 72–80

Smith, A.; Martín, P. (2021). "Going beyond the smart city? Implementing technopolitical platforms for urban democracy in Madrid and Barcelona". *Journal of Urban Technology*, 28(1–2), 311–330

Sorice, M. (2019). *Partecipazione democratica. Teorie e problemi*. Mondadori

10 Collective Candidacies and Mandates in Brazil

Challenges and Pitfalls of a *Gambiarra*

Ricardo F. Mendonça, Lucas Gelape and Carlos Estevão C. Cruz

Introduction

Brazil is famous for its long history of democratic innovations. Participatory Budgeting, Policy Councils and National Conferences are some examples that led the country to be seen as an inventive *laboratory* for democracy (Gaventa, 2004). These experiences were strongly rooted in civil society, and social movements played a key role in their establishment (Avritzer, 2017). Despite the empowerment of these participatory institutions, however, they also had flaws and weaknesses. After all, even if they had some decision-making prerogatives, final policy decisions still depended on parliaments.

Social movements soon realised they had to enhance their capacity to "occupy" parliaments, resulting in a different type of democratic innovation (Almeida and Lüchmann, 2022). Collective candidacies emerged in the Brazilian political landscape, challenging established electoral rules and patterns (Campos, 2021). In essence, a collective candidacy can be defined as a group formed within a party list to run together for one seat in parliament. In the 2020 local elections, there were 313 collective candidacies in Brazil. More than 20 of these groups were elected to office, developing collective arrangements to exert their mandates (Secchi and Leal 2020). These *collective mandates* constitute attempts by citizens to shape new institutions through practices derived from previous mobilisation processes.

On the one hand, these experiences are relevant innovations, addressing some of the gaps inherent to the crises of representation. They are reshaping not only campaigns but also conceptions about how representation is exerted. Several democratic practices are being tested to make these odd structures work in a political system which was not conceived to accommodate them. On the other hand, they are fragile structures which lack full institutional status from a legal point of view. Several collective mandates are facing huge challenges spanning from situations regarding the allocation of resources to the resignation or leave of absence of the individual who has officially registered the candidacy on behalf of a group.

This chapter seeks to discuss this democratic innovation in contemporary Brazilian politics. It introduces the notion of *gambiarra* (which can be translated as a *kludge*, *workaround* or *stopgap*), arguing that it can shed light on these practices, which reinvent electoral politics through improvisation. We argue

DOI: 10.4324/9781003218517-12

that collective mandates present themselves as a practical and creative solution to the crisis of legitimacy of representative institutions, fostering experimentation in an area not particularly open to innovation. Challenged both by the constraints of electoral politics and by the fragilities of other participatory innovations in times of democratic erosion, many collective actors innovated in the attempt to amplify their capacity to exert political influence. These experiments generate ruptures in politics as usual, and such ruptures can lead to short-circuits, meaning that they may create other political problems and instabilities in the political system.

The chapter is structured in three sections. First, we briefly introduce the context of the Brazilian political system; we define collective candidacies and mandates and explore some elements of this democratic innovation. In the second section, we mobilise the notion of *gambiarra* to examine the innovative nature of collective mandates. We argue that institutional innovations, such as this one, often emerge as quick-fixes to respond to situations spontaneously, evolving in different directions. Finally, in the third section, we focus on some of the key challenges and problems involving these innovative attempts to exert political representation through collective practices. Creative citizen-led fixes can generate rich innovation but also trigger chaotic consequences.

A dynamic political system

Brazilian democracy has a history of political changes, with democratic advancements and setbacks. Since its independence, in 1822, the country has had seven constitutions (1824, 1891, 1934, 1937, 1946, 1967 and 1988), which marked this tortuous history (Carvalho, 2015). Throughout this whole history, one element stands out in the Brazilian political system: the centrality of individuals in elections. The open-list proportional representation system currently adopted is a candidate-centred system (Carey; Shugart, 1995), aggravated by the large number of candidates (hundreds or even thousands) and the weakness of parties as cognitive shortcuts for voters (Nicolau, 2006). In general, this combination makes elections more expensive, as candidates are running *intra* and *inter* parties against an enormous number of high-quality competitors (Ames, 2001; Nicolau, 2006). In addition, candidates tend to attribute their electoral success to their own efforts and not to the parties' strength (Lemos; Ricci, 2011).[1]

Another element that stands out is that most political transformations of the country have been elite-driven (Carvalho, 2015). Nevertheless, civil society has also played an important role in generating change and innovation. In the years following the re-democratisation of the country in the 1980s, a vibrant civil society (Sader, 1988) was particularly relevant in the elaboration of the new democratic constitution (Araújo, 2013; Cassette, 2016; Doimo, 1995; Mendonça and Gurza-Lavalle, 2019). The bottom-up push for democratic innovations in this period was at the very heart of a blossoming field of experimentation in the country.

Participatory Budgeting, Policy Councils and Policy Conferences have become particularly famous among the enthusiasts of participatory democracy due to their scope, magnitude and empowerment (Avritzer, 2009; Baiocchi, 2005; Pogrebinschi and Samuels, 2014; Martelly, Almeida and Lüchmann, 2019; Wampler, McNulty and Touchton, 2021). These participatory institutions reinvented forms of civic engagement, overcoming the fake dichotomy between participation and representation (Gurza Lavalle and Isunza Vera, 2011) and establishing new ways to foster the circularity between the state and civil society (Urbinati, 2006). Empirical research shows that a lively civil society was a key condition for the success of these innovations in promoting democratic participation (Avritzer, 2017). Social movements played important roles, frequently acting as legitimate political representatives in decision-making arenas.

Since the massive 2013 demonstrations (Bringel and Pleyers, 2015; Mendonça et al., 2019), nevertheless, Brazilian political life had witnessed drastic changes and instabilities (Avritzer, 2019). These demonstrations started against a rise in public transportation fares, and soon expanded to involve a wide range of issues strengthening anti-politics and anti-corruption movements. The push for democratic innovations was weakened and, since 2016, the country had witnessed a government-led attempt to destroy its participatory system (Avelino, Alencar and Costa, 2017; Almeida, 2020). The fragility of the participatory institutions became clear, despite their legal status. The need to *occupy* more formal and established arenas of decision-making became evident (Campos, 2021). Building on a key dimension of the contemporary repertoire of contention (Mendonça and Bustamante, 2020), many social movements framed their entrance on electoral politics as a form of *occupation,* due to the traditional asymmetries embedded in the Brazilian political system.

It is in this context that social movements sought to occupy electoral politics, and collective candidacies and mandates emerged as a possible tactic. As a new bottom-up democratic innovation, they gathered different individuals, frequently with diverse associative bonds (Almeida and Lüchmann, 2022), to provide allegedly stronger and more plural forms of representation. In doing so, they also challenged the aforementioned person-centred nature of the Brazilian political system.

Collective Mandates as Democratic Innovations

In the past two Brazilian elections (2018 and 2020), there was a significant growth in candidacies that presented themselves as collective (Secchi and Leal, 2020; INESC, 2020). A study carried out by the Municipal Legislature of Belo Horizonte (MG/Brazil) defines collective candidacies as those in which "a group of people collectively demand the same seat in parliament, affirming the commitment to share decisions and other actions of the mandate among the members of that specific group" (CMBH, 2021). This means that a group of individuals run together for the same seat in parliament is a *collective candidacy*. If elected they try to exert a *collective mandate,* developing procedures and strategies to create a unified position, which is translated into one vote in parliamentary processes, with varying levels of success, as discussed below. *Collective mandates* usually "present a reduced number of co-representatives, who generally know each other or are close to each other, and have a clear ideological perspective" and whose decision-making is often based on deliberation aimed at consensus (RAPS, 2019: 24). The fact that a collectivity pleads for the same seat in parliament and their collective decision-making processes distinguishes collective mandates from other types of shared mandates.[2]

Collective candidacies and mandates are not regulated by Brazilian electoral legislation, which entails legal and organisational challenges that will be discussed below. They are not explicitly prohibited, however, and legal conflicts have been dealt with on a case-by-case basis. There are legislative proposals under evaluation in Congress, which seek to introduce the formal recognition of collective candidacies and mandates.[3] At this moment, nevertheless, they still inhabit a legal limbo of uncertainty and open possibilities.

The argument that collective mandates represent a novelty is sometimes challenged. After all, traditional mandates are also somehow collective, as they are linked to parties which are supposed to maintain broader relations with their supporters. The novelty of collective mandates is, however, that they hypothetically build and deliver a different type of representation, capable of challenging current institutional politics. For instance, Campos (2021) highlights that they are marked by attempts at collective decision-making (through different formats) and the use of new tools for popular participation. Her study of three mandates[4] points out that parliamentary action was also attentive to intersectionality, with an emphasis on issues such as women's rights, the environment, human rights and culture, with co-representatives acting as bridges between social movements and institutional arenas of decision-making (Campos, 2021). Collective mandates often give, therefore, emphasis to overlooked issues and bring different *bodies* to representative politics.

A growing number of exploratory and descriptive studies are trying to map this phenomenon (Almeida and Lüchmann, 2022; Campos, 2021; Silva, Secchi and Cavalheiro, 2021; Secchi and Leal, 2020; INESC, 2020; RAPS, 2019). These studies have offered important contributions to the comprehension of the diversity inherent to the phenomenon. The frequent conclusion is that collective candidacies and the mandates eventually derived from them are still "an imprecise experiment, based on trial and error; on learning from successes and failures in the various formats already adopted" (RAPS, 2019: 24).

Data from the 2020 elections[5] (Secchi and Leal, 2020) show that, despite the greater number of collective candidacies in the Southeast region (52.1%), especially in the state of São Paulo, the distribution of collective candidacies followed the pattern of the total candidacies in each region of the country (considering only candidates for city council). In regard to the profile of the individual candidates, the number of women running in collective candidacies (47.3%) is proportionally higher than the total number of women running for city councils (34.6%) (Secchi and Leal, 2020; Almeida and Lüchmann, 2022).

Despite the fact that the majority of collective candidacies have spokespersons[6] who declare themselves white (52.58%), it is noteworthy that the percentage of self-declared black individuals in collective candidacies is 28.4% against only 10.9% in the total number of candidacies. The existing scholarship also points to a generational distinction. The proportion of collective candidacies led by young people (aged 18–24) is 8.31%, against 3% in total candidacies. More than half of the collective candidacies were represented by people under 39 years of age.

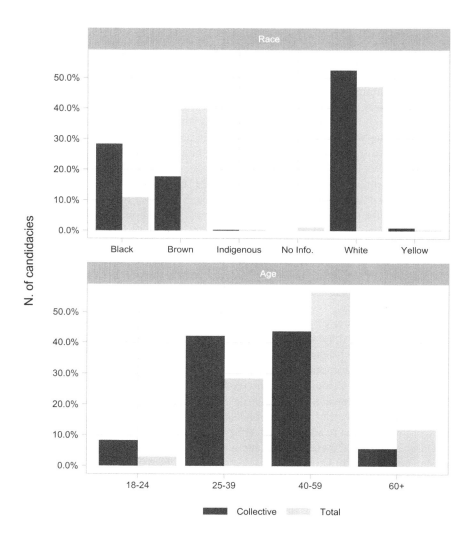

Figure 10.1 Percentage of city council candidacies per race/ethnicity and age in the Brazilian 2020 elections. *Source: Created by the authors using data from Secchi and Leal (2020).* Note: Collective candidacies data considers only the spokesperson's characteristics.

Lastly, data shows that collective candidacies from left and centre-left parties represent 80.83% of the cases (Secchi and Leal, 2020), which makes sense due to the collective tradition of organisation by left-wing movements in the country and the repertoire of horizontal politics developed within leftist groups. Almeida and Lüchmann (2022) show that 84.3% of candidates have associative bonds to social movements, parties and public policy councils. More than 65% of collective candidacies are new (Almeida and Lüchmann, 2022), indicating that they are an attempt to change politics as usual, through the occupation of institutional politics and the change in party hierarchies. Collective candidacies can, hence, be seen as a strategy more frequently employed by less powerful actors, who use this improvised solution to try to level the playing field in a political context with deeply marked asymmetries.[7]

The elected mandates amplify the trends observed in the candidacies. According to Almeida and Lüchmann (2022), 28 out of 30 elected mandates have links to associations, with half of them having multiple links. The strongest links are with more consolidated and organised social movements. The data support the hypothesis that social movement activists are investing in the electoral path to overcome the current limits of participation and interaction with the state (Almeida and Lüchmann, 2022). But they do so through innovative practices, such as the collective mandates.

Regarding political inclusion, elected collective mandates are more plural than traditional mandates, and have shown to be an actual tool to break down some of the barriers of political parties and the misrepresentation of oppressed groups (Almeida and Lüchmann, 2022). While 16% of the total elected mandates are represented by women, among the collective mandates, women represent 60%. Some of the mandates prefer to be called WoMandates[8]. In relation to colour, half of the elected individuals representing collective mandates declare to be non-white, with 33% declaring themselves black – in the aggregate of mandates this percentage is only 6.2% (Almeida and Lüchmann, 2022).

These different investigations on collective mandates converge in pointing out their innovative nature, which pushes the boundaries of what representation means and how it is exerted. There is also a shared diagnosis that such mandates promote diversity, transparency and bottom-up participation in institutional politics, through the occupation of legislative arenas (Secchi and Leal, 2020; Almeida and Lüchmann, 2022; Campos, 2021).

An Innovative *Gambiarra*

Collective candidacies and mandates are a result of strong demands for inclusion and participation in the electoral dynamics of representation in Brazil. However, these mandates are not clearly foreseen in the electoral legislation or the constitution. Even if the open-list proportional system adopted for legislative elections in the country can generate a collective form of representation – since mandates belong to parties – individuals, and not groups, occupy seats and exert mandates. And, currently, collective mandates have no formal institutional existence.

These candidacies and mandates emerged out of improvisation, in an attempt to address existing problems and fix how representation is actually exercised. As the state deputies from the *Mandata Ativista* (2020) state: "we're inventing our own office", or as participants of these mandates frequently mention, they are *hacking* political institutions (Campos, 2021). Collective mandates are, hence, a form of political quick fix or *gambiarra*. In Portuguese, *Gambiarras* are improvised solutions to fix something with the usage of things at hand (Priberam, 2021). At first sight, they are usually frowned upon, given their precariousness. However, under scenarios of many constraints, they can also be seen in a positive light as the expression of ingenuity and creativity.

Assunção and Mendonça (2016) shed light on the political dimension of *gambiarras*, in a broader sense. They argue that, beyond the specific solution generated by the quick-fix, *gambiarras* have a displacing potential to affect the way we look at certain things and make sense of them. They affect the way we perceive reality and attribute meaning to it. Kludges often make us smile, when we notice their ingenuity, their simplicity and their precarious nature. They embody human creativity, but also its risky consequences.

In this chapter, we argue that *gambiarras* may be an instrument of institutional change. Historical institutionalism has shown the strength that institutions have in surviving the test of time. One of the main arguments for this capacity is related to *path dependence*, that is, "the dynamics of self-reinforcing or positive feedback processes in a political system" (Pierson; Skocpol, 2002, p. 699). Once institutions reach an equilibrium, these processes reinforce their inner workings, making them more stable. The literature also shows that exogenous factors may break up institutional stability, either by a gradual accumulation of forces or by a strong rupture (Rezende, 2012). In this scenario, *critical junctures* are the temporal configurations that can lead to these ruptures (Rezende, 2012). In Brazilian politics, the numerous crises since the 2013 demonstrations worked as a critical juncture, challenging the political system, and when collective candidacies and mandates emerged as *gambiarras*.

Gambiarras can foster change in at least two ways. First, at a critical juncture, political actors can produce a whole set of new rules and institutions. Second, under a scenario of disputes, political actors work on the margins of existing norms (Monteiro, 2018) to establish new institutions and/or give new meanings to the existing ones.[9] Collective candidacies and mandates did not completely change the structure of representation in Brazil (or even created any relevant formal rules yet), but they emerged as important innovations in this context. As Blanco, Lowndes and Salazar (2021) argue in the context of participatory governance, formal rules are harder to change, but institutions can also be changed through practices and/or narratives, as might be the case with these *gambiarras*.

Political *gambiarras* emerge from the need to deal with concrete problems. They are signs of the practice of improvisation that involves the deployment of available resources in a given context to deal with an actual problem demanding a solution. These improvised artefacts are, nevertheless, inherently ambivalent.

Collective Candidacies and Mandates in Brazil 161

On the one hand, they are fragile and potentially dangerous. They are unsteady: a quick fix that can lead to many and bigger problems.[10] On the other hand, *gambiarras* express human ingenuity. They are artefacts produced by a practical creativity in the face of the need to work around a problem and solve it with the available resources and possibilities. They emerge from the fleeting operation of agents reinventing the structures and relations of power in which they are immersed. As Michel de Certeau (2000) argues, there is room for reflexivity and creativity, and human beings can reinvent the situations in which they play a role by appropriating the elements that constitute these situations. Certeau focuses on the tactical behaviour of the weak, who take advantage of the right moment to reinvent, through their practices, what is defined by others. This can be noted, for instance, when social movements seize the opportunity of certain events to reshape the political landscape.[11]

We claim that collective candidacies and mandates are *gambiarras*. They emerged as quick fixes to deal with concrete problems of political representation, re-signifying elements of the Brazilian electoral system without major reforms. They are creative ways to overcome problems such as the misrepresentation of oppressed groups and the insulation of individuals in formal politics. Due to the high barriers of entry and the country's representative deficits, some political actors aim at subverting existing rules to produce some institutional change. They do so by bending existing rules, thus reshaping them through practices (Blanco, Lowndes and Salazar, 2021). The innovation here (as in many contexts) does not involve, at least in its origins, the establishment of new rules or deep reforms. Rules are appropriated in innovative ways through practices that creatively seek to fix a set of problems.

Innovations that deepen democracy are often more chaotic and less organised than what is usually considered under the umbrella of democratic innovations (Asenbaum, 2021). They often start in more precarious and unforeseen ways through the acts of citizens. The notion of *gambiarra* seeks to grasp the practical and shaky dimension of some innovations, expanding the idea in itself of what counts as innovation.

Democratic innovations are usually conflated with well-designed participatory institutions aimed at promoting deliberation (Asenbaum, 2021). Elstub and Escobar (2019) present an encompassing survey of the definitions and varieties of democratic innovations to advance the following characterisation:

> Democratic innovations are processes or institutions, that are new to a policy issue, policy role, or level of governance, and developed to reimagine and deepen the role of citizens in governance processes by increasing opportunities for participation, deliberation and influence.

Innovations are not restricted, therefore, to minipublics and participatory experiments, but can be related to other forms of influence, including electoral politics. Despite the amplitude of this definition, however, it misses a more practical dimension of innovations.

Political *gambiarras* are precarious and unstable. They are risky and have bred hazards of different types not only to the actors involved but to the political system. Collective candidacies and mandates are *gambiarras* exactly because they are not institutionalised, which explains their displacing capacities but also their risks. Their capacity to survive in the long run is, therefore, uncertain due to the challenges they face. The last section of the chapter will focus on some of the existing challenges, mobilising concrete illustrations to evince problems actually faced by collective mandates in their practical reinvention of electoral politics in Brazil.

Short-Circuits and Dilemmas of an Emerging *Gambiarra*

While collective mandates can be understood as new political actors challenging the current institutional arrangement, they are also *arenas* of different types of interaction. This perspective sheds light on the different dynamics and relationships cutting across the varied initiatives of this diffuse experimentalism. Different experiences have been marked by different problems, and diverse solutions have been tried in the face of the challenges experienced.

We will now identify some of the challenges that these experiences are facing in their attempt to prosper as viable alternatives to innovating representative politics. These challenges, we argue, can be seen as short-circuits inherent to these *gambiarras*. The unstable nature of quick fixes often causes disruptions and "accidents". Their hazards should not be neglected as they can cause damages to political institutions, such as parties, legislative chambers and the mandate. For the sake of clarity, we will organise these challenges into three blocks, although they are obviously interrelated.

Absence of Regulation and Legal Recognition

One of the most significant limits faced by collective mandates is the lack of legal recognition and regulation in electoral laws. This limit leads to constraints in electoral campaigns, at the time of registration of a candidacy and in regard to the accountability of collective candidacies to the electoral courts. If electorally successful, a collective mandate faces an endless friction with the internal regulations of the legislative chambers.

The moment in which a candidacy is registered already leads to frictions with the current rules. The formalisation of a candidacy requires that one (and only one) person must be registered and that this person must fulfil several legal requirements. There is, nevertheless, some flexibility in the selection of the name displayed in the ballot. There are cases, such as *Juntas* (PSOL/PE) and *Coletivo Nós* (PT/São Luis-MA), which used collective names, while other experiences mixed the name of the person legally registered with the name of the group, such as *Monica da Bancada Ativista* (PSOL/SP) and *Sonia Lansky da ColetivA* (PT/Belo Horizonte-MG). In some cases, the collective candidacy simply adopted the name of the individual candidate, such as Henny Freitas (REDE/Alto Paraíso de Goiás-GO).

This situation has challenged the Electoral Justice and, in most cases, the courts have been permissive with the registration of the name shown in the ballot box, although they demand the fulfilment of the other requirements from just one individual. There are cases, however, in which the courts prevented the registration of candidacies with collective names, as a case decided by the Regional Electoral Court of Pernambuco (TRE-PE) illustrates.[12] A recent resolution from the Superior Electoral Court (23.675/2021) authorised the adoption of "the group or collective of supporters in the composition of the candidate's name" (Tribunal Superior Electoral, 2021) for the 2022 elections.

The frictions over collective mandates become even more evident after the inauguration and in the exercise of parliamentary activity. In this case, too, there is a lack of clear standards and patterns. Collective mandates are not actually recognised or fully anticipated in the internal regulations of legislative houses, which tend to restrict many of the parliamentary prerogatives to the individual considered as formally elected. In the face of threats to its members, the collective mandates *Bancada Feminista* and *Quilombo Periférico,* for instance, required an escort for all its co-councillors from the São Paulo City Council (CMSP). In response, the CMSP Attorney instructed the presidency of the house to refuse the request, since the institution does not recognise the existence of collective mandates.[13]

Some collective mandates are, however, taking advantage of regulatory loopholes to open spaces for the action of co-representatives. Recently, the City Council of Salvador held a Special Session promoted by the collective mandate *Pretas por Salvador* (PSOL/Salvador-BA), which had the participation of its three co-councillors.[14] The co-representatives of *Mandata Ativista* in the State Assembly of São Paulo invented strategies to make themselves present in plenary sessions. Since only the formally elected individual has access to this key arena of legislatures, this individual (i.e., Monica) often used her time on the floor to reproduce videos recorded by the other co-representatives, thus assuring their collective visibility (Campos, 2021, p. 170). In the State Assembly of Pernambuco, all the co-representatives of *Juntas* successfully required access to spaces of the house which are restricted to members of parliament (Campos, 2021).

Relationships with parties and other representatives

Collective candidacies are part of broader party lists and it is often the case that not all members of the collective candidacy are affiliated to the same party, or even to any party (Almeida and Lüchmann, 2022; Campos, 2021). This creates a situation that increases the risk of contradictions between the positions advocated by the members of the collective candidacy and the programme of the party in whose list the candidacy was elected.

In relation to parties, this dilemma can bring challenges of three kinds. First, there is the question of the freedom that each party gives to collective mandates to exercise representation. The formation of the *Mandata Ativista*'s candidacy in São Paulo, for example, considered the "degree of independence" that the mandate would have in relation to the party in case of victory (Campos, 2021, p. 105–106). Gabinetona (in the state of Minas Gerais) also made this choice considering the opening for experimentation that the party would provide, and they had to deal with significant problems along the way (Campos, 2021, p. 102–103).

Then, there is the possibility of conflict due to different party orientations within the same mandate, as a collective mandate may include co-representatives from more than one party. The case of *Bancada Ativista* (PSOL/SP) became the paradigmatic example, given its multi-party character and the conflicts derived from this situation (Campos, 2021). In early 2021, party differences made a significant impact on how co-representatives positioned themselves (Barifouse, 2021).

Lastly, one can note the conflict arising from how parties deal with collective mandates in cases of resignations or leaves of absence. The electoral legislation establishes that, in cases of resignation, the following name on the party list must take office. This means that parties may have to deal with situations in which a mandate is transferred to a different individual, while members of a former collective mandate still believe they have the right to continue exerting some form of representation. This is what happened in the case of *ColetivA* (PT-Belo Horizonte/MG), with the resignation of the individual formally elected as the representative. The resignation was not foreseen by any internal agreement of the group or the party. The surrogate was another candidate without any connections to the collective mandate. The situation led to a political arrangement in the party that ensured that the former co-representatives would be informally considered. As a representative in the City Council, however, the collective mandate ceased to exist. In the case of the health leave requested by Monica Seixas, from the *Mandata Ativista* (PSOL/SP), an agreement was made with the surrogate to preserve the mandate's model and keep the appointed co-representatives in the functions of parliamentary advisors.

Challenges for the Organisation and Socialisation of Power

This challenge involves the difficulties in the organisation of the exercise of parliamentary activity, leading to different internal attempts to distribute responsibilities, empower co-representatives, make decisions, resolve internal conflicts and share the costs and benefits of political action.

In several ways and with different degrees of formalisation, collective mandates have structured their organisation through agreements and internal regulations (RAPS, 2019). Most of them are grounded on tacit agreements, but there are also some cases of formalisation of these agreements. *Mandato Coletivo de Alto Paraíso* (PTN-Alto Paraíso de Goiás/GO), for instance, registered in a notary's office a regulation which was signed by all of its members during the electoral period. In this regulation, the members agreed to take decisions and guide their position through deliberative plenary sessions. Consensus was defined as the key procedure to define rules for inclusion and exclusion of members, regulate the use of parliamentary resources and organise the division of tasks and functions. Likewise, *Coletivo Nós* (PT-São Luis/MA) drafted a regulation with the support of a legal committee outside the co-representatives. The statute characterises the collective mandate, defines goals and values, sets the main principles and establishes the internal structure and responsibilities of each co-representative.

The absence of internal rules can lead to burnout for the mandates, as happened with the *Mandata Activist* (PSOL/SP). Elected without the establishment of clear rules and commitments, this WoMandate faced "insecurity, many conflicts and frustrations" immediately after the electoral victory (Campos, 2021, p. 136), which demanded a restructuring of the mandate to establish functions and give more autonomy to co-representatives (Campos, 2021, p. 136).

Concluding Remarks

This chapter presented the recent experience of collective mandates in Brazil as a democratic innovation in representative politics. It argued that collective mandates are a source of creativity and change, despite their frailty and dangers. To develop this argument, the chapter mobilised the notion of *gambiarra*. Like other *gambiarras*, collective mandates have emerged as a quick fix to several problems of representative politics, such as the underrepresentation of women and black communities and the elitist dimension of electoral politics in Brazil. Collective mandates often emerge from grassroots social movements in an attempt to occupy decision-making arenas and reinvent politics.

Their problems and dilemmas often get much attention in the press and should not be overlooked. We discussed several challenges pointing in the same direction: collective mandates are unstable structures operating in a *space between order and disorder*, to use Monteiro's (2018) words. They are innovative reinventions of representation, displacing the way representation is conceived of and institutionally exerted, but they are fragile and vulnerable. The informal power of this *gambiarra* lies in its capacity to push the boundaries of what is established and institutionalised. It is exactly because it is somehow outside the boundaries of institutional politics, however, that this *gambiarra* can easily fall apart (by simple resignations or personal leaves) or can cause short-circuits in administrative and political arenas (for instance, when different parties fight to influence a given mandate or when institutions do not know how to deal with a simple request for protection).

These bottom-up *gambiarras* tell much about how innovation actually happens. It is through the practice of actors in the face of problematic situations that institutions may be challenged and displaced. This process is not riskless. There is no safe way to foster innovation, and experimentalism implies challenges and unanticipated short circuits. *Gambiarras* can go awfully wrong. But *gambiarras* are a sign that creativity requires agency and practice. They show innovation might be possible in areas where nothing new seemed conceivable. Paradoxically, they may show that simple things may challenge very complex problems.

In this sense, notwithstanding their hazards and vulnerabilities, we argue that the *gambiarra* of collective mandates has an enormous potential to displace institutions and reinvent them. If nothing else, they shed light on tacit elements of crystallised institutions and their constructed nature. *Political gambiarras*, such as collective mandates, denaturalise established institutions, bringing a mix of amazement, surprise and instability to deal with existing problems. In a certain way, they shake politics as usual up, by introducing awareness, reflexivity and creativity in areas of politics that tend to be extremely stable. Although it is unclear to what extent they can provide effective solutions to existing problems of democracy, they are an innovative attempt to tackle them. They may become a viable solution, but this still requires significant steps towards their institutionalisation.

Notes

1 The Workers' Party has been a notable exception since the 1980s (Samuels, 1999). One should not be mistaken to fully characterize Brazilian parties as weak, since they are a relevant part of its electoral structure. Indeed, the electorate hardly ever look to parties as an electoral cue in the country's proportional representation elections (Nicolau, 2006). However, they are important institutions in this arena. First, party affiliation is a requirement for anyone to be a candidate. Second, in elections heavily influenced by campaign finance (Mancuso, 2015; Speck, 2015, 2016), parties have a crucial role in the balance of the playing field. This became even more relevant with the 2016 Supreme Court decision banning corporations from donating to political campaigns (Speck, 2016), and the creation of the Electoral Fund for Campaign Finance, that currently adds up to almost US$1 billion and is controlled by party leadership. Third, parties have access to a quota of visibility in TV channels which is proportional to the number of members of parliament elected by each party.
2 Shared mandates, in turn, are those that "stand out for the plurality and heterogeneity of a medium to large group (usually over 100 people)", and in which the power is exerted in a more individualized way, by majority rule, based often on electronic polls (RAPS, 2019: 24). The characteristics of shared mandates bring them closer to international experiences that emerged in the last 15 years, such as those of Demoex/Direktdemokraterna, in Sweden; the Pirate Party, in more than 30 countries; Senator Online – Online Direct Democracy, in Australia; and Partido de la Red – DemocracyOS, in Argentina.
3 Notably the Proposal for Amendment to the Constitution 379/2017 and Bills 4.475/2020 and 4724/2020.
4 Campos (2021) studied the experiences of Gabinetona (in the state of Minas Gerais), Mandata Ativista (in São Paulo) and Juntas (in Pernambuco).
5 Data compiled by Secchi and Leal (2020) does not include complete results from Amapá, a state in the North region.
6 Since Brazilian electoral law only allows individual candidacies' registration, collective candidacies are registered under the name of one person, the "spokeperson". The data in this section considers only spokespeople data and not all members of collective candidacies.
7 We are thankful to Adrian Bua for suggesting this articulation.
8 In Portuguese, the word "mandate" is a masculine word ("mandato"), as most of the substantives are gendered. Since several collective mandates are composed by women, a neologism has been used with a feminine version of the word (i.e. "mandata"). To make this clear we have translated "Mandatas" as "WoMandates".
9 Under a different perspective, Mahoney and Thelen (2009) stress that institutional changes are not necessarily the result of exogenous sources, such as the one generated in a critical juncture, and can be endogenously generated through processes similar as these.

10 The short experience of Parliamentarism in Brazil in the early 1960s, for instance, emerged as a stopgap in an alleged attempt to avoid an institutional crisis. After the resignation of president Jânio Quadros in 1961, political and military elites agreed on the implementation of parliamentarism in Brazil, given military leaders' resistance to allow vice-president João Goulart to take office (Figueiredo, 1993). This solution was enshrined in a constitutional amendment that put this new system of government standing, in a *gambiarra* destined to weaken the presidency in that critical juncture. But, this new regime was never institutionalized. President Goulart and his allies worked to undermine the new system, in order to avoid its institutionalization and make a return to Presidentialism viable (Figueiredo, 1993). This 17-month experience ended with the return to Presidentialism in 1963, and was not capable of preventing a major crisis, marked by fragmentation, radicalization and decision-making paralysis, which ended up in a military coup in 1964 (Santos, 1986; Amorim and Rodriguez, 2016). The quick fix actually contributed to delegitimize and weaken President João Goulart.
11 In the Brazilian case, which grounds our discussion, this was evident in the constitutional process of 1988 or when the Workers' Party won the municipality of Porto Alegre, opening the opportunity for the reinvention of the budgetary discussion.
12 Available at: https://www.tre-pe.jus.br/imprensa/noticias-tre-pe/2020/Outubro/tre-pe-impede-nome-que-faca-mencao-a-candidatura-coletiva. Accessed December 15, 2021. / Confirmation available at. https://www.tse.jus.br/imprensa/noticias-tse/2020/Novembro/ministro-nega-pedido-de-candidata-ao-cargo-de-vereador-para-registrar-nome-de-urna-de-carater-coletivo. Accessed December 15 2021.
13 Available at: https://g1.globo.com/sp/sao-paulo/noticia/2021/02/04/procuradoria-da-camara-de-sp-diz-que-nao-reconhece-a-existencia-de-bancadas-coletivas-bancada-do-psol-pede-escolta-para-covereadoras.ghtml. Accessed December 15, 2021.
14 Available at: https://www.facebook.com/tveradiocam/videos/4144018752370553. Accessed December 15, 2021.

References

Almeida, Débora; Lüchmann, Lígia. 2022 (forthcoming). Movimentos sociais e representação eleitoral: o fenômeno das candidaturas e dos mandatos coletivos. In: Almeida, D; Tatagiba, L; Gurza Lavalle, A; Kunrath, M. *Participação, ativismos: entre retrocessos e resistências*. Porto Alegre: Zouk.

Almeida, D. R. (2020). Resiliência institucional: para onde vai a participação nos Conselhos Nacionais de Saúde e dos Direitos da Mulher?. *Caderno CRH*, v. 33, p. 1–24.

Ames, Barry. 2001. *The Deadlock of Democracy in Brazil*. Ann Arbor: University of Michigan Press.

Amorim, Octavio; Júlio César Cossio Rodriguez. 2016. O novo método histórico-comparativo e seus aportes à ciência política e à administração pública. *Revista de Administração Pública*, v. 50, n. 6, p. 1003–1027.

Araújo, Cícero. 2013. O processo constituinte brasileiro, a transição e o poder constituinte. *Lua Nova, São Paulo*, v. 88, p. 327–380.

Asenbaum, H. 2021. Rethinking democratic innovations: A look through the Kaleidoscope of democratic theory. *Political Studies Review*, v. 20, n. 4, p. 680–690.

Assunção, Helena S.; Mendonça, Ricardo F. 2016. A estética política da gambiarra cotidiana. *Revista Compolitica*, v. 6, n.1, p. 92–114, 2016.

Avritzer, L. 2009. *Participatory Institutions in Democratic Brazil*. Johns Hopkins. University Press.

Avritzer, Leonardo. *The Two Faces of Institutional Innovation: Promises and Limits of Democratic Participation in Latin America*. Cheltenham, UK: Edward Elgar Publishing, 2017.

Avritzer, L. 2019. *O Pêndulo da Democracia no Brasil*. São Paulo: Todavia.

Baiocchi, Gianpaolo. *Militants and Citizens: The Politics of Participatory Democracy in Porto Alegre*. Stanford: Stanford University Press, 2005.

Blanco, Ismael, Vivien Lowndes and Yunailis Salazar. 2021. Understanding institutional dynamics in participatory governance: How rules, practices and narratives combine to produce stability or diverge to create conditions for change. *Critical Policy Studies*, v. 16, n. 2, p. 204–223.

Bringel, Breno; Pleyers, Geoffrey. 2015. *Junho de 2013... dois anos depois. Polarização, impactos e reconfiguração do ativismo no Brasil*. Nueva Sociedad: Especial em português, 2015.

Câmara Municipal de Belo Horizonte. 2021. *Estudo Técnico sobre Candidaturas e Mandatos Coletivos no Brasil*. Diretoria do Processo Legislativo. Belo Horizonte: Câmara Municipal de Belo Horizonte.

Campos, Bárbara Lopes. 2021. Juntas em um único número na urna? Uma análise das experiências de mandato coletivo no Brasil. PhD dissertation, Universidade Federal de Minas Gerais.

Carvalho, José Murilo de. 2015. *Cidadania no Brasil: O longo caminho*. Rio de Janeiro: Civilização Brasileira.

Carey, John and Matthew Shugart. 1995. Incentives to cultivate a personal vote: A rank ordering of electoral formulas. *Electoral Studies*, v. 14, n. 4, p. 417–439.

Cassette, Mariah. 2016. *A construção da soberania inacabada e a experiência constituinte de 1987–88*. PhD. Dissertation in Political Science. Federal University of Minas Gerais, Belo Horizonte.

Certeau, Michel de. 2000. *A Invenção do Cotidiano: artes do fazer*. Petrópolis: Editora Vozes, 2000.

Doimo, Ana. 1995. A voz e a vez do popular: Movimentos sociais e a participação política pós *1970*. Anpocs: Relume Dumará.

Elstub, Stephen, and Escobar, Oliver. 2019. *Handbook of Democratic Innovation and Governance*. Cheltenham: Edward Elgar Publishing.

Figueiredo, Argelina Cheibub. 1993. *Democracia ou Reformas? Alternativas democráticas à crise política: 1961–1964*. São Paulo: Paz e Terra.

Gaventa, John. 2004. Prefácio. In: Coelho, Vera Schattan P.; Nobre, Marcos (Org.). *Participação e deliberação: Teoria democrática e experiências institucionais no Brasil contemporâneo*. São Paulo: Ed. 34, p. 7–9.

Gurza Lavalle, A.; Isunza Vera, E. 2011. A trama da crítica democrática: Da participação à representação e à accountability. *Lua Nova*, v. 84, p. 95–140.

INESC. 2020. Análise das candidaturas coletivas nas eleições de 2020. Available at: https://www.inesc.org.br/analise-das-candidaturas-coletivas-nas-eleicoes-de-2020/?cn-reloaded=1. Accessed December 15, 2021.

Lemos, Leany and Paolo Ricci. 2011. Individualismo e partidarismo na lógica parlamentar: o antes e depois das eleições. In: Power, Timothy J. and Zucco Jr, Cesar. *O Congresso por ele mesmo: Autopercepções da classe política brasileira*. Belo Horizonte: Editora UFMG, p. 207–238.

Mahoney, James and Kathleen Thelen. 2009. A theory of gradual institutional change. In: Mahoney, James and Kathleen Thelen. *Explaining Institutional Change: Ambiguity, Agency and Power*. Cambridge University Press, p. 1–37.

Mandata Ativista. 2020. Candidaturas e mandatos coletivos. *Folha de S. Paulo*, São Paulo, Tendências/Debates, 13.ago.

Martelli, Carla Giani, Carla Almeida, and Lígia Lüchmann. 2019. The Meanings of Representation and Political Inclusion in the Conferences of Public Policies in Brazil. *Brazilian Political Science Review*, v. 13, n. 1.

Mendonça, Ricardo F.; Gurza Lavalle, Adrian. 2019. Brazil, 40 Years of Struggles Over Political Legitimacy Through the Lenses of Representation. *Representation*, 55:3, 239–250.

Mendonca, Ricardo F. and Bustamante, Márcio. 2020. Back to the Future: Changing Repertoire in Contemporary Protests. *Bull Lat Am Res*, 39: 629–643.

Mendonça, R. F.; Ercan, S.; Ozguc, U.; Reis, S. and Simoes, P. G. 2019. Protests as Events: The Symbolic Struggles in 2013 Demonstrations in Turkey and Brazil. *Revista de Sociologia e Política*, v. 27, n. 69, p. 1–27.

Monteiro, Pedro Meira. 2018. Precariousness rocks: Brazilian counterculture, from Hélio Oiticica to Daniela Thomas. *Asymptote* journal. Available at: https://www.asymptotejournal.com/special-feature/pedro-meira-monteiro-on-brazilian-writers/. Accessed December 15, 2021.

Nicolau, Jairo. 2006. O Sistema Eleitoral de Lista Aberta no Brasil. *Dados*, v. 49, n. 4, p. 689–720.

Pierson, Paul and Theda Skocpol. 2002. Historical institutionalism in contemporary political science. In: Katznelson, Ira and Helen V. Milner. *Political Science: State of the Discipline*. p. 693–721.

Priberam. 2021. Gambiarra. In: *Dicionário Priberam Online de Português Contemporâneo*. Available at: https://dicionario.priberam.org/. Accessed December 15, 2021.

Pogrebinschi, Thamy, and David Samuels. 2014. The impact of participatory democracy: Evidence from Brazil's national public policy conferences. *Comparative Politics*, v. 46, n. 3.

RAPS. 2019. *Mandatos coletivos e compartilhados: Desafios e possibilidades para a representação legislativa no século XXI. Rede de Ação Política pela Sustentabilidade*. São Paulo: RAPS/Arapyaú/UDESC

Rezende, Flávio da Cunha. 2012. Da exogeneidade ao gradualismo: inovações na teoria da mudança institucional. *Revista Brasileira de Ciências Sociais*, v. 27, n. 78, p. 113–130.

Sader, Eder. 1988. *Quando novos personagens entraram em cena: experiências, falas e lutas dos trabalhadores da Grande São Paulo (1970–80)*. Rio de Janeiro: Paz e Terra.

Santos, Wanderley G. dos. *Sessenta e quatro: anatomia da crise*. São Paulo: Vértice, 1986.

Secchi, Leonardo and Leal, Leonardo 2020 (coord). As candidaturas coletivas nas eleições municipais de 2020: análise descritiva e propostas para uma agenda de pesquisa sobre mandatos coletivos no Brasil. Relatório de Pesquisa. Universidade do Estado de Santa Catarina; Universidade Federal de Alagoas; Universidade de Brasília; Universidade Federal de Santa Catarina. Editora IABS

Silva, William Quadros, Secchi, Leonardo and Cavalheiro, Ricardo. 2021. Mandatos coletivos e compartilhados no Brasil: análise descritiva de inovações democráticas no Poder Legislativo. *Revista Debates, Porto Alegre*, v.15, n.1, p. 168–190.

Speck, Bruno Wilhelm. 2016. Game over: Duas décadas de financiamento de campanhas com doações de empresa no Brasil. *Revista de estúdios brasileños*, v. 3, n. 4, p. 125–135.

Tribunal Superior Eleitoral. 2021. Resolução nº 23.675, de 16 de dezembro de 2021. Available at: https://www.tse.jus.br/legislacao/compilada/res/2021/resolucao-no-23-675-de-16-de-dezembro-de-2021

Urbinati, Nadia. 2006. *Representative Democracy: Principles and Genealogy*. Chicago: University of Chicago Press.

Wampler, Brian, Stephanie L. McNulty, and Michael Touchton. 2021. *Participatory Budgeting in Global Perspective*. Oxford: Oxford University Press.

11 Democracy-Driven Governance and Governance-Driven Democratisation in Barcelona and Nantes

Adrian Bua, Sonia Bussu and Jonathan Davies

Introduction

The growing popularity and worldwide diffusion of forms of participatory governance over recent decades highlight an important paradox: "democratic innovations" (Smith 2009) promise to open up new opportunities for citizen participation at a time when the space for political choice and democracy has been constrained by neoliberal technocracy (Baiocchi and Ganuza 2016). This raises fundamental questions on the space for projects to "deepen democracy" (Fung and Wright 2003) within contemporary capitalist political economy. In this chapter we examine the relationship between participatory governance and these broader processes, with a view to assessing opportunities for emancipatory and democratic transformations. We do so by comparing two approaches to participatory governance: the first one is what Warren (2014) termed "governance-driven democratization" (GDD); the second one is an alternative form which in other work (Bua and Bussu 2021; Bua and Bussu, introduction to this volume) we have labelled "democracy-driven governance" (DDG).

Warren's work offers the best description of the dominant form of participatory governance: an elite-led form where the aim is to address the legitimacy crisis of institutions and experts and to improve policymaking on complex issues, by involving new voices and interests. The rationale is therefore functionalist in nature and the agenda is often shaped by agencies "inviting" citizen participation (Cornwall 2004). DDG is more critically oriented and bottom-up. It emerges through popular mobilisation, attempts to bring social movements into the state and has transformative aspirations (Bua and Bussu 2021; Sintomer 2018). The key difference is that whereas GDD accepts the basic parameters of neoliberal political economy and is therefore easily incorporated into good governance discourses, DDG has more radical ambitions; it challenges the separation of politics and economics that characterises liberal democracy, and it is driven by a social justice orientation.

The chapter develops an analytical framework derived from previous work explaining the institutionalisation of participatory governance (Bussu 2012; Fung and Wright 2003; Heller 2001). Our aim is to use this framework to develop knowledge as to the conditions under which DDG-like forms of participatory governance develop, flourish and are sustained or undermined. To this end, we draw on a comparison of Nantes and Barcelona, two cities with similar governance histories and contextual features, but with variations on the recent development of DDG in Barcelona and the sustenance of GDD in Nantes. This chapter explains this divergence, seeking to identify conditions that support DDG. The next section presents our analytical framework, which we then use to examine key features of both cases. Finally, we draw out comparative lessons on the conditions for the development of DDG.

Analytical Framework

Different forms of participatory governance can be placed on a spectrum between those seeking to revitalise and improve the internal efficacy and legitimacy of existing democratic systems (GDD) and those seeking to expand the scope of democratic regulation and challenge the way existing institutions function (DDG). Different approaches to participatory governance can be compared using this continuum. However, it is important to emphasise different forms of citizen participation exist in a dynamic relationship and interact with each other. Both GDD and DDG spaces can generate "new fields of power" (Barnes et al. 2007: 54), where what Blaug (2002) refers to as "critical" and "incumbent" concerns interact. Despite being elite-led, citizens invited to participate in GDD-like spaces often "transgress positions as passive recipients and assert their rights" (Cornwall and Coelho 2007, see also Baiocchi and Ganuza, 2016), and DDG spaces originally "claimed" through social mobilisation can become functional to incumbency through assimilation and co-optation (Cornwall 2004; Gaventa 2004).

What drives this dynamism? In this section we draw on previous work (Bua and Bussu, 2021; Bussu 2012) to outline a framework combining agential variables (political leadership and civil society) and institutional variables (local autonomy and socio-economic context) which can act as a constraint or trigger for change. We theorise how these variables interact to produce conditions (un)favourable to the development of DDG-like governance processes and apply them to explain different participatory governance trajectories.

Political Leadership

Local leadership plays a crucial role in facilitating or hindering social mobilisation and social innovation (Pares et al. 2017). Political elites might have an interest in opening an inclusive process, in order to alter the balance of power with opponents to increase their visibility and widen their support base. Local leaders might be stronger or weaker, enjoy more or less personal support, and have a greater or lower incentive to increase their legitimacy through participation. Leadership eager to build support might foster alliances with excluded or weaker social actors against political opponents (Heller 2001). An innovative and autonomous leadership with a clear development project might be interested in building social capacity and furthering redistributive strategies, to widen its own support base. Social movement theorists (Della Porta and Diani 2006; Tilly and Tarrow 2012) have argued convincingly that only social mobilisation can push for redistribution of power and resources. Thus, alliances between local leadership and social movements seem to be crucial not only to the emergence, but also to the resilience of a DDG regime. Without the ongoing support of these alliances, a weak leadership might be more vulnerable to co-optation, party pressures or clientelistic ties with strong interests within and outside state institutions. We hypothesise that the *emergence* of DDG is facilitated by the development of a close relationship between social movements and political leadership with the aim of occupying state institutions (Martínez & Wissink, 2021). This latter aspiration differentiates DDG strategies from Blaug's (2002) concept of "critical democracy" (for more on this difference see Bua and Bussu, 2021), which is concerned with building autonomous, radically democratic spaces that maintain a critical distance from the state. Following Bua and Davies' (2022) analysis of failed attempts to institutionalise radical participation, we hypothesise that maintaining close alliances with social movements and the grassroots base is a key determinant of the *resilience* of DDG once formal institutional power is achieved.

It is important to emphasise that the type of leadership required within any participatory project entails a capacity to coordinate and organise different interests and to foster mutual trust within coherent and committed partnerships. It has to be capable of motivating and aggregating interests, as well as guaranteeing continuity between the initial phase and the operational phase (Piselli 2005). DDG leadership often works within arenas infused "with value differences, conflicts, and mutual interdependence", whereby leadership requires "something other than traditional leaders with formal political authority which they exercise over others" (Bussu and Bartels 2014). Leadership thus becomes facilitative, which ensues not from formal political authority over others, but from working with others to achieve results through an inclusive process (Susskind and Crushank, 2006; Svara, 2008). In the context of radical municipalism in Spain, which generated multiple attempts at constructing DDG-like regimes (Roth et al. 2019), this was reflected in an ambition to "feminise" politics and political leadership, entailing a move towards more horizontal and cooperative styles of political leadership (Russell 2019). Within this context, political institutions are expected to play a different role in stimulating "multilateral exchanges, which will produce norms of behaviour and reciprocity" (Pinson 2002:14). This participatory and collaborative approach to local governance can often trigger resistance from local institutions, which may lack the capacity or willingness to decentre political power and competency. Displaced political agents can continue to constrain transformative projects, by mobilising enduring links to other layers of the state, business, civic and media interests (Bua and Davies, 2022). Furthermore, coalitions advocating DDG are likely to be homogeneous, resulting in internal feuds and disagreements that might weaken their governing capacity, or they might lack political experience and savviness to navigate complex local interests and address political and legal constraints (Blanco et al. 2019; Bua and Bussu 2021; Bua and Davies, 2022).

Civil Society and Social Movement Organisation

We expect high levels of associational activity to increase opportunities for social mobilisation, supporting progressive and transformative political projects and sustaining participatory governance (Fung and Wright 2003; Heller 2001). Stone (1993) argues that a key condition for progressive urban regime change is the sustenance of informed and engaged public support, which provides a crucial resource enabling greater regulation and extraction of concessions from elites. Following Tarrow's (2012) political opportunity structure framework, we can expect opportunities for these alliances to break through into state institutions at times of political or economic crisis, where increases in both incentives for collective action and associations' capacity to mobilise social capital combine with cleavages amongst governing elites to provide opportunities for change.

We should not, however, ignore that strong associations could also use participatory arenas to further corporatist interests and participatory governance could thus encourage collusive behaviours between community leaders and political elites while excluding weaker or non-organised interests (Tarrow 2012). Brought under the control of party and state structures or substituted with more technocratic forms of decision-making, even highly mobilised civil society can be subsumed, as the latter inevitably remains "dependent on the institutional and political environment for finding effective modes of engagement with the state" (Heller 2012: 661). Local associations themselves can be more or less collaborative, although this will often depend on the degree of inclusiveness displayed by the local leadership and/or how substantive the participatory project is perceived to be by social stakeholders.

Local State Autonomy

Institutional constraints and dynamics of multilevel governance inevitably affect the role and impact of local political projects. Political rivalries between national, regional and local government and political party formations at different tiers might affect policy outcomes, as certain local projects or partnerships might be ostracised at higher levels. With regard to higher jurisdictional levels the main constraints are often of an institutional nature, as the lack of coordination and a different approach to local planning and social policies might determine fragmentation of local initiatives. Devolution of responsibilities to regional and municipal authorities has been notionally advocated across many European countries since the 1990s (Bussu 2015). This has also raised expectations of a more active role on the part of the local leadership in addressing economic and development issues, particularly in the context of de-legitimised national parties. However, the remit of European local government is limited and reduced through austerity (Bua et al. 2018). The political platform of new grassroots coalitions is often beyond the regulatory scope of local government (Roth et al. 2019; Bua and Bussu 2021). Even in the context of a decentralised polity with high levels of effective local state autonomy, radical political projects and policy agendas, such as those underpinning DDG, are subject to higher-order constraints of the capitalist political economy (Culpepper, 2015; Dryzek, 1996). Indeed, the socially transformative ambitions of DDG make it a political project that necessarily connects the local to the global, and different scales of government, as it aims to transform liberal democratic institutions and the political economy that unpins them. Finally, resistance from public servants and technocrats at different tiers can combine with the administrative inexperience of activists-turned-politicians to curb more radical ambitions, which in turn will diminish support from social movements, as initial ambitions are not realised (Blanca & Ganuza, 2018); Bua and Davies, 2022).

Economic Context and Socio-economic Performance

It is important to emphasise two dynamics in terms of economic context. On the one hand, globalisation appears to distance the economy from the locality, due to deregulation processes and high mobility of firms. On the other hand, there is renewed interest in the local context, beyond the endowment of natural resources and the geographical proximity to markets or what is referred to as the territory's comparative advantage. During the 1990s and 2000s, the focus was on the so-called competitive advantage (Crouch et al., 2001), or the local collective competition goods that a place can produce. As urban elites were increasingly forced to respond to the pressures of international capital and competition for job creation, issues of housing, social exclusion and social conflicts faded from the political agenda, while lower taxation became the indicator of good management (Le Galès 2002). The rhetoric of image and identity was given political priority to attract investments, with increasing emphasis on public-private partnerships. This was conducive to the emergence of GDD regimes across several European cities, with a strong focus on governance and partnership, as well as a growing rhetoric on citizen participation, which was easily incorporated into discourses of good governance, transparency and open government. However, the global economic crisis in 2008 and associated austerity policies (Blyth, 2013) refocused attention on social issues and played a crucial role in the rise of social mobilisation (Davies, 2021). The social fallout of austerity unleashed progressive movements and right-wing populism (Hopkin & Blyth, 2019). The two cases examined in this chapter illuminate these dynamics.

From this framework, we hypothesise that poor socio-economic performance within a context of political fragmentation generates opportunities for participatory regime change towards DDG, given the existence of progressive political leadership emerging from and working with a critical and organised civil society. The rest of the chapter tests this framework through a comparative analysis of GDD continuity in Nantes (Griggs et al., 2020) and the shift from a GDD to a DDG-like regime in Barcelona (Blanco et al. 2020, Bua and Bussu, 2021).

DDG and GDD Trajectories in Barcelona and Nantes

We focus on the cases of Nantes and Barcelona for their analytically relevant divergence in participatory governance trajectories (Bua et al., 2018).[1] Nantes is paradigmatic of a functionalistic form of collaborative governance (Griggs et al., 2020) that strongly resonates with GDD. Barcelona was selected because it is paradigmatic of radicalisation witnessed since the financial crash and austerity politics (Blanco et al. 2020; Bua et al. 2018) leading to DDG (Bua and Bussu 2021). Until the implementation of austerity measures post-2008, the two cities shared similar GDD models of participatory governance, within a context of relatively successful post-industrial conversion and stable and continuous centre-left political leadership. With the global economic crisis, the onset of austerity and sharpened distributional conflict, the trajectories of participatory governance in each case diverged.

Political Leadership

Since the 1980s, Nantes City council has been governed by centre-left Socialist Party mayors, implementing a relatively successful post-industrial conversion to a service-oriented economy, accompanied by a "consensual and pragmatic" approach that makes heavy use of public-private collaboration and citizen engagement. This is the so-called "system Ayrault" (Griggs et al. 2020), named in reference to the mayor from 1989 to 2012. Jean-Marc Ayrault's term and legacy have provided a stable political context to carry out reforms and develop a style of governance, which is equated by admirers to the slick touch-pass and move style of Nantes Football Club in the 1970s: "le jeu à la Nantaise". The metaphor evokes images of collaborative and inclusive governance in the City, where all actors play an equally important part in constructing policy. This approach appears to have generated an important sense of local identity and pride among political elites. Since 2014, the current mayor, Johanna Roland, also made citizen participation a hallmark of her political style, renewing commitment to participatory governance and branding Nantes as the "citizen city", promoting policies aimed at generating well-being, sustainability and citizen engagement (Griggs et al. 2020). The council committed itself to reinvigorating its participatory governance infrastructure, aiming to generate "constant dialogue" between councillors and citizens. Nantes's approach continues to be touted as a good practice model in building a more democratic, efficient and green city, offering alternative forms of dialogue and resource coordination and innovation to overcome "wicked problems" associated with moves towards sustainable development.

The idea of collaboration in Nantes is firmly embedded, with practices of participation providing spaces for citizen input and for government to justify decisions. Griggs et al. (2020) argue that the "Nantes Game" is a novel way of dealing with the French model of public service delivery and the crisis of legitimacy considered to be engulfing the French Republic, whilst drawing on citizen expertise for effective and responsive service delivery and policy development. However, following Republican principles, decision-making ultimately resides with politicians and participatory spaces exclude actors engaged in contestation, including a wide range of urban activist groups who often avoid participating due to suspicion of top-down agendas. Fundamental discourses and decisions do not appear to change as alternative views often become absorbed and transformed in the participatory process – raising questions as to how meaningful collaboration is in practice.

Like Nantes, political leadership in Barcelona City Hall during the transition to democracy was marked by long-standing electoral hegemony of the centre-left, led by Socialist Party Mayors Pascual Maragall (1982–1997) and Joan Clos (1997–2005). Under this context, the City developed an extensive political infrastructure for public engagement, alongside a tradition of intensive collaboration amongst public authorities, private interests and community groups, part of the so-called "Barcelona Model". Many of these crystallised around the preparations for the 1992 Olympics, including public-private partnerships in urban regeneration and regulations establishing a series of participatory processes and advisory councils, particularly in social policy (Blakeley, 2007; Blanco, 2009). Alongside post-industrial conversation, this participatory infrastructure was made functional to a neoliberal growth model based on services and tourism. Opposition was successfully placated through the incorporation of actors from neighbourhood assemblies. By the turn of the century, this extensive GDD-like political infrastructure was mostly reduced to non-binding consultations heavily orchestrated by the council (Blakeley, 2007; Degen & Garcia, 2008) and had come to be perceived by critics as hollow, generating more fatigue than empowerment (Blanco et al. 2020).

Reflecting patterns observed throughout Spain, the 2011 elections returned changes in long-standing political leadership. For the first time since the transition to democracy a politically conservative administration was elected to city hall, led by Xavier Trias (2011–2015). His urban austerity agenda compounded provincial- and national-level measures, emphasising an intensified neoliberal logic, sought to boost the tourist economy, with enhanced public–private partnerships and subcontracting. The City's participatory infrastructure was not rolled back, but neither was it invested in: it was left to wither on the grapevine (Blanco et al. 2020). However, as in so many other parts of Spain, Barcelona witnessed a sharp intensification of mass mobilisations against austerity during the early 2010s. The Indignados movement led to the emergence of a new national party, Podemos, which gained 21.2% of the votes in the 2016 general elections. At the municipal level, the 2015 elections were characterised by the victories of local movement-parties across Spain's major urban centres (Roth et al. 2019). Barcelona was one of several cities where street movements became part of radical left platforms to contest municipal elections, bringing together the traditional left with new anti-austerity forces. In May 2015, led by a leading activist against housing evictions, Ada Colau, the BeC coalition won the municipal election, forming a minority administration. Under the banner of the "New Municipalism" (Blanco and Gomà, 2020), Barcelona City Council rolled out many initiatives in support of social justice, participatory democracy and feminism. The influence of social movements on agenda setting meant that participatory governance processes became linked to material concerns related to sharpened austerity, neoliberalisation and touristification. Colau was re-elected in 2019, with substantial support from social movements but upon weaker electoral position due to political developments to be explained related to the rise of Catalan nationalism and the waning 15-M cycle of contention (Davies et al. 2022). Political leadership in Barcelona is therefore characterised by social movement collaboration, for example through public-commons partnerships, and much of its agenda seeks to advance radical democracy, cooperative economics, and develop new forms of social protection and de-commodification (Vlahos, this volume).

Civil Society and Social Movements

Much of civil society contention in Nantes revolves around social exclusions generated by its urban growth model. In the 2000s plans to construct a new airport at Notre-Dame-Des-Landes, some 20 km to the north-west of the city, became a nodal point for contentious politics (Griggs et al. 2020). Bubbling up since the announcement by central government of the new airport construction in 2000, conflict peaked in 2012 with the intervention of riot police to clear out protesters. The City's refusal to support local protesters initiated a crisis of legitimacy for both the sustainable development credentials of the city and its style of governance. Indeed, social movements had long disassociated themselves from the City's participatory infrastructure, seeing little strategic value in engaging. Griggs et al. (2020) describe the harsh criticism by oppositional actors of what they perceived as the tokenism of Nantes's GDD regime. Demands for deeper and more meaningful engagement, which the Nantes model no longer satisfies, are becoming more widespread amongst actors in civil society. Furthermore, anti-capitalist protesters organising against airport expansion occupied the construction land and sought to work alongside local farmers and citizens to generate autonomous spaces. Such critical actors have yet to constitute a counter-hegemonic discourse comparable to that of Barcelona en Comú but have succeeded in questioning the approach to urban governance, revealing the inability of managerial forms of participatory governance to accommodate more radical alternatives (Baiocchi and Ganuza, 2016).

In Barcelona, during the 1980s and 1990s, social opposition was contained by the incorporation of actors from neighbourhood assemblies (Blakeley 2005; Blanco 2009). Nevertheless, as social fallout accumulated and economic returns from the neoliberal boosterism of the so-called "Barcelona model" diminished (Delgado 2007), counter-hegemonic spaces emerged where social movements collaborated with critical public servants to develop alternative regeneration models. The hosting of the Universal Cultures Forum to showcase the city's burgeoning tourism industry also provided a focal point for protests from a variety of movements organising around urban privatisation and touristification. Such movements would find their claims vindicated by the sharpening of neoliberalisation and austerity during the Trias administration. Whilst some autonomous spaces for social innovation were met with acquiescence by the council for their potential to compensate for a retreating welfare state (Sánchez Belando, 2017), the social fallout from austerity fuelled and radicalised mobilisations. Movements such as the platform of mortgage victims (PAH) and the Indignados were especially strong in the city, protesting against the privatisation of water, housing, public space, health and education. PAH emerged in 2009 in Barcelona and successfully spread around Spain, in protest to draconian mortgage and repossession laws. It successfully framed housing as a collective issue rather than one of individual responsibility over debt. Whilst the Indignados movement that famously swept Spain in 2011 had fizzled out by 2014, the political agenda it had articulated was incorporated by Podemos nationally, and at the municipal level by grassroots coalitions such as Barcelona en Comú (BeC).

Social movements such as the PAH were instrumental for BeC, providing channels for non-state actors to define priorities, as is evident in the content of policies, but also in BeC's horizontal style of governance (Font & Garcia-Espin 2019). BeC's platform was open and shaped by social movements' demands but sought to institutionalise participation by individual citizens rather than solely relying on associations' representatives. Therefore, citizens, even when members of social movements, political parties, trade unions or other organisations, participated on an individual basis together with non-affiliated citizens (Baiocchi & Ganuza 2016; Eizaguirre et al. 2017). Having entered office, a key strategy for BeC to overcome the structural and institutional barriers faced by DDG was to continue to leverage the political power of social movements, helping the administration strengthen the legitimacy of its message as well as exert pressure on higher tiers of authority to call for changes in regulations outside the scope of municipal action (Blanco et al. 2020). Indeed, under the conceptual umbrella of notions such as the urban commons and the social and solidarity economy, the new BeC government aims to foster an active and autonomous society capable of acting beyond the state sphere (see Salazar et al., this volume).

Local State Autonomy

During the 1980s and 1990s, both France and Spain were deeply influenced by the structural shifts away from national redistribution and urban managerialism towards urban self-reliance and entrepreneurship (Harvey, 1989). France is a highly de-concentrated state, with over 36,000 municipalities and mayors enjoying considerable powers and autonomy. Some scholars talk of "municipal presidentialism" (Mabileau 1995), whereby although mayors are not directly elected, there is growing personalisation of the municipal system (Kerrouche 2005). Political elites in Nantes were important actors and advocates of these metropolitanisation processes and promoted the setting up of ad-hoc mechanisms for intermunicipal co-operation in the metropolitan area (Pinson and Le Gales, 2005), which came to be known as "Nantes Metropole" by 2004. In formal terms, local autonomy would enjoy an added boost during austerity politics. In 2014 the French state devolved tax-raising powers as well as competencies in economic development and transport. The city of Nantes led the region's economic development planning, with broadly positive results. Nantes enjoyed generally positive socio-economic performance in the aftermath of the global economic crisis, which enabled local elites to develop urban development strategies that avoided the harshest impact of austerity. Metropolitanisation has strengthened the city mayor, other mayors, and the executive, arguably leading to pork-barrel politics and risking citizen marginalisation from democratic decisions taken at the metropolitan scale (Bussu 2015). As seen in other European countries undergoing similar processes, participatory governance has often served to strengthen the visibility of mayors and their unmediated relationship with civil society to pursue flagship projects, whilst bypassing more structured participatory institutions (ibid.). At the same time, reductions in national government transfers, and tax reforms introduced in the early 2010s created greater fiscal pressure on the City Council, exposing it to significant budget cuts from 2016. Yet, the council retained a degree of fiscal autonomy, regulations allowing it to lengthen its balanced-budget cycle to mitigate these pressures. As Davies et al. (2022) explain, "perhaps the most significant lesson from Nantes ... is that with a modest degree of fiscal autonomy, a city can differentiate or even contrast itself politically with the national situation around it".

The Spanish state is characterised by an asymmetric and relatively decentralised system of "autonomous communities". Regional governments take responsibility for key services including education and health. Provincial governments have a more limited role, balancing service delivery between rural and urban areas, and municipalities have variable powers, which increase in large urban centres such as Barcelona. However, repeating a pattern observed throughout several European countries, including France, (Bua et al. 2018), the era of austerity signified substantive (re)centralisation of powers through cuts to services managed at the local level. Spain was one of the countries where this was exacerbated by the EU austerity memorandum, which led to the enforcement of fiscal consolidation targets for all Spanish administrations. The Organic Law on Budgetary Stability and Financial Sustainability in 2012 mandated balanced budgets and imposed debt ceilings for all levels of governments. The infamous "Montoro laws" for the Rationalisation and Sustainability of Local Administration forced local authorities to use any financial surplus for debt repayment, and an "independent" authority for Fiscal Responsibility was established to monitor compliance – similar entities were established in a number of Eurozone countries (Davies, 2021).

Centralisation exacerbated the aforementioned mismatch between the ambitious BeC policy agenda and the regulatory capacity of City Hall, and it is an important terrain of struggle. BeC made efforts to free municipal politics from the economic relations and institutions to which they are usually beholden, for instance through investment in community-wealth building, whilst deconstructing and rethinking the notion of the state–society relationship as a binary opposition. For this, and much like other "new municipalist administrations" it earned the outright hostility of actors at higher state scales, which obstructed otherwise routine governance arrangements (Bua and Davies, 2022; Blanca and Ganuza, 2018). Moreover, austerity rescaling measures added grist to the mill of the independence movement in Catalonia, which grew considerably after 2010 and provided an electoral competitor to BeC. Thus, the re-politicisation of the city and the democratisation of local institutions opened up new possibilities and imaginaries but also coincided with an intensification of constraints on autonomy. Combined with relatively low levels of administrative-political experience of activists-turned-politicians and the tumultuous political environment of the Catalan independence conflict and the Spanish state's counter-attack to the municipalist movement (Bua and Davies, 2022), these severely limited BeC's capacity for government.

Economic Context and Socio-economic Performance

The recent history of Nantes is that of a relatively successful post-industrial conversion, from an economy based on shipbuilding to a service-led one specialising in IT and banking (Griggs et al. 2020). Under the context of political stability described above, urban regeneration policies aimed at strengthening the international competitiveness and distinctiveness of the city. For example, Nantes positioned itself as a "green city" (Griggs et al., 2020) culminating with the award of European Green Capital in 2013. This success is widely attributed to an urban growth agenda based on large-scale urban regeneration projects in neighbourhoods and industrial heritage sites, and a city branding strategy based on sustainability (Davies et al. 2022).

In Bua et al.'s (2018) analysis of urban austerity governance in five European cities, Nantes appears as somewhat of an anomaly for its relatively positive socio-economic performance. A growing population and tax base meant that it managed to avoid the sharpest edges of austerity, despite being affected by national-level issues such as increased unemployment and cuts to local government services (also Davies et al. 2022). However, inequality increased following the global economic crisis with poorer households experiencing sharp reductions in income, leading policymakers to focus on how to engender more inclusive growth, but within the same political and economic model. City officials used the term "décrochage" to capture the idea that these neighbourhoods had become de-coupled from the vibrant growth of the rest of the city (Griggs et al. 2020). The policy challenge was thus framed as re-connecting these communities rather than questioning the current socio-economic model. The possibility of this endeavour is underscored by political elites in terms of differentiating economic management in Nantes from broader patterns of urban austerity, a language which local politicians found uncomfortable (Davies et al. 2022). Instead, they articulated a confident sustainable growth mentality, emphasising the city's capacity to employ counter-cyclical strategies to mitigate the impact of national-level cuts.

Barcelona also underwent similar processes of urban restructuring during the 1980s. Centre-left city leaders engaged in a form of neoliberal urban boosterism based on leveraging international events such as the 1992 Olympics to build the City's profile as a tourist attraction. Facilitated by further permissive planning law implemented by 1990s national-level conservative governments (Martí-Costa & Tomàs, 2016), as well as the substantial liquidity of global financial markets at the time, the construction of new homes and other forms of urban construction accelerated substantially, as did private debt and broader processes of financialisation (Blanco et al. 2020). The staging of the 1992 Olympics crystallised the "Barcelona Model" of urban governance (Blakeley 2005; Blanco 2009), including the development of a service and tourist-based economy, with the use of great events as catalysts for regeneration.

Whereas the Barcelona post-Olympic growth model is widely touted as a success, critics argue that it led to increased inequalities, gentrification, touristification and resulting displacement and social cleansing (Delgado 2007; Martí-Costa and Tomas 2017). The socio-economic fallout from these processes was exacerbated by national austerity policies following the financial crash of 2008. Unemployment rose to 18.6% in 2012, with 18.2% of the population at risk of poverty in 2011 (Bua et al. 2018). The Trias administration (2011-2015) sharpened neoliberal boosterism and touristification. The social fallout led to the radicalism and popular appeal of the urban change agenda espoused by BeC. Since 2015, their economic strategy has focussed on regulating tourism, overturning privatisation and engaging in community-led forms of economic development, often based on cooperative ownership and the social economy. However, this ambitious agenda has been constrained by the limited regulatory capacity of City Hall, compounded by hostility from other state scales and a local "pro-status quo coalition" (Blanco et al. 2020).

Discussion

The previous section tells a story of two cities which developed post-Fordist economies and relatively similar participatory governance infrastructures. The ability of both to generate consent and legitimacy diminished as the neoliberal boom years subsided, with latent urban alternatives growing against established urban governance models in both cities. However, in Nantes, this model would survive the social fallout from austerity, whereas in Barcelona this provided the basis for radicalisation in pursuit of democracy-driven governance. The analysis we have provided contributes to explanations of this divergence. Table 11.1 summarises the key details from each case.

In Nantes, the decades-long leadership of socialist mayors ensured a stable political context while at the same time reducing the space for political contestation and closing down windows of opportunities for a more radical project of democratisation. This political environment has opened the path to a top-down vision of transformation, which has shifted power from non-state actors to technocrats and consultants. Similarly to what Heller (2001: 664) observed when examining the missed opportunities for civil society in South Africa under the ANC, "the power that flows from electoral dominance has, in other words, come directly at the expense of participatory democracy". Griggs et al. (2020) note that the French republican tradition sees the state as the primary actor to advance social solidarity, whereby "public officials and politicians claim to embody the general interest, while negating opposition from groups who are deemed to promote merely sectional interests" (Griggs et al. 2020: 14). As the power and visibility of local political elites, and mayors in particular, grew through decentralisation reforms, it also curbed the significance of other democratic structures, making participatory governance ancillary to the mayor's vision of economic development.

Table 11.1 A Framework to Understand Emergence of DDG

Dimensions	Nantes GDD	Barcelona DDG
Leadership/ Political Context	• Sustained centre-left leadership since the 1980s, successfully adapted to urban entrepreneurialism • Commitment to collaborative governance and citizen participation • Lack of effective opposition	• Political stability and successful adaptation to urban entrepreneurialism • Competing governance imaginaries with rise of counter-hegemonic movement after global economic crisis • Heightened political contestation post-economic crisis and window of opportunity for social movements to "enter the state" • Alternative urban agenda pursued since 2015, in connection to material concerns raised by social movements and attempts at establishing more radical forms of participatory governance
Civil Society	• Development of alternative movements around airport protests successfully questioning urban governance but falling short of establishing counter-hegemonic movement • Opposition partially contained by GDD	• Co-option of critical civil society until alternative movements developed in response to sharpening social fallout and diminishing returns • Radicalisation and consolidation of alternative forms of governance with 15-M cycle of contention • Emergent "New Municipalism" bringing social movement agendas into local state
Local Autonomy	• Contextual shift from redistribution and managerialism to urban self-reliance and entrepreneurialism • Successful adaptation by urban political elites to neoliberal shift • Relative autonomy from central state allows for economic strategy containing impact of austerity	• Reduction in state autonomy with EU and national austerity measures • Mismatch between DDG aspirations and municipal powers • Hostile state constrains governance
Local Economy	• Successful post-industrial conversion (Banking and IT) • Avoids sharp edges of austerity due to growing population and tax base • Increases in inequality and "décrochage" post-2008 crisis	• Successful post-industrial conversion (service and tourism) • Diminishing returns to urban model during the 2000s • Sharpening of neoliberalisation and social fallout post-2008 economic crisis

In Barcelona, similar patterns of citizen engagement had developed under the stable leadership of the Catalan Socialist Party between 1979 and 2011. When in 2011, following the economic crisis triggered by the global economic crisis and in a context of widespread discontent with punishing austerity measures, a Conservative-liberal coalition took power, the electoral arena became more competitive. This dramatic change in government, by destabilising local power dynamics, also opened opportunities for more radical political projects led by a well-organised civil society already galvanised by the momentum of widespread protests across the country. Barcelona's civil society vaunts a long history of mobilisation and enough operational autonomy to be able to align with the local state whilst containing risks of co-optation. A new national-level movement party, Podemos, had emerged from a coalition of intellectuals and social movements and helped to orchestrate the necessary political consensus for reform at national level. Getting the politics right, and specifically having a proper balance between political power and civil society, was therefore crucial for DDG to emerge. This fortunate conjunction of different factors in Barcelona appears highly dependent on the heightened political contestation of the post-financial crash period. Political instability might also make any new institutional gains precarious. Changes in government will represent a litmus test for the resilience of new participatory institutions, unveiling genuine popular consensus (or exposing lack thereof) on the role of participatory democracy in redefining the relationship between citizens and state institutions.

Both Nantes and Barcelona's experiences show how GDD and DDG relied on routinised forms of participation to facilitate dialogue between citizens and the administration, highlighting a preference for permanent and embedded structures. This proceduralisation poses a dilemma: if it is too loose, it is difficult to safeguard the process against the erratic developments of political cycles; however, where it is excessively rigid it could constrain the experimental nature of democratic innovations and, like in Nantes, turn participatory spaces into a hollow site of legitimation of top-down decisions (Bussu 2012). DDG sits between routinised participation and protest politics. Thus, in the long term, continuous alliances with social movements and local civil societies might be able to guard it against risks of bureaucratisation. Furthermore, international constituencies for radical reforms and cross-border alliances with other new municipalist cities, and the local and global social movements supporting them, might prove an effective strategy to reform democracy from the local level up.

One of the interesting differences that emerged from the comparison between Barcelona and Nantes was the impact of socio-economic conditions combined with varying degrees of autonomy enjoyed by local government. Relatively positive economic performance in Nantes, combined with relatively more flexibility in meeting debt obligations under the leadership of a centre-left national government under Francois Hollande, allowed City leaders to use their powers in pursuit of different strategies of economic development from the national government, shielding the urban economy from the harshest impacts of austerity. Barcelona, although enjoying considerable autonomy compared to many European cities of similar size, was subjected to the harsh (re)centralisation of fiscal powers by a Conservative government responding to the 2012 EU memorandum, as a consequence of deeper cuts to public services, privatisation and outsourcing of many of its functions. The grievances fuelled by these recentralisation processes also contributed to already complex centre-periphery relations, with growing popularity of separatist parties on the left and right of the political spectrum. A combination of economic and political instability opened a window of opportunity for a transformative political project.

Barcelona's alliance between left-wing political formations and social movements that led to local institutions' occupation and transformation vaguely resembles the relationship between the Workers' Party and the neighbourhood associations that transformed Porto Alegre's budget approval process by introducing Participatory Budgeting, in the aftermath of the long military dictatorship in Brazil (Baiocchi 2005). However, Barcelona en Comú's ambitions have been curbed by the relatively limited remit of local government's financial autonomy and decision-making powers. In a context of centralisation and privatisation, where citizens are now primarily consumers, the project for a deeper democracy must align necessarily with one for a decentralised democracy and strengthened local government (Bua and Escobar, 2018; Bussu 2015). BeC's DDG regime is still fragile, as it faces age-old power equations pitting bureaucrats against civil society and institutional logics against mobilisational logics and de-mobilisation associated with the waning of the 15-M cycle of contention, whilst the media often rallies against policies that threaten local powerful interests. However, Barcelona's case also shows how local government is "often an arena where alliances across the state-society boundary can develop and produce synergistic outcomes" (Heller 2012: 660).

Conclusion

This chapter has reflected on factors that might favour the emergence of a DDG regime, by comparing two European cities which initially shared similar post-industrial economies and DDG-like governance structures: Nantes and Barcelona. The global economic crisis and ensuing austerity politics had different impacts in each of these two cities, whereby Nantes was able to shield its economy and municipality from the worst effect of austerity and therefore safeguard the legitimacy and stability of its political elites. On the contrary in Barcelona, the social and economic fallout destabilised the political environment, leading to greater contestation, which a well-organised civil society was able to exploit, carving out a window of opportunities. The fragile DDG regime in Barcelona with its ambitions for radical reforms is however constrained by local state capacity, as reduced competencies of local government following cuts and outsourcing pose severe limits to the impact of radical forms of participatory governance. This makes DDG vulnerable to political cycles – in many other Spanish cities, changes in government marked the end of the new municipalist experience (Bua and Davies, 2022). Ultimately, the resilience of DDG initiatives will likely depend on whether there is a popular consensus for deepening the scope of democracy.

Note

1 This research mainly draws upon UK Economic and Social Research Council-funded research (ES/L012898/1) undertaken in eight cities between 2015 and 2018, exploring dynamics of collaborative governance under austerity. It references now-published work on both cases from this project (e.g., Blanco et al., 2020; Bua et al., 2018; Davies, 2021; Davies et al., 2022; Griggs et al. 2021; Griggs and Howarth 2020).

References

Baiocchi, G. and E. Ganuza (2016). *Popular Democracy: The Paradox of Participation.* Stanford University Press.
Barnes, M. et al. (2007). *Power, Participation and Political Renewal: Case Studies in Public Participation.* Policy Press.
Belando, M.V.S. (2017). "Building alternatives to the creative turn in Barcelona: The case of the socio-cultural centre Can Batllo", *City Culture and Society* 8: 35–42.
Blanca, R., & Ganuza, E. (2018). Les labyrinthes du pouvoir : les mairies du changement face aux administrations. *Mouvements*, 94(2): 36–44.
Blanco, I. (2009). Does a 'Barcelona Model' Really Exist? Periods, Territories and Actors in the Process of Urban Transformation, *Local Government Studies*, 35(3): 355–369.
Blanco, I., et al. (2019). Urban governance and political change under a radical left government: The case of Barcelona. *Journal of Urban Affairs*: 42:1, 18-38, DOI: 10.1080/07352166.2018.1559648.
Blanco, I., Bianchi, O. and Salazar, Y. (2020). "Urban governance and political change under a radical left government: The case of Barcelona." *Journal of Urban Affairs.* 42, (1): 1–21.
Blaug, R. (2002). Engineering democracy. *Political Studies* 50(1): 102–116.
Blyth, M. (2013). *Austerity: The History of a Dangerous Idea.* Oxford: Oxford University Press.
Bua, A. and S. Bussu (2021). Between governance-driven democratisation and democracy-driven governance: Explaining changes in participatory governance in the case of Barcelona. *European Journal of Political Research* 60(3): 716–737.
Bua, A. and J. Davies (2022). Understanding the crisis of New Municipalism in Spain: The struggle for urban regime power in A Coruña and Santigo de Compostela. *Urban Studies*, online before print: https://doi.org/10.1177/00420980221123939
Bua, A. and O. Escobar (2018). Participatory-deliberative processes and public policy agendas: Lessons for policy and practice. *Policy Design and Practice* 1(2): 126–140.
Bua, A. Davies, J. Blanco, I. Chorianopoulos, I. Cortina-Oriol, M. Feandeiro, A. Gaynor, N. Griggs, S. Howarth, D. and Salazar, Y. (2018). "The Urban Governance of Austerity in Europe", in Kerley, R. Liddle, J. and Dunning, P. (eds) *The Handbook of International Local Government.* Routledge: 280–295.
Bussu, S. (2012) Governing with the citizens: strategic planning in four Italian cities. LSE Thesis.
Bussu, S. (2015) Between a rock and a hard place: The councillor's dilemma between strong mayors and citizens' needs. *Local Government Studies* 41(6): 841–860.

Bussu, S. and K. Bartels (2014) Facilitative leadership and the challenge of renewing local democracy. *International Journal of Urban and Regional Research*, 38 (6):2256–2273.
Cornwall, A. (2004). Spaces for transformation? Reflections on issues of power and difference in participation in development. in Hickey, S., Mohan, G., Eds *Participation: From Tyranny to Transformation:..* London, UK; New York, NY, USA: Zed Books, 75–91.
Cornwall, A. and V. S. Coelho (2007). *Spaces for Change? the Politics of Citizen Participation in New Democratic Arenas* (Vol. 4). London, UK; New York, NY, USA: Zed Books.
Culpepper, P. (2015). Structural Power and Political Science in the Post-Crisis Era. *Business and Politics*, Vol, 17. (3): 391–409
Crouch, C. Le Gales, P. Triglia, C. Voelzkow, H. (2001). *Local Production Systems in Europe: Rise or Demise?* Oxford: Oxford University Press.
Davies, J.S. (2011).*Challenging Governance Theory: from Networks to Hegemony.* Bristol: Polity Press.
Davies, J. Blanco, I. Bua, A. Chorianopoulos, I. Feandeiro, A. Gaynor, N. Gleeson, B. Griggs, S. Hamel, P. Henderson, H. Howarth, D. Keil, R. Pill, M. Salazar, Y. and Sullivan, H. (2022). New Developments in Urban Governance: Rethinking Collaboration in the Age of Austerity. Bristol University Press.
Delgado, M. (2007). *La Ciudad Mentirosa: Fraude Miseria en el Modelo Barcelona*. Catarata.
Della, P. D. and M. Diani (2006). *Social Movements: An Introduction*. Blackwell Pub.
Dryzek, J. S. (1996). Political inclusion and the dynamics of democratization. *American Political Science Review* 90(3): 475–487.
Eizaguirre, S. Marc Pradel-Miquel and Marisol García (2017). Citizenship practices and democratic governance: 'Barcelona en Común' as an urban citizenship confluence promoting a new policy agenda. *Citizenship Studies*. https://doi.org/10.1080/13621025.2017.1307609
Font, J. and P. Garcia-Espin (2019). From Indignad@s to mayors? Participatory dilemmas in Spanish municipal movements. *Routledge Handbook of Contemporary European Social Movements*, edited by Flescher Forminaya, C. and Feenstra, R. Routledge.
Fung, A. and E. O. Wright (2003). *Deepening Democracy: Institutional Innovations in Empowered Participatory Governance*. Verso.
Gaventa, J. (2004). Towards participatory governance: Assessing the transformative possibilities. *Participation: From Tyranny to Transformation*: 25–41.
Griggs, S., Howarth, D. and Feandeiro, A. (2020). "The logics and limits of "collaborative governance" in Nantes: Myth, ideology, and the politics of new urban regimes." *Journal of Urban Affairs*.1-18.
Harvey, D. (1989) from managerialism to entrepreneurialism: the transformation in urban governance in late capitalism, Geografiska Annaler. *Series B, Human Geography*, 71 (1) 3–17.
Heller, P. (2001). Moving the State: The politics of democratic decentralization in Kerala, South Africa, and Porto Alegre. *Politics & Society* 29(1): 131–163. https://doi.org/10.1177/0032329201029001006
Heller, P. (2012). Democracy, participatory politics and development. *Polity* 44(4): 643–665.
Hopkin, J. and Blyth, M. (2019). The Global Economics of European Populism: growth Regimes and Party Systems Change in Europe. *Government and Opposition.* 54(2): 193–225.

Kerrouche, E. 2005. The powerful French Mayor: Myth and reality. In *Transforming Local Political Leadership*, edited by R. Berg and N. Rao. Palgrave.

Le Galès, P. (2002). *European Cities, Social Conflicts and Governance*. Oxford University Press.

Mabileau, A. (1995). De la Monarchie Municipal à la française [On municipal monarchy french style]. *Pouvoirs* 73: 7–17.

Marti-Costa, M. and Tomas, M. (2017). "Urban governance in Spain: From democratic transition to austerity policies." *Urban studies* 54(9): 2107-2122.

Martínez, M. A., & Wissink, B. (2021). Urban movements and municipalist governments in Spain: alliances, tensions, and achievements. *Social Movement Studies*. Online before print: https://doi.org/10.1080/14742837.2021.1967121

Parés, M., et al. (2017). *Social Innovation and Democratic Leadership: Communities and Social Change from Below*. Edward Elgar Publishing.

Pinson, G. (2002) Political government and governance. Strategic planning and the reshaping of political capacity in Turin. *IJURR* 26(3): 477–93.

Pinson, G. and P. Le Galès (2005). State restructuring and decentralisation dynamics in France: Politics is the driving force. Cahier Européen 7, Centre d'Études Européennes de Sciences Po.

Piselli, R. (2005). Capitale sociale e società civile nei nuovi modelli di governance locale. *Stato e Mercato* 75(December): 455–485.

Roth, L. A. Monterde and A. Calleja López (eds). (2019). *Ciudades Democraticas: La Revuelta Municipalista en el Ciclo post-15M*. Icaria.

Russel, B. (2019). Beyond the local trap: The New Municipalism and the rise of fearless cities. *Antipode* 51(3): 989–1010.

Sintomer, Y. (2018). From deliberative to radical democracy? Sortition and politics in the twenty-first century. *Politics & Society* 46(3): 337–357.

Smith, G. (2009). *Democratic Innovations: Designing Institutions for Citizen Participation*. Cambridge University Press.

Stone, C. N. (1993). Urban Regimes and the Capacity to Govern: A Political Economy Approach. *Journal of Urban Affairs*, 15(1): 1–28.

Susskind, L.E. and J.L. Cruikshank (2006). *Breaking Robert's Rules*. New York University Press.

Svara, J.H. (2008). *The Facilitative Leader in City Hall: Reexamining the Scope and Contributions*. CRC Press.

Tilly, C. and S. Tarrow (2012). *Contentious Politics: [With a Brief Preface Update on the Arab Spring, the Occupy Movement, and Connections to Contentious Politics Over Time]*. Oxford University Press.

Warren, M. (2014). *Governance-Driven Democratization. Practices of Freedom: Decentered Governance, Conflict and Democratic Participation*. Edited by S. Griggs, A. J. Norval and H. Wagenaar, Cambridge University Press.

Section 3
Assessing the Challenges to Projects of Radical Reform

12 Expanding Participatory Governance through Digital Platforms?
Drivers and Obstacles in the Implementation of the Decidim Platform

Joan Balcells, Rosa Borge and Albert Padró-Solanet

Introduction

The implementation of the *Decidim* ("We Decide" in Catalan) platform by local governments across Catalonia illustrates how the use of new digital tools for citizen participation can have a complex effect on local governance, due to the combination of elements of radical democratisation with a top-down managerial logic. This interplay can be characterised through the contrast between governance-driven democratisation (GDD) and democracy-driven governance (DDG). GDD refers to an elite-driven form of participation oriented to improving the performance of policymaking (Warren, 2014), whereas DDG involves participation pushed by social movements aimed at deepening democracy (Bua & Bussu, 2021). These forms of participatory governance are not mutually exclusive but can coexist and interact with each other, though not unproblematically (Blanco et al, 2020; Bua & Bussu, 2021). Some practitioners and scholars fear that online participation can lead politicians and administrations to implement participative experiences bypassing the transformative demands claimed by social movements. However, technology does not necessarily imply a technocratic and managerial bias: free and open-source participatory platforms devised by a community devoted to promoting citizens' participation can be combined with other forms of locally based participation to leverage its potential, although this process is not devoid of tensions (Borge, Balcells & Padró-Solanet, 2022).

Participatory platforms like Decidim were designed as a tool to radicalise democratic governance by bringing the participatory know-how of social movements to public institutions. In Spain, since the 2008 Great Recession, 15-M activists critical of the existing representative democracy had pushed for a more direct, participatory and deliberative model of democracy through civic technologies. After a new left coalition coming from these protest movements gained power in Barcelona in 2015 (Barcelona En Comú), the platform Decidim was adopted by the local government as the main tool for participatory processes. Up to November 2021, 85 municipalities in Catalonia and more than 400 local and regional governments, organisations and institutions in the world have implemented this platform, with more than 1 million users.[1]

DOI: 10.4324/9781003218517-15

Although born with radically democratic expectations, aligned with DDG purposes, open-source and free-software participatory digital platforms tend to be used and institutionalised by local public administrations in a way more akin to managerial goals. Nevertheless, the participatory drive underpinning the platform is backed up and sustained in the Catalan local agenda by alliances between social movements, local associations, activists and political confluences, some of them as part of the new municipalism (Thompson, 2021). In addition, the process of implementation of these participatory tools has the potential of disrupting traditional working patterns of public administrations and clashing with previously institutionalised routines and structures of citizen participation.

Thus, this convergence between social movements and public administrations has not been as seamless as it might appear. It raises problems and contradictions, namely between the technocratic bureaucratisation of citizen participation and the logic of grassroots democracy. To what extent do the institutionalisation and bureaucratisation of participatory digital platforms interfere with bottom-up initiatives and participation? Has the implementation of participatory platforms met resistances and obstacles? Which are the drivers that favour the deployment of the platform in its full participatory capabilities? Our analysis sheds light on the tensions between the two models of participatory governance behind digital platforms.

To answer these questions, we collected data through an online questionnaire and in-depth interviews targeting managers in charge of implementing Decidim in 34 Catalan local administrations, who experienced first-hand the challenges raised by the digitisation of participatory processes. This information was complemented with users' data from the platforms' web pages.

Our analysis of public managers' perceptions highlights three different tensions: between the goals of transparency and participation, between innovation and previous structures of participation and between acceptance and reluctance from key actors, particularly among well-established local organisations who may feel displaced because of disintermediation in favour of direct individual participation.

Drivers and Obstacles

Open-source participatory platforms like Decidim enable crowd-sourced participatory processes, communication and collaboration in multiple directions, citizens' self-organisation and autonomy, and traceability and accountability of all stages of the participatory processes. In that sense, these platforms have the potential of fostering a more democratically driven form of governance. However, this potential is mostly dependent on factors such as the will of local representatives or the constrictions and resources of the public administrations who are in charge of implementing them.

The tensions between managerial and more radically democratic expectations can be a continuous source of conflicts and problems. On the one hand, the adoption of ambitious participatory policies and their transition to digital platforms can alter the existing power structures and relations that define local governance. As Ganuza et al. (2016, p. 330) pointed out, "both critics and proponents of participation tend to overlook how any participatory project requires allies, and how such project provokes tensions and conflicts". On the other hand, purely managerial strategies that do not look for genuine participation risk alienating citizens or triggering protests and opposition (Fung, 2015).

To approach the phenomenon, we analysed the way Decidim is perceived by the public managers in charge of its implementation. Being at the front line and acting as liaisons between public administration and civil society, these managers are well positioned to assess the institutional and organisational conditions that may foster or hinder the development of digital platforms as a tool for citizen participation, as well as the reactions of the different actors involved. Thus, an analysis of their perceptions can provide very useful information for better understanding the challenges at play when implementing participatory projects through digital channels. That is in line with other studies relying on interviews to detect barriers and enablers for the implementation of participatory and technological innovations in public administrations (Bua & Escobar, 2018; Mergel et al., 2019; Smith & Prieto-Martín, 2021; Rodríguez-Bolíbar 2014).

Perceptions are organised around three main factors or drivers that explain the implementation of participatory digital platforms following findings in previous literature: (1) institutional and organisational factors (Criado et al, 2017; Borge, Colombo & Welp, 2009; Falcó & Kleinhans, 2018); (2) an organisational culture in favour of participation and transparency (Aikins & Krane, 2010; Meijer, 2015; Falcó & Kleinhans, 2018); and (3) a supportive reception by key actors, namely the political leaders of the local government, public administrators, individual citizens and local associations (Bherer et al, 2016; Ganuza et al, 2016).

Institutional and Organisational Factors

A supportive institutional environment can facilitate the adoption and implementation of technological innovations for citizen participation by reducing costs and barriers. For example, technical support from supra-municipal organisations can help reduce implementation costs that would otherwise be insurmountable for municipalities with fewer resources. Similarly, the open-source nature of technology can also reduce the impact of technological barriers (Criado et al., 2017). In addition, isomorphic pressures (Di Maggio & Powell, 1983) can make governments prone to using the participatory digital tools that other administrations are implementing. On the one hand, the Spanish normative framework favours participation and the use of digital technologies.[2] On the other hand, as happens with other innovations, local governments tend to adopt the digital platforms that surrounding municipalities are using (Borge, Colombo & Welp, 2009).

Also crucial is understanding how the implementation of digital platforms fits in with previous citizen participation structures. Past experience with participatory processes and platforms can ease the implementation of new ones, as there is already a set of resources and an organisational culture with a positive attitude towards responsiveness and digitally enabled citizen involvement (Meijer, 2015). However, new digital platforms can also introduce a certain degree of complexity, as they can disrupt public administrations' work routines and require the adaptation of firmly established processes, which can obviously generate resistance and imbalances (Aikins & Krane, 2010).

Organisational Culture

The use of digital platforms to strengthen the role of citizens and external stakeholders requires an organisational culture responsive to the needs and demands of these diverse actors. Previous studies show that exploiting the interactive potential of digital technologies requires that public managers believe in the opportunities these technologies provide to gather citizens' inputs (Aikins & Krane, 2010; Voorberg et al, 2015). Besides resources and organisational capacity, motivation and commitment are key elements for the success of innovative practices (Atkin et al., 2015; Schedler et al., 2019). Digital platforms may help to expand participatory governance through citizen involvement and transparency if these goals are mutually shared by the actors involved. Public administrations commonly see participation and transparency as two complementary goals that constitute the basic pillars of the so-called "open-government" agenda (Oszlak, 2013). In this line, digital technologies are the channel that facilitates this conjoint achievement (OECD, 2016). However, public administrations more comfortable with a governance-driven form of participation (GDD) may prefer to put technology at the service of information and transparency while limiting participation (Meijer & Bekkers, 2015; Schnell, 2020). Indeed, scaling up to more empowering forms of participation brings more demanding expectations and organisational requirements to ensure due responsiveness.

Reception by Key Actors

For a digital platform to become a successful instrument for citizen participation, the interests of the different actors involved – such as politicians, public officials, citizens and other stakeholder groups like civic associations – need considering and balancing. Equally important is the ability to manage the expectations, conflicts and tensions that may eventually arise between actors whose incentives and motivations are not necessarily aligned. Digital platforms risk changing the way actors involved in participatory policies interact with each other, especially for those whose power or ability to influence (in terms of gatekeeping, agenda-setting or access) might be more at stake.

Support from the politicians who head municipal governments is crucial in participatory processes, as only they can delegate authority. Normally, politicians who are most favourable towards such decisions are also more open to experimenting with new institutional forms (López Ronda & Pineda Nebot, 2013). However, providing citizens with a participatory platform may also expose a party in government to criticism from political adversaries, as the discussions and discontent there could give the opposition ammunition to use against the government.

Public administrations and their managers and officials need to have sufficient resources, including expertise and time, to design and manage online participatory processes. Presumably, larger municipalities are better equipped for this task. Adopting participatory processes, especially when this means handing over decision-making powers, involves changes to routine government processes and a significant degree of coordination between the area in charge of citizen participation, the departments responsible for technical assessment, implementing decisions and budgeting, and the thematic areas affected by the citizens' proposals. Furthermore, digital platforms can yield a large amount of input from citizens, which can further increase coordination problems and conflicts of authority (Bekkers et al., 2013). Local officials and managers can be overwhelmed by both an increasing workload and the requirements of technological adaptation to a new digital platform (Aikins & Krane, 2010).

To generate citizens' interest and input, participatory processes need to be perceived as having a real impact on decision-making. When there is no real transfer of sovereignty, the public's response tends to be disappointment and distrust of politicians (Font & Galais, 2009). Also, digital initiatives are in need of even more acceptance due to the digital divide and certain population sectors' lack of trust in technology (Schedler et al., 2019).

Finally, local associations and collectives are also important stakeholders in the participatory processes. In Spain, since the 1980s, local organisations and groups have been commonly represented in sectorial or territorial municipal advisory councils. Governments with solid support from local organisations are more likely to conduct participatory experiments transferring power to citizens because such processes involve reaching supportive electoral segments and collectives (Shah, 2007). However, by opening up a direct line of communication and influence between individual citizens and government, digital platforms may unintentionally displace the representative and influential role played historically by local organisations, as usually happens with participatory innovations (Ganuza et al., 2016).

The Decidim Platform

The open-source and free-software Decidim has become a worthwhile example of a new trend in public administration of building digital frameworks that combine websites, programmes, apps and social media to facilitate citizens' participation and political decision-making, sharing the platform licence and working together to develop and improve government services (Kankanhalli et al., 2017). Its functionalities and architecture enable a crowd-sourced model of direct democracy where large numbers of citizens and organisations can assemble, participate, debate and decide online (Barandiaran et al., 2017).

Decidim's main features are its spaces and components for participation. The participation spaces are the framework whereby citizens participate, and the components are the citizens' interaction mechanisms within the spaces. Participation spaces are processes (such as participatory budgets), assemblies (e.g., groups), initiatives/petitions and consultations. The platform has up to 15 participation components (see the description on the decidim.org website) which characterise the participatory spaces in terms of participation, voting, deliberation, collaboration, transparency and accountability. They can be combined, developed, activated or deactivated independently. This modular architecture is a major advantage that has contributed to the widespread adoption of the platform but it also allows politicians and public administrators to decide how far to deepen participation.

Continual improvement of the platform is possible thanks to a development support community composed of programmers, activists from the 15-M movement, researchers, consulting firms and municipal managers from different countries (the so-called Metadecidim community and Decidim Association). This network of activists and technological experts is de facto a vanguard that pushes for a democracy-driven model of governance in the locations and organisations where Decidim is being adopted.

In a more top-down move, the Catalan Government, the consortium of local administrations Localret and the Barcelona Provincial Council (Diputació de Barcelona) promote and coordinate the platform's adoption. In this context, also with the help of the Decidim community, municipal officials and managers can exchange doubts and discuss needs to be met collaboratively.

Data and Methodology

Our research design combines (1) in-depth interviews with managers who pioneered the use of Decidim, (2) an online questionnaire addressed to all local administrations that adopted the Decidim platform and (3) data from the platforms' websites. In-depth interviews helped to identify problems and challenges detected by public managers and to construct a framework for analysing perceptions, while quantitative methods (i.e., online questionnaires, web content data and techniques such as regression analysis) have been used to extend the analysis to a variety of municipal cases and identify common patterns. This combination of methods is particularly useful when the number of cases is relatively low and the researcher is exploring complex phenomena such as organisational processes and needs to identify key variables to study quantitatively (Creswell & Plano Clark, 2010).

The online questionnaire was based on the information collected in nine in-depth interviews, which lasted around one hour each, and was conducted in July 2018 with managers in local governments that pioneered the implementation of Decidim. In this fundamentally qualitative stage of the research, the interviews provided information about the roll-out and use of Decidim including four areas: political context and participatory experience of the municipality; reception by the actors involved; organisation and operation; and assessment of the functioning of the platform (see Borge et al., 2018).

The online questionnaire was administered to individuals who were in charge of the Decidim platform in each local government. It was sent to all local administrations that were using the Decidim platform as of March 2019 (n = 34), with a response rate of 88% (30 municipalities). As for the professional profile, the vast majority were working in citizen participation departments, but some of them were working at the mayor's office or in other departments. This was especially common among small municipalities, where departmental divisions tend to cover a broad range of heterogeneous policy areas. Respondents were asked to express their level of agreement with 29 statements using a seven-point Likert scale, grouped into four sections that mirrored the areas previously identified in the interviews. The online questionnaire also included open-ended questions at the end of each section so that respondents could provide further information and nuances, which allowed us to qualitatively control the responses to the close-ended questions.

Additional data was collected from the websites of each municipality's Decidim platform, namely the number of citizens registered on the platform and the time of the first participatory process's publication. The number of registered citizens is an indicator of both the level of platform acceptance by the citizenry and the actual effort devoted by the municipality to reach out to the population.

We used several techniques to detect relations and groupings among the online questionnaire statements representing the perceptions of managers in charge of Decidim. Firstly, we generated several indices to operationalise the perceived factors affecting the implementation of the platform. Secondly, we used a biplot to visualise how the perceptions were related to each other. The biplot is a technique to compactly represent multivariate data that can be used when – as in our case – there is a relatively disproportionate number of variables (perceptions) over cases (municipalities). The biplot usually displays two dimensions, which are the two first major principal components of the variables, showing the weights of each variable (length of the vectors) on those dimensions and the cases as scattered points projected perpendicularly on the two dimensions (Greenacre, 2010, p. 10). Finally, we ran a linear regression analysis to examine how the proportion of inhabitants registered on the platform was related to the perceptions of drivers and obstacles to its successful implementation. We also included as a control variable the amount of time since the publication of the first process, as we expect the number of registered citizens to increase over time.

Cases

The Decidim platform was first launched by the Barcelona local government on 1 February 2016 at the start of the participatory process for the Barcelona Municipal Action Plan, which concluded in April 2017. A total of 39,049 people participated, 10,860 proposals were presented and 18,192 online comments on citizens' proposals were posted (Luque, 2016). Since then, its use has extended in successive waves up to 85 Catalan municipalities by November 2021, most of them in the Barcelona metropolitan area. The release and expansion of Decidim coincided with a turbulent political period in Catalonia, along with a vigorous cycle of citizen protests pushed by anti-austerity and pro-independence movements that gave birth to new political parties and coalitions. The rise of new parties and the increase of political fragmentation translated into government coalitions at the local level. There is actually a wide variety of parties and coalitions adopting the platform. Besides Barcelona, the first wave involved ten municipalities, mostly medium-sized cities from Barcelona's metropolitan area (with an average population of 136,863 inhabitants, excluding the city of Barcelona), which implemented the platform in 2017. Only two of these municipalities (Barcelona and Badalona) were ruled by the political heirs of the 15-M, but in coalition or with the support of other political forces. The rest were led by other parties such as the Catalan Socialists' Party (PSC), Catalonia's Republican Left (ERC) or the Catalan Democratic Party (PDeCAT). The second wave started in 2018 and generally included smaller municipalities (with an average population of 26,731 inhabitants), mostly from Barcelona province, involving governing parties and coalitions across the ideological spectrum (Table 12.1).

Dependent Variable

The proportion of inhabitants registered on the platform in each municipality is relevant for several reasons. First, it is an indicator of the effort devoted by the administrations to promote the use of the platform. Second, it gives an approximate idea of the success of the platform in attracting citizens' interest and trust. Third, it is a reasonable standard measure that allows comparing different municipalities. Although the actual reasons for registering in Decidim can be multiple and therefore the interpretation cannot be straightforward, this indicator provides an idea of the relative importance of the platform within each municipality. The appropriateness and potential of this measure are unveiled when matched with the managers' perceptions about the platform, as we will see in the results section.

Table 12.1 List of Catalan Municipalities That Have Implemented the Decidim Platform (March 2019)

Wave	N	Municipalities
–	1	Barcelona
1st wave	10	Badalona, Calafell, Gavà, L'Hospitalet de Llobregat, Mataró, Reus, Sabadell, Sant Cugat del Vallès, Terrassa, Vilanova i la Geltrú
2nd wave	23	Arenys de Munt, Begues, Calaf, Castellbisbal, Esparreguera, Esplugues de Llobregat, Figaró-Montmany, La Torre de Claramunt, Malgrat de Mar, Mollet del Vallès, Olesa de Montserrat, Palamós, Premià de Mar, Rubí, Salt, Sant Boi de Llobregat, Sant Esteve Sesrovires, Sant Feliu de Llobregat, Sant Pere de Vilamajor, Teià, Vacarisses, Vic, Viladecans

The mean value for the percentage of registered citizens is 2.5%, with a standard deviation of 1.8. A total of 21 out of 30 municipalities (70%) have a percentage between 0.4% and 2.8%. The two municipalities with the highest registration levels (6.9% and 6.3%) are small towns with 3,547 and 25,444 inhabitants, respectively. The correlation between the size of the municipality and the percentage of registered citizens is very low (−0.02), which shows that the small size of a municipality is not an obstacle to its citizens' acceptance of the digital platform, something observed in past online participatory processes in Catalonia (Borge, Colombo & Welp, 2009). The registration level can depend on multiple factors like the perceived difficulty of online registration and local authorities' actions to overcome such difficulty, the usefulness and decision-making power of participation, the time and quantity of participatory processes since the platform was released or the effectiveness of information campaigns.

Independent Variables

Managers' perceptions were grouped into three broad categories (see Table 12.2), corresponding to the factors identified in the theoretical framework, each of which is divided into different indices. The reliability of each index is indicated by the corresponding Cronbach's alpha.

Institutional and organisational context. We generated two different indices. One includes institutional factors that are exogenous to the local government but can be an important incentive for adoption (such as the imitation of other municipalities' experiences, support from regional and provincial governments or the fact it is an open-source platform). The other index captures an internal organisational dimension and measures the influence exerted by previous experiences in participatory processes as well as the previous use of digital devices for citizen participation. Thus, this latter index can be seen as an indicator of the existence of previous structures for the management of citizen participation.

Organisational culture. The organisational culture of the local government, namely the beliefs, motivation and commitment of its public administrators, must be consistent with the purposes of the platform. Perceptions of the functioning of the platform were structured on two indices, inspired by two of the main pillars of open government initiatives: participation and transparency. Participation includes perceptions of the platform as a channel for collecting citizens' proposals and transferring decision-making capacity to citizens. Transparency refers to perceptions of the platform as a means of better structuring information on the website and making participatory processes more transparent.

Reception by key actors. Perceptions of support for the platform were divided into four different indices, which include the perceived reactions of four different actors: public officials, politicians, citizens and civic associations. These measures were used to capture the potential conflict between the platform's development and the different actors involved in participatory processes. The index of citizen support adds positive perceptions (such as the level of acceptance) and subtracts negative ones (such as problems of being unfamiliar with the platform

Table 12.2 List of Indices and Corresponding Questionnaire Items

Category	Index	Cronbach alpha	Questionnaire Items
Institutional and organisational context	External influence (Ext_Inf)	0.80	(+) Being open-source as a key factor for adoption (+) Other local governments using it as a key factor for adoption (+) Technical support from supra-municipal entities as a key factor for adoption
	Previous experience (Pre_Exp)	0.55	(+) Previous experience in managing participatory processes (+) Previous use of other online platforms
Organisational culture	Participation (Cit_Part)	0.64	(+) Channel for collecting citizen proposals (+) Gives more decision-making capacity to citizens
	Transparency (Trans)	0.75	(+) Better organisation of information about participatory processes on the website (+) Makes participatory processes more transparent
Reception by key actors	Citizens (Cit_Acc)	0.68	(+) Good level of acceptance among citizens (−) Despite information campaigns, the platform is relatively unknown among citizens (−) It has been difficult to reach specific publics due to the digital divide
	Civic associations (StakAcc)	0.71	(+) Good level of acceptance among local associations (−) Local associations have been reluctant out of fear of losing influence
	Public officials (OrgStress)	–	Local officials are overloaded with work because of the platform
	Political leaders (Pol_Supp)	0.62	(+) It has the consensual support of the local government (−) It has been a matter of political dispute between political parties

or digital divide issues). In a similar vein, the index of civic associations contrasts the perception of acceptance of the platform with feelings of reluctance from civic associations. The political leadership index refers to the level of political consensus vis-à-vis conflict between political groups. Finally, public officials' support is limited to one specific item: public officials' perception of being overloaded with work because of the platform, which indicates the level of organisational stress.

Results and Discussion

The biplot (Figure 12.1) indicates how managers' perceptions are related to each other in a bi-dimensional space. Figure 12.2 displays the distribution of the cases (municipalities) in this same space. The two dimensions explain 56% of the total variance. Broadly speaking, the first dimension (Dim 1), which is the linear function of the original variables that capture most of their variance, is related to a more internal view of the platform's operation. As can be seen in Figure 12.1, the more influential variables (i.e., those that have the largest projection of their vector on the first dimension) are the ones related to organisational viewpoints, including the indices of transparency and participation and support from political leaders and organisational stress. The external influence is also aligned with this dimension. The second dimension (Dim 2), which is the linear function of the variables which is uncorrelated to the others and captures the second amount of data variance, is related to the support given by the external public, such as citizens and

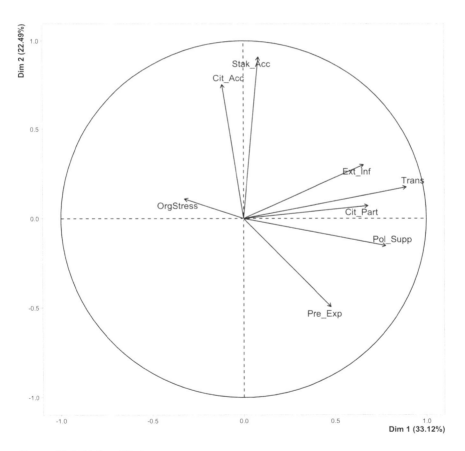

Figure 12.1 Biplot of Indexes.

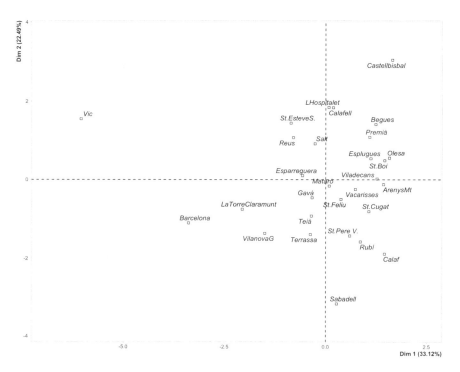

Figure 12.2 Distribution of Cases in the Biplot.

civic associations. The index of the previous existence of participation structures contributes to both dimensions. The regression model provides further insights into understanding this pattern and shows how all these perceptions are related to the platform's performance.

The regression model in Table 12.3 shows the managers' perceptions that are aligned with a higher proportion of inhabitants registered on the platform. All the independent variables are statistically significant or on the verge of statistical significance with a 10% level of confidence. Overall, the regression model performs remarkably well. It explains 64% of the variance of the dependent variable, and the independent variables pass the tests of multicollinearity – the mean of the VIF is 2.56, all of them being below 5.

The regression analysis points out several obstacles related to the use of the Decidim platform. While some variables show the expected positive sign, meaning that they are positively related to the proportion of citizens registered, some other variables (such as the perceptions of transparency, the existence of previous experience and support by civic associations) are negatively related.

Unsurprisingly, external factors associated with a supportive institutional environment are aligned with the proportion of inhabitants registered. However, at

Table 12.3 Regression Analysis. Dependent Variable: Percentage of Registered Citizens

	Coefficients*	Standard Error	Significance
Ext_Inf	1.157	0.409	0.011
Pre_Exp	−0.529	0.299	0.094
Cit_Part	0.970	0.339	0.010
Trans	−2.160	0.455	0.000
Cit_Acc	0.647	0.354	0.085
Stak_Acc	−1.250	0.330	0.001
Pol_Supp	0.852	0.329	0.018
OrgStress	−1.010	0.337	0.008
Platform_Duration	0.003	0.001	0.004
Intercept	0.973	0.564	0.101
Number of obs.	28		
R^2	0.76		
Adj. R^2	0.64		

*The additive indices that summarise perceptions (independent variables) were standardised to facilitate the comparison of coefficients.

the internal level, the existence of previous structures of participation has a negative impact. This result confirms the ubiquitous location of the previous existence of participation structures in the biplot: positively related to organisational and institutional support for the platform but negatively associated with citizens' and local associations' support. Although often considered a facilitator for the adoption of democratic innovations, past experience in participatory practices may also paradoxically limit the full deployment of new ones because previous ways of doing things, interests and expectations can interfere and collide. Illustrative of this is the fact that some interviewed managers argued that adapting the existing participatory processes to the language and functionalities of the digital platform was demanding and not straightforward (see Borge et al, 2018, 24–25).

As expected, positive perceptions of the platform's potential to increase citizen participation are positively and significantly related to the proportion of inhabitants registered. However, perceptions of transparency go in the opposite direction. In-depth interviews also revealed that local managers often did not know about the platform's modules and capacity for transparency despite belonging to municipalities with a high percentage of registered citizens. As discussed in the theoretical section, all of this could indicate that transparency and participation are goals that do not necessarily correlate. Some studies show that these objectives can be at odds with one another (Grimmelikhuijsen, 2010; Schnell, 2020). The areas, tasks and officials responsible for transparency and participation are usually different and separate and not necessarily aligned. Transparency is commonly understood in terms of a top-down managerial objective such as service delivery and regulatory compliance, whereas digitally enabled participation and co-design of public policies are seen as a more transformative objective (Meijer & Bekkers, 2015).

Perceived support from political leadership is positively and significantly related to the proportion of inhabitants registered. Similarly, organisational stress is negatively related, which can be alternatively read as positive support from public officials. Remarkably, the perceived reactions of external actors clearly differ. The perception of support from citizens keeps a positive sign, as happens with politicians and public officials, though to a lesser degree. However, and interestingly enough, the perception of support from civic associations is strongly and negatively related. This point confirms the idea that the disruptive potential of the platform can be seen with reluctance from actors who may feel disempowered. This is especially notable in the case of associations that might feel bypassed by the government engaging directly with individual citizens who have gained a more direct and disintermediated line of influence over administrators. Some interviewees explained that the local associations were concerned about the new influential role of citizens (see Borge et al, 2018, 29), as shown in this excerpt from the in-depth interviews with a local manager and a city councillor from an important municipality of the Metropolitan Area of Barcelona:

Local manager: "The fact that citizens can make so many proposals looks like we are cancelling the local associations: there is this feeling of loss of prominence that all the District Councils have addressed to us and it seems that one must always weigh what comes from a citizen and an association ... it seems to be a threat for them".

Local councillor: "When implementing the platform, there are associations that have taken it as a problem: 'you have taken away my ability to influence'. But there are other associations, perhaps newer ones, that are less than 30 or 40 years old that have a different way of looking at things and that have taken advantage of the platform ... They present a proposal on the platform as an association and they look for the support of any neighbour even if they are not members of the association".

In several municipalities, in order to compensate local associations for the potential loss of influence, citizens' proposals and initiatives need to collect many more votes and signatures and there are quotas that imply that the majority of the proposals selected are from local associations instead of individual citizens (ibid.). That is a clear example of the concessions made by some local governments when trying to foster citizen participation without altering the role played by intermediary actors.

Finally, as logically expected, the variable of time since platform launch (Platform_Duration) is positively related to the proportion of citizens registered, meaning that time helps to increase the number of registrations.

Conclusions

This chapter presented some obstacles, drivers and trade-offs that condition the development of digital platforms for wider participation, by analysing the relation between the number of citizens registered in digital platforms and the perceptions of public managers who are in charge of their implementation. Public managers witness the problems and tensions regarding the deployment of participatory platforms from within public administrations and occupy a central position to assess the interactions between the different stakeholders involved.

As expected, the analysis of perceptions reveals some tensions that emerge as the number of registered citizens on the platform increases. One of the main conclusions derived from this research is that the transition of pre-existing participatory structures to digital platforms such as Decidim, which can function as a spearhead of democracy-driven governance, requires the collaboration and commitment of multiple actors who, to the greatest extent possible, need to see this move as mutually beneficial. That puts participatory processes in a difficult position to satisfy managerial goals and respond to the democratic pressures from below at the same time.

The empirical findings point towards the identification of several tensions and problems. First, we observed that a higher proportion of citizens registered on the platform is associated with perceptions of support by public officials and political leaders. That is barely surprising since that kind of support is crucial for the decision of adopting and implementing any innovations. In contrast, we observed some remarkable reluctance from local associations. Traditionally associations play a representative and intermediary role in local politics in Catalonia. The transition towards digital forms of participation, which may give more weight and force to individual citizens' participation, is likely to increase reluctance among local associations, which can feel displaced. The distrust of well-established local associations towards democratic innovations has been also detected in other contexts and can become an important hurdle in the first stages of its development (Bherer et al. 2016).

Second, similarly, we also found that the existence of previous participatory experiences and platforms is negatively associated with the proportion of citizens registered on the Decidim platform. Past experience in participatory processes is probably a strong predictor of the future implementation of new ones. However, the implementation of changes in already working structures of citizen participation adds to the cost and difficulty of adapting to new forms of interaction, which highlights the need to deal with path-dependency problems and organisational costs regarding adaptation.

Third, interestingly enough, the perceptions of transparency and participation are related differently to the proportion of citizens registered on the platform. This indicates that transparency and participation can have different organisational logic and be conceived differently by public administrators. A common understanding of open government binds them together (Oszlack, 2013), but some studies warn against simplistic implementations of the two objectives (Grimmelikhuijsen, 2010; Meijer & Bekkers, 2015). In fact, the focus of public administration on transparency to the detriment of participation can be seen as a feature of a government driven by effective decision-making and good governance, rather than by more participatory models of democracy (Schnell, 2020).

The focus on public managers' perceptions has some limitations. For a more complete picture, we would need to expand the research to include in-depth interviews and questionnaires targeting other actors involved in participatory processes, namely random citizens and users of the platform, local organisations and activist networks defending the democratic potential of the platform.

To sum up, the implementation of digital platforms may redefine the ecosystem of participation, but not without raising new problems and conflicts. Although the dominant role of the local public administration and the game of representative politics will remain, the implementation of digital platforms introduces elements of disturbance, opening up opportunities for widening citizen participation, which could incommode the previous participative actors and procedures and trigger shifts in power relations. Of course, without the capacity to involve citizens and to provide spaces for autonomous and bottom-up initiatives, there is a danger that the platform simply turns into a new fancy technological solution at the service of a top-down model of governance. Nevertheless, the emergence of conflicts and difficulties we observed can also be understood, as Ganuza et al. point out (2016: 329), as revealing the presence of a genuine struggle to expand democratic borders.

Notes

1 See https://decidim-census.digidemlab.org/
2 The legal framework in Spain and Catalonia binds local governments to deploy mechanisms and processes for citizen participation, in addition to guaranteeing measures to ensure open government through digital tools. Among the most important laws in this area are Law 57/2003 on local government modernisation measures and Law 19/2014 on transparency, access to public information and good governance.

References

Aikins, S. K., & Krane, D. (2010). Are public officials obstacles to citizen-centered E government? An examination of municipal administrators' motivations and actions. *State and Local Government Review*, 42(2): 87–103. https://doi.org/10.1177/0160323X10369159

Atkin, D. J., Hunt, D. S., & Lin, C. A. (2015). Diffusion theory in the new media environment: Toward an integrated technology adoption model. *Mass Communication and Society*, 18(5): 623–650. https://doi.org/10.1080/15205436.2015.1066014

Barandiaran, X., Calleja, A., Monterde, A., Aragón, P., Linares, J., Romero, C., & Pereira, A. (2017). Decidim: Redes políticas y tecnopolíticas para la democracia en red. *Recerca. Revista de pensament i anàlisi.*, 21: 137–150. https://doi.org/10.6035/Recerca.2017.21.8

Bekkers, V., Tummers, L. G., & Voorberg, W. H. (2013). *From Public Innovation to Social Innovation in the Public Sector: A Literature Review of Relevant Drivers and Barriers*. Rotterdam: Erasmus University Rotterdam.

Bherer, L., Fernández-Martínez, J.L., García Espín, P. & Jiménez Sánchez, M. (2016). The promise for democratic deepening: The effects of participatory processes in the interaction between civil society and local governments. *Journal of Civil Society*, 12(3): 344–363, DOI: 10.1080/17448689.2016.1215957

Borge, R., Balcells, J., & Padró-Solanet, A. (2022) Democratic disruption or continuity? Analysis of the decidim platform in catalan municipalities. *American Behavioral Scientist*. Online first. doi:10.1177/00027642221092798

Borge, R., Balcells, J., Padró-Solanet, A., Batlle, A., Orte, A., Serra, R. (2018) "La participación política a través de la plataforma Decidim: Análisis de 11 municipios catalanes". Paper presented at *IX Congreso Internacional en Gobierno, Administración y Políticas Públicas GIGAPP*. Madrid, September, 24–27.

Borge, R., Colombo, C., Welp, Y. (2009) Online and offline participation at the local level. *Information, Communication & Society*, 12(6): 899–928, doi: 10.1080/13691180802483054.

Blanco, I., Salazar, Y. & Bianchi, I. (2020). Urban governance and political change under a radical left government: The case of Barcelona. *Journal of Urban Affairs*, 42(1): 1–21.

Bua, A. & Bussu, S. (2021). Between governance-driven democratisation and democracy driven governance: Explaining changes in participatory governance in the case of Barcelona. *European Journal of Political Research* 60(3): 716–737. https://doi.org/10.1111/1475-6765.12421

Bua, A., & Escobar, O. (2018). Participatory-deliberative processes and public policy agendas: Lessons for policy and practice. *Policy Design and Practice* 1(2): 126–140. https://doi.org/10.1080/25741292.2018.1469242

Creswell, J. W., & Plano Clark, V. L. (2010). *Designing and Conducting Mixed Methods Research*. SAGE Publications.

Criado, J. I., Rojas-Martín, F., & Gil-Garcia, J. R. (2017). Enacting social media success in local public administrations: An empirical analysis of organizational, institutional, and contextual factors. *International Journal of Public Sector Management*, 30(1): 31–47. https://doi.org/10.1108/IJPSM-03-2016-0053

DiMaggio, P. J. & Powell, W. W. (1983). The iron cage revisited: Institutional isomorphism and collective rationality in organizational fields. *American Sociological Review*, 48(2): 147–160.

Falco, E., & Kleinhans, R. (2018). Beyond technology: Identifying local government challenges for using digital platforms for citizen engagement. *International Journal of Information Management*, 40(January): 17–20. https://doi.org/10.1016/j.ijinfomgt.2018.01.007

Font, J., & Galais, C. (2009). *Experiències de democràcia participativa local a Catalunya: Un mapa analític*. Generalitat de Catalunya, Departament d'Interior, Relacions Institucionals i Participació, Direcció General de Participació Ciutadana.

Fung, A. (2015). Putting the public back into governance: The challenges of citizen participation and its future. *Public Administration Review*, 75(4): 513–522. https://doi.org/10.1111/puar.12361

Ganuza, E., Baiocchi, G., & Summers, N. (2016). Conflicts and paradoxes in the rhetoric of participation. *Journal of Civil Society*, 12(3), 328–343. https://doi.org/10.1080/17448689.2016.1215981

Greenacre, M. (2010). *Biplots in Practice*. Madrid, Spain: BBVA Foundation.

Grimmelikhuijsen, S. G. (2010). Transparency of Public Decision-Making: Towards Trust in Local Government? *Policy & Internet*, 2(1), 5–35. https://doi.org/10.2202/1944-2866.1024

Kankanhalli, A., Zuiderwijk, A., & Tayi, G. K. (2017). Open innovation in the public sector: A research agenda. *Government Information Quarterly*, 34(1), 84–89. https://doi.org/10.1016/j.giq.2016.12.002

López Ronda, S., & Pineda Nebot, C. (2013). Experiencias de presupuestos participativos en el País Valenciano: Análisis de variables que intervienen en su paralización. *OBETS. Revista de Ciencias Sociales*, 8(2). https://doi.org/10.14198/OBETS2013.8.2.03

Luque, S. (2016). *L'experiència participativa del Pla d'Acció Municipal a través de la plataforma*. Ia Jornada METADECIDIM, November 25, Barcelona.

Meijer, A. (2015). E-governance innovation: Barriers and strategies. *Government Information Quarterly*, 32(2), 198–206. https://doi.org/10.1016/j.giq.2015.01.001

Meijer, A., & Bekkers, V. (2015). A metatheory of e-government: Creating some order in a fragmented research field. *Government Information Quarterly*, 32(3), 237–245. https://doi.org/10.1016/j.giq.2015.04.006

Mergel, I., Edelmann, N., & Haug, N. (2019). Defining digital transformation: Results from expert interviews. *Government Information Quarterly*. https://doi.org/10.1016/j.giq.2019.06.002

OECD (2016). Open Government: The Global Context and the Way Forward. OECD Publishing, Paris, https://doi.org/10.1787/9789264268104-en.

Oszlak, O. (2013). Gobierno abierto: Hacia un nuevo paradigma de gestión pública (No. 5; Colección de documentos de trabajo sobre e-Gobierno, p. 35). Red de Gobierno Electrónico de América Latina y el Caribe – Red GEALC.

Rodríguez-Bolívar, Manuel Pedro. (2014). *Measuring E-Government Efficiency: The Opinions of Public Administrators and Other Stakeholders*. New York: Springer.

Schedler, K., Guenduez, A. A., & Frischknecht, R. (2019). How smart can government be? Exploring barriers to the adoption of smart government. *Information Polity*, 24(1): 3–20. https://doi.org/10.3233/IP-180095

Schnell, S. (2020). Vision, voice and technology: Is there a global "Open Government" trend? *Administration & Society*, 52(10): 1–20. https://doi.org/10.1177/0095399720918316

Shah, A. (Ed.). (2007). *Participatory Budgeting*. The World Bank. https://doi.org/10.1596/978-0-8213-6923-4

Smith, A., & Prieto Martín, P. (2021). Going Beyond the Smart City? Implementing Technopolitical Platforms for Urban Democracy in Madrid and Barcelona. *Journal of Urban Technology*, 28(1–2), 311–330. https://doi.org/10.1080/10630732.2020.1786337

Thompson, M. (2021) What's so new about New Municipalism?. *Progress in Human Geography*, 45(2): 317–342. https://doi.org/10.1177/0309132520909480

Voorberg, W. H., Bekkers, V. J. J. M., & Tummers, L. G. (2015). A Systematic Review of Co-Creation and Co-Production: Embarking on the social innovation journey. *Public Management Review*, 17(9), 1333–1357. https://doi.org/10.1080/14719037.2014.930505

Warren, M. (2014). Governance-driven democratization. In S. Griggs, A. J. Norval & H. Wagenaar (Eds), *Practices of Freedom: Decentered Governance, Conflict and Democratic Participation*. Cambridge: Cambridge University Press, 38–60.

13 The Embeddedness of Public-Common Institutions

The Citizen Assets Programme in Barcelona

Marina Pera, Iolanda Bianchi and Yunailis Salazar

Introduction

In this chapter we focus on the embeddedness of participatory structures within social and political contexts, through an analysis of the "Citizen Assets Programme" (CAP) in Barcelona. This is a policy that seeks to establish institutional support for the urban commons, that is, spaces and facilities rooted in the community that are susceptible to being transferred to citizens' collectives to be managed democratically (Ajuntament de Barcelona, 2017). We define policies as being embedded when they are situated in their social and political environment with a "productive relation to the other institutions of the democratic system" (Bussu et al. 2022a, p.3). Embeddedness is considered a crucial element in the fruitful implementation and sustainability of innovative participatory structures.

Moreover, the CAP is a clear case of "Democracy-Driven Governance" (Bua and Bussu, 2020), henceforth DDG, since the formulation of the policy takes into account practices of self-government that have a long tradition in the city of Barcelona, and also sets out an institutional design, backed by the Barcelona en Comú (BComú) local government, that recognises and protects urban commons. The CAP aims to recognise, protect and promote "public-common institutions" since it considers them an opportunity for democratic innovation (Bianchi, 2022; Russell, 2019). These institutions intend to substitute traditionally formal spaces of participation in order to create embedded and enduring participatory governance structures in which decision-making power is formally shared between active citizens, social movements and public actors, thus combining the principles of representative democracy with those of direct democracy (Blanco and Gomà, 2019).

The notion of commons has become increasingly popular within civil society, as a reaction to the privatisation of public resources and as an alternative form of democratic management (Laval and Dardot 2015). It is also one of the ideas underpinning the *Barcelona en Comú* (BComú) platform: an "in-movement and in-practice" (Russell 2019, p.991) political party born of the 15M mobilisations in Spain.[1]

The practice of citizen involvement in public policy and management has a long tradition in the city. Bottom-up demands for developing legal frameworks for citizens' management of municipal facilities have existed for decades and resulted in policies such as the Civic Management regulations in the 1990s that partially responded to citizens' demands to manage resources directly (Pera, 2022). The Citizen Assets Programme, however, is more ambitious and looks to create a more robust political and legal framework that can implement commons-based democratic administration and public-commons institutions (Russell and Milburn, 2019; Bianchi, 2022) on a greater scale.

In order to better understand the factors that influence the embeddedness that is required to implement DDG policies, we address two issues: the instruments that BComú has used to create new public-common institutions, and the challenges that have arisen in implementing these instruments. Thus, drawing on the qualitative discourse analysis of official documents and 17 interviews conducted with politicians, civil servants, academics, and activists between 2015-2021,[2] this chapter analyses the opportunities that the CAP opens up for social movements and community-based groups to translate their proposals into a new framework for participatory governance in the city (Blanco et al., 2021), and examines the main constraints that hinder the embeddedness of participatory structures.

Our findings show that one of the key elements that enables the embeddedness of DDG policies in their institutional and social environment is effectively promoting civil society and administrative actors' trust in new democratic institutions. Trust had already been identified as an important element in the study of citizen participation in governance networks (Ansell and Galsh, 2007; Brugué, 2010), and we underline that trust also remains important in the embedding of participative politics. Thus, by analysing this programme, one that recognises and promotes public-common institutions, we contribute to understanding the challenges faced by DDG in contexts of pre-existing administrative practices and cultures.

We begin by describing the concept of embeddedness and the different conceptions of commons, and how it is articulated into policies. After briefly contextualising the spread and development of commons in civil society, we present the CAP and how it is being implemented. Finally, we analyse the main challenges that have appeared in the implementation process. We conclude by discussing how the analysis of the CAP highlights the role of trust in facilitating embeddedness, so that new democratic institutions can be developed effectively.

Embeddedness and Commons in Theory: Dimensions and Evolution of Two Interrelated Concepts

One of the recurrent traits of DDG policies is how they take on board knowledge and practices that come from social movements and community-based organisations; this aims to create new forms of deliberative decision-making that involve citizens and attempts to increase the quality of democracy (Bussu et al., 2022b).

Embeddedness in Participatory Policies

Embeddedness is considered one of the main elements that aids legitimacy and efficiency in participatory governance (Bussu et al., 2022b). Although embeddedness is a concept that has been used in different disciplines for decades, few clear definitions of it have been formulated.

In The Great Transformation (2001) Karl Polanyi was the first to apply the concept of embeddedness to explain the integration and dependence of economic activities within the social context, and the influence of non-market institutions on economic activities, such as kinship, religion or political institutions. However, the advent of capitalism led to the dis-embeddedness of economic activities from their social context. In this way, the market was conceived as an independent system with its own rules, independent of social institutions. Based on Polanyi's notion, Bussu et al. (2022a) propose a definition of embeddedness in the field of participatory governance as the integration of participatory policies in the political and social context in which they are developed, one that establishes an efficient and fruitful relationship with the other democratic institutions and key actors in public administration and civil society.

However, embeddedness is not a stable, given characteristic of participatory structures. Instead, it has a weak and dynamic nature that needs to be reshaped to adapt constantly to the context in which is integrated (Escobar, 2021). Embedded participatory governance, which is not the same as the institutionalisation of participatory policies (see Bussu et al. 2022a), has a relationship of mutuality with actors and institutions in its context. This reciprocal relationship levers efficiencies and offers a potential for durability.

Embeddedness consists of three dimensions: *temporal* and *spatial*, and its *practices*. These refer to when, where and how to embed policies (Bussu et al. 2022a). The *temporal* dimension concerns the importance of iteration over time. This dimension underlines the need for participative structures to become permanent and work in conjunction with the political cycle and policy system (Chwalisz, 2020) as well as with civil society. On some occasions, embeddedness can be promoted through the recognition of informal spaces of deliberation within community and public administration structures as formal spaces of participation.

The *spatial* dimension aims to visualise the most appropriate level of government for embedding participatory structures. While there is general agreement in the literature on citizen participation that the local level is the most suitable one in which to embed new participatory institutions (Fung and Wright, 2003), Bussu et al. (2022a) point out two further characteristics which are not focused on scale but rather on where new democratic institutions should be situated to become efficient and productive: first, within the power structures that are related to decision-making spaces, and second, within civil society, conceived as either individual citizens or organisations.

The third and final dimension, *practices*, refers to the mechanisms that enable the process of embedding participatory governance. Thus, this dimension largely refers to the study of the design of formal mechanisms and regulations that frame new democratic institutions. However, it is also crucial to consider the informal practices that enable embedding. These include behaviours, attitudes, and bonding strategies within and across the community, that aim to include different cultures and interests in participatory structures (Bussu et al., 2022a). Moreover, informal practices that take place within the scope of participatory structures can be used as guidance and drivers for reshaping formal institutions that are moving towards more participatory ecology (Blanco et al. 2021).

In what follows, we reflect on embeddedness by examining the CAP policy that aims to recognise and promote public-common institutions (Bianchi, 2022; Russell, 2019) as new participatory structures in which citizens can decide on and directly manage certain public assets.

The Concept of the Commons and Its Articulation into Policies

The development and the design of the CAP were inspired by the concept of the commons, which has been the subject of growing scholarly and political attention over recent decades (Ferreri and Vidal, 2021). Beginning with the extensive research carried out in the framework of Ostrom's neo-institutionalist studies (1990), academic research on the commons has expanded to include other disciplines, such as critical legal studies, political economy, geography and political theory. This burgeoning interest in the concept has made it somewhat controversial and disputed but has also enriched it with multiple approaches that highlight different facets of the study of participatory governance.

Initially, the notion of the commons had few points of convergence with local participatory policies literature. Ostrom's neo-institutionalist approach dominated the debate on the commons from the 1960s until the onset of the neoliberal project. Her approach saw commons as tangible and intangible resources that are managed collectively by a community of individuals who establish rules and enforce them (Ostrom, 1990; Ostrom and Hess, 2007). In this way, the commons can include areas where villagers establish rules for fishing, urban gardens where neighbourhood residents take turns planting and harvesting vegetables, or digital archives where groups of scholars share scientific knowledge. The focus of this discipline was primarily to understand the motives and variables affecting the regulatory capacity of the commons. However, it was not generally concerned with the relationship the commons had with other political institutions, nor did it extensively examine its interaction with capitalism or its own modes of governance.

The notion of commons acquired a different meaning when it began to be used by critical theorists in disciplines such as law, geography and political economy. This new reflection on the commons emerged as a response to the accelerated processes of privatisation and commodification witnessed from the 1980s onwards. Commons are a social relationship based on the principle of direct democracy, use value and reciprocity that is established between a group of people and a tangible and/or intangible resource (Harvey, 2012; Federici and Caffentzis, 2013; Mattei, 2011). The construction of the social relationship between the group and the resource means that the commons do not only include horizontal, de-commodified and autonomous forms of collectively managed resources, such as urban gardens or digital archives, but also other types of resources, such as water and health services, that are managed by other institutions, but for which the community is campaigning for a more equitable, more democratic and more de-commodified form of management. In this way, the concept of commons is now set within a broader political debate, which is concerned with the identification of strategies, practices and modes of governance that are at odds with neoliberal capitalism.

However, above all, it has been contributions from political theorists that have caused the commons to become more strongly embedded in the debate regarding social change and participatory democracy (Hardt and Negri, 2009; Laval and Dardot, 2015). The work of Laval and Dardot (2015) has been inspirational for understanding how the concept of the commons can drive social change by pushing for a radical democratisation of government institutions and enhancing participatory democracy. The authors argue that state institutions can be democratised by following the principle of self-government, or the capacity of citizens to co-produce rules and norms, in Ostrom's sense. Despite pondering the risk of commons becoming co-opted by state institutions, Laval and Dardot (2015) underline their capacity to create new governance structures that allow civil society to go beyond institutional participation when the principle of commons is introduced into state institutions. They argue that the commons can lead a paradigm shift: it can help participation move forward from being carried out on a case-by-case basis – which has opened up some avenues of democratisation but has rarely led to effective social transformation – in order to build stronger forms of popular control that are based on a form of self-government which is permanently embedded in institutions.

The two authors illustrate this with the example of the re-municipalisation of the water service in Naples carried out by the new municipalist government of De Magistris. Here, the new governance structure of the service is made up of a supervisory committee of workers, civil society representatives and users, who have the task of ensuring that the management of water services follows the principles of justice, sustainability, and good governance (Mattei, 2011).

As we have argued, Naples and Barcelona are two paradigmatic cities in the development of policies that include the notion of commons. Thus, in this chapter, which focuses on policies regarding the commons in Barcelona, we analyse how public-common institutions can be inserted in their political and social context, innovatively connecting the concept of embeddedness with the notion of commons when these take the form of public policy.

Commons in Practice in Barcelona: Between Civil Society and Party Politics

The city of Barcelona has a long tradition of public-commons collaboration. This was consolidated over several successive social-democratic leaderships, from the first democratic elections in 1979 until 2011, when a liberal-conservative coalition won power. However, this consolidated tradition is not only thanks to the farsightedness of local government investment in these types of collaborations. It is also thanks to the particularly active role of Barcelona's civil society, which has always tirelessly put forward demands and claims for a fairer, more equal, and more liveable city (Blakeley, 2007).

The fact that these forms of public-common collaboration are widespread does not mean that this is or has always been the dominant model of governance in the city. The reality is quite the opposite: over the years Barcelona has made extensive use of forms of public–private partnerships (PPP), which are a feature of the notorious Barcelona Model, devised in particular to strengthen the city's economic and urban development (Balibrea, 2005), such as the remodelling of the seafront and the extensive outsourcing of local public services that has been carried out especially since the Olympic Games in 1992. However, the proliferation of PPPs has not excluded other forms of public-community collaboration. These have become increasingly important in recent years due to advocacy for commoning practices carried out by both the ruling coalition of the BComú government and by organised civil society (Rubio-Pueyo, 2017).

Many groups from organised civil society and from social movements have used the commons to define socially transformative projects, aiming to build spaces of self-government inside and outside the state. Paradigmatic in this respect is the case of the *Fundación de los Comunes* (2015), created in 2011 by several organisations linked to social movements – such as the research and consultancy cooperative *La Hidra Cooperativa* (Barcelona) – whose aim is to collectively produce tools to develop critical thinking for political intervention. Although this foundation has been involved in the production and dissemination of critical knowledge on various topics, the commons represent an important part of its work.

In addition, in Barcelona, the concept of commons has recently been introduced into public institutions, in part due to the victory of BComú. In its electoral programme, BComú emphasises "new forms of public-common collaboration that strengthen the sense of belonging to what is common" (Barcelona en Comú, 2015 p.61), taking up the public-common collaborative tradition mentioned previously and strengthening it through the deployment of new policies and legal tools.

Public Policy for the Commons: The Citizen Asset Programme

The first BComú mandate in 2015 saw the beginnings of the CAP, which was designed and developed as part of the innovation programme of the Participation Department. The design of the programme went through a series of participatory workshops with different social actors (social movement activists, citizens, critical scholars) before it became operational in 2017. Its main objectives are:

> Supporting, encouraging and consolidating the community use and management of municipal public assets, through the construction of an institutional and regulatory framework that allows the recognition and promotion of citizens' experiences of community use of the public commons.
> (Ajuntament de Barcelona, 2017 p.3)

The first key element in developing the CAP was drawing up the Citizen Assets Ordinance. This defined the municipal assets that could be managed by organised citizens, as well as regulating the agreements that could be established between the city council and civic groups.

The second element was the Catalogue of Assets. This consists of a list of all the assets and plots of land that have been ceded or that could be ceded to non-profit organisations. It also includes the conditions and criteria for future contracts of this nature. Thus, the aim of this catalogue is to increase transparency and to regulate the concessions that until then had been carried out by different departments or districts of the city council without using shared criteria. As stated by one interviewee, the justification for creating the catalogue was that no official register existed of all the assets owned by the municipality. The sale of public assets to private companies and the lack of transparency resulting from the push towards public-private partnerships had left the council without this essential information.

The third element is known as the Citizen Assets Board. It includes all the city council departments that deal with any aspect of the assets, especially community action services, citizen participation, urban ecology and the social and solidarity economy. The aim is to coordinate the implementation of the policy and assess the demands of non-profit organisations. This is therefore primarily a technical area which evaluates all projects or initiatives that could become part of the programme and benefit from a concession.

The fourth element is the Municipal Citizen Assets and Community Management Board. This participative structure is different from the above-mentioned Citizen Assets Board and is composed of city council representatives and representatives of community-based organisations that manage public assets. The function of this board is to supervise the allocation of municipal assets to citizen groups, as well as to provide a space where the representatives of the commons who are involved with the CAP can express their needs and demands.

The Citizen Assets Office was created to provide support to non-profit organisations in the initial stages of managing assets, as well as to initiatives that were already doing so but might require some assistance, such as in applying the Community Balance metrics (see below). The office is run in collaboration with *Torre Jussana*, the service centre for associations in Barcelona. One of the main forms of assistance it offers is training courses on the main objectives and strategies for community action, participation, governance, communication, gender policy and the management of economic resources.

Sixth comes the Community Balance Report, which is designed to help the non-profit organisations in charge of citizens' assets to self-assess their performance. The metrics within it measure performance internally and externally on the basis of social and environmental criteria, such as participatory and democratic governance, links to the area/neighbourhoods, diversity, inclusion and community relationships. The Community Balance Report has been developed in collaboration with actors from the solidarity economy sector such as XES (Catalonia Social and Solidarity Economy Network) and from non-profit organisations. It therefore represents an innovative instrument that aims to improve the transparency of non-profit organisations' performance and to measure the transformation processes carried out by these initiatives. The plan is to apply these indicators and to implement them gradually for all the facilities and plots of land that form part of the programme. In addition to assessing the territorial and social impact of the projects, the rationale for creating this self-evaluation tool is based on the notion that the collective use of commons does not necessarily imply greater democratisation, especially when criteria such as class, gender, ideology or ethnicity are not taken into account.

To date, the main aspects that have been developed are the Catalogue of Citizen Assets, the Citizen Assets Board, the Citizen Assets Office and the Community Balance Report. Although the CAP is an ongoing policy at an early stage in its implementation, it is worthwhile describing two examples of how it has been implemented: the case of the *Can Batlló* sociocultural centre and that of *La Xarxa de Dones Cosidores* (the dressmakers' network).

Can Batlló is a self-managed community space located in an old industrial complex that was reclaimed by the residents of the areas of Sants and La Bordeta, to be used for socio-community projects and neighbourhood facilities. In 2011, following pressure from the residents, organised groups obtained the concession of one of the buildings to start various sociocultural projects that are open to the community, through the CAP. These include an auditorium, art workshops and urban gardens. In 2019, after fighting for recognition of the social and economic value of Can Batlló, the residents obtained a concession of 13,000 square metres "for private use for non-profit social projects" for a period of 30 years, with the option to extend the concession for a further 20 years. This is one of the most paradigmatic experiences in the application of the CAP and sets a precedent for other organised neighbourhood initiatives.[3]

While Can Batlló is a well-known space for critical urban scholars and activists involved in self-organised spaces in Barcelona and Europe, *La Xarxa de Dones Cosidores* is a recent initiative that supports the self-organisation of groups of women working in dressmaking. They define themselves as a "network based on sustainability, activism, mutual support and care". The project was launched in May 2020, when different neighbourhood groups coordinated to produce 13,000 masks for essential workers in more than 40 municipal health and social services centres in the Nou Barris district[4] and for the city council during the initial months of the COVID-19 pandemic. The municipal Community Action Service stressed that this network is an example of "the need for collective processes in the face of social challenges, as it shows that the community is capable of responding".[5] Groups of women living in precarious conditions were able to organise themselves and generate new self-employment schemes. The CAP now provides them with a space to continue growing and to hold training initiatives to start new projects that have strong ties to their neighbourhoods, while benefitting from mutual support and a feminist approach.

These examples show how the CAP aims to support transformative projects which have participants in vulnerable situations. As stated by a public official in one interview, many of these women are in difficult economic and housing situations (some of them are at risk of being evicted or are immigrants). They have embraced the collective ethos because it is their best opportunity to be economically autonomous. Furthermore, another facility granted to the network includes a community garden to be used and shared with other groups and initiatives in the neighbourhood, thus creating opportunities for bonding and generating a strong social infrastructure (Klinenberg, 2021).

Challenges in Developing New Commons-Based Institutions

The CAP represents a way for the public administration to recognise the capacity of organised citizens to manage certain types of municipal services and facilities autonomously. The programme is therefore based on the recognition of the social value of citizen self-government. However, our analysis of how the CAP has been implemented has revealed legal and administrative challenges that have hindered the creation of trust regarding the policy among public employees and civil society actors, thus impeding the CAP from becoming embedded in an effective way.

First, the main challenge is the need to reinterpret or transform the current multi-scalar legal framework, in order for it to be able to allow public assets to be managed by citizens. With a view to decide which community-based organisations should be granted the common management of public spaces and facilities, the CAP uses social criteria. The legitimacy of the management of public assets as commons is mainly built on how these commons are connected to the local community, the social impact of their projects and how they promote community empowerment. The current legal framework does not foster this process, and the current way of ceding a service to non-state actors works through the Spanish procurement law (9/2017), enabling the outsourcing of services but with economic efficiency as the main criterion for selecting the organisation. Thus, the criteria underpinning the legitimacy and the adequacy of community-based organisations to manage resources differ greatly from the administrative criteria established by the multi-scalar procurement laws (both Spanish and European). For this reason, the implementation of the CAP requires the modification or reinterpretation of the current law for the concession of public spaces and facilities. As stated by some of the academic activists who participated in developing the CAP:

> It is about making a tactical and counter-hegemonic use of law, making an innovative application of the rules to expand what is possible, looking for loopholes and generating new regulations. It is about deactivating the law as an expression of capital and placing legal technicalities at the service of social struggles.
>
> (Castro and Forné, 2021 p. 31)

Thus, the strategy identified among the interviewees was not only to try to reinterpret and foster the CAP within the current legal framework but to advocate for the approval of laws that recognise the idiosyncrasy of public-common institutions. For instance, one of the city council politicians that were interviewed mentioned the need to pass the new law on the social and solidarity economy in Catalonia, as its current draft covers the management of public resources and assets by community-based organisations. Passing this law would give greater strength and legal coverage when awarding assets to organised citizens and would make it easier to set up public-common institutions.

The fact that no robust framework exists that is adapted to public-common institutions negatively affects the embeddedness of the CAP within local governance and public employees. We identified scepticism and resistance among some public employees who were required to participate in the implementation of the CAP. Selection based on social criteria, as well as possible risks of clientelism or transferring assets only to groups that are politically sympathetic to the municipal government has led to some public officers having a sceptical attitude to the scheme. However, the CAP includes tools to avoid clientelism, such as the Municipal Citizen Assets and Community Management Board, which is a plural and participative body representing community-based organisations and city council members, and which monitors the selection process of community-based organisations candidates for managing public assets. Moreover, the Community Balance Report also emphasises the social performance of public-commons institutions in terms of internal democracy, inclusiveness and their connections with the neighbourhood where they are located. Despite the tools that are used to avoid fraud when selecting who manages assets and in monitoring performance, the grassroots management of public services and facilities still generates some resistance among public employees.

Thus, although the local level has been observed as the most adequate arena for developing participatory politics (Fung and Wright, 2003), it is important to remember that the local scale is affected by a multi-scalar combination of laws that can complicate the implementation of new democratic institutions. Poor embeddedness due to the inadequate legal framework at the regional and state level is a key aspect that challenges the capacity of new municipalist platforms to implement policies that radically change the urban agenda of local governments.

Second, the CAP standardises the administrative processes for creating public-commons institutions. This means that the different city council departments have had to adopt new, uniform mechanisms. Over previous decades, the city council had designed specific, less ambitious mechanisms to respond to the management demands of organised citizens, such as civic management (the community management of municipal facilities). In most of these cases, the districts (territorial administrative organisations) were responsible for these arrangements, resulting in substantial differences between them in the criteria used to select the citizen organisations and evaluate their performance in managing the facilities in question.[6]

The standardisation of an administrative process requires public employees to invest a significant amount of their time. In addition, some public employees and politicians are reluctant to change mechanisms that are already in place. Moreover, in some cases, these previous structures, which are less legally and politically robust, can coexist while the new ones are being fully implemented and consolidated.

Third, the implementation of the CAP entails the creation of new governance structures, such as the Municipal Citizen Assets and Community Management Board, that do not fit into an administrative culture that avoids the engagement of citizens in the implementation of public policies. This kind of co-production spaces may generate reluctance from certain public employees who are antipathetic to co-production; some claim that people's engagement tends to be inconsistent because the citizens lack the required technical understanding and administrative knowledge; others claim that the processes become too long and drawn out due to the slow pace of participatory dynamics (Voorberg et al., 2014). For instance, the Municipal Citizen Assets and Community Management Board will begin functioning in 2022. This will be made up of community projects, actors involved in the facilities, and the city council. It is likely that in this space, the main tensions that arise in processes of democratic transformation that involve cooperation between activism and local government will become clear. One government official expressed that it is difficult to even contemplate what these spaces should be like and who should participate, e.g., whether all social organisations should participate or whether they should be represented in another way, something which in turn would be contrary to the idea of direct democracy.

The bureaucratic constraints and functioning of local councils hinder implementation processes either when prior frameworks are applied to new policies (which have key characteristics that cannot be translated into "old" schemes) or because local governments have struggled to generate these new governance structures and public-common institutions, resulting in the dissolution or transformation of traditional patterns of public administration and the reinterpretation of laws at different scales. The kinds of modifications that are needed for implementing the CAP have not contributed to some public officers and politicians committing to it, and have not facilitated the embeddedness needed for the effective implementation of the CAP.

Last but not least, it should be noted that the CAP has not become fully embedded within civil society. No wholescale social mobilisation has occurred in favour of deploying and applying the CAP as a whole. Citizen mobilisation has instead been focused on the implementation of specific aspects of the programme or even focused on the improvement of pre-existing mechanisms. The design of the programme develops the notion of commons and is based on historical demands for citizen management of public resources. However, people have not identified with the programme as a whole or fought for it. The reasons for this low level of mobilisation are multifaceted and complex. However, through our fieldwork, we may be able to identify some factors that influence it.

On the one hand, some community-based organisations that manage municipal facilities stem from an autonomist tradition that has self-managed projects for decades in Barcelona without any support from the state. This leads to some community-based organisations being rather sceptical regarding collaboration with the city council. These community-based organisations, despite not rejecting the current agreements with the state outright, are waiting to see how the programme develops and the effect it might have on their projects.

On the other hand, pre-existing municipal regulations oriented towards the urban commons have also led to mobilisations for them to be improved. Although older regulations are less robust than the CAP, some people have calculated that mobilisations for improving pre-existing participatory regulations might result in more tangible and achievable benefits than mobilising for a programme with a wider scope. This support for improving previous regulations rather than pressing for implementing the CAP is another illustration that trust levels regarding the CAP are low, which does not contribute to embedding the policy among civil society actors.

However, it should be mentioned that collaborative work among community-based organisations and the city council to develop specific tools within the CAP is taking place to develop concrete elements of it. One example is the measuring instrument of Community Balance that was developed based on the social balance of the XES (an association that promotes the social and solidarity economy in Catalonia) in coordination with some community-based organisations, academic activists and the city council.

Discussion

Throughout this chapter, we have shown that although the partial implementation of the CAP has entailed the concession of plots and facilities to community-based organisations, the potential of this ambitious programme has remained limited due to the policy not being embedded firmly enough regarding some public employees, some politicians and community-based organisations.

The margins of manoeuvre within the local state are narrow, even when a sympathetic party, such as BComú, is in power. These margins are mainly outlined by the multi-scale legal framework and by the cultural and organisational working patterns of the public administration. Firstly, the legal framework at the local level, but also at the regional or state level, does not facilitate the recognition of the citizen management of public services and facilities. The CAP involves the conceptualisation and implementation of a more democratic form of public management based on the commons-inspired idea of self-government. However, the implementation of this recognition is hindered by the Spanish public sector procurement law (9/2017) – in turn, informed by the EU procurement regulation – that benefits private companies when contracts for services are granted through outsourcing selection procedures. That is why the insufficient development of the legal framework that covers some of the aspects of the programme and the associated reorganisation of administrative tasks have led to both scepticism and the policy being poorly embedded in the practices of public employees and politicians.

Moreover, the policy inspired by the notion of commons requires some modifications in the organisational culture of the public administration which understands the co-production of policies, such as the CAP, as ceding their power to citizens and as an excessively time-consuming way of developing policies. Thus, the implementation of the new programme requires adaptation processes and must consider training for public officials to develop new forms of organising and collaborating with grassroots and social movements, including the reconceptualisation of the structures for traditional participatory governance in Barcelona.

These legal and administrative implementation challenges lead to public employees not fully committing to the CAP, as well as a series of challenges regarding the mobilisation of civil society in the implementation of the programme. The existence of previous and more detailed regulations that respond to citizen demands for managing public facilities (Civic Management, Empty Plots Programme, etc.) has led to mobilisations to improve these particular regulations, rather than promoting engagement with the CAP and generating mobilisations for implementing commons policies in general. The CAP covers more types of initiatives and involves more city council departments, adding to old mechanisms that were already operational by implementing new ones.

The CAP has had some very successful outcomes, such as the Community Balance Report or the cession of a space to *Xarxes de dones cosidores* (dressmakers' network). However, a major challenge remains in place: promoting trust in the policy in order to implement it effectively while maintaining its main objective. That is, to urge collaboration between local public institutions and citizens' initiatives through the creation of public-common institutions that understand participation as self-government and democratic radicalism but use local government as a space that connects municipalism with the idea of citizens' rights to the commons and the redistribution of power.

Thus, regarding embeddedness and how important it is in participatory governance, our analysis adds complexity to its dimensions: *space*, *temporal* and *practices* (Bussu et al., 2022a). We have identified different elements of the CAP that correspond to the dimensions of embeddedness identified by Bussu et al. (2022a), and we have gone further, pointing out that trust is a key element that influences the implementation of participatory policies. In terms of the *space* dimension, the CAP is designed to engage different areas of the city council that are involved in transferring assets to citizens. Because of this, the policy has highlighted the appropriate actors and departments in the city council that should be involved in the effective implementation of such an ambitious policy. Regarding the dimension of *time*, the CAP is designed to create permanent instruments to build and consolidate participatory bodies that allow public-common institutions to be created, thus guaranteeing a continuity in the policy throughout the years. Third, in terms of *practices*, the implementation of the CAP entails the standardisation of mechanisms for creating public-commons institutions in order to promote transparency and legitimacy and contribute to the embedding of the CAP in the local administration and civil society. However, in order to ensure that it becomes embedded, the CAP also needs to generate trust among those that participate in its implementation and among those that can benefit from it, since innovative and collaborative policies often require social mobilisation from civil society and the engagement of those who have to implement it, as had been previously confirmed in the collaborative and network governance literature (Ansell and Gash, 2007; Brugué, 2010). Thus, trust is a transversal feature that facilitates the creation of

Conclusions

In this chapter, we have analysed the implementation of the CAP in Barcelona. The concept of embeddedness (Bussu et al., 2022a) has led us to focus on how this innovative policy that was inspired by the notion of the commons can be effectively inserted into its immediate political and social context.

This policy has implied reformulating how citizens collaborate with the local state, through the recognition and protection of collective forms of management of public services and facilities, based on the idea of self-government and direct democracy that go beyond traditional forms of collaboration, such as direct management or outsourcing. The CAP can be considered an experience of DDG in which a form of innovative, democratic and grassroots management of services and facilities is recognised and promoted by the city council. Public-common institutions promote citizen participation and community-based lifestyles and attempt to reconceptualise public service management by creating new democratic and institutional participatory structures. However, we have identified some challenges in implementation that underline the difficulty of translating concepts that have emerged from citizens' practices into the realm of policy (Bianchi, 2022). Our analysis finds that lack of trust is one of the crucial elements that has hindered the fruitful implementation of the CAP. This could be a useful addition to Bussu et al.'s (2022b) conceptualisation of embeddedness, since we consider trust as a transversal feature that covers all the dimensions of embeddedness (*space*, *time* and *practices*).

In a context in which local governments are adopting new schemes that are emerging from civil society as a way of renewing the democratic system and of engaging citizens in public policy, more research on empirical cases is needed to better understand the processes of implementation of innovative policies. Our analysis contributes to identifying trust, which had previously been confirmed in collaborative and network governance literature (Ansell and Gash, 2007; Brugué, 2010), as one of the relevant factors in the fruitful embedding of DDG participatory structures. Moreover, this research underlines the relevant role of the actors' involvement in the implementation of DDG policies, and we highlight that these actors should be encouraged to commit further in order to achieve productive and durable participatory structures that can spawn new democratic paradigms.

Notes

1 This movement resulting from demonstrations against the austerity policies and the social consequences of the crisis led to the creation of municipalist candidacies in different cities in Spain, some of them also connected to the national party *Podemos*.
2 This chapter is the result of three research projects in which the authors have been involved: (1) Collaborative Governance under Austerity: An Eight-Case Comparative

Study (Ref. ES/L012898/1); (2) La gestión procomún en el Área Metropolitana de Barcelona: Tipos de experiencias, redes y aprendizaje a nivel territorial (2017 – SGR-1126) and (3) PROTO LOCAL. De la protesta a la propuesta. Ayuntamientos del "Cambio", políticas urbanas y movimientos sociales (Ref. No. CSO2015-68314-P).
3 Agreement of concession (available in English): https://drive.google.com/file/d/1lB EHcfjDg7kXOq4WsL1SN5DFVhVqC7e_/view).
4 Nou Barris is the district of Barcelona with the highest rates of social vulnerability and has also been one of the most affected by the pandemic.
5 Women dressmakers' network participated in the initiative of producing masks during the covid-19 pandemic https://ajuntament.barcelona.cat/acciocomunitaria/ca/noticia/mascaretesenxarxa-una-resposta-de-suport-mutu-que-connecta-els-barris_938057
6 In the case of civic management facilities, in 1999, the first recognition of the capacity of community-based organisations to manage municipal facilities was based on the Municipal Charter, and its application was decentralised to the district administration level. However, it was not until 2015 that legal bases for civic management were approved and thus regulated the criteria to select grassroots candidates (Pera, 2022).

References

Ajuntament de Barcelona (2017). *Programa de patrimonio Ciutadà d'ús i gestió comunitàries*. Retrieved from https://ajuntament.barcelona.cat/participaciociutadana/sites/default/files/documents/comunsurbans_doc_sm_0.pdf

Ansell, C. and Galsh A. (2007). Collaborative governance in theory and practice. *Journal of Public Administration Research and Theory*, 18: 543–571.

Balibrea, M. (2005). Barcelona: Del Modelo a la Marca [Barcelona: from the model to the brand]. In J. Carillo, I. Estella Noriega and L. García-Merás (Eds.), *Desacuerdos 3. Sobre arte, política y esfera pública en el Estado español* (pp.263–267). Granada, Spain: Arteleku, MACBA and UNIA.

Barcelona en Comú (2015). Programa electoral municipal 2015. Retrieved from https://barcelonaencomu.cat/sites/default/files/programaencomu_cat.pdf

Bianchi, I. (2022). The commonification of *the public* under new municipalism: Commons-state institutions in Naples and Barcelona, *Urban Studies* 0 (0).

Blakeley, G. (2007). Local governance and Local democracy: The Barcelona Model, *Local Government Studies*, 31(2): 149–165.

Blanco, I. and Gomà, R. (2019). Nuevo municipalismo, movimientos urbanos e impactos políticos, *Desacatos: Revista de Ciencias Sociales*, 61: 56–69.

Blanco, I., Lowndes, V. and Salazar, Y. (2021). Understanding institutional dynamics in participatory governance: How rules, practices and narratives combine to produce stability or diverge to create conditions for change. *Critical Policy Studies,* 16(2): 204–223.

Brugué, Q. (2010). *Transversalidad: Del concepto a la práctica, de las ideas a los resultados*. Vitoria-Gasteiz: Fundación Kaleidos.

Bua, A. and Bussu, S. (2020). Between governance-driven democratisation and democracy-driven governance: Explaining changes in participatory governance in the case of Barcelona. *European Journal of Political Research*, 60(3): 716–737.

Bussu, S., Bua, A., Dean, R. and Smith, G. (2022a). Embedding participatory governance. *Critical Policy Studies*, 16(2): 133–145.

Bussu, S., Golan, Y. and Hargreaves, A. (2022b). *Understanding Developments in Participatory Governance*. Manchester: Manchester Metropolitan University.

Castro, M. and Forné, L. (2021). *Patrimoni Ciutadà. Un marc per a la col.laboració públic-comunitària. La Hidra Cooperativa.* Retrieved from https://lahidra.net/ca/informe-patrimoni-ciutada-un-marc-de-collaboracio-public-comunitari/

Chwalisz, C. (2020). Reimagining democratic institutions: Why and how to embed public deliberation. In *Innovative Citizen Participation and New Democratic Institutions: Catching the Deliberative Wave.* Paris: OECD Publishing.

Escobar, O. (2021). Between radical aspirations and pragmatic challenges: Institutionalizing participatory governance in Scotland. *Critical Policy Studies*, 16(2): 146–161.

Federici, S. and Caffentzis, G. (2013). Commons against and beyond capitalism, *Upping the Anti: A Journal of Theory and Action*, 15: 83–97.

Ferreri, M. and Vidal, L. (2021). Public-cooperative policy mechanisms for housing commons, *International Journal of Housing Policy*, 22(2): 149–173.

Fundación de los comunes (2015). *Comuns urbans a Barcelona.* Retrieved from: http://bcncomuns.net/

Fung, A. and Wright, E.O. (2003). *Deepening Democracy. Institutional Innovations in Empowered Participatory Governance.* London: Verso.

Hardt, M. and Negri, A. (2009). *Commonwealth.* Cambridge, MA: Harvard University Press.

Harvey, D. (2012). *Rebel Cities.* London: Verso.

Klinenberg, K. (2021). *Palaces for the People.* New York: Random House.

Laval, C. and Dardot, P. (2015). *Común: Ensayo sobre la revolución en el siglo XXI.* Barcelona: Gedisa.

Mattei, U. (2011). *Beni comuni. Un manifesto.* Bari: Laterza.

Ostrom, E. (1990). *Governing the Commons.* Cambridge: Cambridge University Press.

Ostrom, E. and Hess, C. (2007). *Private and Common Property Rights,* Bloomington: School of Public & Environmental Affairs Research Paper No. 2008-11-01.

Pera, M. (2022). *Estudi de la gestió cívica a Barcelona: La gestió d'equipaments municipals com a pràctica democràtica i comunitària.* [Doctoral Dissertation, Universitat Autònoma de Barcelona]. Thesis and Dissertations online, www.tdx.cat

Polanyi, K. (2001). *The Great Transformation: The Political and Economic Origins of Our Time.* Boston, MA: Beacon Press.

Rubio-Pueyo, V. (2017). *Municipalism in Spain. From Barcelona to Madrid, and Beyond.* New York: the Rosa Luxemburg Stiftung's New York Office.

Russell, B. (2019). Beyond the local trap: New municipalism and the rise of the fearless cities. *Antipode*, 51(3): 989–1010.

Russell, B. and Milburn, K. (2019). What Can an Institution Do? Towards Public-Common Partnerships and a New Common-Sense. *Renewal: A Journal of Social Democracy*, 26(4): 45–55

Voorberg, W.H., Bekkers, V.J.J.M. and Tummers, L.G. (2014). A systematic review of co-creation and co-production: Embarking on the social innovation journey. *Public Management Review*, 17(9): 1333–1357

14 How Can Democracy-Driven Governance Turn into Technopopulism?

Arguing on the Case of *Ahora Madrid*

Fabiola Mota Consejero and Cristina Herranz

Introduction

The anti-austerity movements which emerged across western democracies towards the beginning of the last decade brought about the prospect of advancing social justice and deepening democracy (Della Porta, 2015). This outlook appeared especially where movement parties developed from the protest to compete in the electoral arena and eventually entered the state. Such was the case of Spain during the municipal elections of 2015, when many large and medium-sized cities came to be governed by new left and radical municipalist movement parties which were deeply rooted in the 15-M or Indignados movement (e.g., *Ahora Madrid, Barcelona En Comú, Compostela Aberta, Cádiz Sí Se Puede*, among many others). All these administrations were committed to applying new forms of participatory governance in response to the lack of responsiveness of representative institutions in managing the 2008 financial crisis (Tormey, 2015). Moreover, the policy agenda of the so-called Municipalities of Change ("Ayuntamientos del Cambio"), prioritised changing the neoliberal norms ruling the relations of power in the Spanish municipalities in order to reduce the high rates of social exclusion and the sharpened territorial inequalities caused by austerity policies. Whilst these administrations had to deal with similar structural constraints (Blanco et al., 2020, Janoschka & Mota 2021, Roth et al. 2019, etc.), their success in achieving what Bua and Bussu (2021, and introduction to this volume) refer to as "democracy-driven governance" seems to have varied (Martínez & Wissink 2021, Mota & Janoschka 2022). In this chapter we analyse how "*Ahora Madrid*" (*AM, Madrid Now*) tackled social and territorial inequalities through a model of participatory governance that intended to deepen and broaden local democracy as well as to transform the political *status quo* at the urban level (Thompson 2021). Through an in-depth case study of *AM*, we analyse and reflect upon the co-existence of various visions of participatory democracy within the AM administration and go into depth on the conditions shaping what we identify as an intertwining of technopopulism (Bickerton & Acceti 2021, De Blasio & Sorice 2018) with democracy-driven governance.

The analyses are based on empirical evidence collected from face-to-face interviews, conducted between 2016 and 2018, with local government officials, city council representatives of *AM* as well as of political opposition and with activists of urban social movements and civic organisations.[1] Additionally, information gathered from participant observation in public events from 2015 until 2019,[2] official published reports and online data, and municipal opinion poll surveys have also been scrutinised for the research.

The following section outlines the theoretical debate and provides a short description of the origins and features of *AM*. Afterwards, we present a critical analysis of the most outstanding policy initiatives implemented by *AM* with the aim of fighting against inequalities and promoting citizen participation. The chapter ends with a discussion section dealing with some specific conditions underlying the failure to develop democracy-driven governance in Madrid between 2015 and 2019.

The Twofold Goal of Radical Municipalism: Social Justice and Participatory Democracy

In the aftermath of the financial crisis of 2008, anti-austerity, anti-eviction and pro-democracy struggles arose in Spain joining together in 2011 under the umbrella of the Indignados movement, or 15-M, after the march of *Democracia Real Ya* (Real Democracy Now) on the streets of Madrid and other cities the 15th of May that year (Castañeda 2012). The occupation of Sol Square in the Madrid city centre evolved into a huge camp, *Acampada Sol*, that became a symbolic referent for the whole movement. At this stage of the protest cycle, the 15-M shows basic organisational features and repertoire of actions of a typically autonomous movement (Flesher 2015). Based on the practice of direct democracy through face-to-face communication and deliberation, popular assemblies were inclusive, open to everybody engaging as an individual and facilitated the generation by ordinary people of horizontal and decentralised mutual aid networks rooted in place (e.g. autonomous social centres and neighbourhoods). This latest feature was at odds with a technopolitical or cyberactivist ideational framework, which underlies the extensive and innovative use of digital technologies driven by free culture activists during the protest campaign, and which projects the concept of cyberspace as a place open to everyone without geographical restrictions (Flesher 2020, p. 145). Nonetheless, both movement influences share a sharp commitment to a "do it yourself" philosophy without intermediation (Flesher 2020, p.47), which turned out to be crucial for the development of *Podemos*'s populist strategy emphasising the transversality of a popular antagonist subject ("the people") against the elites, or "the caste" (Kioupkiolis & Pérez 2019, Rubio-Pueyo & Fernández 2020). At a later stage, the Acampada Sol was lifted, and social mobilisations focused on popular assemblies spread out across the neighbourhoods. At this point, the strong neighbourhood movement in Madrid gained significance and, with it, the forms of collective organisations rooted in the institutional left. Such a left tradition defends a representative model of collective political subjects (e.g., citizens, neighbours, and workers) which organised in formalised and vertical structures of representation. Thus, the 15-M movement in Madrid brought together at least three distinct traditions, practices and imaginaries for collective action, which also convey different and even conflicting understandings of the meaning of real democracy (Flesher 2020, Mota Consejero & Janoschka 2022): autonomism, technopolitics and institutional left.

The 15-M anti-austerity and pro-democracy mobilisations gave rise to the *confluencias municipalistas* ("municipalist confluences") in many cities on the eve of the local elections of May 2015 (Delclós 2015). One of these, *Municipalia*, would later evolve into *Ahora Madrid* (*AM*) in Spain's capital city. The municipalist confluences were completely new organisations where participation occurs at least ideally at the individual level and not by quotas (nobody representing any collective voice or aggregated political will), trying to adopt the form of popular assemblies with their open and horizontal decision mechanisms. The importance of this organisational form is that it allowed to involve a significant number of people not previously connected with parties or movements (Roth et al. 2019), hence reinforcing inclusiveness. On the other hand, "New municipalism" emphasises the need to begin transformation from the local realm (Russel 2019, Subirats 2016), the closest to citizens' everyday struggles, by fighting against three consequences of austerity policies: economic inequalities (transfer of incomes to the richest), popular disempowerment (transfer of power to the lobbies) and social deprivation (transfer of rights to the market) (Blanco & Gomá 2019, p. 59). Consequently, it aims to build a shared public sphere between social movements and institutions of local government where traditional institutions, social movements and citizens undergo a democratic transformation. Municipalist confluences have thus been theorised as an instance of "democracy-driven governance" to the extent that they represent an attempt by social movements to move into the state and radicalise participatory governance as part of their strategy (Bua & Bussu 2021, p. 720). It involves the need for a participatory governance that opens-up opportunities for bottom-up agenda setting and decision-making, though not with the aim of strengthening the legitimacy of traditional institutions nor the neoliberal distribution of power, but rather for challenging the social order and transforming inherited power relations.

The theoretical question arising from radical municipalism's twofold objective is how can both goals be achieved simultaneously (Roth et al., 2019), or, in other words, how can participatory governance be truly democratising from the bottom-up. Participation has long been associated with democratisation insofar as it provides a means to contest the authority of hierarchical organisations by challenging the status quo, fighting inequality and reshaping authority in order to advance social justice. However, the revival of participation since the seventies, as a management tool rather than a method of democratisation, coincided with an intense expansion in socioeconomic inequalities over the past half a century (Lee et al. 2015). Both changes overlapped with the neoliberal irruption in policy-making and a growing antagonism between institutional elites and ordinary citizens (Swyngedouw 2019). Consequently, the municipalist confluences' twofold goal of fighting inequalities through participatory governance is both timely and challenging.

What is the goal of citizen participation? To the extent that participation is merely understood to promote solidarity by transforming identities and interests that make us better citizens, able to act on the general good and contribute to social consensus, it can conceal the materiality of an unequal society and denies the existence and legitimacy of political conflict (Lee et al., 2015, p.14–15). We believe that this is the main trap the confluences could fall into, and we will argue this was the case in the experience of *AM* with its turn towards a technopopulist governance style that combined the popular will of populism and the competence of technocracy (Bickerton & Acceti 2021).

Governing from Competing Visions of Participatory Democracy

Despite the plural collective traditions coming together under the 15-M movement in Madrid, the creation of the *AM* electoral platform, and its manifesto on the horizon of the local elections of 2015, followed rather faithfully the diverse prefigurative democratic praxis performed during the protest cycle (Mota Consejero & Janoschka 2022). On the one hand, the new organisation was made up of individuals who were likely, but not necessarily, activists in different social movements (e.g., neighbourhood and civic associations, social cooperatives and cultural centres) and political organisations (such as the new movement-party *Podemos*, the ecologist party *EQUO* and local factions of *Izquieda Unida*, a left-wing coalition led by the *Communist Party* of Spain). On the other hand, the electoral programme was drafted through participatory and deliberative procedures taking place in face-to-face, horizontal, open and inclusive assemblies and seemingly following the autonomist modality of democratic activism introduced above. Once a first draft was completed, additional participatory processes took place across all the districts and neighbourhoods to collect policy proposals. Finally, the process culminated by adding up citizen suggestions made through a web platform created for this purpose (performing here as a "techno-politic" movement actor).

The *AM* electoral programme contained a transformative political project in relation to the previous neoliberal model of urban governance, proposing novel ideas for structural and transversal changes based on participatory approaches. Basically, commitments to establish a participatory democracy, achieve more transparency and responsiveness of the local government and replicate democratic innovations from the previous protest cycle were essential electoral promises (*Ahora Madrid*, 2015).[3]

Given the impressive support amongst urban social movements for AM, *Podemos* decided to back the emerging municipalist platform following an agreement on who would lead the confluence. AM's leader, Manuela Carmena, was a retired and charismatic female judge, a former labour lawyer whose office colleagues had been victims of assassination by far-right terrorists during the transition to democracy in Spain in the mid-1970s. The widespread social approval of the 15-M's claims, the popular enthusiasm about the new politics and the acknowledged leadership of Manuela Carmena enabled *AM* to obtain more than half a million votes in the city, almost one-third of the electorate. These electoral results brought Ahora Madrid to form a government, as the number of elected councillors from progressive parties exceeded the representatives from liberal and conservative ones. However, it could only be a minority government that needed the support of the traditional centre-left *Spanish Worker Socialist Party (PSOE)* to pass bills and approve budgets. A progressive movement-party (Della Porta et al., 2017) was set to rule Madrid following more than a quarter of a century of rule by the liberal-conservative *Popular Party* (*PP*).

Spanish law dictates that the members of municipal executive must be elected local councillors (an aspect on which the elected mayor disagreed). As such, the Ahora Madrid government was composed of the ten first candidates on AM's candidate list, which represented the rich plurality of the traditions and activism within the 15-M movement. Each one was entrusted with a specific area within the local executive.

Exceptionally, the Madrid executive was the only new municipalist government in which the responsibilities for citizen participation were shared between two distinct areas: the Department of Transparency and Citizen Participation (TCP) and the Department of Territorial Coordination and Associative Promotion (TC&AP), later re-named as Territorial Coordination and Public Social Cooperation (TC&PSC). The councillors appointed to coordinate these two areas evidence the influence of the previous protest cycle in the composition of the new government. On the one hand, the TCP's Department was directed by Pablo Soto, a person recognised in the free digital culture movement, and a crucial member of it since the beginning of the *15-M* movement. Its main function was to initiate decision-making mechanisms through direct and individual citizen participation. This was done by transferring some "digital democratic innovations" introduced by free culture activists in the social mobilisations since 2011 (Mota Consejero & Janoschka 2022). In fact, this Department worked in close collaboration with MediaLab Prado, a cultural space and citizen lab created by the Madrid City Council in 2000. Funded by the Department of Culture, MediaLab had housed the free culture activism in previous years, and now it had created a Lab of Collective Intelligence for Democratic Participation (ParticipaLab), which was focused on innovation in digital participation from a technopolitical approach (ParticipaLab 2019).

On the other hand, the councillor responsible for the TC&AP's Department, Nacho Murgui, had previously been active in neighbourhood movements and was the president of the Regional Federation of Neighbourhood Associations in Madrid). The objectives entrusted to this department were to decentralise local democracy by transferring responsibilities and institutional resources to the city districts and to ensure the effective participation of civic associations in the governance process (for instance, by elaborating innovative forms of co-management).

By and large, when it comes to comparing to the historic path of governance in the city, the participatory policies developed by AM may be considered remarkably innovative, even in comparison with Barcelona (Font & García Espín, 2020; Blanco et al., 2020). However, while there was an apparently straightforward implementation of electoral agreements, various incongruities and fine-tuning occurred over time, triggering various conflicts with social movements and organisations despite their close ties to the government. It became clear over time that competing and unbridgeable visions of participatory democracy coexisted within AM, making it difficult to carry out and institutionalise a coherent form of democracy-driven governance. In the words of a representative of a neighbourhood association interviewed in 2017: "We do not know yet if the city council has clearly defined its policy for citizen participation. We do not know whether it is targeted towards citizens, whether it is targeted towards collective entities, or a combination of both". Attempts to reconcile such plural visions when developing policies against inequality through participatory governance are analysed in the next two sections.

Democratic Innovations Driven by Individual Digital Participation and Sortition

No doubt, the most ground-breaking democratic innovation implemented by AM City Council was the "Decide Madrid" (Madrid Decides) online platform for citizen engagement. It has also been considered a directly transferable innovation from the cyberactivist collectives of the 15-M movement to municipal participatory governance (Mota Consejero & Janoschka 2022). Launched by the Department of Citizen Participation and Transparency as early as September of 2015, Decide Madrid was created with an open-source software named "Consul"[4] which allowed the digital platform to be adopted and modified by other institutions and city councils (Herranz et al., 2019).

Decide Madrid enabled any citizen registered as a resident to be involved in participatory processes such as citizen proposals, local consultations, online debates and participatory budgeting. All new institutional mechanisms for citizen engagement in the city. The innovative nature of these reforms was also recognised by the right-wing opposition:

> They have transferred the [participatory] procedure from *Podemos* to an institution such as the City Council, with the inconveniences that this entails, because you leave a lot of people out. But, come on, of course, it is undeniable that it is innovative.
>
> (Local councillor, opposition party)

Between 2016 and 2019, citizens could propose and vote in open-ended bottom-up processes, on specific policy actions, city- and district-wide. Such actions would be implemented under the yearly call of participatory budgeting. As explained by Pablo Soto, the real innovation introduced by his Department was to set direct, individual and digital participation in the well-known mechanism of participatory budgeting.

> What we have done is … setting in a unique platform, various mechanisms for bottom-up decision making, this is, that people themselves can say about

what we should decide, setting the political agenda, and then incorporating those best practices which we have not invented ... citizen initiatives, binding referendum, participatory budgeting, are widespread worldwide since long, (...) And they are implemented in one form or another. And participatory budgeting has mostly extended in a form that is not precisely direct but through intermediaries and that makes that, in the end, are limited processes. And we have wanted to make them very direct, that really any person can make policy proposals ... anyone vote for them, and anyone can win the voting and to have his proposition made real.

(Local councillor of the TCP's Department)

Neighbourhood associations and other collectives criticized the individually oriented nature of Decide Madrid as the exclusive mechanism for engagement in participatory budgeting. As a result, the City Council also fostered collective propositions through on-site participatory activities carried out in so-called "Local Forums for Participation" and temporary initiatives. Additionally, facilitators for participatory processes were allocated to each city district.

In the same line as the new strategy to broaden and deepen participation hinging upon citizen proposals, anyone could suggest concrete policy initiatives, measures and public actions through the Decide Madrid platform. If a proposition obtained support by at least one percent of the electorate (approx. 27,500 votes), it passed to a politically (but not legally) binding consultation. A public multi-consultation was carried out in February 2017, comprising bottom-up citizen propositions (such as the issue of a unique ticket for Madrid public transport) as well as top-down institutional ones (such as the restructuring of the Plaza de España). Voter turnout was quite considerable, above 200,000 participants through three different channels: Decide Madrid, posted voting and at polling stations.

Despite procedures for raising citizen proposals evolved to include collectively organised demands from neighbourhoods and the city, social movements rooted in a left organisational tradition showed their concern about the participatory governance conducted by the City Council. As clearly expressed by a representative of a neighbourhood association:

To my knowledge none of the citizen proposals reached the required percentage (of votes), but they were taken as good (...) because the City Council was interested by them. (...) The proposition we have in our top list (...) I assure you that City Council is not going to pick it up for public consultation because it is contrary to its own interests. Then, the approach they have is a network approach, of social network, which is a very mercantilist approach. Marketing. Then, it does not fit in the culture and usual methodology of the collectives, hence it is little flexible to be used as a resource by them. Moreover, a good part of people involved in there do not want to participate in organizations. They are people who, still among the allied to the municipal government, oppose social organizations because they see them like a burden of the old politics. (...) The truth is that for City Council apparently citizen participation is for citizens, not for organizations where citizens collectively organized to protect themselves from the system's attacks.

Certainly, among those people understanding direct democracy exclusively in individual terms was the mayor, such as she pointed it later in her memoirs:

> This disinterest for permitting individual opinion in public debate has led to some people to mythicize assembly democracy by understanding it as a positive form of direct democracy. Assembly democracy (*democracia asamblearia*) is not direct democracy at all. (…) Assembly participation is enormously controllable by who leads it. (…) Assembly democracy, apart from not allowing reasoning nor the free expression of will, is absolutely inefficient and ineffective.
>
> (Carmena 2021, p. 228)

Two years into the digital participation via *Decide Madrid*, data protection procedures turned out to be a prominent factor limiting the scope of digital deliberative democracy. Consequently, additional democratic innovations were introduced to promote specific forms of deliberation based on sortition democracy, which were developed in the *ParticipaLab* experimentation project. For instance, the first mini-public mechanism took place in March 2017 under the call of G1000 (Navarro, 2017). However, the most innovative mechanism was the City Observatory (Observatorio de la Ciudad), which was created towards the end of the mandate as a permanent participatory body allowing 49 randomly selected citizens to monitor the policies of the City Council and also to propose policy improvements and citizen consultations (Ganuza & Menéndez 2020, Nez & Ganuza 2020). Both mechanisms were justified by their inclusiveness, since random selection may be considered the most direct and wide-ranging form of participation, preventing political bias of organisations and associations, acting also as a filter against intrusion from professional lobbies. As had been expressed by Manuela Carmena "because of the system of election (sortition or by lots) they (participants) did not bring with them any bias" (Carmena 2021, p. 231). Therefore, this type of democratic innovation responded to the goal of developing better local policies and reinforcing the legitimacy of new participatory mechanisms. Yet it can be argued that these aims are pursued through an overtly consensus-oriented decision-making procedure that marginalises social movements (Bua & Bussu, 2021).

Local Power Devolution and Territorial Allocation of Public Funds

Relative to Spain, Madrid is a large and wealthy city, but in 2015 it also had a huge debt burden, crosscut by inequalities. The districts and neighbourhoods of Madrid are very unequal, and such inequality has been historically forged between the centre and the periphery as well as between the northwest and southeast. Still, in the last decade, it had become the most segregated out of the capital cities in Europe and the second highest in social inequality (Leal & Sorando 2017). Consequently, despite their awareness of the strong economic, institutional and legal-administrative limitations imposed on the city council's real power (Janoschka & Mota 2021, Martínez & Wissink 2021), the local executive sought to meet the priority of fighting against social and territorial inequalities in the city. For instance, each councillor was assigned the responsibility of two districts of diametrically opposed social stratification, which should strengthen the commitment of all government members to think about politics transversally across the fractures of social stratification in the city (Janoshcka & Mota 2021). Furthermore, the political role of the districts was upgraded, promoting a noticeable devolution of the decision-making processes which clashed with bureaucratic inertias and financial and legal constraints.

The TC&AP's Department (later TC&PSC one) launched two big policy initiatives to fight against territorial disparities through participatory mechanisms: the creation (with the support of the councillors from the socialist party (*PSOE*) and the liberals (*Ciudadanos*)) of the Local Forums for Participation (LFP), introduced in the 21 districts of the city in February of 2017, and the Territorial Rebalancing Fund.

The LFP intended to promote citizen engagement for local policymaking from the perspective of neighbourhoods and districts, thus encouraging dialogue among individuals, civic associations and district administrations. They came to replace the former Territorial Board of Associations, in which only formally registered associations and a limited number of people could engage. On the contrary, the LFP was conceived for both individual and collective participation; it included associations but also informal collectives like citizen platforms (thanks to the new Public and Social Cooperation Local Regulation, approved in 2018, that politically recognised non-formalised social actors); and it did not limit the scope and number of participants but was completely open. In fact, one main objective pursued by the regulation of the LFPs was to become as inclusive as possible when it comes to public policy making. In the words of a municipal official of AM who described to us the novelty of the LFPs in comparison to the previous territorial model of citizen participation:

> There is participation if there is a political will to translate the result of participation into public policies. Political will is very important for citizen participation. And then, citizen participation can be used to justify democratically or in terms of providing legitimacy for a government team ... What you want to do ... or you can really open the doors of the institution to citizenship. I understand that the previous model was lacking the ability to integrate all positions, all positions of the main agents of the city.
>
> (AM Appointed official)

In contrast to the individual participation mainly channelled through the digital platform *Decide Madrid*, the LFPs relied primarily on collective and on-site forms of participation and deliberation (assembly model), being their final decisions and proposal of "reference" for the district council.

The LFPs evolved over time and were also thought to channel and sort out all the local participatory processes: "those coming top-down from institutions and those going bottom-up from citizens" (AM appointed official). Amongst the latter, a promising participatory process was the electoral proposition for citizen auditing of the local debt and public policies, which had been a claim flag of the 15M movement, then taken on by the Madrid Citizen Debt Audit Platform in 2012 and eventually incorporated through the LFP in 2017. Since it was left to the citizens' initiative, citizen auditing groups of local debt solely came up in 13 LFPs where they worked for a very short period (Villena & Luengo 2019), though there were groups previously informally working in three districts, the most active of which were in the districts Usera and Arganzuela (where AM obtained a majority of the votes).

The relative success of the LFPs could be conditioned by unequal citizen engagement at district level. In fact, the territorial levels of citizen participation show significant disparities among districts over time. Differences appear closely related to socio-economic territorial inequalities (the richer the district, the higher rate of participation would be expected) on one hand and the vote for *AM* (the larger electoral support at district level, the higher rate of citizen participation) on the other hand.

As shown in Figure 14.1, growth of participation from 2016 to 2019 was more intense in the northwest districts of the city as compared to the southeast, where the electoral support for *AM* was larger in relative terms and where citizen engagement with City Council participatory policies used to be the highest in the beginning. Consequently, the AM City Council's participatory policy succeeded in fostering citizen participation in all the city, thereby spreading citizen engagement within local policies beyond deprived areas where more people were mobilised by the municipalist confluence. In fact, the individual participation growth from 11% in 2016 to 18% in 2019 is sharper among voters of the liberal party, *Ciudadanos*, and of the socialist, *PSOE*, in the latest local elections.

By and large, although some associations perceived LFPs as an attempt to control and institutionalise autonomous activities, opinions from territory-based social activism tended to be more hopeful:

> What novelties do I think brings the Local Forum? I think it further opens citizen participation (…) I think there is a possibility for working groups of the local forums to deliver policy proposals to the district council, which can be discussed there, and so to become an additional voice over there. (…) I think it has many potentialities, it is still starting, but they seem interesting to me.
> (Participant in Arganzuela LFP)

Notwithstanding, an important message delivered by the Department of Territorial Cooperation was that:

> The potential scope of the Local Forums is very conditioned by the process of local devolution. (…) If the district council, which is the first institution

How Can DDG Turn into Technopopulism? 235

Figure 14.1 Percentages of participation[5] by year and district, and relative variation by district. Source: Quality of life and satisfaction with public services of Madrid city (2016, 2017 and 2019). Authors' own elaboration with Geopandas Python Library, with maps and data from Open Data Portal from Madrid City Council.

responding to citizens, does not have implementation capacity, that may provoke frustration, inhibit participation. Therefore, the LFP's success is largely dependent on that district councils have more competencies, enough budget, and more decision capacity in the future.

(Appointed official of AM City Council)

In this regard, the nationally imposed restrictions on the replacement rate for public sector employees had not been allowing any expansion of the municipal workforce, hence, the implementation of a fully territorial devolution became unrealisable in practical terms. Notwithstanding, the municipal budget was remarkably transformed over time, providing more financial margin thanks to the increasing reduction of debt interest and repayment (for instance, by getting rid of the rating agencies) as well as to the increasing incomes from restructuring property-related taxes (Sánchez Mato & Garzón 2019). As a result, a certain leeway was enjoyed, expanding the budget in line with electoral promises in strategic policy realms. One of those priority objectives was territorial rebalancing, hence a second local participatory mechanism implemented by the TC&PSC's Department was the Territorial Rebalancing Funds (TRFs), a mechanism to allow citizens to decide about a part of the municipal budget that is allocated to districts and neighbourhoods. TRFs were part of the Strategic Plan of Municipal Decentralization in its economic dimension and were introduced as a tool for the cohesion of the city and an instrument designed to intervene in deprived neighbourhoods or areas, as well as to fulfil specific needs for facilities, urban and social improvement of the city as a whole. Proposals for actions to be implemented under the TRF were decided by the district council in a process of consultation with the collective entities taking place at the LFP of the corresponding district. According to one Department official, "it is another mechanism for citizen participation like participatory budgeting". During its mandate, the *AM* City Council allocated more than 100 million euros to implement 423 projects distributed in the 21 districts (e.g., employment workshops, restoration of soccer fields, basic sports facilities, urban squares, public schools and so forth). Nonetheless, as expressed by Baiocchi & Ganuza (2014), more popular participation in neighbourhood-oriented decision-making may justify and legitimise political decisions that reproduce social and territorial inequalities.

Whilst the former Special Plan for Investments and the Neighborhood Plans were acknowledged antecedents of the TRFs, what was unanimously highlighted as real innovative about the TRFs has to do with the technical criteria and scientific procedures applied in the policymaking and implementation. "All actions were distributed according to the Vulnerability Index, to bring more resources to the most disadvantaged areas" (Murgui Parra, 2020: 113). According to the General Director of Devolution and Territorial Action,

> accurately defining rebalancing needs was not an easy task. For this reason, the Government Area of Territorial Coordination and Public Social Cooperation contacted a team from the Carlos III University in which people

belonging to the Applied Artificial Intelligence Group and the Department of Social Sciences participated. This team proposed the methodology of Hierarchical Analysis (AHP) as the ideal tool to determine the vulnerability of the neighbourhoods and districts of Madrid and its application to the case through the technology and knowledge of the University.

(Díaz Méndez 2019)

The emphasis on technical expertise applied to public policies and management by the AM City Council was clearly expressed by the mayor, Manuela Carmena, in her speech presenting the TRFs in 2017:[6]

> We make public policies that we honestly believe should serve to reduce inequality (…) We are determined that the public policies that we put in place produce results, and if they do not produce results we will change them, **we will do** something else, whatever it may be, to make those public policies work. (…) And we have a great field that I don't know if you scientists have thought about (…). (…) we have designed public policies, (…) all of them should pursue to return a dignity that generates something that I would like the advice of scientists on how it can be measured, something that, I believe, it is extraordinarily transcendent: it is hope, hope that things can be different. I believe that when hope is transmitted to urban areas, when it is transmitted to groups of citizens, the solution begins, because one has the capacity to imagine the future and to make it possible. Therefore, we need to be able to measure that, but I know that you will help us (addressing the scientists).

Nonetheless, by strongly relying on expert knowledge and technical procedures, was the City Council admitting that not all questions are usefully open to compromise and deliberation? But then, why not decide on the basis of agonistic contests between organised interests groups? All in all, by greatly emphasising the goodness of scientific and apparently objective criteria for policy and decision-making (such as the territorial allocation of funds), AM seemed to elude political confrontation and, by doing so, dimmed its political response to their supporters from social movements. This appeared to be the opinion of activists from anti-eviction and housing rights movements when expressing in face-to-face interviews that the City Council participatory governance ruled out unavoidable social conflict. Paradoxically, the ensuing municipal coalition government of the *PP* and *Ciudadanos* updated in 2022 the Vulnerability Index for territorial rebalancing by applying Artificial Intelligence (through a digital tool named IGUALA developed by the international firm Accenture), and it turns out that one of the richest neighbourhoods (by income per capita) ranks at the top of deprived ones (Leenhouts 2022). Likewise, the current conservative-liberal government has used the Decide Madrid platform to launch public consultations aiming at revoking innovative norms and participatory institutions such as the Municipal Regulation for Public and Social Cooperation (2018) that legally recognised non-formalised citizen collectives as political actors.

Democratising from Social Movements and Surfing the Wave of Technopopulism?

AM City Council demonstrated strong political will to make citizen participation more inclusive in policymaking by establishing various well-known participatory mechanisms (e.g. participatory budgeting, citizen initiatives and public consultations). Overall, it can be considered a great breakthrough in face of practices of former conservative local governments which used to hinge upon a culture of patronage, thus disregarding citizens' and social organisations' engagement in public decision and policymaking. On the contrary, AM's participatory model put a great emphasis on open government, public transparency and efficiency and also a quest for social consensus that in practical terms entailed a neutralisation of social conflicts. By and large, they fostered a model of "democracy-driven-governance" insofar as attempts were made to institutionalise some forms of democratic organisation that arose from the "critical democracy" of citizen mobilisations (Bua & Busu 2021, p. 4). Concretely, it was mainly the technopolitics approach to democracy, conveyed by cyberactivists and the free culture movement in the protest cycle of the 15-M. From this approach, individual and direct participation is understood as an end in itself, instead of as a means to transform the political *status quo* of power relations that impeded social justice. Likewise, the autonomous ethic of "do it yourself" (Flesher 2020), without intermediaries, underlies the implementation of deliberative forms of participation by lots.

By and large, the analysis of AM's participatory governance demonstrates how the combined goals of the municipalist confluence to tackling inequalities through citizen participation evolved into a participatory model of governance that we can describe as a technopopulist fashion of ruling social conflicts (Kioupkolis & Seoane 2019). Understanding technopopulism as a new logic of political action, and not exclusively of electoral competition replacing the left-right divide, the popular will of populism and the competence of technocracy are not opposed to each other but are deeply connected. Both share an unmediated conception of the common good (Bickerton & Acceti 2021, p.3), opposing themselves to the mediated system of party democracy and organised social interests too.

This study has singled out certain factors accounting for the technopopulist shift in AM, independently of the structural constraints faced when in power. Firstly, a technocratic leadership in the leading figure of the mayor. Technopopulist leaders emphasise the ability to transform the popular will into public policies, thus driving a depoliticisation of policy making. Despite the rhetoric of the "politics of doing", what really occurs is a "desubtantialization" of public policies (Bickerton & Acceti 2021). In Manuela Carmena's own words:

> I have been very criticized because of my conviction that we must govern for everyone. (…) they insisted that we only must govern for those who vote for us. No, I don't think so. (…) Governing is, above all, managing the public. Changes may have to be decided for management to work, but changing management patterns rarely requires new laws, but new ideas, imagination,

and enthusiasm. (…) I conceive of political life as the activity of managing the public.

(Carmena 2021, pp. 188–189)

Secondly, AM agreed on an ill-defined objective of democratic transformation which materialised into two different institutional ways to broaden and deepen citizen participation, each one leading the City Council Departments of TCP and TC&AP. Thirdly, divisions within the 15-M movement in Madrid, in which three political cultures and collective action traditions came to act synergistically but also competed with each other (autonomous, technopolitics and institutional left), came to hindering the harsh process of institutionalisation of the social movement that entered the state. All in all, these characteristics help to understand how technopopulist governance can arise as an unintended consequence of democracy-driven governance.

Notes

1 The interviews were recorded, transcribed and analysed following the approaches of critical discourse (Wodak & Meyer 2001).
2 Including over a dozen of local workshops and gathering convened, either sporadically or on regular basis, by the municipal Departments for Citizen Participations and for Associative Promotion as well as by municipal agencies such as MediaLab Prado, civic organisations such as the Observatory of Participation (Observatorio de la Participación de Madrid) and Neighborhood Popular Assemblies (Asambleas Populares de Barrio).
3 The mayor Manuela Carmena (2021) states in her memoirs that "Ahora Madrid made a large and peculiar program, because of its content as much as the bottom-up process of drafting it (…)" (p.169). "This program was being done when I arrived (…) Though it was an admirable collective task it does not mean it was a true electoral program" (p. 172–173). "I did not feel identified with the long list of very concrete proposal of the Ahora Madrid program" (p.174). "Looking back, perhaps I should not have accepted the Ahora Madrid program, given its final prolix configuration because of accumulation of proposals" (p. 175).
4 Web page and platform code accessible at the following link: https://github.com/consul/consul
5 https://www.madrid.es/portales/munimadrid/es/Inicio/El-Ayuntamiento/Calidad-y-Evaluacion/Percepcion-ciudadana/Encuesta-de-Calidad-de-Vida-y-Satisfaccion-con-los-Servicios-Publicos-de-la-Ciudad-de-Madrid/?vgnextfmt=default&vgnextoid=87fcc6ba1d244410VgnVCM2000000c205a0aRCRD&vgnextchannel=5134261f46839710VgnVCM1000001d4a900aRCRD; https://geoportal.madrid.es/IDEAM_WBGEOPORTAL/index.iam
6 https://www.youtube.com/watch?v=uNp_Yik9-Rc "Manuela Carmena presenta los Fondos de Reequilibrio Territorial 2017". Manuel Carmena's speech at the public presentation of Territorial Rebalance Funds in 2017.

References

Ahora Madrid Electoral Manifesto (2015). It can be retrieved from: https://www.documentcloud.org/documents/2086732-ahoramadrid-programa-municipales-2015?sidebar=0 (Latest accessed 24th March 2022)

Baiocchi, G., & E. Ganuza (2014). Participatory budgeting as if emancipation mattered. *Politics & Society*, 42(1): 29–50.

Bickerton, J., & Acceti, C.I. (2021). *Thecnopopulism. The New Logic of Democratic Politics*. Oxford: Oxford University Press.

Blanco, I., & Gomá, R. (2019). Nuevo Municipalismo, movimientos urbanos e impactos políticos. *Desacatos*, 61: 59–69.

Blanco I., Salazar Y., & Bianchi I. (2020). Urban governance and political change under a radical left government. The case of Barcelona. *Journal of Urban Affairs*, 42(1): 18–38.

Bua, A., & Bussu, S. (2021). Between governance-driven democratisation and democracy-driven governance: Explaining changes in participatory governance in the case of Barcelona. *European Journal of Political Research*, 60(3): 716–737.

Carmena, M. (2021). *La joven política. Un alegato por la tolerancia y crítico con los partidos*. Barcelona: Península.

Castañeda, E. (2012). The Indignados of Spain: A precedent to occupy wall street. *Social Movement Studies*, 11(3/4): 309–319.

De Blasio, E.D. and M. Sorice. (2018). Populisms among technology, e-democracy and the depoliticisation process. *Revista Internacional de Sociología* 76(4): e109. https://doi.org/10.3989/ris.2018.76.4.18.005

Delclós, C. (2015, May 26). Towards a new municipal agenda in Spain. *Open Democracy*. https://www.opendemocracy.net/can-europe-make-it/carlos-delcl%C3%B3s/towards-new-municipal-agenda-in-spain

Della Porta, D. (2015). *Social Movements in Times of Austerity*. Polity Press.

Della Porta, D., Fernández, J., Ouki, H., & L. Mosca (2017). *Movements Parties Against Austerity*. Cambridge Polity Press.

Díaz Méndez, A. (2019). Vulnerabilidad y desigualdad territorial: El proyecto de descentralización y reequilibrio territorial en Madrid. V Congreso Ciudades Inteligentes. Accesible at: https://www.esmartcity.es/comunicaciones/comunicacion-vulnerabilidad-desigualdad-territorial-proyecto-descentralizacion-reequilibrio-territorial-madrid

Flesher Fominaya, C. (2015). Debunking spontaneity: Spain's 15-M/ Indignados as autonomous movement. *Social Movement Studies*, 14(2): 142–163.

Flesher Fominaya, C. (2020). *Democracy Reloaded. Inside Spain's Political Laboratory from 15-M to Podemos*. Oxford University Press.

Font, J., & García-Espín, P. (2020). From Indignad@s to mayors? Participatory dilemmas in Spanish municipal movements. In C. Flesher Fominaya & R.A. Feenstra (Eds.), *Routledge Handbook of Contemporary European Social Movements. Protest in Turbulent Times* (pp. 387–401). Routledge.

Ganuza, E., & Menéndez, M. (2020). Did you win? Sortition comes to the politics of Madrid. *Recerca*, 25(1): 95–110.

Herranz, C., Escudero, R.D., Muelas, D., & Saulière, S. (2019). Estrategias en Comunidades y Redes Sociales Digitales para Fomentar las Prácticas Participativas. *GIGAPP Estudios Working Papers*, 6(111–115): 28–48.

Janoschka, M., & Mota, F. (2021). New municipalism in action or urban neoliberalisation reloaded? – An analysis of governance change, stability and path dependence in Madrid (2015–19). *Urban Studies Journal*, 58(13): 2.814–2.830.

Kioupkiolis, A., & Pérez, F.S. (2019). Reflexive technopopulism: Podemos and the search for a new left-wing hegemony. *European Political Science* 18: 24–36. https://doi.org/10.1057/s41304-017-0140-9

Leal, J., & Sorando, D. (2017). Economic crisis, social change and segregation processes in Madrid, in Tammaru, T. et al. *Socioeconomic Segregation in European Capital Cities. East Meet the West*. Routledge, 214–237.

Lee, C.W., McQuarrie, M., & Walker, E.T., Eds. (2015). *Democratizing Inequalities. Dilemmas of the New Public Participation*. New York University Press.

Leenhouts, P. (2022). *Iguala. El ranking de vulnerabilidad del ayuntamiento que no debería darnos igual*. Blog *Público* (2022, May 11) https://blogs.publico.es/otrasmiradas/59505/iguala-el-ranking-de-vulnerabilidad-del-ayuntamiento-que-no-deberia-darnos-igual/

Martínez, M.A., & Wissink, B. (2021). Urban movements and municipalist governments in Spain: Alliances, tensions, and achievements. *Social Movement Studies*. https://doi.org/10.1080/14742837.2021.1967121

Mota Consejero, F., & Janoschka, M. (2022). Transforming urban democracy through social movements. The experience of Ahora Madrid. *Social Movement Studies*. https://doi.org/10.1080/14742837.2022.2028615

Murgui Parra, N. (2020). Las políticas de reequilibro territorial e innovación institucional en Madrid, 2015–2019. *Papers: Regió Metropolitana de Barcelona: Territori, estratègies, planejament*, (63): 110–117.

Navarro, F. (2017). El G1000 de Madrid: Un ejemplo de sorteo y deliberación como complemento de la representación. *Recerca*, 21: 151–157.

Nez, H., & Ganuza, E. (2020, November 14). Del 15M a las instituciones. Las políticas participativas de Ahora Madrid (2015–2019). *Encrucijadas. Revista Crítica de Ciencias Sociales*, 19(a1901): 1–19.

ParticipaLab (2019). *Democracias Futuras. Laboratorio de Inteligencia Colectiva para la Participación Democrática*. Madrid: MediaLab Prado.

Roth, L., Monterde, A., & Calleja López, A. (2019). *Ciudades Democráticas. La revuelta municipalista en el ciclo post-15M*. Barcelona: Icaria.

Rubio-Pueyo, V & Fernández Iglesias, F., (2020). Presentación. Entre movimientos e instituciones: Prácticas, aprendizajes y límites del "asalto institucional". *Encrucijadas. Revista Crítica de Ciencias Sociales*, 19: 1901.

Russell, B. (2019). Beyond the local trap: New municipalism and the rise of the fearless cities. *Antipode*, 51(3): 989–1010.

Sánchez Mato, C., & Garzón Espinosa, E. (2019). *919 días ¡Sí se podía! Cómo el Ayuntamiento de Madrid puso la economía al servicio de la gente*. Madrid: Akal.

Subirats, J. (2016). *El poder de lo próximo. Las virtudes del municipalismo*. Madrid: Los Libros de la Catarata.

Swyngedouw, E. (2019). The perverse lure of autocratic postdemocracy. *South Atlantic Quarterly*, 118(2): 267–286.

Thompson, M. (2021). What's so new about new municipalism? *Progress in Human Geography*, 45(2): 317–342.

Tormey, S. (2015). *The End of Representative Politics*. Cambridge, UK: Polity.

Villena, A., & Luengo, M. (2019). *Una auditoría truncada*. Contexto y Acción, *CTXT 213*, (2019, March 20), https://ctxt.es/es/20190320/Politica/25093/Andres-Villena-Marta-Luengo-auditoria-deuda-Sanchez-Mato-Madrid.htm

Wodak, R., & Meyer, M., Eds. (2001). *Methods of Critical Discourse Analysis*. London: Sage.

15 Surfing Disappointment
The Uneasy Inclusion of Social Movement Activists in Local Participatory Institutions: A Case Study of Madrid (2015–2019)[1]

Patricia García-Espín

Introduction

In May 2015, an electoral platform formed by social movement members, radical left militants and intellectuals gained the local government of Madrid. The platform fell under the umbrella of New Municipalism movements. While this was happening, Miranda was a member of the *Public Education Defence Movement*. Soon after, she decided to engage in the recently created district participatory institutions: *local forums*. In the beginning, she was enthusiastic, and she started to take part in meetings, conferences and workshops in her neighbourhood. However, two years later, she began to feel disappointment due to her poor experience and perception of even poorer outcomes. Miranda's case is illustrative of the disillusionment that many social movement militants feel when they engage in municipal participatory channels: the political scope and the capacity of influence do not meet their expectations.

Feelings of frustration are common after engaging in these institutions: they consist of "a range of feelings that develop when the participatory experience is perceived by participants as falling short of the initial expectations of political influence. These feelings may be manifested in temporary emotional reactions such as disillusionment, grief, or anger" (Fernández et al., 2020: 720; see also Hanson, 2018). Disappointment and frustration can unfold due to many reasons, but crucially, research points to excessive enthusiasm in the initial stages, poor results, lack of real influence or just an unpleasant experience, i.e., when the participatory process is not properly designed considering the capabilities of participants, when real decision-making is not guaranteed or when relational goods do not compensate the time and energy invested by participants (Young, 2001; Fung & Wright, 2001; Bherer et al., 2016; Brugué et al., 2021).

Disappointment has been examined when it develops among association members and individual participants (Talpin, 2012; Font & Navarro, 2013; Funes et al., 2014; Fernández et al., 2020), but has received scant attention in the case of social movement activists (henceforth, SMAs). This chapter focuses on this special category of active, critical and radical participants. Why do SMAs often, and soon, feel disappointment when they engage in institutional participation? Can we detect or imagine potential solutions to discontent? Focusing on SMAs is

DOI: 10.4324/9781003218517-18

helpful for two key reasons. Firstly, it can reveal limitations in participatory procedures which are not apparent to other publics more attuned to state institutions or who are more moderate (i.e., members of neighbourhood or cultural associations). Moreover, SMAs' reactions are relevant to observe how local institutions can deal with structural and social justice demands as those radical social movements carry on (Young, 2001).

In this chapter, the disappointment of SMAs is examined in the context of *local forums*, a new system of citizen councils created in Madrid in 2016 under the umbrella of New Municipalism. Interviews with key agents conducted in 2018–2019 point to a growing process of disillusionment among urban social movements whose causes, processes and strategies are explored throughout the chapter. The rest of the chapter is structured as follows: firstly, the analytical framework is set out. Secondly, the case, methods and data are described, and thirdly, the processes of disappointment are traced together with the potential remedies that agents put forward. Finally, measures to prevent frustration are discussed as an issue that promoters should consider if they want to include, at some point, the contribution of SMAs with structural social justice agendas.

SMAs in Official Participatory Institutions

SMAs are defined as politically active citizens who are members of grassroots organisations with socially transformative goals, inclined to protest and contentious action (Della Porta & Diani, 2011: Ch. 6).[2] They tend to challenge the existing sociopolitical order, promoting radical, anti-establishment and counter-hegemonic goals (Flesher Fominaya, 2017). In contrast to other associations, NGOs, sporting or cultural organisations, they are oriented towards more radical demands and protest action. In certain circumstances, however, these militants take part in institutional participation. If they manage to shape agendas towards socially transformative aims, this may result in what Bua and Bussu (2021) term "democracy-driven" processes, the major theme of this volume.

However, their integration has frequently been complicated (Baiocchi et al., 2011; Lee, 2015; Font & García-Espín, 2019; Janoschka & Mota, 2020; Lima, 2019). Regarding this issue, the literature has pointed to the concepts of autonomy, co-optation and conflict, as if the institutional encounter would lead typically to one of these poles: a moderation of aims due to institutionalisation, versus critical learning which reinforces their autonomy or situations of tense unrest (García-Espín & Jiménez, 2017; Lima, 2019; Holdo, 2019b). In this chapter, I address the problem from a different angle: the disappointment of SMAs and subsequent feelings of frustration are studied as part of their process of institutional contact.

This effect is especially relevant for counter-hegemonic SMAs who occasionally enter "socio-political coalitions" with radical left parties in local governments (Navarro, 1999). On the one hand, left-wing authorities may have come from personal trajectories of radical activism (for example, in housing, feminism or unions), moving from protest organisation to movement-parties and, later, to local governments (Della Porta et al., 2017; Font & García-Espín, 2019). This was the case with union and neighbourhood association members after the Spanish political transition in the 1970s, and it is now the case with housing movement or certain social movement leaders in New Municipalism (Calvo & Álvarez, 2015). On the other hand, the remaining activists may feel sympathy and even support towards these "friendly" authorities, engaging in informal alliances with them. This coalition may result in one-off collaborations and, also, in their engagement in official participatory institutions, which were previously rejected. Consequently, dynamics of co-optation, autonomy and conflict may appear (Lima, 2019; 2020; Talpin, 2015), but also patterns of disappointment and frustration which have received less attention despite their prevalence (Talpin, 2012; Font & Navarro, 2013; Funes et al., 2014; Fernández et al., 2020; Janoschka & Mota, 2020; Caballero, 2020).[3]

Here, I use the terms frustration and disappointment interchangeably. Participatory frustration has been defined as a cultural product including emotions and thoughtful political reasoning (Fernández et al., 2020). It affects experienced and novel participants after engaging in local institutions such as participatory budgeting or citizens' councils. Often, it is the result of four circumstances: excessive expectations; the failure of the design to adapt to participants' needs; failure in the implementation of proposals; and abrupt discontinuations. This scheme draws on Hirschman's cycles of involvement and disengagement (2002),[4] and it underscores the fact that people take part in participatory processes because they expect to exert some influence over political decisions. However, often, the policies ultimately adopted by authorities are too moderate in the eyes of participants, making them feel disappointed and deceived and provoking dynamics of disengagement. Moreover, there can be scarce relational goods that compensate for the perceived lack of influence (Olson, 1989; Uhlaner, 1989).

Processes of disappointment can be quicker and more pronounced among SMAs, for at least two reasons. Firstly, these participants start out with a more critical view of institutional politics (Bennet et al., 2013). For example, members of a squatted social centre who suffered repression at the hands of the police may have reasons to distrust local institutions (Luhtakallio, 2012). Thus, when they get involved in official participation, they need to moderate their repudiation of formal institutions, making a major ideological effort. Secondly, as radical activists normally support structural changes in terms of redistribution, they must similarly work hard to translate their claims into concrete proposals suitable for participatory devices with a limited scope (Baiocchi & Ganuza, 2014; Polletta, 2014; Lima, 2019). Therefore, when activists agree to collaborate and take part in official participation, they tend to be more susceptible to disillusionment. They can quickly transition to that state once they observe that their investments do not lead to acceptable outcomes or rewarding relationships.

One of the key authors who reflected on these processes was Iris M. Young (2001). From a theoretical point of view, she argues that institutional deliberation frequently excludes critical agents because it is framed by fixed agendas and a style of deliberation, which only incorporates limited topics and excludes conflict. Furthermore, it is usually restricted to very constrained local powers, and hegemonic discourses are strongly enforced by authorities and satellite associations. As a result, deliberative bodies frequently fail to include SMAs and collectives with radical agendas. Following this argument, we wonder what happens when actual engagement occurs (they have accessed) and when increasing disappointment is discussed and questioned (not just given as a matter of fact). Participants may put forward solutions to enlarge the scope and the inclusion capacity as they are not passive recipients of institutional framing (Holdo, 2019a).

Activists' insights are significant on account of their potential contribution to improving local participatory processes. Furthermore, the discussion of frustration processes can be useful to understand sociopolitical alliances between agents with social justice and structural goals (Janoschka & Mota, 2020). How can municipal participatory institutions contribute to this entente and to exchange between these agents? How can deliberative institutions include SMAs whilst preventing bitter disappointment, even if there is a healthy distance? These questions are still a topic for debate in the literature, which does not usually distinguish between SMAs and other types of associations (Lima, 2020). The process of disillusionment experienced by activists, and their responses to it, deserves specific consideration.

A Case Study in Madrid: From Protest to District Participatory Institutions

The case study presented here is contextualised in Madrid during the period 2015–2019. The new local government was led by the electoral platform *Ahora Madrid*, formed by *Podemos*,[5] *Izquierda Unida*[6] and activists from different anti-austerity movement sectors (Calvo & Álvarez, 2015). After 26 years of right-wing governments in the capital city, a new authority was formed with the external support of the Socialist Party (PSOE). Many activists were enthusiastic in anticipation of the new political orientation and regarding the opportunities to negotiate with local administrations. SMAs were especially attentive to the process of decentralisation to districts, a local arena that had become increasingly central in contentious politics since the 2011 mobilisations (García-Espín, 2012; Portos, 2019).

The creation of *local forums* in Madrid in 2016 provided a response to the demands made by neighbourhood associations about the lack of an attractive system of participatory institutions at the district level (Caballero, 2019; Medina-García et al., 2021). The former *territorial councils*, established in the 2000s, were deemed overly bureaucratic and ineffective, with little ability to mobilise, and even representatives of the Conservative *Partido Popular* were critical of them (González, 2011). Thus, in 2015, the Ahora Madrid government and its Councillor for Territorial Coordination, Nacho Murgui, promoted a participatory process to change these entities. Members of associations, along with district and municipal political representatives debated the rules governing the new forums, which would replace the old territorial councils. Though the new regulation was approved by the City Council, the Conservative *Partido Popular* opposed on the grounds it was too ideological.

Local forums can be categorised under the umbrella of advisory councils, though they represent a new generation (Nez, 2019). All residents over 16 years of age could register to participate in plenary sessions, and all associations operating within a district could enrol their representatives. The final composition of local forums depended on the associative fabric of the area: individual participants were frequently members of associations or SMAs, even if they participated as individual residents. Another important aspect to consider is their interaction with traditional neighbourhood associations (Ganuza et al., 2014). At the plenary sessions of the forums, decisions were made through majority voting, so members' votes were weighted according to their profile: whether they participated individually or as representatives of associations. An individual had one vote; an association with 100 members, or fewer, had 2 votes; if it had 101–500 members, it was granted 5 votes; and if it had more than 500 members, it got 6 votes.

Regarding decision-making, local forums could operate via plenary sessions or in sectoral committees, which were constituted with the approval of the former. There were three main outputs: *proposals*, *diagnoses* and *conclusions*. *Proposals* were recommendations submitted to the district government: a maximum of three proposals were presented to the Chamber of District Representatives[7] each month, in other words 33 per year. Political representatives had to vote publicly on citizens' submissions. These proposals were, therefore, deemed "referential" because they were discussed by all the represented parties. *Diagnoses* were reports on thematic issues, which were considered relevant by the forums' members. Finally, *conclusions* were declarative recommendations: their purpose was to express the opinion of local forums regarding policy measures. The first output (citizens' *proposals*) reinforced the forums' advisory function. Despite the high level of authorities' approval of citizen proposals (more than 90% in the first year) (Nez, 2019), many surpassed the scope and powers of district administrations. According to Caballero (2020), from February 2017 to April 2018, 28.2% of citizen proposals dealt with district services, while 42.2% were municipal and 6.9% were regional in their scope.

This chapter examines a working-class district in the south of Madrid, with high levels of migrant workers, dynamics of deprivation and a high degree of associational activity. The local forum flourished there, with more than 490 participants registered during the first year (2017–2018) and 15 committees with around 300 members. There was, for example, an *education committee* composed of forty people: education professionals, members of parents' associations ("AMPAS"), associations with educational aims (NGOs) and members of critical social movements. This example of a local forum ties in with the "democracy-driven" model proposed by Bua and Bussu (2021), in the sense that it was created and developed through the drive of social movements and associative agents. For instance, before its creation, a general conference promoted by district administrations gathered SMAs and associations to analyse the main problems of the area. The people who attended organised themselves into several thematic committees, which were subsequently integrated into the new local forum. Thus, though the initial invitation came from official district bodies, many activists felt that it might be a good opportunity to redirect their demands towards local administration.

With the purpose of studying the integration of SMAs, and, specifically, those with a programme of structural change, special attention is paid here to the members of the Public Education Defence Platform, which took part in local forums and education committees. This social movement can be considered a regional branch of a state-wide organisation, which was especially active in Madrid during the period 2008–2015. It was formed by left-wing unions (CGT, CC. OO, UGT, STES),[8] students' unions (*Sindicato de Estudiantes*), the main parents' associations (CEAPA) and other education activists. In 2011, they became known as "La Marea Verde" (*Green Tide*), because many education professionals started to wear green t-shirts with the slogan "State schooling for everyone" to protest against privatisations. The *Green Tide* platform was especially robust in Madrid, calling for strikes, demonstrations and symbolic occupations in 2011–2012, fighting back against the privatisation of regional education services (Rogero-García et al., 2014). Many activists remained committed in 2015–2019 when local forums were launched and decided to collaborate with the purpose of advancing some of their aims.

During the fieldwork, ten semi-structured interviews were conducted, with their profiles summarised in Table 15.1. The strategy of research was exploratory.

Table 15.1 Interviews and Profile of Informants

Interviewee Num.	Profile	Area and Activity
1	Political cadre. Woman, around 40 years old.	District-Local Forum
2	Public official. Woman, public administration personnel.	Education
3	Political cadre. Man, around 40 years old, sociocultural professional.	Territorial Coord. Dep. And Local Forums
4	Political cadre. Man, sociocultural professional.	Territorial Coord. Dep. And Local Forums
5	Association and individual participant. Man, around 60 years old, retired teacher and pedagogist.	Local forum and education committee
6	Social movement participant. Woman. School teacher in her fifties.	Local forum and education committee
7	Social movement participant. Man. High school teacher in his early sixties.	Local forum and education committee
8	Social movement participant. Man. Teacher and union leader. Around 40 years old.	Local forum and education committee
9	Social movement occasional participant. Woman, around 50 years old, teacher and school principal.	Local forum and education committee
10	Social movement participant. Woman, Member of parents' association. Around 40 years old. Sociocultural professional.	Local forum and education committee

Source: Own elaboration.

Interviews were conducted with politicians from the *Territorial Coordination Department*, one district political representative and one district public official, along with one individual participant and five social movement militants. Conversations lasted between 40 minutes and 1 hour, and they followed a script with questions about the characteristics of participation, deliberation, decision-making in the institution and its relationships with other forms of public engagement. Interviews were transcribed and coded with NVivo. An interpretive report was written to contextualise and interpret the discourses of the interviewees, considering their evaluations of local forum entities. All active participants (six interviewees) expressed disappointment after a period of strong commitment. Interviews were complemented with an examination of official documentation, external evaluations, academic reports and media news.

Regarding the limitations, one may argue that the case is narrow or context dependent. It was an exceptional period in which Madrid's New Municipalism was leading the capital city, and some (previous) SMAs took public office. This is certainly a special situation, however, the fact that the context was unusual reinforces our findings: even under such circumstances, activists' processes of disappointment emerge, and they are comparable to those observed in other cities. The case is specific; the processes that it reflects (Burawoy, 1998) are quite frequent. In the next section, the phases of involvement are presented together with participants' processes of fatigue and disenchantment.

Phase #1: Participatory Investment and Commitment

Many SMAs shared personal and ideological bonds with the elected authorities in Madrid in 2015 (Janoschka & Mota, 2020). Furthermore, most local government members had taken part in anti-austerity mobilisations, including the Councillor for Territorial Coordination, Nacho Murgui, who had also been leader of the Federation of Neighbourhood Associations (Nez, 2019). There was a degree of convergence around the agenda of political decentralisation: in some districts, SMAs had retained district assemblies with ups and downs since 2011 (Nez & Ganuza, 2017), while new Councillors wanted to create a totally new system of district participation. Thus, municipal, district authorities and some SMAs started to collaborate to organise decentralised "general conferences" to discuss priority measures for neighbourhoods. As Jerónimo (interviewee num. 5), a retired teacher, argues, "We, most people who are in the forum now, decided to take part in general conferences". The climate of collaboration was such that the announcements of these meetings were even publicised by some 15-M assemblies.[9]

During the meetings, different agents shared organisational practices. For example, education activists came from spaces where contentious action was coordinated at the district level. In our case, there was an *education forum* formed by SMAs and education professionals, and there was a tradition of collectives dedicated to protesting against the privatisation of state school services. As Jerónimo describes,

There was a precedent in [the area], there was an education forum, which was meeting every two or three months, and we also met whenever there was a conflict. And there was also a tradition of many different collectives around education. One was the Defence of Public Education Platform.

The previous organisation in sectoral social movement platforms, at a territorial level, fitted with the official structure of local forums, which was also thematically organised and allowed for the creation of sectoral committees.

As Holdo (2019a) has argued, all processes of institutional participation imply the recognition and partial acceptance of the rules imposed by authorities. Investing time and intellectual capabilities in official activities entails learning organisational rules, norms of communication and established procedures to interact with authorities (Eliasoph, 1998: Ch. 7). In our case, when SMAs started to work with the district administration, they accepted some rules that had not been accepted in earlier periods. Education activists, for example, assumed that if previous struggles had been against privatisation and the regional government, now they would divert some of their efforts and demands towards local institutions, accepting, in part, the limited powers of municipalities, particularly in education. Despite this, activists decided to engage. As Jerónimo explains, "When local forums emerged, I found that it was a very interesting initiative, which was innovative, a break with previous [district] structures" And later, he reflects that, "There was a problem, powers in education, the few powers that the municipality has […] The district administration only has powers regarding maintenance and infrastructure: repairing a window, heating, rooms, playgrounds". He and his peers were conscious of this distribution of authority, but this did not prevent them from engaging.

High levels of adaption to the new institution were witnessed when SMAs took on an active role in the design of proposals according to the established rules and criteria. In the first year (2017), education activists worked on several proposals, which were approved by the local forum and later transferred to the Chamber of District Representatives. One was a declarative conclusion about the protection of state-owned education in the area, which was decreasing in favour of private businesses. A second proposal was a requirement for information aimed at the city's administrative services: activists asked for data about schooling rates in state and private schools. Both demands were approved by the Chamber of District Representatives, but they did not have any real effect. Other proposals were channelled through participatory budgeting because they did not align with district powers either. For example, the creation of a psychology service for poor families did not tally with the district's functions, so it was channelled through participatory budgeting. SMAs such as Malena (interviewee num. 10) were against this decision, "Those projects are too basic, they do not need to be voted on by the general public [in participatory budgeting] for the authorities to implement them".

Despite these complaints, during the first year, interviewees were committed to the local forum, investing a great deal of time and effort in its activation and dynamism. SMAs were acting as enthusiastic counterparts to the sociopolitical coalition even when they maintained their autonomous demands (such as the defence of public education). They accepted, albeit with some critiques, that certain proposals could not be addressed by the district administration but could be channelled to other new participatory institutions. They consented to play the institutional game to an extent which was unprecedented for them.

Phase #2: Do-It-Yourself Participation and Fatigue

SMAs' investment in local forums reached its pinnacle when they decided to promote several projects with the support of the administration. These policy actions could be termed "co-production" (Subirats, 2017), as both administration and activists collaborated in the design, implementation and evaluation of the measures. For example, there was a project for a conference on an "Educating District", which included workshops, talks and meetings, bringing together more than 120 people to discuss priorities in education. This conference required a tremendous effort on the part of activists, as Carmela describes:

> It was quite a feat [*muchísimo trabajo*]. We had to do everything: buying the materials, getting in catering, finding speakers, organizing debate groups and facilitating these sessions – without any previous training. We had also to collect proposals, summarize them and present them publicly. We also did the publicity.
>
> (Carmela, int. num. 8)

This project was, therefore, organised by activists but had the financial and administrative support of the district. Activists felt proud of the outcome as they could deliver a critical diagnosis of the situation in education, and they increased their contact with people outside of associations. However, they also felt a sense of fatigue and exhaustion, after assuming an excessive overload of participatory work. Their commitment and the dynamic of co-production, which was previously seen as appealing, became too costly and tiring for volunteers. As Carmela deduces from her experience,

> I feel overloaded [*exceso de responsabilidad*] considering the work of the local forum, the work we do in the platform […] I think that the issue of participation is not yet properly established. Engaging brings with it too many responsibilities, you have to attend meetings, carry out tasks, read documents and draw up proposals. If you propose a conference, you do everything by yourself. Everything. I feel so tired.

The peak level of SMA commitment entailed co-production, and it was exhausting. As Malena (interviewee 10) explains,

> We should put limits on volunteer work. I did the evaluation of the participatory conference: we ran the sessions, we organised everything. That workload

is two months of regular work for a full-time employee. I'm not here to do someone else's job.

Here, there was tension between the ideal of co-production and the actual capacities of activists. These practices of "do-it-yourself democracy" (Lee, 2015), which entail projects that follow a participatory style in which associations, volunteers and individual residents are responsible for the design, implementation and evaluation of public services or actions, may substitute the work of state agencies and professionals. As the case of Madrid shows, the problem is that they relocate public obligations and workloads to volunteers who have their own political, work and family responsibilities, overwhelming them and causing fatigue.

Phase #3: Increasing Disappointment

From this state of fatigue, SMAs moved towards a degree of disappointment, even when they had been previously accustomed to excessive obligations within organisations. Previous studies have pointed to four origins for frustration in participatory institutions (excessive expectations, poorly designed processes, lack of results and abrupt discontinuations), which also hold true for SMAs albeit with certain specificities.

Firstly, a sense of fatigue after their initial passionate commitment facilitated a moment of reflection in which the beginnings of disappointment became palpable. The excessive work dedicated to institutional participation was compared (contrasted) with the perceived *poor results* of local forums. In this sense, the SMAs interviewed argue that most of the measures proposed were approved by authorities but were not implemented. Furthermore, they did not have any certainty about their upcoming execution. As Carmela (int. num. 8) says,

> The measures were approved, they were approved, but there has been a problem with finance. I don't know, there is a financial problem at City Hall [she is referring to the state limitation on municipal budgets], so the proposals are frozen for the moment. They have not been executed. They are paralysed for the moment […]. I think they will be carried out at some point … but the feeling is that we talk a lot, and we are not really getting any results.

The perception of poor results is even stronger regarding demands approved by the local forum which did not imply a significant amount of money. As stated previously, local forums were a sort of advisory council with reinforced powers to the extent that they could propose three measures per month to the Chamber of District Representatives. Taking advantage of this entitlement, SMAs proposed two additional demands: (a) a declaration about the defence of state education in the area, which was supported by the Chamber and "communicated" to the City Department for Education; and (b) a request for information about district schooling data (the number of school places in state and private schools and planning statistics), which met a similar fate. The first declaration did not deliver any results, and no response was received to the second demand. As Jerónimo explains, "There is a black hole [*agujero negro*]. Time goes by, and we don't get any answers".

The second cause of disappointment was precisely related *to the limited scope of participation* in local forums or the range of topics available for public debate. In this regard, SMAs felt in a permanent state of contradiction: on the one hand, proposals are restricted to district powers, which are limited in areas such as education; on the other, if proposals exceed district functions, they become conclusions or public declarations with no guarantee that the authorities will respond. Therefore, structural or transformative aims such as the defence of state-owned schools, preserving the number of state school places or struggling against segregation, become too broad, exceeding the scope of forums. As Malena (int. num. 10) reflects,

> We have asked for information to continue with our analysis and protests, to analyze the reality, but we have received no information from municipal institutions. We are respectful of regulations and channels, but they are not paying us any attention [...] We have done our job [...] This situation is frustrating [*me está agotando*].

With a similar discourse, Carmela argues, "I've lost confidence in the system. I get the impression that it is through protest, when it is powerful, that you get things done. But the administrative machinery does not accept us". Uneasy integration is connected to this lack of response, even when SMAs had accepted the institutional framing.

Growing disappointment was an effect of the (perceived) lack of achievement and, also, resulted from the limited scope for participation, which pushed transformative proposals (and agents) out of everyday administrative dynamics. The reasons for disappointment are related to how the participatory institution was designed and inserted into state/administration structures (Baiocchi & Ganuza, 2016), but it is also the result of the clash between SMAs' transformative aims and the limited scope of local forums.

Phase #4: Walking Out or Searching for Alternatives

Considering their increasing frustration, SMAs found themselves at a crossroads: they could accept their defeat, walk out and concentrate on their speciality, namely protest action; otherwise, they could consider alternative ways of engaging. In our case, both alternatives are identified among the different participants. *Walkouts* were the strategy pursued by some who were unable to resolve the conflict between increasing fatigue and a lack of results. Carmela links the departure of many peers to this conflictive experience,

> At the beginning there were more than 200 of us in the forum, but now many people have disappeared [...] Only those who are really determined remain,

and those who have business interests [she is referring to NGOs or associations that provide public services].

Thinking about alternatives that mitigate disappointment, SMAs were discussing a *reduction of commitment* regarding local forums. They referred specifically to "do-it-yourself" projects and co-production, which involved too much time and energy on the part of volunteers. In their view, these activities demand such a degree of attention, time and concentration that they are unable to undertake other independent protest actions. Malena, for example, arrived at this conclusion: "I have said that I am against volunteering for conferences, reports or projects. I told them they couldn't count on me next time it was proposed". She did not fully abandon her engagement in the local forum, but she was not willing to offer such a level of volunteering any longer. As she declared, "These projects need hired professionals [...] I don't want to substitute them". Reduction of commitment implied the rejection of co-production dynamics.

Similarly, other participants discussed a *redefinition of their roles* as participants. If they were previously willing to be involved in policy implementation, now, they only want to "voice" their genuine demands as they would in any other institutional space. This is the solution some have found to their feelings of disappointment, as Carmela proposed, "I only want to chirp, to chirp loudly [*gritar fuerte*], but don't ask me to do pirouettes,[10] because I can't". As a potential answer, SMAs discuss institutional changes which could improve their work as demands-makers: a more responsive administration (improving mechanisms for responsiveness) could enhance this demand-making role.

Along the same lines, SMAs debated strategies to use the participatory space as *a source of information*. For them, local forums could work as platforms to disseminate and distribute relevant administrative knowledge, so that social collectives could improve demand-making, control and, ultimately, protest activity. They might use official information to enrich their goals and critical approaches. In our case, this was attempted by SMAs, who decided to use the local forums to collect evidence on local and regional school policies, to write reports on public education challenges, which would substantiate future protest actions. They wanted to ask for and study official data to gain a better understanding of why state schools were being reduced in the area, while there was overcrowding and segregation. In this latter phase, institutional participation could be useful to gather information and enrich protest.

Finally, in their attempt to not disengage, SMAs imagined procedures to strengthen the *connection between municipal administration and local forums*. As Jerónimo (int. num. 5) stated, they felt as if there were a "black hole" in municipal administration, especially when proposals were not met or answered. Thus, activists thought that there should be professional figures who could act as intermediaries between administrations and lay participants. This was supposed to be the case of hired facilitators; however, as they were not permanent members of staff, their access to administrative units and files was limited. Considering this situation, participants imagined other mediation figures, which might improve the integration of participatory institutions and popular decisions in everyday bureaucratic logics.

Conclusions

This case of local forums showcases certain lessons learned regarding the disappointment produced by local participatory institutions. First and foremost, the process of disenchantment among SMAs – see Figure 15.1 – shares certain common features with the frustration felt by other association members (Fernández et al. 2020). The lack of solid outcomes is one central cause, as other studies confirm, because, sometimes, participatory institutions receive more resources allocated to deliberations than to the implementation of real decisions (Polleta, 2014; Baiocchi & Ganuza, 2014; Font et al., 2018). Furthermore, as in other examples of participation, in local forums, people started out engaging with high expectations which soon fell due to their limited impact. This process was exacerbated by dynamics of co-production which were seen as too costly and time-consuming, despite their positive representation in the specialised literature (Nabatchi et al., 2017). In the end, in terms of the perceived lack of results or limited influence, the disappointment of SMAs was not particularly unusual or special.

However, SMAs' disappointment was also caused by the lack of "relevant" outcomes in their view since social movement members were committed to the defence of structural and transformative aims in education. They took part despite a continuous contradiction between their political aims (defence and extension of public education) and the limited scope of official participation. The conflict between "first-order" and "second-order" aims (referring to short-term versus social justice goals) sparks particular anger among SMAs, as Young (2001) reported regarding deliberative

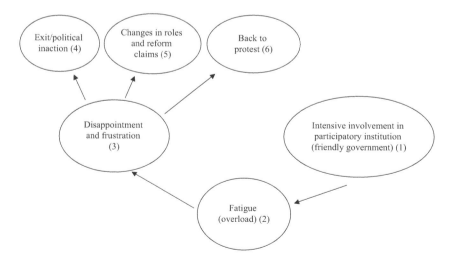

Figure 15.1 The Process of SMAs Disappointment. Source: Own elaboration.

events. The specifics of activists' disappointment are related precisely to this conflict: they did not only feel a lack of results but a lack of "relevant" outcomes according to their transformative views. Furthermore, another particularity of SMAs was that they were proactive and creative in imagining procedures which could improve their inclusion, which is also a missing point in the previous literature. Disappointment was not interpreted just as an invitation to disengage (exit), but as an opportunity for reflection and theorisation. They did not passively accept their exclusion but instead considered potential changes in their roles and in administrative devices. These reflections contributed to the redefinition of their positions regarding participatory institutions (Lima, 2020), reducing their initial commitment, adopting demand-making roles, using the participatory space as a source of relevant information and, ultimately, calling for the incorporation of institutional mediators, who would open up local bureaucracies to lay people such as them.

We may argue that, in the end, SMA disappointment was not a consequence of stratospheric demands or an ill-judged excessive expectation about local forums. It was rooted in moderate requirements regarding the accomplishment of decisions, and a view in which participatory democracy should be connected – somehow – to more redistributive goals. In this sense, the integration of activists was not difficult *per se*; they did not display any defective characteristics which would impede institutional engagement, especially when there was a friendly government (as there was in Madrid 2015). But there was tension between the scope of these institutions and the SMAs' goals, which can be seen in many other experiences and which deserves empirical and theoretical reflection. The sensibility of activists together with their tendency towards "metadeliberation" (the discussion of participatory official norms) (Holdo, 2015) make them especially creative in the proposal of workable solutions, such as those indicated above.

Moreover, the case of social movement activists and their disappointment with local forums, suggests some concerns regarding the Bua and Bussu's concept of democracy-driven processes. Firstly, as these authors reflect, SMAs had a decisive initial influence over the district policy, including the creation of new "routines" or procedures for popular participation which were open to all neighbours, including social movement militants. Secondly, as democracy-driven processes, local forums suffered internal tensions and interacted with straitjacketed bureaucratic logics which hampered the consideration of transformative aims (i.e., interventions over the educational system). This case shows the need for a greater reflection on the inertia and strong dominance of traditional governance methods (i.e., when activists do not receive any answer due to district limited powers or when their proposals are not accomplished for a long period). Facing these issues, radical participants envisioned measures such as mediation positions to help citizens navigate the complex bureaucratic sea of agencies and official information. Democracy-driven processes tend to find similar institutional obstacles (Martínez-Palacios, 2021), which spur disappointment at best and predict disengagement ultimately. As I have shown in this chapter, this latter scenario is not inevitable, but it would require a more careful listening of activists' suggestions and concerns.

Acronyms

SMAs	Social movement activists
NGOs	Non-governmental organisations
PSOE	Spanish Socialist Party
AMPAS	Mothers and Parents' Associations
CGT	Confederal Workers' Union
CC. OO	Workers' Commissions
UGT	General Union of Workers
STES	Confederal Union of Education Workers
CEAPA	Confederation of Mothers and Parents' Associations

Notes

1 This chapter is part of the project AssoD-And (P18-RT-2785), funded by the Department of Innovation, Science and Enterprise of the Regional Government of Andalusia, Spain.
2 They are dedicated mainly to protest action, and their organisations are assembly-based and loosely organised. They can be contrasted to NGOs, unions and other associations, which are more prone to the provision of services and collaboration with public administrations.
3 Following the "keyhole technique" (Hochschild, 2018), the focus on disappointment allows one to concentrate on the standing of social movement militants and their internal dilemmas in relation to local policies.
4 I owe the idea of using Hirschman's ideas to explain processes of frustration to Manuel Jiménez Sánchez (UPO, Seville, Spain).
5 Radical left party created in 2014 after anti-austerity mobilisations.
6 Traditional radical left party created in 1986.
7 The City of Madrid has 21 district councils made up of elected political representatives.
8 See the final list of acronyms.
9 Protest movement starting in 2011.
10 Meaning to do "difficult" and costly tasks while volunteering.

References

Baiocchi, G., and Ganuza, E. (2014) "Participatory budgeting as if emancipation mattered." *Politics & Society*, 42(1): 29–50.
Baiocchi, G., and Ganuza, E. (2016) *Popular Democracy: The Paradox of Participation*. Stanford: Stanford University Press, 2016.
Baiocchi, G., Heller, P. and Silva, M. (2011) *Bootstrapping Democracy*. Stanford: Stanford University Press.
Bennett, E., et al. (2013) "Disavowing politics: Civic engagement in an era of political skepticism." *American Journal of Sociology*, 119(2): 518–548.
Bherer, L. et al. (2016) "The promise for democratic deepening: The effects of participatory processes in the interaction between civil society and local governments." *Journal of Civil Society*, 12(3): 344–363.
Brugué, Q., Font, J., and Ruiz, J. (2021) "The closer, the better? Comparing advisory councils at different government levels." *Administration & Society*, 53(6): 844–871.
Bua, A., and Bussu, S. (2021) "Between governance-driven democratisation and democracy-driven governance: Explaining changes in participatory governance in the case of Barcelona." *European Journal of Political Research*, 60(3): 716–737.
Burawoy, M. (1998) "The extended case method." *Sociological Theory*, 16(1): 4–33.

Caballero Ferrándiz, J. (2019) "La necesidad de aprender a participar: neocorporativismo y repliegue burocrático en la participación institucional de los Foros Locales del Ayuntamiento de Madrid." *Inguruak. Revista vasca de sociología y ciencia política*, 66, 1–24.

Caballero Ferrándiz, J. (2020) "Cierre deliberativo y miedo al desborde en la participación ciudadana de los Foros Locales del Ayuntamiento de Madrid." *Encrucijadas: Revista Crítica de Ciencias Sociales*, 19, 35–53.

Calvo, K., and Álvarez, I. (2015) "Limitaciones y exclusiones en la institucionalización de la indignación: Del 15-M a Podemos." *Revista Española de Sociología*, 24: 115–122.

Della Porta, D., and Diani, M. (2011) *Los movimientos sociales*. Madrid: CIS.

Della Porta, D., et al. (2017) *Movement Parties Against Austerity*. Hoboken: John Wiley & Sons.

Eliasoph, N. (1998) *Avoiding Politics: How Americans Produce Apathy in Everyday Life*. Cambridge: Cambridge University Press.

Fernández-Martínez, J. L., García-Espín, P. and Jiménez-Sánchez, M. (2020) "Participatory frustration: The unintended cultural effect of local democratic innovations." *Administration & Society*, 52(5): 718–748.

Flesher Fominaya, C. (2017) "European anti-austerity and pro-democracy protests in the wake of the global financial crisis." *Social Movement Studies*, 16(1): 1–20.

Font, J., and Navarro, J. (2013) "Personal experience and the evaluation of participatory instruments in Spanish cities." *Public Administration*, 91(3): 616–631.

Font, J., and García-Espín, P. (2019) "From Indignad@ s to Mayors? Participatory dilemmas in Spanish municipal movements." In Flesher Fominaya, C., and Feenstra, R. A. (eds.), *Routledge Handbook of Contemporary European Social Movements*. London: Routledge, 387–401.

Font, J., et al. (2018) "Cherry-picking participation: Explaining the fate of proposals from participatory processes." *European Journal of Political Research*, 57(3): 615–636.

Funes, M. J.; Talpin, J. and Rull, M. (2014) "The cultural consequences of engagement in participatory processes." In Font, J. et al. (eds.), *Participatory Democracy in Southern Europe: Causes, Characteristics and Consequences*. London: Rowman & Littlefield.

Fung, A., and Wright, E.O. (2001) "Deepening democracy: Innovations in empowered participatory governance." *Politics & Society*, 29(1): 5–41.

Ganuza, E., Nez, H., and Morales, E. (2014) "The struggle for a voice: Tensions between associations and citizens in participatory budgeting." *International Journal of Urban and Regional Research*, 38(6): 2274–2291.

García-Espín, P., and Jiménez-Sánchez, M. (2017) "Los procesos participativos como potenciadores de la democracia. Explorando los efectos, mecanismos y evidencias en la sociedad civil." *Revista de estudios políticos*, 177: 113–146.

García-Espín, P. (2012) "El 15M: De vuelta al barrio como espacio de lo político." *Revista internacional de pensamiento político*, 7: 291–310.

González, A. (2011) "Los desafíos de la participación ciudadana local. Un estudio comparado entre las ciudades de Madrid y Helsinki." *Revista del CLAD Reforma y Democracia*, 49: 203–240.

Hanson, R. (2018) "Deepening distrust: Why participatory experiments are not always good for democracy." *The Sociological Quarterly*, 59(1): 145–167.

Hirschman, A. O. (2002) *Shifting Involvements*. Princeton: Princeton University Press.

Holdo, M. (2015) "Strategies of deliberation: Bourdieu and struggles over legitimate positions." *Political Studies*, 63(5): 1103–1119.

Holdo, M. (2019a) "Power and citizen deliberation: The contingent impacts of interests, ideology, and status differences." *Journal of Deliberative Democracy*, 13(3): Article 2.

Holdo, M. (2019b) "Cooptation and non-cooptation: Elite strategies in response to social protest." *Social Movement Studies*, 18(4): 444–462.
Janoschka, M., and Mota, F. (2020) "New municipalism in action or urban neoliberalisation reloaded? An analysis of governance change, stability and path dependence in Madrid (2015–2019)." *Urban Studies*, 58(13): 2814–2830.
Lee, C. W. (2015) *Do-it-yourself Democracy: The Rise of the Public Engagement Industry*. Oxford: Oxford University Press.
Lima, V. (2019) "The limits of participatory democracy and the inclusion of social movements in local government." *Social Movement Studies*, 18(6): 667–681.
Lima, V. (2020) "The institutionalisation of social movements: Co-optation and democratic policy-making." *Political Studies Review*, 19(2): 245–261.
Luhtakallio, E. (2012) *Practicing Democracy: Local Activism and Politics in France and Finland*. London: Palgrave Macmillan.
Martínez-Palacios, J. (2021) "La burocratización neoliberal de la participación ciudadana en España." *Revista Internacional de Sociología*, 79(2): 184.
Medina-García, C., de la Fuente, R., and Van den Broeck, P. (2021) "Exploring the emergence of innovative multi-actor collaborations toward a progressive urban regime in Madrid (2015–2019)." *Sustainability*, 13(1): 415.
Nabatchi, T., Sancino, A., and Sicilia, M. (2017) "Varieties of participation in public services: The who, when, and what of coproduction." *Public Administration Review*, 77(5): 766–776.
Navarro, C. (1999) *El sesgo participativo: Innovación democrática en municipios del Sur de Europa (1960–1995)*. Madrid: CSIC.
Nez, H., and Ganuza, E. (2017) "Among militants and deliberative laboratories: The indignados." In Tejerina, B. and Perugorría, I. (eds.), *Crisis and Social Mobilization in Contemporary Spain*. London: Routledge, 2017. 15–35.
Nez, H. (2019) "La démocratie participative à Madrid (2015–2019). Entre héritages des mouvements sociaux et influences internationals." *Pôle Sud*, 2: 23–41.
Olson, M. (1989) *The Logic of Collective Action*. London: Palgrave Macmillan.
Polletta, F. (2014) "Is participation without power good enough? Introduction to 'Democracy Now: Ethnographies of contemporary participation'." *The Sociological Quarterly*, 55(3): 453–466.
Portos, M. (2019) "Keeping dissent alive under the Great Recession: No-radicalisation and protest in Spain after the eventful 15M/indignados campaign." *Acta Politica*, 54(1): 45–74.
Rogero-García, J., Fernández Rodríguez, C. and Ibáñez, R. (2014) "La "marea verde". Balance de una movilización inconclusa." *Revista de Sociología de la Educación*, 7(3): 567–586.
Subirats, J. (2017) "La ciudad como espacio de identidad, de exclusión e inclusión." *Cuestión Urbana*: 1, 9–20.
Talpin, J. (2012) *Schools of Democracy: How Ordinary Citizens (Sometimes) Become Competent in Participatory Budgeting Institutions*. Colchester: ECPR Press.
Talpin, J. (2015) "Silent suppression: How local politicians stifle collective action in working-class neighborhoods." *Metropolitics* 19 October 2018. URL: https://metropolitics.org/Silent-Suppression-How-Local-Politicians-Stifle-Collective-Action-in-Working.html.
Uhlaner, C. (1989) "Relational goods and participation: Incorporating sociability into a theory of rational action." *Public Choice*, 62(3): 253–285.
Young, I. M. (2001) "Activist challenges to deliberative democracy." *Political Theory*, 29(5): 670–690.

16 Institutionalising Participation from Below

From the Shack to Municipal Elections in Commercy, France

Sixtine Van Outryve

Introduction

Participatory democracy designs to engage individuals in existing institutions tend to be developed by experts and policymakers. What happens when grassroots politics reimagine spaces of participation? What are the institutions that movements themselves envision to allow the people to have a say over public life? The purpose of this chapter is to show how a local movement designed the institution that would enable individuals to exercise public power. Emerging from the Yellow Vests mobilisation against the rise of fuel prices on 17 November 2018, the assembly direct democracy movement in the French town of Commercy undertook this task. Heterogeneous in terms of its socio-economic composition, its modes of organisations and its political orientations, the Yellow Vests movement nevertheless shared common criticisms of tax injustice leading to declining purchasing power, of political elites disconnected from the daily life of the majority, and of representative government as a mode of exercising power. This last criticism, reflecting the democratic aspirations of the Yellow Vests, was translated under many different forms and propositions by the thousands of Yellow Vests groups occupying roundabouts throughout France (Bedock et al., 2020; Gourgues, 2020). In Commercy, the local group first organised in popular assemblies at their shack, to then attempt to institutionalise this participatory space by presenting its own list to the French municipal elections of March 2020, with the sole purpose to give public power to the assembly gathering the town residents through city councillors' mandates.

In contrast to forms of participation designed by policymakers, coined by Warren (2014) under the term "governance-driven democratization", Commercy's experiment comprises a case of "democracy-driven governance" (Bua and Bussu, 2021), insofar as a grassroots movement envisioned a process through which people could exercise public power gained through popular mobilisation. Whilst the task of democratic innovation's institutional design is often left to policymakers or theorists, this contribution aims to show that it can also be undertaken by a social movement and that, when it happens, it can yield results that are better suited to the unfolding of the democratic innovation. Contributing to the literature on social movements (Talpin, 2015; della Porta, 2020), democratic innovations

(Elstub & Escobar, 2019; della Porta & Felicetti, 2019; Bua & Bussu, 2021) and communalism (Bookchin 2015), this chapter describes the process of grassroots institutional design that unfolded in Commercy. Theoretically, it focuses on a problem that any movement aiming to institutionalise democratic innovation encounters: that of attendance.

The problem of attendance arises when a democratic project seeks participation in the collective exercise of public power by the assembled people, instead of through electoral representation. Insofar as the new system would no longer rest on the legitimacy provided by electoral representation, it needs to put the conditions in place to ensure the democratic legitimacy of this new body, which includes facilitating *attendance* by individuals at the assembly. A basic premise that all participatory democrats can agree on is that individuals should have greater opportunities to participate in politics than voting at periodic elections. This, nevertheless, leaves open the question: How do we ensure that political participation beyond voting does not exclude individuals or groups (a fault representative government purports to avoid)? This chapter explores how social movement activists tackled the issue of "physical" attendance when designing a participatory institution: seeking to ensure that everybody could enter the assembly room despite socio-economic, political and cultural constraints imposed among others by work, social reproduction tasks, mobility, the digital divide and so on.

This contribution is structured in three parts. The first establishes the theoretical framework. It connects the literature on social movements and democratic innovations, by specifying the communalist project from which this innovation stems and by showing the gap in the literature that this contribution addresses. The second traces the evolution of the experiment of Commercy, from the beginning of the Yellow Vests assemblies to the municipal elections, and relates this strategy to the literature. The third explores the problems, constraints and possibilities encountered by the movement as it attempted to engage in bottom-up institutional design. It analyses more specifically how actors, during this institutional design process, answered one of the numerous problems any direct democracy movement would face, that of attendance.

This contribution reflects on the data from fieldwork in Commercy that combined participant observation during meetings, assemblies and activities; two rounds of semi-structured interviews with 36 participants; participation in a two-day group interview of a dozen participants; and textual analysis of documents.

From Social Movement to Democratic Innovation: A Communalist Perspective

To fully grasp the complexity of how a social movement inspired by the ideas of communalism goes from occupying public space to engaging in grassroots institutional design, it is necessary to explore and combine literatures on social movements, democratic innovations and communalism.

This case connects the study of social movements with that of democratic innovations, fields which are often separated despite some interactions (della Porta,

2020; Talpin, 2015). The demand for more participation made by social movements is not new (della Porta & Felicetti, 2019: 6). It has, at times, led to the creation of democratic innovations, defined as "processes or institutions that are new to a policy issue ... and developed to reimagine and deepen the role of citizens in governance processes by increasing opportunities for participation, deliberation and influence" (Elstub & Escobar, 2019: 11). Indeed, historically, democratic innovations have often been created in response to demands made by social movements to have a greater say in politics (Talpin, 2015). As such, social movements are increasingly considered "promoters of democratic innovations" and "incubators of emerging ideas about democracy", who are involved in "the ideation and implementation of innovations in institutional politics" and are playing a "key role in introducing democratic innovations . . . in public institutions" (della Porta, 2020: 7, 18, 156). In this contribution, I argue that, as well as stimulating the development of democratic innovations by the state, they can play a critical role in their design.

Most movements demanding democratic innovations share a constitutive trait: that of not having access to public power. To remedy this lack of power, they develop "created spaces", defined as "the spaces which are claimed by less powerful actors from or against the power-holders, or created more autonomously by them" (Gaventa, 2004: 35). A crucial question concerning created spaces this contribution addresses is that of their institutionalisation. Indeed, "besides engaging in internal practices of democratic innovation, social movements are in fact also carriers of innovation in institutions" (della Porta, 2020: 15). This analysis takes seriously the endeavour to "institutionalise the forms of democratic organisation that arise from the 'critical democracy' of citizen mobilisations" (Bua & Bussu, 2021: 719), where a social movement of "critical democracy" mobilises "people normally excluded from political activity" in "resistance to elite governance" (Blaug, 2002: 106). Insofar as it "emerges through popular mobilisation" and "attempts to bring social movements into the state", a movement of critical democracy can be qualified as one of "democracy-driven governance", as conceptualised by Bua and Bussu (2021: 717), as opposed to "governance-driven democratization" (Warren, 2014).

Della Porta and Felicetti (2019: 3–4) find that "the rootedness of citizen-led democratic experiments in popular mobilizations shapes their nature in profound and little explored ways". This chapter addresses this gap by attempting to understand how the social movements' experience of democratic practices affected institutional design. Focusing on democratic practices allows us "to look in new directions in institutional design" (Felicetti, 2021: 1589), where democratic innovations are "devised by civil society actors to respond to a popular need for countering a profound political crisis" (della Porta & Felicetti, 2019: 9). Indeed, "unlike top-down democratic experiments, in which institutions and the interests they pursue are of primary importance, bottom-up ones, which give citizens the central stage, spring from protest and respond to the need for radical democratic reform" (ibid.: 14).

The process designed by this social movement was never institutionalised since it did not enter city hall. Therefore, this chapter cannot carry out the analysis of the input, throughput and output legitimacy of this democratic innovation (Caluwaerts & Reuchamps, 2015). However, what this contribution aims to do is to understand the problems, constraints and possibilities encountered by the movement when acting as "institutional designers" of this democratic experiment (della Porta, 2020: 158). While the results of some democratic innovations crafted by social movements have been explored (Caluwaerts & Reuchamps, 2015), the problems encountered by a social movement during design are rarely studied.

More specifically, it aims to understand how the movement reflected upon one of the biggest obstacles to the creation of democratic innovation: that of attendance. In representative government, political participation is materialised by representation through elections and the legitimacy of representatives stems from the fact that they are authorised by, and accountable to, the represented (Parkinson, 2006: 29–36). On the contrary, in assembly direct democracy, political participation is secured by participation in the popular assembly which directly exercises public power. Such an assembly is deemed only possible at a small scale (Dahl, 1989: 214–215, 226; Parkinson, 2006: 27) as no room can hold the entirety of the people (Arendt, 1963: 236). As such, the problem of attendance is paramount to the legitimacy of the latter system because, if everybody is supposed to gather to exercise public power, and not everybody comes, then the absentees might not be represented and rely on unelected representatives to make claims on their behalf. Their political participation, an essential feature of a democracy (Dahl, 1989), would suffer. This could threaten the legitimacy of the new system. Some argue that the problem of attendance has "enough force to stop the project as direct democracy" (Plotke, 1997: 25).

The difficulties encountered when involving participants in democratic innovations have been pointed out in the literature (Ryfe, 2002: 365). However, "participation in 'invited spaces' is framed by technocrats, whose interventions produce and limit what is possible" (Cornwall, 2004: 7). As such, the benefits of having the grassroots, rather than policymakers, reflecting on such an obstacle have not been identified. Nor has the way in which movements, during the development of their democratic practices, can act as a "learning site" (Welton, 1993) and "producer of knowledge" (della Porta, 2020: 11) and that this, in turn, shapes the solutions that can be brought to this problem.

The transfer of democratic practices from the streets to the institutions has been analysed in the case of movement-parties, defined as "coalitions of political activists who emanate from social movements and try to apply the organization and strategic practice of social movements in the arena of party competition" (Kitschelt, 2006: 280). The literature has explored how movement-party implementing democratic innovations are drawing from the political culture and practice of actors involved in the movement, in the case of *Ahora Madrid* (Consejero & Janoschka, 2022: 5), *Barcelona en Comú* (Bua & Bussu, 2021) or *Podemos* in Spain and the *Movimiento al Socialismo* in Bolivia (della Porta, 2020). In the same way as these movement-parties, movements have also realised a shift of process: "as institutions remained closed and mobilisation in the streets declined, a 'destituent' process mutated into a constituent process, based on the 'assault on institutions', also through participation in the electoral process" (ibid.: 108–109). However, the constituent process of movements that are similar, but that explicitly reject political party organisation, seeking instead to create a platform for direct participation, has received less attention.

It is now crucial to clarify the political project followed by the movement at hand. Developing spontaneously under the form of popular assemblies functioning in direct democracy in the first days of the movement, the Commercy experiment presents common features with the theory of communalism. While most participants were first-time activists, some Yellow Vests had political experience or some theoretical knowledge, especially on communalism. They proposed elements of this theory when they saw that such propositions could give an articulated form to the democratic functioning and aspirations of the assembly, which were already present independently of any theoretical ideas. Also called libertarian municipalism, the political project of communalism has been developed by the American thinker Murray Bookchin (2015). This theory sees the municipality as the place where communities collectively manage their affairs – political, social and economic – through popular assemblies open to all residents of the commune. For matters going beyond the municipality boundaries, these autonomous entities organise themselves in a confederal model, that is, a network of councils composed of delegates who are recallable and strictly mandated by their assemblies to administer policies decided by them (Bookchin, 2015). Indeed, when there is a need to decide on a large scale, the task of representation becomes inevitable (Dahl, 1989: 215). As such, communalism does not do away with representation, when understood generically as the making present of that which is absent (Pitkin, 1967: 8-9), but relies on imperatively mandated delegates to make present the already deliberated will of their respective assembly at the confederal level. As such, communalism seeks to enable everybody who is subjected to a rule to deliberate and decide on it, thereby combining "deliberation of *all* those subject to a regime" through presence at the popular assembly, with large-scale decision through the delegation system, thereby preventing the lack of legitimacy traditionally attached to deliberative and direct democracy (Parkinson, 2006: 6). In order to bring about this society, one of the strategies communalism proposes is to radically restructure municipal institutions by running candidates for municipal elections who would, once elected, give power to the popular assembly by taking their mandates from this entity (Van Outryve, 2019). Such a strategy aims to do what representative government refuses: "to give an institutional role to the assembled people" (Manin, 1995).

Importantly, the direct democracy project carried out by communalism goes beyond aiming to establish participatory governance. While democracy-driven governance attempts to "safeguard critical spaces for social movements to act as a counterbalance to the administration" (Bua & Bussu, 2021: 731), direct democracy in a communalist sense aims to give the entirety of decision-making power to the people by institutionalising it, not simply ensuring it to act as a counterbalance. Indeed, insofar as it aims to radically change the logic of power by giving an institutional role to the assembled people so that it can directly decide on public matters, communalism goes beyond only *involving* individuals in order to *improve* the quality of democracy. It rather aims to *give back* the entirety of public power to the people, without leaving any decision-making power to the elected representatives. As such, communalism fundamentally *alters* the paradigm of democracy, from a representative one to a direct one, rather than improve the functioning of existing democratic institutions. Communalism is also distinguished from the new municipalism (Roth, 2019). Indeed, the former is in radical opposition to the state and representative democracy and aims to establish the institutions of communal and confederalised popular self-government. Contemporary municipalist experiments, meanwhile, have difficulty in breaking away from the framework of municipal sovereignty to go beyond "the form of a participatory municipalism combining municipal administration by renewed elected officials with a set of participatory devices that mostly attracts the most educated citizens" (Cossart & Sauvêtre, 2020, my translation).

Direct Democracy in Commercy: Popular Assemblies from the Shack to Municipal Elections

Located in the Meuse region of Eastern France, Commercy is a small rural sub-prefecture of about 5,400 people. This working-class city, host of various industries, was an ancient military base. The population mainly voted for the left in the presidential elections, until the far-right candidate Marine Le Pen gained most votes during the first round of the 2017 elections. Locally, the town was governed by an unaffiliated right-wing representative who arrived at city hall at the last 2014 elections, replacing a decades-long municipal rule by the socialists.

In Commercy, local assemblies have been the privileged form of democratic organisation since the beginning of the Yellow Vests movement. Corresponding to the criticism of political abstraction of representative government that animates the movement (Jeanpierre, 2019: 157-162), the desire to anchor democratic mechanisms in lived experience is reflected in the daily general assemblies that the Yellow Vests had at the shack that they built in two nights in the main square after a few days of blockade. A place of "human warmth, contact, fraternity" in the words of two retired participants, but also of meeting, debate and collective decision-making during daily general assemblies, the shack was the cornerstone of Commercy's direct democracy experience in its early days. These assemblies allowed everyone to express themselves, to be listened to and to vote by the majority rule on everything concerning the local movement, without institutionalised leaders. From this shack, the Commercy Yellow Vests called onto other Yellow Vests of France to refuse representation, elect delegates with imperative, recallable and rotating mandates and organise into popular assemblies. As such, the experience of Commercy reflected ideas of communalism as formulated by Bookchin (2015).

In March 2019, the mayor had the Commercy Yellow Vests' shack destroyed, despite their democratic mobilisation through a grassroots local Citizens' Initiative Referendum (CIR) aimed at gathering the population support. The movement was then forced to adapt to the loss of its collective space and to the absence of a fixed place for the democratic organisation of its assembly, which led to dissociating the association of collective life and political life that the shack allowed. Part of the group then decided to institutionalise the assembly as a forum for discussion and to open it up to all residents of Commercy, even those who did not identify as Yellow Vests. This became the Commercy Citizens' Assembly (CCA). After several assemblies in May, June and September 2019, participants in the CCA mandated a group of people among them to present a list for the March 2020 municipal elections, marking a split in the Commercy Yellow Vests group with those who saw such an electoral strategy as "non-Yellow Vest". The list, entitled *Let's Live and Decide Together*, had only one programme: direct democracy. In other words, its only electoral commitment was to give power to the CCA by linking the mandate of elected municipal officials to the decisions of the assembly – the electoral strategy of communalism (Bookchin, 2015; Van Outryve, 2019). As such, the members of the list, as pledged when they signed the "Charter of the elected person", would, if elected, endorse the assembly's decisions as their own in city council.

This shift shows that, as the movement and its assembly evolved, so did its relationship with the municipal government. Indeed, the municipal government was first seen as an enemy to the Yellow Vests' direct democracy project because they considered it "a central front line in the fight between [them] and the executive" (Jeanpierre, 2019), as evidenced by the destruction of the shack. However, the movement used this hostility from the mayor as a springboard to stimulate their direct democracy project. City hall progressively shifted from an enemy towards an institution to be conquered to allow the people of Commercy to decide. In the general movement by the Yellow Vests to relocalise politics (Jeanpierre, 2019), the seizure of power in a local representative institution was conceived as a strategy to bring about direct democracy through a radical restructuring of this institution (see Van Outryve, 2023). Such a "radical democratic reform" constituted the group's answer to the demands carried out by the Yellow Vests movement calling for direct democracy (Bedock et al., 2020). However, what separates the Commercy group from the rest of the Yellow Vests constituted in assemblies throughout the country is their strategy to institutionalise the "created space" (Gaventa, 2004) of "critical democracy" (Blaug, 2002) that emerged from the experiment of face-to-face assembly during the Yellow Vests movement. Indeed, the CCA aimed to bring into the institution the democratic practices of assemblies they developed in the streets to create a democratic innovation stemming from its own democratic practices as a social movement (della Porta, 2020: 15; Felicetti, 2021). Giving power to the assembly as the main deliberating and decision-making body of the municipality, that is to give "an institutional role to the assembled people" (Manin, 1995), through the elections would require transferring the power devolved to elected municipal officials to the CCA. As such, the list's goal was to create and institutionalise a democratic innovation, by subverting and radically transforming existing institutions from the inside. In doing so, the strategy pursued by the list is that of "interact[ing] with traditional institutions to transform them rather than adding to their legitimacy" (Bua & Bussu, 2021: 719).

However, unlike movement-parties, they did not form a party to do so. They used the vehicle of the list at the occasion of the elections, but only as a way to give power to the CCA gathering the residents of the city, not to remain structured as one, as that is incompatible with communalism's commitment against representative government.

Giving an Institutional Role to the Assembled People: An Experiment of Grassroots Institutional Design

Tensions Surrounding Grassroots Institutional Design

During the electoral campaign, intense and in-depth reflections were carried out by the list on the role and functioning of the assembly in the event of victory. These reflections occurred through the process of drafting a Local Constitution: an initiative to institutionalise the assembly, give it a role and operating rules and elaborate its relation to the city council. Before turning to one of the solutions the movement found to the problems any movement seeking to establish direct democracy would face, and under which form it constitutionalised this solution in the Local Constitution, let us first dive into the genesis of this text to understand the stakes of this process.

The existence of these moments of reflection on the functioning of the assembly did not go without tensions within the group. While some preferred not to spend time on the technicalities of running an assembly that had not yet been born, and might never do, others wanted to take the time to develop a coherent and serious project, with a twofold aim. Firstly, they wanted to have a solid basis in case of an electoral victory to realise the promise made to the population to change the political system towards direct democracy in a communalist sense. This required being able to think about the various scenarios that could threaten the proper functioning of direct democracy (e.g., the risk of a low rate of participation due to work, social reproduction tasks, mobility, the digital divide or the ability to express oneself in public). Secondly, the members of the list wanted to explore whether the project was viable, so as to convince themselves and, in turn, be able to convince the population. As said by a female retired participant during a meeting on the functioning of the assembly (23.11.2019), "the more we believe in our project, in our objective, the more plausible we will be to share it". Developing arguments to defend the direct democracy project in the eyes of the residents of Commercy was therefore a matter of being "credible" – an expression met numerous times during individual interviews and which is deemed by them as necessary to run for the municipal elections. Since the electoral campaign aimed to convince the residents that this system of direct democracy could work, it seemed important to be able to offer collectively thought answers to their concerns and questions about how this direct democracy programme could be realised, and how it could overcome obstacles.

Participating in Participatory Spaces: An Obstacle to Direct Democracy?

Once the institutional design endeavour was agreed upon, the list dived into the multiple problems surrounding the institutionalisation of the assembly, to which they gave solutions in the Local Constitution. Among these numerous questions – agenda-setting, articulation with the municipal council, effective participation, the articulation between procedural and substantive democracy through the establishment of safeguards – I will elaborate on only one of them: the problem of participation, or attendance. Though it is interrelated with that of effective participation (Dahl, 1989: 109), as it touches on actors' motivation to participate by making their experience meaningful (Parkinson, 2006: 36–41), I only deal with the former to capture the full extent of how the movement tackled it.

In its preamble, the Local Constitution defines the assembly as follows:

> The term "Citizens' Assembly" generally refers to all moments of debate and decision-making open to all residents, in the form of a physical meeting and by any other means (internet …). It offers to all the residents of Commercy the possibility to decide by themselves and for themselves.

As such, the assembly is open to all residents and does not have any mechanism of selection, whether elections or random selection. This lack of selection mechanism, and subsequent openness to all, however, begs the question of participation, which has animated the CCA participants since its creation. They were indeed very well aware of the fact that, following the words of a female retired participant, "it is not easy to assemble people" and that the residents of Commercy constitute a "silent mass" that is necessary to "reach out to in order to give them the right to express themselves", according to a female education worker participant.

During the first assembly (10.5.2019), gathering approximately 80 people in Commercy, a male Yellow Vest organiser of the assembly put in perspective the requirement that everybody should immediately participate in the assembly in order for the direct democracy project to work:

> If we organise a popular assembly in Commercy or elsewhere, not everybody will come, but a small minority. The principle of the popular assembly is to open the possibility to decide, not merely participate in the debate, but participate in the decision. We open the possibility. Of course, seeing the formatting and the centuries of conditioning that we endured by delegating our power to others, it is not in eight days, nor even in one year or five that we would get a majority of people to decide. But the possibility will be open. So some people will come, people who would never have thought about it at first, or who were disgusted, but then who heard about the fact that they could come and vote on specific matters. We are starting a process, it is not a definitive solution that will revolutionise society overnight. We are entering into a process, that is the idea of direct democracy.

The answer of this participant contains several elements to understand how Commercy Yellow Vest activists saw their project as viable in tackling the problem of attendance. First, opponents of direct democracy often object that some individuals would not be willing to engage in the public sphere, but rather remain satisfied within the boundaries of their private one. The respondent argues that individuals' political passivity under the current representative system is not a natural, almost necessary, aspect of human nature, but rather one cultivated by centuries of centralisation of the exercise of public power in the hands of the political and economic elite. Far from an immutable essence, this conditioned feature of modern individuals could be changed over time by the "process" of direct democracy, thereby placing their endeavour as a long-term one. As such, they start from the premise that participation triggers a process of political education that will make participants competent to deliberate and decide collectively on political affairs, a premise shared by democratic theorists (Rousseau, 1968; Mill, 1910: 347-348; Pateman, 1970). It has proven difficult to test empirically on traditional modes of political participation (Pedersen, 1982), but has been attested in case studies of specific democratic innovations (Talpin, 2011).

Second, in relation to the motivation of individuals to participate, the respondent argues that being invited to decide, and not only to debate, might intrigue and motivate people to join the assembly. To them, the best way to ensure attendance is to give real power to the assembly to decide on matters that are important in their lives (in this sense, see Abers, 2003; Pateman, 1970: 45-50; Font et al., 2021; van der Does, 2022).

Third, the respondent makes an assertion that is crucial to the legitimacy of the project: that direct democracy remains legitimate even if not everybody attends the assembly, thereby contradicting the claim that "in direct democracy, everyone needs to attend" (Plotke, 1997: 25). Though having a community in which every single member takes part in the deliberation and decision on public affairs should certainly be the horizon for which communalist direct democracy projects strive, full attendance to popular assemblies might never be reached even after the adoption of measures to ensure participation (see below). As stated by the participant, fundamental to the project is that the doors of the popular assembly are open: that they are, Bookchin puts it, always "open to whoever lives in the neighborhood ... for all who wish to attend and participate" (2015: 53–54). In the constitution, they nevertheless decided to set a minimal threshold of 30 people for the assembly to be able to convene (article 7). During a meeting on the functioning of the assembly (9.12.2019), they considered this number sufficient to ensure that an assembly would be legitimate to decide since it "corresponds to the number of elected people at the municipal council". However, this choice begs the question as to the democratic legitimacy of the decisions taken by the assembly in the absence of the principal-agent relationship provided by the elections. In the eyes of participants, there are at least three reasons rendering the assembly's decisions legitimate, even if not attended by all: the fact that their political project would have been voted upon by the population should they win the elections (Van Outryve, 2023), the openness of the assembly to all who are affected by its decisions, and measures taken to enable their attendance.

Indeed, despite the questions of motivation and legitimacy surrounding the problem of attendance, participants are very well aware that measures need to be taken so that everybody can, in fact, attend, if they wish to. Such a question has been central during the reflections about the concrete functioning of the assembly, guided by the principle that they should organise the assembly "in such a way that they allow the participation of the greatest number of residents" (article 3). To this end, the group discussed various questions: that of the schedule to hold assemblies, especially for workers and people in charge of social reproduction tasks, that of older people and people who would have difficulty (financially or physically) to move, that of people who do not have time and that of the location of the assembly.

In relation to the problem of transport, they found inspiration in previous forms of daily tasks organisation in the town and decided to organise a shuttle service to bring people to the assembly, as a municipal public service. Regarding social reproduction, a childcare service was proposed. Scheduling was also deliberated, since a unique time and date might not allow everybody to participate in a given question, resulting in the group's decision (6.2.2020) to organise "several assemblies at various times in the week", later constitutionalised in article 3: "Similar meetings organised at different date and time can be considered in order to foster the participation of the greatest number of people". As such, they envisioned to organise three assemblies for deliberation during a given period of time, and a subsequent one for decision. However, deeply convinced of the power of deliberation by their months of assemblies at the shack, they realised that organising several assemblies of deliberations would mean that people would not take part in the same exchanges of arguments, and, thereby, might take a different decision depending on the deliberative assembly they would have attended. To solve this, it was decided that a pre-vote video summing up the various arguments presented throughout the three deliberative assemblies would be disseminated before and during the decision assembly. For the people who would not have time to come to this last assembly, they thought of setting up an online application that would allow people to vote only after watching the pre-vote video. In order to develop such a digital application, they submitted a project called "local democracy application" to the Meuse department's participatory budgeting. Two female retired participants thought that technology could be "a very precious tool", but were nevertheless wary of the digital divide, considered especially sharp in Commercy. Therefore, they proposed to duplicate every moment of vote: either people could vote online or they could take a shuttle to city council.

Lastly, on the physical location of the assembly: participants deliberated that residents might feel excluded by holding assemblies in city hall, an imposing castle previously occupied by Polish nobility, and informally called "the castle" by residents. Though this question has not been definitively answered, they nevertheless attached a great deal of importance to that matter, demonstrating their understanding of the stakes raised by the question of attendance in terms of the legitimacy direct democracy can pretend to.

The Problem of Participation Rethought by the Grassroots

What this contribution aims to show is that when social movements *themselves* design democratic innovation, we can think anew about the problem of attendance, in at least three ways.

First, when activists aimed to institutionalise the assembly through the municipal elections, they built on their experience gained during the Yellow Vests movements. The knowledge mobilised during the design of the citizens' assembly, therefore, stems from their democratic practices. As such, "democratic practices take their own specific forms in light of the contexts in which they emerge", often to address the problems encountered by the movement (Felicetti, 2021: 1594). The practices of the general assembly, the desire to go beyond the Yellow Vests struggle to have a long-term citizens' assembly, the necessity to overthrow the mayor and take city hall by giving the power to such an assembly, could not have emerged if it were not for the daily general assemblies at the shack, its destruction by the mayor and the need to gain access to power to put in place ideas developed during assemblies.

Moreover, this movement acted as a "learning site" (Welton, 1993) and a "producer of knowledge" of new notions of democracy (della Porta, 2020: 11). Because they were actors during the grassroots direct democracy experiment of the Yellow Vests of Commercy, the knowledge they mobilised for building institutions of direct democracy for the whole town is situated, and therefore better suited than abstract and disembodied knowledge used in governance-driven democratic innovations to overcome problems such as that of attendance through top-down design. Indeed, they produced knowledge "embedded in and embodied through lived, place-based experiences, [which] means they produce *different* kinds of answers from more abstract knowledge: knowledges that are situated and embodied, rather than supposedly neutral and distanced" (Casas-Cortés et al., 2008: 42–43). The solution actors developed to the problem of attendance suggests the possibility that knowledge relevant to institutional design solutions can emerge through participation, action and praxis. Not only were they the subjects of the democratic form of the assembly, but they also learned from it. As such, "they experiment with new ideas in their internal life, prefiguring alternative forms of democratic politics, and they spread these ideas within institutions" (della Porta, 2020: 13).

For example, having several assemblies deliberating on the same topic to enable participants with different schedules to attend the assembly is a solution built from their practice of having to deal with the question of attendance of assemblies during their struggle, as is their realisation of the need to multiply deliberation fora to overcome the issue that not everybody who wishes to participate on a given question, could in fact participate. Moreover, realisation that they would need to organise a video that would synthetise all arguments expressed during these various deliberative assemblies came from their lived experience regarding how deliberation can change participants' opinions.

Second, the fact that this democratic innovation was designed by a movement anchored in social justice demands and constituted mostly of people in situations of precarity (Alexandre, 2019) enables us to think about the participation of traditionally excluded groups. Indeed, social movements have proven able "to broaden the social distribution of participants (Smith, 2009: 41 and ff) with greater involvement by the popular classes" (della Porta, 2020: 158). Since the Commercy

Yellow Vests participated themselves in the democratic form of the assembly they later aimed at institutionalising, they were best suited to understanding the hurdles to individuals' participation in assemblies in this exercise of drafting a model for non-professional politicians, by non-professional politicians. They knew what enables working-class people to participate in assemblies, because, unlike policy professionals, they themselves have encountered these issues to attend assemblies during the Yellow Vests movement. As such, their constant attention to the rhythm of the assembly, its schedule, the mobility to enable people to attend it, as well as the location of the assembly testifies to their will to facilitate *real,* rather than formal, participation. In this sense, though the discussion on the location of the assembly (within city hall or in other more sober municipal premises of the city) was not settled, their attention to this potential obstacle to popular participation attests to a motivation to not only open the assemblies' doors but to establish the conditions for people to actually walk through them.

Third, how direct democracy social movements think about participation is qualitatively different than how policymakers think about it. Indeed, "participation in 'invited spaces' is framed by technocrats, whose interventions produce and limit what is possible" (Cornwall, 2004: 7). As such, participation as understood by technocrats is different than that as understood by social movement. While the former sees it in terms of threshold for a democratic innovation to functionally work, the latter sees it as a long-term question (ibid.), since it is a way to alter the paradigm of how power is exercised, and how politics should be the everyday activity of all rather than the profession of the few. As stated by the respondent cited at length above, developing a participatory culture is a process that will take time, and which is constitutive of the ideal of direct democracy. The problem of attendance is therefore seen as one that would not be solved once and for all by technocratic solutions, but as one intrinsically linked with the paradigm of how public power is exercised. To be solved, it requires a change of paradigm through practices of direct democracy, through allowing people to learn that they can, and should, decide together. Despite aiming to find solutions to enable participation, and especially of traditionally excluded groups (working people, people in charge of reproductive work, people with mobility issues), thinking the problem of attendance through the necessity of a paradigm shift legitimates an initiative of direct democracy that would otherwise be discredited on the sole basis of attendance, as a prefigurative experiment from which can contribute knowledge towards the development of new radical forms of self-government.

Conclusion

Commercy Yellow Vests have created several forms of assembly direct democracy: daily general assemblies, local CIR, a citizens' assembly, followed by a project to institutionalise it through municipal elections in order to radically change the mode of exercising power from representative to direct democracy. The list suffered an electoral defeat in the first round of municipal elections on 15 March 2020 with 9.76 per cent of the votes and failed to reach the 10 per cent threshold and qualify for the second round by four votes. However, the process undertaken by the group in creating and institutionalising this democratic innovation provides an insight into the constraints faced and possibilities opened up by bottom-up institutional design. Castoriadis (1989) put the goal well: "to create forms of democracy that are not alienating, where people participate in modern society, that can only be the work of the people as a whole and not of a theorist". In this vein, this chapter has suggested that social movements can be better situated to create democratic innovations and answer questions of institutional design than policymakers or theorists.

More specifically, this chapter shows the extent to which the grassroots character of the design's authors impacted the answers they brought to institutional design issues. What this case study points towards is that institutional design led by the grassroots can identify shortcomings and develop solutions that top-down policymakers or thinkers might not. Indeed, because they learned from their experience of democratic practices during the social movement and developed situated knowledge, because they are from the same class as the majority of the people who would participate, and because they see direct democracy as a long-term process and increasing participation as correlated to the unfolding of this process, this movement could develop contextualised solutions to the attendance problem affecting direct democracy. Further research on grassroots institutional design could reveal new solutions to democratic innovation design problems and enhance the emancipatory potential of social movements.

Acknowledgments

I am grateful to Adrian Bua and Sonia Bussu for their thorough reading and stimulating feedback, as well as to Oliver Escobar for useful advice. My thanks also go to Michèle Riot-Sarcey for the group interview she organised and invited me to. Lastly, my sincere and deepest gratitude goes to the members of this social movement who kindly welcomed me and allowed me to witness the evolution of their movement and participate in its activities. As an *aspirante FNRS*, this research is supported by the Belgian *Fonds National de la Recherche Scientifique* (FNRS). This article has been drafted during a research stay at the University of Edinburgh supported by the FNRS and Vocatio.

References

Abers R. (2003). Reflections on what makes empowered participatory governance happen. In A. Fung and E. O. Wright (eds), *Deepening Democracy*. London: Verso.

Alexandre C. et al. (26 January 2019). «Qui sont vraiment les 'gilets jaunes'? Les résultats d'une étude sociologique». lemonde.fr.

Arendt H. (1963). *On Revolution*. London: Penguin Books.

Bedock C. et al. (2020). Une représentation sous contrôle : Vision politique et réformes institutionnelles dans le mouvement des Gilets jaunes. *Participations* 28(3): 221–246.

Blaug R. (2002). Engineering democracy. *Political Studies* 50(1): 102–116.

Bookchin M. (2015). *The Next Revolution. Popular Assemblies and the Promise of Direct Democracy.* London & New York: Verso.

Bua A. & Bussu S. (2021). Between governance-driven democratisation and democracy-driven governance: Explaining changes in participatory governance in the case of Barcelona. *European Journal of Political Research* 60: 716–737.

Caluwaerts D. & Reuchamps M. (2015). Strengthening democracy through bottom-up deliberation. *Acta Politica* 50(2): 151–170.

Casas-Cortés M.I., Osterweil M. & Powell D.E. (2008). Blurring boundaries: Recognizing knowledge-practices in the study of social movements. *Anthropological Quarterly* 81(1):17–58.

Castoriadis C. (1989). Une leçon de démocratie. Interview by Chris Marker. Available at http://derives.tv/cornelius-castoriadis-une-lecon-de/.

Consejero F.M. & Janoschka M. (2022). Transforming urban democracy through social movements: The experience of Ahora Madrid. *Social Movement Studies*: 1–18.

Cornwall A. (2004). Introduction: New democratic spaces? The politics and dynamics of institutionalised participation. *IDS Bulletin* 35: 1–10.

Cossart P. & Sauvêtre P. (2020). «Du municipalisme au communalisme». *Mouvements* 101(1): 142–152.

Dahl R. (1989). *Democracy and Its Critics.* New Haven: Yale University Press.

della Porta D. (2020). *How Social Movements Can Save Democracy: Democratic Innovations from Below.* Cambridge: Polity.

della Porta D. & Felicetti A. (2019). Innovating democracy against democratic stress in Europe: Social movements and democratic experiments. *Representation* 58(2): 1–18.

Elstub S. & Escobar O. (eds) (2019). *Handbook of Democratic Innovation and Governance.* Cheltenham: Edward Elgar Publishing.

Felicetti A. (2021). Learning from democratic practices: New perspectives in institutional design. *The Journal of Politics* 83(4): 1589–1601.

Font J., Pasadas S. & Fernández-Martínez J.L. (2021). Participatory motivations in advisory councils: Exploring different reasons to participate. *Representations* 57(2): 225–243.

Gaventa J. (2004). Towards participatory governance: Assessing the transformative possibilities. In S. Hickey & G. Mohan (eds), *Participation: From Tyranny to Transformation.* London: Zed Books.

Gourgues G. (2020). Peut-on ensauvager la participation ? Radicalité démocratique et Gilets Jaunes. *Réfractions* 45: 105–118.

Jeanpierre L. (2019). *In girum. Les leçons politiques des ronds-points.* Paris: La Découverte.

Kitschelt H. (2006). Movement parties. In R. Katz & W. Crotty (eds), *Handbook of Party Politics.* London: Saige: 278–291.

Manin B. (1995). *Principes du gouvernement représentatif.* Paris: Flammarion.

Mill J.S. (1910). *Representative Government.* London: Everyman.

Parkinson J. (2006). *Deliberating in the Real World: Problems of Legitimacy in Deliberative Democracy.* Oxford: Oxford University Press.

Pateman C. (1970). *Participation and Democratic Theory.* Cambridge: Cambridge University Press.

Pedersen J. (1982). On the educational function of political participation. *Political Studies* 30(4): 557–568.

Plotke D. (1997). Representation is democracy. *Constellations* 4(1): 19–34.

Pitkin H.F. (1967). *The Concept of Representation.* Berkeley and Los Angeles: University of California Press.

Roth L. (2019). (New) municipalism. In M. Peters & R. Heraud (eds), *Encyclopedia of Educational Innovation*. Singapore: Springer.

Rousseau J.-J. (1968). *The Social Contract*. London: Penguin Books.

Ryfe D.-M. (2002). The practice of deliberative democracy: A study of 16 deliberative organizations. *Political Communication* 19(3): 359–377.

Smith G. (2009). *Democratic Innovations. Designing Institutions for Citizen Participation*. Cambridge: Cambridge University Press.

Talpin J. (2011). *Schools of Democracy. How Ordinary Citizens (Sometimes) Become Competent in Participatory Budgeting Institutions*. Colchester: ECPR Press.

Talpin J. (2015). Democratic innovations. In D. della Porta & M. Diani (eds), *The Oxford Handbook of Social Movements*. New York: Oxford University Press.

Van der Does R. (2022). Citizen involvement in public policy: Does it matter how much is at stake? *Public Administration*: 1–16.

Van Outryve S. (2019). Becoming mayor to abolish the position of mayor. Thinking the line between reform and revolution in a communalist perspective. *Unbound: Harvard Journal of the Legal Left* 12(55): 1–46.

Van Outryve S. (2023). Realising direct democracy through representative democracy: From the Yellow Vests to a libertarian municipalist strategy in Commercy, *Urban Studies, Special issue: Municipalist Strategy in Crisis?*: 1–17.

Warren M. (2014). Governance-driven democratization. In S. Griggs, A.J. Norval & H. Wagenaar (eds), *Practices of Freedom: Decentered Governance, Conflict and Democratic Participation*. Cambridge: Cambridge University Press, 38–60.

Welton M. (1993). Social revolutionary learning: The new social movements as learning sites. *Adult Education Quarterly* 43(3): 152–164.

Section 4
Conclusion

17 Towards the Messy Middle

The Next Generation of Democracy-Driven Governance Research

Gianpaolo Baiocchi

It is hard to remember today, but not so long ago the idea of participatory democracy was exclusively associated with social movements and, to a lesser extent, Left political projects. There was the famous Paris 1968 student graffito: *Nous participons, vous participez, ils décident*. Similarly, social movements of the 1960s such as Mexico's *Movimiento Estudantil* or the United States' Students for a Democratic Society helped define a terrain of debate about the role of participation. The SDS (1962) Port Huron Manifesto called for a system in which "the individual share in those social decisions determining the quality and direction of his life" and laid out the terms for a desirable participatory democracy, including "decision-making of basic social consequence be carried on by public groupings" and "channels should be commonly available to relate men [*sic*] to knowledge and to power so that private problems—from bad recreation facilities to personal alienation—are formulated as general issues".

In subsequent years, all manner of New Left parties began to incorporate participatory democracy into their programmes, whether in Europe as part of new Marxist thinking or in Latin America when new parties were founded in rejection of Leninist practices and took a "local and a social turn", with a central focus on ideas of civil society and participation (Castañeda 1993: 200). This new thinking was eclectic, influenced by sources as wide as debates with European New Left, Liberation Theology and Popular Education. As it is well known, throughout Latin America in the 1990s there were demands and claims from social movements and new progressive actors who sought to reform the state and deepen democracy through participation. This discourse ranged from the Zapatistas in Chiapas, to the Civil Society Assembly in Guatemala, to local administrations run by the Workers' Party in Brazil, to the Movement for Socialism in Bolivia, among many others.

If contemporary ideas of participation emerged among social movements in the 1960s, these ideas were first appropriated by mainstream policymakers three decades later. It was in the 1990s that agencies like The Inter-American Development Bank, USAID, the World Bank and other bilateral and multilateral donors like DFID (UK), CIDA (Canada), UNDP and major foundations like Ford, Kettering, Rockefeller and MacArthur began to adopt the language of civil society and participation. Interest in participation continued to increase in the 2000s, what Caroline Lee, Michael McQuarrie and Edward Walker (2015: 7) have called a "participatory revolution".

Ernesto Ganuza and I have discussed this trajectory before (Baiocchi and Ganuza, 2016), but it is worth remembering it when we reflect on where this excellent collection of chapters leads us.

Much of the current discussion on participation references debates that began in the late 1990s and early 2000s, the fleeting historical moment after participation seemed to have achieved some institutional success, but, crucially, before it became clear to many of us what the impact of multilateral interest in participation would be. It was impossible to imagine the behemoth that participatory institutions would become in the coming years. Much of the critical tone in the years since about participation implicitly or explicitly derived from a comparison with an earlier time when movements seemed to demand participation, and a present when participation was most often introduced by government agencies in concert with consultancies and non-profits with little or no movement participation. That this seemed to happen at the same time as neoliberal reforms only added to the "troubling paradox" that Adrian Bua and Sonia Bussu discuss in the introduction: "As new and innovative forms of citizen participation in policymaking and public service delivery are used globally and at different tiers of government, the space for meaningful citizen input is increasingly constrained by technocratic decision-making and global economic pressures". Further, Henk Wagenaar's chapter (see Chapter 5, this volume) effectively sketches the political-economic obstacles to realising the democratic ambitions of social movements and citizen associations. He argues that: "The occupation of the state by an increasingly assertive, detached, exploitative and rapacious globalised corporate-financial sector, and the ideological surrender of the state to this state of affairs, has imperilled democratic governance worldwide". This inevitably closes down the space for meaningful democratic innovation.

But the case is hardly closed, as this volume shows. The world has dramatically changed in recent years, for one thing. Principles like democratic dialogue, inclusion and the respect for difference – the *sine qua non* of participation – have acquired new valence as polity after polity around the world falls prey to the seduction of far-right anti-democratic politics. What may have seemed a trivial space of deliberation with its attendant civilising pressures in the early noughties now appear to be endangered and valued resources. But it is not only that. What people in movements will tell you, and what many scholars have found empirically over the years – though we have not often analytically engaged with it – is that there is such a thing as an engaged critical position. Movements will engage a space while being fully aware of and pushing against its limits. This is as true of imported Participatory Budgeting in the US (Baiocchi and Ganuza 2016) as it is of anti-dam movements in the Amazon (Klein 2022), or even environmental decision-making in New York City for that matter (Araos 2021). There are many instances of a kind of movement activism that acknowledges "the critique advanced by radical democratic theory but embraces the challenges of institutionalisation" (see the introduction in this volume). It is as if movements have returned to the scene once again.

But what happens when movements try to reclaim these very arenas? Can they, as Bua and Bussu ask in the introduction to this volume, "open up space for a deeper critique of the minimalist liberal democratic institutions and the neoliberal economy these sustain"? If Mark Warren's (2009) Governance-Driven Democratisation ("democratic innovations mostly initiated by public agencies to respond to specific policy issues") had the accent on official institutions, Bua and Bussu's Democracy-Driven Governance puts the accent back on the side of agents.

The DGG framework opens up a set of analytic possibilities between a determinist political economy approach (which a priori assumes the impossibility of agency) and a normative experimentalist approach (which assumes the opposite, that is, that democratic innovations imply agency). It very helpfully joins other recent scholarship on "innovative capacity in terms of nurturing and spreading new ideas – about, among other things, democratic institutions" (della Porta, 2020, p. 3). It is an important adjunct to other discussions, such as the Empowered Participatory Governance approach of Archon Fung and Erik Wright (2003). The EPG discussion of Wright and Fung was, of course, a different kind of intellectual project altogether – its proposal, as all other real utopian proposals, was to identify institutional design principles of real utopian institutions, like participatory budgeting (Baiocchi 2003). EPG points to features, like recombinance, that "work". It is agnostic about origins, and there are many instances of EPG that are initiated by public agencies. And it is silent about the implication of institutions being "driven" by political dynamics one way or another. DDG helps train our attention on the messy middle of political action, which is also the messy middle between the scholarly positions that separate the world into "either/or". DDG recognises the scope of action in constrained but always changing contexts. Elsewhere this has been discussed as "disavowed political action" – that is, political action that is premised on recognising constraints on it (Baiocchi, Bennet, Cordner, Klein and Savell 2014). The framework thus sets up several important questions explored in the various contributions to the book:

- The sustainability of DDG initiatives
- The existence of new forms of participation and new usages of extant forms
- The obstacles to DDG broadening democracy
- The impact of social movement engagement
- The potential for radical democratic renewal
- Tensions between participants, organised sectors and officials

The chapters together give us a valuable snapshot of DDG worldwide and help point the way forward. Every single chapter has contradictory outcomes – some elements of DDG are prominent, while others are muted. And unsurprisingly, perhaps, the overall answer to most of the guiding questions of the framework is that "it depends. A lot". No political scientist or sociologist would deny the importance of context, and indeed, contextual factors account for a lot of the analytic work of the chapters.

These contributions do not shy away from providing a realistic analysis of the structural constraints. Adrian Bua, Sonia Bussu and Jonathan Davies (Chapter 11, this volume) offer a powerful contrast between Barcelona and Nantes. In the former, participatory institutions come to be Democracy-Driven, while in the latter they are Governance-Driven. To make sense of the distinction, they argue, we need to look at the complex interactions of agency-side and institutional-side factors. To put it another way, what are the political openings and who is able to take advantage of them? This is more than a story about more movements making for more democracy. It is an account of a relatively progressive status quo (Nantes) that was "able to shield its economy and municipality from the worst effect of austerity" and thus preserve political elite legitimacy and not provide openings for more expansive democracy. In Barcelona, the social and economic fallout destabilised the political environment, leading to greater contestation, which a well-organised civil society was able to exploit, carving out a window of opportunity.

Other chapters focus on the processes of ongoing contestation that underpin these spaces. Joan Balcells, Rosa Borge and Albert Padró-Solanet's chapter on Catalunya's Decidim platform (Chapter 12, this volume), a digital innovation emerging out of the 15M movement that is meant to radicalise democracy, unveils some contradictions. Local associations, used to playing an intermediary role in Catalonia's local politics, were reluctant to engage, as the transition towards digital forms of participation gave more weight and influence to individual citizens' participation. Similarly, the participatory programme instituted by *Ahora Madrid*, a Left coalition in Madrid in 2015 which is the subject of two chapters, is a powerful reminder that just as GDD can be subverted by movements occupying its spaces, the innovations of DGG are as susceptible to transformation as well. As Fabiola Mota Consejero and Cristina Herranz show (Chapter 14, this volume), while Ahora Madrid was a "great breakthrough in face of practices of former conservative local governments which used to hinge upon a culture of patronage", it in the end lent itself to "a neutralization of social conflicts" and, ultimately, became an instrument of "technopopulism". Patricia Garcia Espin's chapter (Chapter 15, this volume) shows, in a careful and nuanced way, how Ahora Madrid's process was understood by activists and how it ultimately produced profound disappointment and activist demobilisation after participation in a process that was straitjacketed from the start, particularly concerning its redistributive goals. Democracy-Driven Governance processes, Garcia Espin writes, "tend to find similar obstacles".

Many of the chapters point to the importance of *domain-specific enabling and constraining features*, often beyond formally stated goals. Marina Pera, Iolanda Bianchi and Yunailis Salazar analyse the implementation of the "Citizen Assets Programme" in Barcelona (Chapter 13, this volume). While they document significant tensions, it is hard not to notice constraints, particularly when it came to assets. Vlahos's chapter on planning processes in Toronto makes a number of important rejoinders to the overall DDG framework, specifically that it more explicitly foregrounds commodification and decommodifications within the welfare state. It compares a Neighborhood Planning Table that, while in principle having goals of decommodification, faces "structural barriers" for the issues brought up that would require "more than working around the problems of capitalism". While the Neighborhood Planning Table winds up being closer to GDD, the other case in the chapter is closer to DDG. The participants in the Parkdale People's Economy, a community development project leading to a Community Land Trust, "do not separate an equitable local economy from the redistribution of decision-making power away from the local government to the community". The biggest point here is not that DDG is more de-commodifying, but rather that there are fundamental structural constraints when it comes to the domains over which DDG projects can exert influence. In the case of Toronto, it might well be that "the participatory governance of social wellbeing is better situated in communities rather than integrated in municipal governance", but fundamentally Community Land Trusts tend to be small interventions in the larger context of urban housing markets, as "the scale of activities that are required for larger levels of decommodification [...] requires policy interventions that support actors in collectively devising and securing social wellbeing".

Markus Holdo, in reference to participatory budgeting in Rosário, Argentina, reminds us of the ethos of caring that is implicit in participation and fostered by it (Chapter 4, this volume). But it ultimately is a paradoxical act, because to care for democracy is to resist the neoliberal credo of selfishness and help make space for solidarity and collective mobilization. But on the other hand, it provides neoliberal societies with the bonds of trust and legitimacy needed to sustain them.

Similarly, Falanga's chapter on the participatory process of Lisbon around the Martim Moniz Square makes important points about structural constraint (Chapter 8, this volume). A major process on urban redevelopment of a key area of the city, the process stands out for its inclusiveness, even though the "Right to the city" that was enacted was relatively limited. Falanga's chapter, however, points to one process that recognised new actors for the first time; indeed, one of the interesting collective findings of the volume has to do with the appearance (and recognition of) new practices and identities in DDG processes, an element that was present in most of the chapters, and that it is captured poignantly by Giovanni Allegretti's case of anticolonial protests in Greenland (Chapter 9, this volume). Ricardo F. Mendonça, Lucas de O. Gelape and Carlos Estevão C. Cruz (Chapter 10, this volume) also describe one of the innovations emerging from Brazil – the collective candidacies for political office, often by women of colour. Taking advantage of a quirk in Brazilian laws that permits a juridical person to run for office, women of colour throughout the country have decided to run on left-party platforms for elected office, sometimes winning. In some ways, it is indeed a "quick fix" and a "hack" to the political system, but it is an institutional innovation that emerges more or less out of a recognition that participatory democracy, so diffused in Brazil, in itself is not enough.

There are inspiring cases of democratic energy and critical renewal. Sixtine Van Outryve d'Ydewalle's fascinating chapter on the unfolding of Commercy's participatory democracy after the "Yellow Vests" movement in France (Chapter 16, this volume) is an account of how a movement experience fed directly into participatory design; features as "having several assemblies deliberating on the same topic to enable participants with different schedules to attend the assembly" was a "solution built from their practice of having to deal with the question of attendance of assemblies during their struggle". Paola Pierri's chapter on climate action and the adoption of the Assises model in the Orleans (Chapter 6, this volume) provides an interesting case of "strange bedfellows" in the crafting of DDG, in particular how movements "put pressure on the local conservative government by translating the global demands of climate movements to the local political context". Interestingly, "their actions also managed to galvanise support among the local population for the left and green parties, that played a stronger role in the last election". It is one of the more hopeful accounts in the volume because it shows a set of reforms in what might be an unexpected context, but more than that because it shows the formation of new political identities in the process.

These cases remind us of the value of prioritising "radical openness" over rational consensus. Dannica Fleuss uses the Icelandic Initiative for Constitutional Reform and Germany's "Bürgerrat Demokratie" as a moment to reflect back on Deliberative Democracy from the point of view of DDG experiences (Chapter 2, this volume). She convincingly argues that Deliberative Democrats ought to give up some of their stronger rationalist assumptions. The bigger point here might be that democratic theorists ought to not abandon normative theory, but they should leave their offices more often and engage with the world of amazing, contradictory and constrained experiences out there in the messy middle of political action. And when they do, the DDG agenda and the chapters in this volume can be an important and helpful guide.

References

Araos, M. (2021). "Democracy underwater: Public participation, technical expertise, and climate infrastructure planning in New York City." *Theory and Society*. https://doi.org/10.1007/s11186-021-09459-9

Baiocchi, G. (2003). "Emergent public spheres: Talking politics in participatory governance." *American. Sociological Review,* Vol. 68, (1): 52–74.

Baiocchi, G. and Ganuza, E. (2016). *Popular Democracy: The Paradox of Participation.* Stanford University Press.

Baiocchi, G., Bennett, E.A. Cordner, A., Klein, P. and Savell, S. (eds) (2014). *Civic Imagination Making a Difference in American Political Life*. Routledge.

Castañeda, J. (1993). *Utopia Unarmed: The Latin American Left After the Cold War*. Knopf.

della Porta, D. (2020). "Protests as critical junctures: Some reflections towards a momentous approach to social movements." *Social Movement Studies* 19(5–6): 556–575.

Fung, A. and Wright, E.O. (2003). *Deepening Democracy: Institutional Innovations in Empowered Participatory Governance*. Verso.

Klein, P. (2022). *Flooded: Development, Democracy, and Brazil's Belo Monte Dam*. Rutgers University Press.

Lee, C.W., McQuarrie, M. and Walker, E. (2015). *Democratizing Inequalities: Dilemmas of the New Public Participation.* NYU Press.
Students for a Democratic Society (1962), Port Huron Statement, available at Port Huron Statement, 1962 (hanover.edu), accessed 31/01
Warren, M.E. (2009). "Governance-driven democratization." *Critical Policy Studies* 3(1): 3–13.

Index

Note: Page numbers in *italics* indicate figures, **bold** indicate tables in the text, and references following "n" refer endnotes.

15-M movement 196, 198, 225–230, 238, 239

administrative bureaucracy 71–72
adversarial countervailing power 92, **92**, 100
Agency for Public Infrastructure 73
Ahora Madrid (*AM*) (Spain) 245; digital participation of 230–232; electoral programme 228; Local Forums for Participation in 233–236; percentages of participation *235*; social movements 238–239; territorial disparities in 232–233; Territorial Rebalancing Fund 233, 236; *see also* 15-M movement; Indignados (Indignant) movement (2011)
Almeida, D. R. 159
Alterglobalisation and Occupy movements 105
anticolonial protest (Greenland) 137–141
anti-trust legislation 75
Arnstein, S.R. 7
Artificial Intelligence 237
Asenbaum, H. 147
Assunção, Helena S. 160
Attoh, Kafui A. 123
autonomy 23
Ayrault, Jean-Marc 175

Banting, K. 40
Barcelona: Citizen Asset Programme in *see* Citizen Asset Programme (CAP); civil society in 177–178; commons in 213–214; democracy-driven governance in 174–184; economic context and socio-economic performance in 180–181; local autonomy in 179; political leadership in 176–177; post-Olympic growth model 181; social movements in 177–178
Barcelona en Comú (BeC) 177, 178, 184, 209, 262
Belda-Miquel, S. 123
Berthelsen, A. 150n3
bipartisan credibility 54
BipZip programme 126, 129
Bishop, C. 106–107
Black Lives Matter movement 137–138
Blanco, I. 160
Blaug R. 6, 171, 172
Boal, A. 111–112
Boggs, C. 105
Bookchin, M. 263
bottom-up legitimacy 19, 108, 143, 155, 227, 230; crucial value of 21; deliberative theory and 20–23; initiatives 28, 31–32; requirements of 24; strategies for 25–28
Brazil: collective candidacies in 154; collective mandates in 156–159; dynamic political system in 155–156; *gambiarras* 159–165
Brown, W. 54
bureaucracy, administrative 71–72

Caballero Ferrándiz, J. 246
Campos, B. 157
Can Batlló 216
capitalism 39–40, 43, 74, 107; advent of 211; cross-sectional actions against 123; (de)commodification in 36, 37; and

Index

democracy 35; global 54; neoliberal 51, 105, 213; primacy of 121; in right to city 121; urban 41; welfare 37
capitalist democracy 36; core features of 38; democratic innovations in 39; inequality in 46; participatory governance in 37–39; problem of 37
care, defined 55; *see also* democratic care
caring democracy 56, 62–63; *see also* democratic care
Carmena, M. 228, 238–239
Castells, M. 124
Castoriadis C. 272
Certeau, Michel de 161
Citizen Asset Programme (CAP) 209–210, 219; Catalogue of Assets 215; Citizen Assets Board 215; Citizen Assets Ordinance 215; Community Balance Report 215–216, 218, 221; elements in developing 215; Municipal Citizen Assets and Community Management Board 215, 218, 219; public-common institutions and 214–222; successful outcomes of 221
Citizens Assembly on Electoral Reform (British Columbia) 28–29
Citizens' Assembly on the Future of Democracy (Bürgerrat Demokratie) (Germany) 20, 28–31, 282
citizenship, defined 123
Citizens' Initiative Referendum (CIR) (Commercy) 264–265
civic associations 69–73
classical deliberative theory: bottom-up legitimation and 20–23; limits to theory 26; radical openness and 23–28; shortcomings of 20–23
climate change: climate-related governance processes 93–94; decentralising 93; and democracy 89–90; Orléans Metropole 90, 95–100; transition governance, participatory and 94–97
Climate-Knowledge and Innovation Community (Climate-CKIC) 94
collaborative countervailing power 90–2, **92**, 96–97, 99
collective candidacies: *Bancada Ativista* (PSOL/SP) 162, 164; in Brazil 154; *ColetivA* (PT-Belo Horizonte/MG) 162, 164; defined 154, 156l; *see also gambiarras*
collective mandates 154; *Bancada Feminista* 163; challenges of 157–159;

defined 156; as democratic innovations 156–159; presenting 154–155; *Pretas por Salvador* (PSOL/Salvador-BA) 163; *Quilombo Periférico 163*; race/ethnicity and age *vs. 158*; *see also gambiarras*
Colon-Rios, J. 27, 31
Commercy (France) 259–260; direct democracy in 264–266; grassroots institutional design of, experiment of 266–271
Commercy Citizens' Assembly (CCA) 265–267
commoning art 107
commons 70, 74; in Barcelona 213–214; -based institutions, challenges in developing 217–220; childcare 78; concept of 212–213; defined 79; and progressive municipal politics 80; public policy for 214–217
communalism 260; direct democracy and 263–264; electoral strategy of 265; municipalism *vs.* 264
community development unit (CDU) 42, 43
community land trust (CLT) 44, 281
consensus, defined 164
constitutional change 19, 23–24; bottom-up initiatives for 31–32; genuinely democratic 31–32; radical 26; reconsidering 25–28
Cooke, B. 106
Co-op Cred Program 44, 45
Cornwall, A. 123
corporate-financial order 76–77, 79, 81, 278
corporate social responsibility 75
countervailing power 93; adversarial 91–92, **92**; collaborative 90–2, **92**, 96–97, 99
critical democracy 6, 136–137, 172, 238; in Commercy Citizens' Assembly 265–267; created space of 265; social movement of 261
cyberactivism 122

daily general assemblies 264, 270
Dardot, P. 213
Davies, J. 172, 179
Decide Madrid 230–232
Decidim 191, 195–197; cases 197–198; Catalan municipalities implementing **198**; dependent variable 198–199; features of 195–196; independent

Index   287

variables 199–200; institutional and organisational factors 199, **200**; key actors, reception by 199–200, **200**; obstacles to use of 202–203; online questionnaire for 196–197; organisational culture 199, **200**; public managers' perceptions 196, 201; regression analysis 202, **203**
(de)commodification of social wellbeing 37–40; indices 39; stratification in participation and 40
deliberative democracy 31; core values of 24; Habermasian 19; notions and ideals to develop 24; political ideals of 26; *see also* classical deliberative theory
della Porta, D. 3, 98, 125, 131, 261
democracy-driven governance (DDG) 4–6, 36, 67–68, 104, 136, 170, 246, 259, 261, 279–280; in Barcelona 174–184; challenges 6–12, 73; governance-driven democratisation *vs.* 78; participatory democracy and 5; participatory governance and 43–46; research, next generation of 277–282; resilience of 172; risks of 78–79; role of social movements in 91–94; into technopopulism 225–239; in Toronto, Canada 43–46
democratic care 55–58; ethics of participation 59–60; feminist thinking on 56–57; limits of practices 62–63; politics of participation 60–62; in Rosario, Argentina 58–59; solidarity 59–60
democratic ecosystems 115
democratic innovations (DIs) 1, 2, 136; citizen engagement and *see* Hans Egede Statue; citizenship and 124; collective mandates in Brazil as 156–159; defined 161, 261; by individual digital participation 230–232; in participatory governance 39–40; social movements and 260–264
Department of Territorial Coordination and Associative Promotion (TC&AP) (Ahora Madrid) 229
Department of Transparency and Citizen Participation (TCP) (Ahora Madrid) 229
de Sousa Santos, B. 4
dialogical aesthetic 113–114
digital participation; Decide Madrid 230–232; Decidim 195–204; drivers and obstacles of 192–193; institutional and organisational factors for 193–194; key actors, reception by 194–195; organisational culture for 194; *see also* digital platforms
digital platforms 191–192
direct democracy: in Commercy 264–266; communalism and 263–264; legitimacy and 268; motivation of individuals to participate 268; obstacle to 266–269; opponents of 267–268
double movement 36–39, 46
Dryzek, J.S. 3
Dyson, J. 107

economic democracy 70; international, interconnected and multipolar 75; issue of 74; mirage of 73–79
economy, defined 74
Elstub, S. 161
embeddedness 209; application of 211; defined 211; in participatory policies 211–212; practices 211–212, 221; spatial dimension of 211, 221; temporal dimension of 211, 221
empowered participatory governance (EPG) 91–92, 99–100, 279
Escobar, O. 161
Esping-Andersen, G. 36, 38–40, 46
ethics of care 52, 55; *see also* democratic care
ethics of participation 59–60
European Institute of Innovation and Technology (EIT) 94
European Social Surveys 125
Extinction Rebellion movement 93, 100n1

Feandeiro, A. 175, 177, 181
Felicetti A. 98, 125, 261
Financial Sustainability 179
formal political equality 37
Frediani, A. 123
Fung, A. 90–92, 279

G1000 project (Belgian) 5, 29
gambiarras 154, 159–162; challenges of 164–165; emerging 162–165; legal recognition and regulation in electoral laws 162–163; relationships with parties and representatives 163–164
Ganuza, E. 52–54, 193, 236, 278
Garden Martim Moniz Movement (GMMM) 120, 127–131

288 *Index*

Gaventa, J. 74
giant transnational firm 75
Gilets Jaunes's mobilisation (France) 93
governance-driven democratisation (GDD) 4, 27, 36, 67–68, 91, 104, 136, 170, 259, 261, 279–280; challenges 72–73; democracy-driven governance *vs.* 78; limitations 73; in Nantes 174–184; participatory governance 40–43; progressive public administration *vs.* 80–81; success of 77–78; in Toronto, Canada 40–43
Greenland: anticolonial protest against Hans Egede Statue 137–140; cause-effect relations between poll 144–145; legacies of poll 141–145
Greenland4Nature 141
Griggs, S. 175, 177, 181

Habermas, J. 19–28, 31
handbag economy 76
Hans Egede Statue *138*; anticolonial protest against 137–140; cause-effect relations between local poll on 144–145; legacies of poll on 141–145; memory of referendum 140
Hanusch, F. 147
Harvey, D. 123
Healey, P. 5, 8
"*Healthy, Clean Cities Deep Demonstrations*" programme 94, 100n3
hegemony 70, 76–77; electoral 176; neoliberal 78, 79, 81
Heller, P. 181
Høegh-Dam, Aki-Matilda 138
Holloway, J. 109
Howarth, D. 175, 177, 181

Icelandic Initiative for Constitutional Reform 28–31, 282
Indignados (Indignant) movement (2011) 3, 177–178, 225, 226
institutionalised democracy 70–71
institutional reforms 19, 23–24; bottom-up initiatives for 31–32; genuinely democratic 31–32; radical 26; reconsidering 25–28
Inter-American Development Bank 53
"Inuit Nutaa" collective 141
Irish Citizen Assemblies 29

Jeffrey, C. 107
Jensen, Paninnguaq Lind 138

Kalaallit Nunaat *see* Greenland
Katersugaasivik Nuutoqaq (Nuuk Lokalmuseum) 140
Kester, G.H. 113
Kohn, M. 54
Kothari, U. 106

Laval, C. 213
La Xarxa de Dones Cosidores 216
leadership, concept of 141
Lee, C.W. 278
Lefebvre, H. 120–123, 131
Les Mouvements Zéro 101n6
libertarian municipalism 263
Lisbon city council 125–127
local autonomy 78, 173–174, **182**; in Barcelona 179; in Nantes 178–179
Local Forums for Participation (LFP) 233–236
Lowndes, V. 160
Lüchmann, L. 159
Ludvigsen, C. 138–139

Madrid 242–243; creation of local forums in 245–248; *Green Tide* platform in 247; *see also* social movement activists (SMAs)
Maeckelbergh, M. 114
Mandata Ativista (PSOL/SP) 164
Mansbridge, J. 3, 56
Marcuse, P. 122, 131
Martim Moniz Square (MMS) 125, 127–128; participatory process of 128–129
Marxist theory 121, 123
Maryhill Integration Network (MIN) 115–116n2
Mayer, M. 122
McQuarrie, M. 278
MediaLab Prado 229
Mehr Demokratie e.V. 29–30
Mellor, M. 76
mini-publics 1, 232
Miraftab, F. 125
Mirowski, P. 76
Moury, C. 125–126
movement-parties, defined 262
Movimiento Estudantil (Mexico) 277
municipalism: communalism *vs.* 264; libertarian 263
Municipal Legislature of Belo Horizonte (MG/Brazil) 156
Municipal Platform for Civic Dialogue (Kommuneqarfiga) 139
Myles, J. 40–41

Naegler, L. 107
Nalik Kalaallit Nunaat 140
Nantes: economic context and socio-economic performance in 180; governance-driven democratization in 174–184; local autonomy in 178–179; political leadership in 175–176; social movements in 177
Navarro, Z. 54
Neighborhood Planning Table 281
neighbourhood improvement area (NIA) 42–43, 45
neighbourhood planning tables (NPTs) 40–43
neo-institutionalist approach 212
neoliberalism 70, 76, 81, 176; care for democracy and *see* democratic care; -driven disinvestment 123; economy 75, 76; participation and 53–55; sharpening of 177
New Municipalism movements 3, 5, 122, 176, 242
Nuuk Art Museum 140
Nuuk Nordic Culture Festival 140

ocular democracy 147
Organic Law on Budgetary Stability 179
Orléans Metropole Assises for the Ecological Transition 90, 95–100
Ostrom, E. 212

paradox of participation 51–55
Parkdale-Activity Recreation Centre (PARC) 44
Parkdale Community Economic Development (PCED) Planning project 44–45
Parkdale Neighbourhood Land Trust (PNLT) 44
Parkdale People's Economy (PPE) 43–46, 281
ParticipaLab 229, 232
participatory arts 104; under New Labour 106; other names of 105; in political and apolitical 108–110; political context in 107; present and future 112–114; rehearsal and performance of 111–112
participatory budgeting 51, 155, 230, 249; in Brazil 154–156; implementing 43; individual and digital participation in 230–231; in Lisbon 126; in Porto Alegre 4, 184; in Rosário, Argentina 53–54, 58–62, 281; in US 278

participatory democracy 259, 277; commitments to establishing 228; competing and unbridgeable visions of 228–230; democracy-driven governance and 5; social movements and 2–4
Participatory Institutional Design 26–27
Pateman, C. 52
Peck, J. 54
Peris Blanes, J. 123
"PHOENIX" project 150n20
platform of mortgage victims (PAH) 177–178
Polanyi, K. 36, 38, 40, 46, 211
Policy Conferences, Brazil 154–156
Policy Councils, Brazil 154–156
political-administrative system 67, 68, 80
political leadership 78, 171–172, 204; in Barcelona 176–177; index 200; in Nantes 175–176
political song 110–111
politics of participation 60–62
Polletta, F 124
Port Huron Statement (1962) 277
Prainsack, B. 76
prefiguration, defined 105
prefigurative social movements 104; arts-based interventions in 105; critiques of 107; participatory arts and 108; in political and apolitical 108–110; present and future 112–114; rehearsal and performance of 111–112
progressive public administration 70, 72, 80
Pruijt, H. 124
public-common institutions 209–210; in Barcelona 213–214; challenges in developing 217–220; Citizen Asset Programme and 214–217, 220–222
Public Education Defence Movement 242
Purcell, M. 123

Qom community 59

radical democratic theory 5, 6, 265
radical municipalism in Spain 172, 226–227
radical openness 25–28; deliberative theory and 23–28; from normative theorists' perspective 25; prioritising 282
"right to the city" theory 120; citizen participation for 123–124; conceptual frame of 121–122; in Lisbon 125–127;

Martim Moniz Square 127–131; political claims 122–123; urban movements and participatory processes 124–125
Rosario (Argentina): democratic care in 58–59; ethics of participation 59–60; politics of participation 60–62

Seattle WTO protests (1999) 105
shared mandates 157, 166n2
shareholder value doctrine 75
Short-Term Scientific Mission 137, 149n1
Smith, G. 6, 124
Social Development Finance and Administration (SDFA) 37, 42
social movement activists (SMAs) 242–243; alternatives 252–254; defined 243; disappointment, degree of 251–252; do-it-yourself participation 250–251; frustration and disappointment of 242–254; investment and commitment 248–250; in Madrid 245–254; in official participatory institutions 243–245
social wellbeing: governance of 35–47; indicators of 45; strategy for elevating 43; themes of 42
solidarity 59–60, 114–115
sortition democracy 232
Spanish procurement law (9/2017) 217, 220
Standring, A. 125–126
state economy 74–75
Stone, C. N. 173
Strategy for Citizens Involvement 140
Students for a Democratic Society (United States) 277
Subirats, J. 123, 147
Summers, N. 193
Sustainable Energy, Climate and Air Plans (SECAP) 95

Talpin, J. 97
Tarrow, S. 173
technopopulism 238–239, 280
Temporary Autonomous Zone, concept of 112

Territorial Rebalancing Fund (TRF) 233, 236
Theodore, N. 54
Thorpe, J 74
Toronto: democracy-driven governance in 43–46; governance-driven democratisation in 40–43
Toronto Strong Neighbourhoods Strategy (TSNS 2020) 37, 42, 45
transition governance, participatory 94–95; à l'orléanaise 95–96; defined 100n4; design principles for 97–99; strategies 99–100
Tronto J.C. 55–57, 60, 62

UN-Habitat 53
Urban Heart Index 42

Valesca, L. 127
voluntarism 22
Vox Sessions 112, 116n3
Vox Unbound community 114, 116n4

Waldron, J. 24
Walker, E. 278
Warren, M. 4, 27, 36, 69, 70, 91, 170, 259, 279
welfare state decommodification 37–39
Wolin, S. 4
WoMandates 159, 165
women dressmakers' network 216, 223n5
Workers' Party (Brazil) 166
World Bank 4, 53
Wright, E.O. 90–92, 279

Yellow Vests movement (France) 259, 264, 282; direct democracy and 264–266; face-to-face assembly during 265; participating in participatory spaces 266–269; problem of participation 269–271
Young, Iris M. 244
youth Group Theatre (Tasiilaq) 141

Zechner, M. 78, 80